THE UNCIVIL UNIVERSITY

The American university is suffering from a moral crisis unseen since the great social upheavals of the 1960s. In the name of academic freedom, the core values of higher education—honest scholarship, unbiased research, and diversity of thought and person—have been corrupted by an academy more interested in preserving its privileges than in protecting its own integrity. Aided and enabled, sometimes unwittingly, by faculty, administrators, trustees, philanthropists, and even the government of the United States, the American university has lost its civility.

Nowhere is this loss more apparent than in the rise of anti-Semitism and anti-Israelism on college campuses. *The UnCivil University*, documents the alarming rise in bigotry and bullying in the academy. Using a range of evidence, from first-hand accounts of intimidation of students by anti-Israel professors to anti-Semitic articles in student newspapers and marginalization of pro-Israel scholars, *The UnCivil University* exposes the unspoken world of double standards, bureaucratic paralysis, and abdication of leadership that not only allows but often supports a vocal minority of extremists on campus.

The UnCivil University tells a cautionary tale for all readers, whatever their background, of how higher education, an institution so touted for its open-mindedness, has become a prime vehicle for politically motivated prejudice. With millions of students passing through American universities each year, an attack against some should be of concern to all.

INSTITUTE FOR JEWISH & COMMUNITY RESEARCH

The Institute for Jewish & Community Research, San Francisco, is an independent national and international think tank providing policy research for the Jewish community and society in general. It educates both the public and opinion leaders through publications and conferences in three areas: religious tolerance and intolerance; philanthropy; and religious identity and behavior.

the
UNCIVIL
University

the UNCIVIL *University*

Intolerance on College Campuses
Revised Edition

GARY A. TOBIN
ARYEH KAUFMANN WEINBERG
& JENNA FERER
FOREWORD BY MARC DOLLINGER
INTRODUCTION TO THE REVISED EDITION BY
KENNETH L. MARCUS

LEXINGTON BOOKS
A division of
ROWMAN & LITTLEFIELD PUBLISHERS, INC.
Lanham • Boulder • New York • Toronto • Plymouth, UK

LEXINGTON BOOKS

A division of Rowman & Littlefield Publishers, Inc.
A wholly owned subsidary of The Rowman & Littlefield Publishing Group, Inc.
4501 Forbes Boulevard, Suite 200
Lanham, MD 20706

Estover Road
Plymouth PL6 7PY
United Kingdom

British Library Cataloguing in Publication Information Available

Library of Congress Cataloging-in-Publication Data

Tobin, Gary A.
  The uncivil university : intolerance on college campuses / Gary A. Tobin, Aryeh K.
Weinberg, and Jenna Ferer.
      p. cm.
  Includes bibliographical references and index.
  ISBN 978-0-7391-3266-1 (cloth : alk. paper) — ISBN 978-0-7391-3267-8 (pbk. : alk.
paper) — ISBN 978-0-7391-3268-5 (electronic)
  1. Discrimination in higher education—United States. 2. Jewish students—Crimes
against—United States. 3. Antisemitism—United States. I. Weinberg, Aryeh Kaufmann.
II. Ferer, Jenna. III. Title.
  LC212.42.T64 2009
  378.1'012—dc22   2009005461

Printed in the United States of America

♾™ The paper used in this publication meets the minimum requirements of American
National Standard for Information Sciences—Permanence of Paper for Printed Library
Materials, ANSI/NISO Z39.48–1992.

For Mia

Those learned societies have chosen to remain, for a long time, the sanctuaries in which exploded systems and obsolete prejudices found shelter and protection after they had been hunted out of every other corner of the world.

Adam Smith
An Inquiry into the Nature and Causes of the Wealth of Nations, 1776

Contents

FOREWORD by Marc Dollinger

San Francisco State University has gained widespread notoriety as a haven for anti-Israel, and, at times, anti-Semitic behavior. Over a decade ago, the imposition of anti-Semitic images onto a campus mural of Malcolm X dismayed the Jewish community, and all those who respect higher education. On May 7, 2002, a Yom Ha'atzmaut (Israel Independence Day) rally turned ugly when a verbal confrontation between Jewish and Palestinian students led to anti-Semitic epithets, and as the day unraveled, Jewish students vacated university grounds under the much-needed protection of the campus police. Accounts of that incident reached news outlets around the world and brought renewed focus on the limits of campus free speech. Few had ever seen anything quite like it, and certainly not on a college campus in contemporary America.

But it was not the first time I had experienced something strange and unsavory on a campus concerning Jews and the university. Two years earlier, I engaged in a high-profile campaign against campus anti-Semitism, but at the time it was not at San Francisco State University. A group of professors at the college where I had previously taught, a community college of 30,000 students, announced plans to turn an undergraduate lecture on the Holocaust into what was privately described as "an episode of the Jerry Springer show." In a unit on World War II, the instructors designed a fabricated debate between a controversial Jewish extremist (one who advocated violence against Muslims and others) and a local rabbi on the topic, "Responses to Anti-Semitism after the Holocaust." The rabbi, a disciple of Dr. Martin Luther King Jr., was to speak in favor of non-violent resistance while the extremist would press for more confrontational approaches in the fight against bigotry. It became clear in conversations with the seven professors sponsoring the debate that this event was not intended to raise the intellectual profile of students. It was meant, instead, to "titillate" students, an unfortunate nod to the shouting matches and physical free-for-alls all too typical in staged reality television talk show culture.

I thought it was inappropriate to bring such a Jewish extremist on campus. I do not believe any college or university should be the formal host to such hate speech. Shouting, screaming, drama, and invective are not the building blocks of learning. Students can find plenty of these in other places throughout our society. Faculty teach subject matter, but we should also serve as examples about how to communicate intelligently. Those who violate civilized customs, I thought, are not the best role models to teach our students.

The planned debate, part of the school's Humanities Block Interdisciplinary Program, violated our profession's most basic educational standards. The program faculty valued sensationalist affect more than scholarly integrity. The invited "guest" did not possess academic training in the subject he was asked to teach. Beyond questions of intellectual merit, the invitation also raised concerns for student safety. The extremist invited to speak headed a fringe Jewish defense organization with a long history of violence and an eagerness to engage in direct confrontations with those who oppose its inflammatory tactics. The normative Jewish community has successfully marginalized such violent organizations. Why feature them?

My offers to find a Jewish Studies scholar trained in the history of anti-Semitism and the Holocaust were rebuffed. In a rather tense, and terse sixty-minute meeting, I pleaded with my colleagues to rescind their invitation to the unqualified speaker that they had selected. I asked them not to present the Jewish world's most tragic moment in a circus-like atmosphere. I worried that the planned debate would cloud the real history of anti-Semitism and the Holocaust for the 100 undergraduates enrolled in the course. Aside from the inflammatory nature of the program it was simply low quality.

In a secret ballot following our meeting, the Humanities Block Faculty voted 5–2 to go forward with the invitation. One of the problems around these kinds of controversial issues is the fraternity-like secrecy, and the unwillingness to speak openly and honestly. They defended their decision by invoking their right to academic freedom, affirming that their classroom belonged to them and only to them, under all circumstances and at all times. My critique, according to their analysis, proved tantamount to censorship and they would take a principled stand in defense of their right to control their own course content and method of delivery. No one would argue against that right. I was trying to interject both common sense and quality control to go along with that right.

They also positioned themselves as centrists and categorized my views as extremist, someone who was advocating a dangerous assault on the college's most cherished free speech principles. I was not alone in my assessment, and those of us who opposed the invitation framed the question in far different terms. Acknowledging our colleagues' right to free speech, academic freedom, and autonomy in their own classrooms, we also pressed for academic responsibility and the right to dissent. If academic freedom means that professors have great latitude in what they say and do on campus, then academic responsibility demands that they exercise those rights very carefully. Professors need to maintain the highest levels of professional conduct and accept accountability for the actions they take. Without academic responsibility, academic freedom devolves into anarchy, as was happening on my campus.

Moreover, academic freedom includes academic openness, the willingness to hear different sides of a debate, and even to change one's mind as a result. Academic freedom should not be reduced to a stonewalling defensiveness of, "I don't have to listen to you," or "I don't have to do what you say." Rather than affirming the university as a center committed to the expression of diverse ideas and opinions, the Humanities Block faculty rejected our calls for dialogue, educational forums, and debates.

The tensions grew. The Humanities Block faculty did not appreciate the attention brought to their decision by "outside faculty." They argued that the principles of academic freedom excused them from peer review on their decisions of who to invite and how to construct a panel. Of course, just the opposite is true. Academic freedom is built around peer review. Neither did they recognize any community obligations: to national professional organizations that demand academic excellence, to their campus colleagues concerned about educational standards, or to individuals in the wider Jewish community who objected to an offensive carnival about anti-Semitism and the Holocaust.

To buttress their position, the Humanities Block Faculty called on the school's administration. They appealed to the college president, claiming that academic freedom priorities trumped the concerns raised by individuals whom they characterized as disgruntled colleagues wrongly influenced by their own political biases. Backed with personal assurances from the Humanities Block faculty about the quality and propriety of their choice, the president expressed confidence that the invited speaker did not pose a threat to student safety and was competent to teach the class. With the authority of the president behind them, the Humanities Block faculty were able to legitimate their position and brand as radical those who advocated a different view. This is when the disagreement turned ugly.

In a meeting I convened to offer an alternative perspective on the issue, the president challenged my academic credentials and cautioned me not to adopt such an "extremist" position. I was making trouble by offering a different perspective. How sad, I thought, that this kind of censorship was at play. I urged the president to reconsider and implored him to use his office as a bully-pulpit to advocate for the values and mission of the college: academic quality, diversity of opinion, and freedom from bias. He needed to show some moral leadership because we were dealing with a moral issue as well as an intellectual controversy. It was wrong to trivialize the Holocaust, it was wrong to endorse a speaker who advocated violence, it was wrong to be so callous about the concerns of the Jewish community. I invited him to address the faculty involved in the dispute, sponsor a debate within the social sciences division (where the Humanities Block program was located), or call a public forum for interested individuals: all ways in which to explore complex ideas. He declined all of these. Similar calls to department chairs, the teacher's union, and the academic senate all failed.

The college leadership's refusal to protect the right to dissent and the failure to recognize the critical link between academic freedom and academic responsibility turned a low-level campus dispute into a much larger and contentious conflict. While the right of the sponsoring faculty to stage the debate enjoyed institutional protection, the rights of dissenting faculty to give voice to their concerns did not. Academic freedom proved to be a one-way street, entitling one group of professors the right to intellectual shoddiness, but denying others the forum to present another position. When the college leadership refused to protect the dissenters and demand responsible conduct among its faculty, it failed in its obligation to make the college a haven for the free, open, and safe exchange of ideas. It exposed the Achilles heel of campus-based free speech: the failure of university administrations and faculty governance groups to link the expression of academic freedom to the obligations of academic responsibility. This failure is at the heart of what Gary Tobin and his coauthors have named *The UnCivil University.*

Buoyed by their newfound institutional support, the Humanities Block faculty unleashed a vicious campaign, under the guise of protecting academic freedom, to squash dissent. In the first few months of the controversy, I made a concerted effort to express my concerns in private, to keep the debate within the walls of academe. I believe that faculty and administrators should try to self-regulate whenever possible. As I explained my view to the Humanities Block faculty, this was an issue among academic colleagues and needed to remain closed and quiet. But at some point the failure to resolve the problem widened its importance. After all, the "outside world" was at the heart of the dispute and others needed to help address the issue if the college itself would not.

When word eventually leaked about the proposed "lecture," a steady stream of colleagues, most of whom were African American and Latino, came to my office. They too were upset about the Humanities Block invitation and concerned that I had elected to keep the issue quiet. One by one, they shared their own painful stories about campus life. I heard tales of intimidation, example after example of attempts to push them into one kind of conformity or another. Each faculty member let me know that the attempt to silence me was more widespread than I had imagined. I was reintroduced to the concept of "invisibility," a metaphor drawn from Ralph Ellison's famed work, *Invisible Man.* Dissenters at my college, like Ellison's protagonist, became invisible.

Before the controversy, I had been rewarded with interesting teaching assignments, favorable class schedules, a number of college-based grants, and the greatest privilege the school can offer a junior faculty member: two all-expense paid semesters teaching students in the Florence, Italy, study-abroad program. All that ended when I challenged the Humanities Block.

The Humanities Block controversy demonstrated the fragility of protected dissent on campus. I had become accustomed, as a middle-class Jewish intellectual, to a certain kind of status. Jews are typically overrepresented on the college campus, and the days of Jewish powerlessness have long passed. Moreover, I am part of the post-Holocaust generation. American society has been open to me, and I do not experience much anti-Semitism, certainly not off the campus.

I lived in two social worlds simultaneously. While I enjoyed the highest level of academic and professional training in Jewish Studies, I could not seem to gain intellectual legitimacy among the Humanities Block faculty, who designed curriculum in my field without my input. That duality positioned me to speak from both privilege and powerlessness, even as I understood that I was not entirely a part of either.

About a month before the scheduled debate, a small campus protest movement formed. Students from a variety of classes who had learned about the controversy joined together. They gathered information on the invited speakers, produced leaflets that they distributed after Humanities Block class meetings, and called for a student boycott of the event. I developed a deep respect for the student leaders and the initiative they displayed. During one afternoon of leafleting, a student protester was physically restrained by a college administrator who released the undergraduate only when the student threatened to call the police. Still, copies of their flyers, posted on bulletin boards on campus, were removed. It was hard for me to believe that an institution that promoted free speech could allow the destruction of materials that advocated an opposing opinion. Even more shocking, some protest leaders, fearful that their transfer applications to four-year schools might be compromised, retreated from their activism.

A political science professor, fascinated by the issues raised during informal discussions, asked faculty from both sides of the debate to present their views to her class. Another professor of African American and ethnic studies saw the controversy as a way to dramatize the challenges of invisibility in American society and offered his own request for all of us to speak to his class. I thought it was an excellent idea. The Humanities Block instructors turned down all invitations, in turn, criticizing their faculty colleagues for "dragging" students into the debate.

The school newspaper began almost weekly stories covering the unfolding controversy. The local media also began to follow the debate. I appealed to local rabbis and Jewish community organizations for support. With the controversy in full public view, internal pressure on the campus continued to mount against those who advocated dissent. Tenure-track faculty were pulled aside and advised not to "associate" with the supporters of an open and honest dialogue. Several tenured faculty members came to me in private to share stories of the pressures they were facing to distance themselves. In one of those cases, a professor who had been a powerful supporter advised me that he wanted to finish his career at the college, and he needed to withdraw from the debate. In stating his fear, he revealed a powerful truth: the tenure system did not always protect the right to dissent. Some may be surprised that assaults on tenured faculty come more often from other faculty and administrators, for a wide variety of reasons, and not from outsiders looking to punish faculty for their political views.

On the day of the scheduled debate, the Jewish extremist speaker opted to forgo his discussion on anti-Semitism and the Holocaust and speak instead against "people like me," who had opposed his visit and whom he described as a "self-hating leftist Jew." Campus police, advised to maintain a presence inside the lecture hall, instead formed a line outside the hall to ensure that a planned counter-demonstration did not materialize. Another group of police officers assembled inside a utility closet as reinforcements.

College administrators had also quietly changed the start-time of the event. Some students came to my classroom, informed me that the event was taking place as they spoke, and offered to escort me past the police lines and out the door to my car. How strange that was! Here I am, a Jew, needing my own students to protect me against a Jewish extremist appearing with the unconditional blessing of the College. The students' concerns were not unfounded. The following day, I arrived on campus to find a visibly upset officemate who had just discovered the extremist speaker's calling card taped to our office door. Under these circumstances, I did not feel secure on campus and phoned the city's police department for advice.

They recommended that I program their number into my cell phone and keep it with me whenever I walked on campus.

In the months that followed, the situation continued to deteriorate. Internal college memos that I had written to administrators on the unfolding controversy found their way, along with my picture, to the website of the militant Jewish organization headed by the invited speaker. My call to the board of trustees for an investigation into the source of the leaks was ignored. By this point, only two other individuals, an African American sociologist and the social sciences dean, were willing to continue advocating for institutional accountability.

And in the most bizarre twist imaginable, to demonstrate their absolute "free speech" rights, some faculty re-invited the offending speaker for continuing lectures. In a class on logic, students heard a seventy-five minute oration on the subject, "Marc Dollinger's cowardice," a reference to my refusal to participate in the Jerry Springer-like debate. The professor in that class then rewrote his final examination so that he could test his students on their response to the question: "Was Professor Dollinger a coward?"

My demand that the administration inform me of future campus lectures or visits by this potentially dangerous person fell on deaf ears. The dean of personnel explained that anyone, including this extremist, had a right to come to campus whenever they wished. The school newspaper offered print space to the extremist speaker, who published an op-ed piece calling for my firing and that of the social sciences dean, who continued to support me. Next, he went before the college's board of trustees and made the same demand.

Two months later, the college president summoned the social sciences dean to his office, where he fired her, citing her conduct during the Humanities Block controversy as justification. My African American colleague, though tenured, faced his own form of retribution. In the middle of a class on the sociology of ethnicity and race, campus police entered and removed him on false charges that he had made a threat against a white female colleague.

This controversy lasted as long as it did largely because it came to symbolize far more than the Humanities Block invitation or even the question of academic responsibility. It represented the college's failure to address critical issues of intellectual diversity and its willingness to impose invisibility on those who dissented. It became a chilling example of the damage wreaked by what the authors of this book rightly deem the loss of civility on campus. As events unfolded, I spent hours and hours engaged in dialogue with my African American colleague. A former community college president himself, he narrated our journey through this controversy. With great precision and accuracy, he predicted administrative responses and gave me keen advice on how to conduct myself under pressure.

My colleague did not view this as a Jewish controversy at all and asked if I would be willing to explore the ways my experience paralleled those of other marginalized groups. I agreed and we decided to organize the city's first-ever Town Hall Meeting on Diversity. Anchored by the local chapter president of the Anti-Defamation League, we gathered representatives from across the ethnic, racial, and religious spectrum to speak about their own personal experiences with powerlessness and invisibility. We eschewed canned organizational speeches and challenged our panelists to speak from their hearts.

The event exceeded expectations. In the months of publicity preceding it, we gathered the co-sponsorship of over three dozen community organizations as well as most local politicians and state representatives. Long past our deadline for organizing the speaker's panel, the city's chief of police, an Armenian whose family had perished in the Turkish genocide, requested an opportunity to speak. He wanted the opportunity to stand with members of his community and share how his life story led him into a career in law enforcement. The Anti-Defamation League leader shared stories from his childhood, reflecting on the pain he experienced when faced with anti-Semitism. Over 300 people attended, including, to his credit, the college president. A personal invitation to the director of the Humanities Block program was rejected. The success of our forum was an indication that the ideals of the university had been diminished: the best intellectual interchange about racial and ethnic diversity, the heart and soul of campus sensibility, had to take place without university sanction.

As difficult as it was, I enjoyed a great deal of personal and professional growth from this experience. I developed primary social relationships with African American and Latino colleagues who shared with me a depth of trust nourished by the sacrifices we made during the controversy. I located in my own Jewishness the impulse to bear witness, to align myself with similar-minded people, and to push past my own fears in order to remain true to my principles.

As one who never really likes to break the rules, I learned what happens (and what doesn't happen) when you challenge the status quo on campus. A few articulate and disciplined voices can bring attention to important issues. I also was disappointed with many campus and community organizations and leaders, whom I perceived as unwilling to take the necessary steps for effective social change. In terms of my own professional future, I also knew that I could not continue my career on that campus. When a new job opportunity arose, I decided to move on. The Humanities Block controversy taught me that the school would not open itself to change, and I would always face categorization and marginalization as a "leftist, self-hating Jew."

Until I arrived at San Francisco State University.

Colleagues across the country warned me not to take a position at a school that the Hillel Jewish student organization once designated as the nation's most anti-Semitic university. At San Francisco State University, Zionists face public rebuke for supporting Jewish nationalism. Jewish students recount their apprehension over wearing clothing or jewelry that identifies them as Jewish. I once witnessed a student rally that included a ten-foot effigy of the university president with the sign "Zionist" hanging on its back.

The moment I arrived on the San Francisco State University campus, I ceased to be seen as a leftist Jewish activist. While day-to-day campus life is fairly routine, the occasional high profile student rallies, often centered on the Palestinian–Israeli debate, impose clear political categories on members of the campus community. Zionists, regardless of political profile or ideological approach, are labeled as imperialists and colonialists. When Jewish progressives proclaim their support for the state of Israel, conversation with the leftist community often stops. A Zionist's backing of other progressive social causes gets silenced by the left's singular rejection of Jewish nationalism. While Jewishness meant marginality at my old school, it is equated with power and privilege by the left at San Francisco State. In just one short summer vacation, I morphed from a leftist Jew seeking radical change to an imperialist Zionist apologist for the conservative status quo. As this book makes clear, Jews are whoever anti-Semites want them to be. All I had to do to transform from the left to the right, from powerless to colonial master, was to change campuses.

Experiences at these two schools revealed how Jews are caught between conventional political boundaries. They share attributes from both sides of the aisle but no longer find a stable home in either. On the left, Jews are often sympathetic to many social justice movements, but they also face marginalization when the conversation turns to Zionism and the state of Israel. Jews on the right enjoy newfound access to the highest echelons of power, but they must also distance themselves from the religious fervor of some parts of the right.

I MORPHED FROM A LEFTIST JEW SEEKING RADICAL CHANGE TO AN IMPERIALIST ZIONIST APOLOGIST FOR THE CONSERVATIVE STATUS QUO. AS THIS BOOK MAKES CLEAR, JEWS ARE WHOEVER ANTI-SEMITES WANT THEM TO BE.

Yet, San Francisco State University, despite its negative public image on Jewish issues, provides a safer environment for dissent than my former campus ever could. San Francisco State University's administration and faculty understand the necessity of balancing one side's right to speak with the other side's right to dissent. The university links academic responsibility to academic freedom and holds individuals accountable for their words. Most of all, in the face of anti-Semitism, the university president shows moral leadership and openly condemns this form of prejudice. He hasn't won the battle yet, but he does not shrink from the controversy.

When I first arrived at San Francisco State University, I noticed banners hanging throughout campus, posted after the September 11 attacks, saying, "Hate speech is not free speech." When Palestinian students threatened Jewish students at the May 7th rally, university officials forwarded videotapes of the episode to law enforcement officials for criminal prosecution. Days after the rally, the university president published an open letter in the local Jewish newspaper offering his own perspective on the confrontation. Over the summer, the university president welcomed representatives from a broad range of political constituencies to gather together and engage the issues raised. When the university's own investigation was completed, the president suspended the Palestinian student group as a consequence of its actions that day.

That demand for accountability recalled the president's action during the infamous Malcolm X mural incident a decade earlier. When an artist included anti-Semitic images in a painting of the Nation of Islam leader, the president, amid intense university and community pressure on many sides, ordered the offending mural removed and completely repainted according to the guidelines established during the university's initial approval process. He demanded responsibility in the face of free speech. If San Francisco State University beats back anti-Semitism on campus, the moral courage of its president will have played a key role.

It is impossible to control all hate speech, or eliminate irresponsible or inaccurate statements uttered by professors. But, as Gary Tobin and his coauthors bravely propose, university communities can—and indeed must—demand a high standard of professional conduct and impose consequences on those who abuse the school's trust. I applaud the publication of this book, not only for its insightful and unflinching analysis and essential recommendations but also for its own civility in the face of the outrages it documents. *The UnCivil University* approaches the deep fissures on the campuses of American universities much the same way the universities themselves were intended to function: as places of learning where difference is encouraged and ideas challenged in constructive ways. Whatever their political ideology and affiliation, all responsible members of the academy should heed the calls for reform contained in this book. If we do not, the university will break down, leaving marginalized faculty (and students) to fend for themselves. It is better to teach in the civil university imagined in this book, complete with harsh speech and accountability, because without accountability, without civility, any speech can become harsh.

POSTSCRIPT

The United States Civil Rights Commission conducted an investigation into the Humanities Block controversy. Its lead investigator offered specific critique of the administration's failure to hold faculty accountable for their actions. Under threat of another investigation by the Equal Employment Opportunities Commission, the College administration negotiated a cash settlement with the social sciences dean, who along with my colleague in sociology, found academic positions elsewhere.

Sixteen months after his lecture on campus, FBI agents raided the home of the Humanities Block program's extremist guest speaker and arrested him on charges of conspiring to bomb a mosque, as well as the offices of an Arab-American member of the United States Congress. Police records indicate that he was involved with this plot at the time he was lecturing on campus. On the morning of his first day of trial, federal officials announced that he committed suicide in prison.

Marc Dollinger is the Richard and Rhoda Goldman Chair in Jewish Studies and Social Responsibility, San Francisco State University.

Acknowledgments

The staff of the Institute for Jewish & Community Research worked together to complete this volume. Dennis Ybarra provided valuable assistance in guiding the preparation of the revised edition. He was extremely helpful in reading the manuscript and providing important commentary. Caitlin Collentine prepared the additional manuscript. We want to thank Bruce Purdy for his work in production and design. We are grateful for all their hard work. Diane Tobin managed the research and production team with her usual skill and drive. The book would not have been completed without her guidance.

Introduction to the Revised Edition
by Kenneth L. Marcus

The Long Slumber

The resurgence of anti-Semitism on American college campuses documented in Gary Tobin, Aryeh Weinberg, and Jenna Ferer's *The UnCivil University* has been an unfolding scandal of the twenty-first century. On highly politicized campuses in particular, Jewish students have faced increasing anti-Semitism and anti-Israelism, often cloaked as academic or political expression. I saw these problems mount at American colleges while serving as the head of the U.S. Education Department's Office for Civil Rights (2003–2004) and later as director of the U.S. Civil Rights Commission (2004–2008). Yet few in the community have been willing to confront this issue with the forcefulness that it deserves. Fewer still have grasped the systemic connections among the various incidents that Tobin and his colleagues have identified.

The first wake-up call came in 2002, at San Francisco State University. There, an angry mob chased dozens of Jewish students and faculty, under police escort, away from a peace protest and into the nearby Hillel.[1] Flyers reignited the ancient anti-Semitic blood libel, speaking of "Palestinian Children Meat Slaughtered According to Jewish Rites Under American License."[2] That year, a spate of anti-Jewish incidents flared from coast-to-coast. After a flurry of concern by Jewish and higher education institutions, these incidents were, however, soon forgotten.

Then in 2004, in New York, the David Project's *Columbia Unbecoming* documentary revealed the extent of student intimidation by faculty of Columbia's Middle East and Asian Languages and Cultures (MEALAC) department. Israeli students were publicly denigrated. In one scene, a Jewish American student told of how a MEALAC professor insisted that she should have "no voice in this debate," because she is not a "Semite" but a Jew. This film, too, sounded a sharp alarm but has not been widely enough heard.

Later that year, the Zionist Organization of America (ZOA) filed a complaint with the U.S. Department of Education's Office for Civil Rights (OCR) describing an extraordinary pattern of anti-Semitic intimidation, harassment, threats, and vandalism at the University of California, Irvine.[3] Despite the magnitude of the problems at that campus, OCR dismissed the complaint in November 2007.[4] There are no signs to indicate that it will treat a pending companion case differently.

Surprisingly, the Jewish and higher education communities have been more reluctant to confront these problems even as their severity has increased. In lectures at across the country, I have noted the dearth of information that even active, engaged students, faculty and community members have about this situation. Worse is the unwillingness of many Jewish community or higher education professionals to address this problem for fear of antagonizing others.

THE "GOLDEN AGE" OF AMERICAN JEWISH STUDENT LIFE

Some have failed to see the problem because there are so many signs that Jewish college students are thriving. Just a few years ago, our times were described by knowledgeable commentators as a "golden age" of Jewish student life in the United States; some speak in such terms even today.[5] After all, Jewish students have unprecedented access to Jewish Studies courses, chaplaincy services, Jewish faculty, Jewish administrators, and Hillel chapters. Jews no longer face institutional discrimination in academic admissions, undergraduate housing, club membership, faculty hiring, or administration appointments.

Moreover, faculty attitudes toward Jews are, by and large, quite positive. Indeed, Tobin and Weinberg's own work has shown that American college faculty view Jews more favorably than any other religious group.[6] Specifically, 73 percent of faculty report warm/favorable feelings toward Jews, while only 3 percent report unfavorable feelings. This contrasts sharply with faculty attitudes toward other religious groups, such as Evangelical Christians, who are viewed unfavorably by 53 percent of faculty members.[7]

At the same time, an insurgent campus minority has undertaken an extraordinary number of disturbing recent acts of anti-Semitism and anti-Israelism on American college campuses. Incidents at a few campuses have become widely publicized, but the problem is now undoubtedly national in scope. Jewish students—especially when visibly identified and when vocally supportive of Israel—have been repeatedly threatened, stalked, cursed, bullied, and harassed, while Jewish property is vandalized or destroyed. In my estimation, there are now at least hundreds of anti-Semitic hate and bias incidents each year on U.S. college campuses and perhaps thousands of anti-Israeli incidents. The shear volume of problems belies any suggestion that the phenomenon consists only of a series of unrelated incidents.

In light of these incidents, the "golden age" appellation now rings with a tone of grim irony, somewhat like the phrase, "the Best and the Brightest," used to describe the Kennedy-era architects of the Vietnam War. In each case, the term is not inaccurate in a literal sense: many Jewish students are indeed thriving. Its denotation is now eclipsed, however, by its ironic sense, intended in the latter case if unintended in the former. What is surprising in both cases (as the late David Halberstam reportedly lamented as to his title) is that people often hear only the denotation and miss the irony.

THE PARABLE OF THE BOILED FROG

While the UC Irvine complaint was pending, I met with a group of mainstream Jewish undergraduate leaders from the university to hear their perspectives. Having spoken previously with several current and recent Israel activists on that campus, I knew the fear, anger, and frustration that they experienced. One young woman, who had led Irvine's pro-Israel group just a couple of years before, had spoken of her fear at being stalked by Islamist activists after she had been identified as a strong supporter of Israel. A graduate student had described Jewish student fears of retaliation if administrators became aware of their support for the pending anti-Semitism investigations. But those had been outspoken, strongly identified supporters of Israel. I wanted to know how the more moderate, Hillel-affiliated students perceived the situation.

Over soda at a campus hang-out, the leaders of Irvine's student Jewish organizations told me that they had become "numb" to the hatred of Jews that surrounded them. As freshmen, they had watched in fear as Islamic activists castigated Israelis, Zionists, and Jews. Over time, they had become inured to pervasive anti-Semitism. They realized that their complaints were going nowhere. They had wearied of fighting back against people who despised them. Moreover, they resented community activists who were urging them to become more vocal.

After hearing these students repeatedly describe their numbness to Jew-hatred, I told them a story: the parable of the boiling frog, made famous in Al Gore's movie, *An Inconvenient Truth*. As the story goes, a man drops a frog in hot water, and it immediately jumps out. Even a frog knows, instinctively, how to avoid being scalded. The same man later drops a frog in cool water and then very slowly raises the heat. The frog, comfortable at tepid conditions, adjusts to the increasing temperature and remains in the water. At some point, the frog, paralyzed by the heat, is boiled alive.

None of the students had heard this parable before. As I related the story to them, a flush of recognition crossed their faces.

CHANGING THE SUBJECT

Jewish community groups are invariably startled to hear what is happening on college campuses—when they are willing to listen. As a federal civil rights official, I addressed many communities and activist organizations to discuss the hate and bias problems which they face: African Americans, American Indians, women, Sikhs, the disabled, and others. While each of these groups has its own distinctive history and contemporary challenges, there is one respect in which they are all alike, and Jews are different.

In Indian country, Native American audiences do not ask why people would want to discuss Indian rights. Black audiences do not ask why there is so much focus on issues facing African Americans. Disabled groups do not ask why disability-rights lectures address only disabilities when there are so many important issues facing different groups of non-disabled persons. And so on. But at lectures about anti-Semitism, some member of the audience invariably asks why other forms of bigotry are not addressed. Why just anti-Semitism? Why not talk about racism and bigotry of all kinds, including (but not limited to) anti-Semitism? It does not seem to matter that all of these other issues are discussed at other times and places. In any sizable Jewish audience, there is invariably at least one person who will articulate uneasiness about the focus on anti-Jewish discrimination. There are, I believe, six explanations for this idiosyncratic Jewish response.

First, American Jews inherit a profound and ancient social justice tradition. This tradition calls many Jews, admirably, to seek justice for everyone in the world and not just members of their own group. In some cases, however, Jewish activists may think that Jewish suffering is less important than that of other groups. In particular, they may believe that the anti-Semitism question distracts attention away from either domestic racial conflict or the plight of the Palestinians.

Second, many Jewish Americans are uncomfortable with anything suggestive of Jewish exceptionality or with what they consider to be undue attention to Jewish particularity. They believe that others, either in prior generations or in other parts of the community, have focused too much on what is "good for the Jews." In some cases, this concern is exacerbated by the sting of outside critics who charge the Jewish community with excessive parochialism or perceived exceptionalism. Indeed, those who challenge anti-Semitism on American college campuses are frequently accused of bad faith, hidden agendas, or censorial intent.

Third, some Jewish people, especially among older generations, may be reluctant to dwell on anti-Semitism because the horrors of the *Shoah* are so close. They may want to change the subject precisely because it is so painful. Given both the painfulness of this issue, and the conflicts which it generates, many would prefer to focus instead on what they consider to be more positive messages regarding the Jewish community or the State of Israel.

Fourth, like other groups that face bigotry, Jews may internalize some of the attitudes of those who are biased against them, including those who have belittled the suffering of Jewish people for centuries. In extreme individual cases, this can lead to the well-documented, if controversial, phenomenon of Jewish self-hatred. At a collective level, this can lead to institutional paralysis.

Fifth, Jewish groups are internally divided over the politics of campus anti-Semitism. The relationship between much contemporary anti-Semitism and the political Left is an embarrassment to many Jewish progressives who have long been committed to the anti-racist strands within progressive politics. Moreover, the source of much contemporary anti-Semitism within Arab and Muslim groups has been frustrating to those Jewish activists who are committed to building coalitions with outside organizations.

Finally, aggressive anti-Semitism advocacy by conservative Jewish organizations may lead some mainstream organizations to withdraw from the issue to avoid association with Jewish activists whose politics they disdain. In this way, internal divisions prevent the Jewish community from coalescing in opposition to a common threat.

THE FIGHT AGAINST CAMPUS ANTI-SEMITISM

Despite these obstacles, much progress has been accomplished, particularly since 2004. Dr. Gary Tobin, his Institute for Jewish & Community Research (IJCR), and the first edition of The UnCivil University all played a role in that progress.

In 2004, the U.S. Department of Education's Office for Civil Rights issued its new policy announcing, for the first time, that it would prosecute anti-Semitism cases in a manner similar to its handling of race, sex, and disability matters.[8] Specifically, OCR announced its interpretation that anti-Semitism cases, when sufficiently serious, could violate Title VI of the Civil Rights Act of 1964. This was critically important, because OCR had previously declined to prosecute such cases, despite the severity of anti-Semitism on many college campuses in recent years.[9] The new policy was embodied in two guidance letters which I issued while heading OCR. The second of these letters was directed to Gary Tobin's organization, the Institute for Jewish & Community Research.[10] Already at that time, IJCR had emerged as an important player in an issue for which larger, better-known organizations had not been adequately prepared.

The following year, The UnCivil University made its first appearance, demonstrating the extent, connectedness, and nature of the problem of campus anti-Semitism. Significantly, Tobin, Weinberg, and Ferer's work demonstrated that the new campus anti-Semitism is symptomatic of broader pathologies in our post-secondary system. As their work shows, the contemporary university has been politicized to the expense not only of academic quality but also of basic civility norms. With this loss of civility, an ideology of anti-Israelism and anti-Semitism has become widespread. This ideology, *The UnCivil University* shows, has found expression in student newspapers, classroom syllabi, campus posters, rallies, and elsewhere.

Dr. Tobin launched this book at a briefing before the U.S. Commission on Civil Rights, where I then served as director. I had invited Dr. Tobin to testify based not only on the breadth and timeliness of his research, but also because he clearly grasped the systemic character of this problem. Based in part on Dr. Tobin's research, the Commission issued its 2006 report on *Campus Anti-Semitism*.[11] This report marked a watershed in contemporary understandings of domestic university-based Judeophobia, announcing that anti-Semitism had become, once again, a "serious problem" on many college campuses around the country. Moreover, the Commission pierced one of the most dangerous misperceptions of the new campus anti-Semitism. Addressing the political rhetoric in which much of the new anti-Semtism is wrapped, the Commission announced that "Anti-Semitic bigotry is no less morally deplorable when camouflaged as anti-Israelism or anti-Zionism."[12] At several campuses, students and faculty have reported that this work inspired them to speak out against campus anti-Semitism.

THE BACKLASH

Unfortunately, these important steps have not yet proven sufficient. On some campuses, such as the University of California, Irvine and Wayne State University, the problems described in these pages have continued unabated. At others, such as San Jose State University and the University of California, Davis, new problems have arisen. Moreover, the Civil Rights Commission's directives have not been universally embraced. At OCR, new leadership has actually repudiated at least part of the 2004 anti-Semitism policy, raising doubts as to whether OCR will protect Jewish students at all.[13] In the Irvine case, amazingly, OCR found preliminarily that it had insufficient evidence to bring suit against Irvine. Worse, OCR's opinion is written in a manner that appears to confirm the worst fears about its current treatment of Jewish students.

Ironically, in early 2008, an independent task force investigating the Irvine allegations concluded that the "acts of anti-Semitism are real and well documented" and that "Jewish students have been harassed."[14] Most strikingly, the Task Force urged that "students with a strong Jewish identity should consider enrolling elsewhere unless and until tangible changes are made."[15] This has led several members of Congress to ask pointed questions of the Department of Education, expressing concern that the Department is not abiding by the portions of its 2004 policy which remain official policy.[16]

THE ROAD FROM HERE

Sadly, we have learned from this experience that campus anti-Semitism is now a politically intractable problem which requires both serious study and decisive action. The revised edition of *The UnCivil University* contributes substantially to the need for further scholarship by updating and expanding upon the first edition's analyses. As for the need for decisive action, there is much work to be done.

At a national level, the Education Department needs to reconfirm its commitment to eradicating campus anti-Semitism. The inexplicable failure of OCR's current leadership to apply its official policy requires correction. Congress has made tentative steps toward encouraging this resolution through oversight, but these efforts have not yet been successful. Ultimately, a full governmental approach to this problem will require legislation. Specifically, Congress should pass a statute to prohibit religious discrimination in education, just as it has long prohibited religious discrimination in such areas as employment and housing.[17] In this way, Jewish and other religious minority students will receive the same level of protection as, for example, black, Hispanic, or Arab students.

Locally, university students, faculty, and administration all have a role to play in defeating campus anti-Semitism. In some cases, local activists have successfully channeled their efforts through activist organizations such as Scholars for Peace in the Middle East, StandWithUs, the David Project, and the Zionist Organization of America. The important thing is to heed the admonition of the Civil Rights Commission's campus anti-Semitism initiative: "Silence is an Ally of Hate."[18] The new campus anti-Semitism can only be defeated if good people speak out against this resurgent evil. To those who have been numbed by the slowly gathering heat, I can only urge you to remember the parable of the boiling frog, and jump. Wake up and jump!

Kenneth L. Marcus is the Lillie and Nathan Ackerman Chair in Equality and Justice in America, Baruch College School of Public Affairs, The City University of New York and Senior Research Associate, Institute for Jewish & Community Research. He is former Staff Director, U.S. Commission on Civil Rights.

CHAPTER ONE

SOMETHING AMISS IN HIGHER EDUCATION

ACADEMIC FREEDOM AND THE PUBLIC TRUST

At the University of California, Berkeley, renowned both for its academic rigor as well as for its progressive, if not radical political history, there is a six-foot seal embedded in the pavement of the main walkway, Sproul Plaza, the staging ground of legendary student protests in the 1960s and 1970s. At the center of the seal is a six-inch ring of dirt, around which lies the inscription, "This soil and the air space extending above it shall not be a part of any nation and shall not be subject to any entity's jurisdiction." While many wanted the seal to be a monument to the Free Speech Movement, which began on the Berkeley campus in 1964, the university disavowed that connection. Nonetheless, campus folklore alleges that this spot is uniquely protected and that anyone standing on the seal may claim immunity from arrest or prosecution.

Despite the myth surrounding the seal and its ring of soil, it is not—it cannot be—an absolute sanctuary for those who wish to abuse the right of free speech, because no such place exists, not even on the grounds of the University of California, Berkeley. Both the rules of the larger society and the social norms of the campus require reasonable boundaries on what can be said. Perhaps the campus has fewer constraints, but safety and civility necessitate that some limits are imposed. While universities

1

encourage expansive speech, they tend to draw the line on what they consider hate speech, even at Berkeley.

Assigning extralegal status to the seal in Sproul Plaza is as misguided as the oft-cited notion that college campuses themselves are untouchable spaces that must remain separate from the communities in which they exist in order to protect their own rights of free speech. Despite whatever desires students and faculty may have to live within an imaginary seal of immunity from which they may disregard the rules of the outside world, college campuses operate—or at least they should—by a well-defined code that allows for a greater level of freedom than in the non-academic world and simultaneously requires a higher level of accountability in exchange for that freedom. When students and faculty invoke the First Amendment to protect their right to express unpopular ideas, they are mistakenly conflating free speech with academic freedom. Free speech and academic freedom are not the same. Free speech is essential for academic freedom, but it is only one component. Overemphasis on free speech hints at a trivial aspiration: the desire to protest for the sake of protest, to remain on the outside purely for the status such a position confers.

Academic freedom is part of a system unique to the university. It allows for the unfettered exploration of unpopular ideas, but only within the context of meaningful scholarship. Academic freedom, even more than free speech alone, means that teachers and researchers can pose—without fear of repercussion and without their own biases clouding their inquiry—every reasonable and honest hypothesis. Such a privilege exists only when scholars subscribe to the system of safeguards set up to ensure both their own immunity from politics (tenure, for example) and the integrity and worthiness of their work (peer review in academic journals, among others).

Academic freedom requires, not opposition to the larger society, as so often happens when free speech is invoked on campus, but rather a contract with society. This distinction seems mainly forgotten, and under the banner of free speech, universities increasingly define themselves by their independence from, and often adversarial relationship with, authorities of all sorts, including the government, the private sector, and even the communities that support them and in which they flourish. If they see their primary purpose as bastions of free speech, they must feel particularly beleaguered when the outside world requests accountability. In their self-conceived role as havens for otherwise persecuted or unpopular points of view, universities see themselves as counterweights, watchdogs, and dissenters from established norms, rather than as primary contributors to and shapers of those norms. While these contrarian roles are sometimes appropriate, they are only part of the picture. Over the past forty years, the independence of the university has come to trump all other aspects of its mission. As a result, they have become, in many ways, obstructionist rather than facilitating entities, defeating the very principles that freedom of speech is supposed to ensure.

ACADEMIC FREEDOM REQUIRES, NOT OPPO-SITION TO THE LARGER SOCIETY, AS SO OFTEN HAPPENS WHEN FREE SPEECH IS INVOKED ON CAMPUS, BUT RATHER A CONTRACT WITH SOCIETY.

It was never meant to be this way. From their early days in the United States, universities were intended to be civil institutions in all senses of the word. Initially they were places where young men could learn the skills and knowledge necessary to teach and preach Christian values and scripture, then considered the mark of a civilized person. As universities became secular institutions (with noted exceptions), their classrooms and lecture halls evolved into models of civil discourse, where professors and their students could engage in respectful, if heated, discussion and debate about the most contentious topics.

Free speech on campus has its origins in such unfettered discourse. In the last half-century or so, universities, both public and private, have grown in size and influence and, as a result, have become even more firmly woven into the civic fabric through their contributions to the greater society. Every member of the populace, even those who never set foot on a campus, benefits from the knowledge, research, innovation, and education that flows from the halls of academia out to the community at large. Colleges are contributors to the commonweal; they are institutional citizens.

As such, universities, both public and private, are part of a public trust owned or financed by the American people. This deep reliance on public funds makes the universities' almost religious adherence to the concept of free speech in opposition to encroachment of the public and the government seem particularly misplaced. The university *is* the public; it is a part of the government. It is a civil institution.

Higher education is highly dependent on federal, state, and municipal governments for financial assistance in numerous forms. Universities are a $250 billion a year enterprise, including a hefty sum coming from public funds.[1] Research contracts, student loans, and tax subsidies provide the university with significant resources.

UNIVERSITIES, BOTH PUBLIC AND PRIVATE, ARE PART OF A PUBLIC TRUST OWNED OR FINANCED BY THE AMERICAN PEOPLE.

Federal assistance to universities extends to all kinds of universities, public and private, and it comes in the form of various grants and allocations. Total federal spending for university and college research and development for the 2002–03 year was nearly $20 billion, which amounted to 58 percent of total higher education spending on research and development nationally.

Grant money comes from a wide variety of federal departments such as Health and Human Services, Defense, Agriculture, and Energy as well as the National Science Foundation, among others.[2] Federal financial support for higher education can be found in the most unlikely places. For example, the Transportation Equity Act of 2005, for $286.4 billion, included more than $500 million going to 142 colleges and universities. Some went for "National University Transportation Centers" and other funds for road improvement and parking garages.[3]

Federal student aid is similarly generous. General available aid includes Pell Grants, Work-Study, Perkins Loans, and Supplemental Educational Opportunity Grants. Designated aid includes Stafford Student Loans, Parents Loans for Undergraduate Students, Veterans Loans, and others. Total 2003–04 federal student aid amounted to over $80 billion, with Pell grants and Stafford loans constituting about 75 percent of the total. Federal student aid provides over 40 percent of all undergraduate students with assistance.

State appropriations for public higher education across the nation totaled more than $63 billion for the 2002–03 academic year, according to the *Chronicle of Higher Education*. This amounts to just below 40 percent of total expenditures by public universities. Some state systems are more and some less reliant upon state funding. California, for example, allocates almost $10 billion, 60 percent of total expenditures. Public universities in Vermont, on the other hand, receive 21 percent of total expenditures from the state. In addition to state appropriations, state student aid totaled over $6 billion for the nation in 2003–04. Nationally, approximately 16 percent of undergraduate students receive some form of state financial aid. Although state research grants are less common than federal support, 7 percent of total spending on research and development comes from state government.

The combination of public university operating budgets, state and federal research grants, student aid, and other government subsidies demonstrates that universities and colleges, whether public or private, are at least partially government-sponsored. The total amount of state and federal dollars that are being injected into the higher education system is around $180 billion.[4] Furthermore, universities are designated as non-profit organizations and, as such, are exempt from taxation on a number of levels.

UN-CIVILITY: CAMPUS ANTI-SEMITISM AND ANTI-ISRAELISM

Because Americans, both individually and through public financing, invest heavily in higher education, colleges and universities have a contractual understanding with the public that teaching and research are to be free of politics and propaganda. An uncivil university, therefore, is an affront not only to the students and faculty within the walls of academe, but to the entire community that treasures and therefore supports the true mission of higher education.

Or, at least what it is supposed to be. What was once conceived as an ethical arena in which young people came to exercise their minds, to practice thinking in a safe and invigorating environment, instead has become more of a stifling museum devoted to preserving itself. The core values that make the ideal university a singular place have been subverted. Moreover, the roles that university stakeholders are supposed to play in how they execute their various responsibilities have become murky. The civil university, despite its good intentions, has lost its civility, and the academy has become vulnerable to the very ills that the deliberately rarefied university system was meant to prevent.[5]

What is the uncivil university? It is an abrogation of the partnership agreement between American society and colleges and universities. The pages that follow tell the story of an institution that is confused about its mission. The net result is a loss of the search for truth, a violation of the purpose of the university and ultimately of the public trust. In our analysis, we detail a set of values and cultural norms that no longer reflect their noble origins nor achieve their stated purpose. In many cases, a "butterfly effect" has taken place, so that, with a small shift here and there, what were once well-intentioned and vital components of the university system, such as an emphasis on academic freedom, the willingness to question the established order, a love of rigorous scholarship, and an embracing of multiculturalism, have become twisted and sometimes barely recognizable versions of their former selves. It is in this unfortunate state that ideologies and practices antithetical to the civil university have flourished on some campuses, an indication of just how far they have diverged from their purpose.

This volume examines one particularly egregious and uncivil violation of the public trust—the ideology and expression of anti-Semitism and anti-Israelism in higher education. We examine these two closely related prejudices on college campuses, because the presence of anti-Semitism in a community has always been a reliable indicator of its ill health.

In a civil university, no group is singled out for slander, no democratic nation is declared illegitimate, no political ideology warps the pursuit of truth. In a civil university, the process of learning supercedes personal biases. In such a university, no one tolerates bigotry, because the protection of pluralism is part of the public ideal. In a civil university, everyone protects each other against bias and hatred. And yet, Jewish students report being intimidated, both inside and outside the classroom, and being intellectually and socially threatened for what they believe. In many universities that otherwise consider themselves to be models of civility, anti-Semitism and anti-Israelism are not only tolerated but allowed to flourish.

This loss of civility should alarm every one of us, not just the Jewish people. All members of society should be concerned, because the existence of bigotry and hatred is an indication of a deep gash in the fabric of the public trust. The ideology and expression of anti-Semitism and anti-Israelism in higher education is not a Jewish problem; it is an American problem.

Anti-Semitism is a belief system, a prejudice against Jews as a mythical enemy. Jews are the origin or cause of the inexplicable problems of life and community—poverty, war, or even natural disasters. Jews are also enviable. They are cast as rich, unusually clever, and powerful. Jews are "other"—people who are not like me, some group that is external to my group. Jews are stereotyped as having beliefs, values, and behaviors that are foreign, mysterious, and destructive.

The ideology of anti-Israelism transfers these stereotypes of traditional anti-Semitism onto discussions about Israel. Israel is often substituted for Jews as the primary source of the world's woes. If only we could solve the Palestinian-Israeli problem (which is really presented as an Israeli problem) the world would be much better off. Indeed, anti-Israelists argue that the very presence of a Jewish state threatens the world's stability. Read traditional anti-Semitism: rid the world of Jews, and we will all be better off. Now the line reads, rid the world of Israel, and we will all be better off. The same sentiment, the same outcome, and the same focus substitute the idea of the Jews with the idea of Israel. As we will show, anti-Israelism on campus labels Israel as Nazi Germany, claims the Holocaust never occurred, that Israel is systematically committing genocide, that Israel and the Jews control the United States government, and other ugly charges.

> ANTI-SEMITISM AND ANTI-ISRAELISM IN HIGHER EDUCATION IS NOT A JEWISH PROBLEM; IT IS AN AMERICAN PROBLEM.

Our analysis does not purport to say whether anti-Semitism and anti-Israelism are rising or declining, to count how many campuses in the United States experience anti-Semitism and anti-Israelism and to what extent, or to be a compendium of all of the incidents of anti-Semitism and anti-Israelism to have occurred in the last few years. Nor does our analysis claim to be a survey of anti-Semitic and anti-Israel attitudes on campus. Rather, this volume focuses on the ideology of anti-Semitism and anti-Israelism on campus and the ways that this ideology is expressed.

Although anti-Semitism and anti-Israelism are national campus phenomena, they are not equally distributed among colleges and universities. Some universities may be relatively free of the ideology or its expression, while others may be more problematic. The incidence of anti-Semitism and anti-Israelism may also vary on a particular campus over time, sometimes more prevalent, sometimes less. Levels may also rise and fall because the traveling anti-Israel road show, in terms of conferences, speakers, and petitions, goes from campus to campus, one year at the University of Michigan, another at Duke University, and so on.

Our analysis has three parts. We define anti-Semitism and anti-Israelism as an ideology. Second, we provide evidence about the expression of anti-Semitism and anti-Israelism to understand how this ideology presents itself as behaviors as well as ideas. And, third, we examine how the presence of anti-Semitism and anti-Israelism on campus reveals where reform is needed in higher education.

Concerns about the pervasiveness of this ideology are similar to concerns about the relationship between anti-Semitic beliefs and anti-Semitic behavior in the general society: higher levels of anti-Semitic belief are the foundation of anti-Semitic behavior. We document that anti-Semitism and anti-Israelism are operative ideologies that find expression in classroom syllabi, student newspapers, posters on campus, rallies, and a host of other ways within the university environment. (Colleges, universities, the campus, and higher education are used interchangeably in this analysis. We do not refer to a specific kind of institution when using any of these terms.)

Our research shows that the ideology of anti-Israelism can be found at many colleges and universities. It is probable that a campus-by-campus study would reveal the ideology and expression of anti-Semitism and anti-Israelism throughout much of the higher education system, even if embraced by relatively small segments of the faculty or student body. However, this minority has molded the campus culture concerning Israel. Of our many examples of both ideology and expression, we chose those that best represent our findings, which are illustrative, not unusual or unique. Similar expressions and incidences can be found on campuses all over North America. Our discussion includes a few examples from Canadian colleges and universities, because anti-Semitism and anti-Israelism are North American phenomena and extend beyond the borders of the United States. Because anti-Semitism and anti-Israelism also affect Europe and elsewhere, we occasionally discuss their expression in higher education around the world. While trends in academia can be global in scope, this study focuses primarily on the United States.

Anti-Semitism and anti-Israelism are allowed to flourish because the loudest voices, which embrace this bigotry, dominate the campus culture. It is symptomatic of what is happening in American society as a whole. Those who are the most activist and the most ideologically driven capture the organizational apparatus of political parties, religious institutions, or other parts of our society, and "the extremes are overrepresented in the political arena and the center underrepresented."[6] The campus, like American society, is less polarized than popular image might have one believe. Those with the most extreme views often dominate the ranks and decision-making processes of many institutions and seem—falsely—to represent the majority.

Indeed, anti-Semitism and anti-Israelism are nurtured on college campuses by the energetic focus of a determined minority, and their willingness to dedicate themselves to this cause. Anti-Israelists spend time and energy to promote their cause, while most everyone else is not all that engaged. Most faculty do not endorse anti-Israelism as an ideology. Many simply tune it out on their campus or on other campuses around the country. Advertisers have long known that readers tend to ignore ads for washing machines unless they are looking to buy one. Most faculty are involved in their own disciplines, and their own social and intellectual circles. Occasionally, what they consider to be the "sideshow" of the Palestinian–Israeli debate may attract their attention, but fleetingly, and with no real impact.

The irony of the campus endorsement (through action or by default) of anti-Israelism is that for the most part, campuses are not very active at all about most critical international issues. In spite of all the hype about social activism, embracing liberal causes, and fighting for the underdog, the campus community is disappointingly complacent about genocide, slavery, abuse of women and children, horrific criminal justice systems, and other social and political tragedies around the world. Taking up the anti-Israel cause is all the more curious in the context of the blasé response to the world's tragedies.

Addressing anti-Semitism and anti-Israelism is not a call for censorship or limiting free speech. Israel is not a perfect society. There are social and political inequities in Israel. Policing millions of Palestinians in Gaza and the West Bank has proved to be a failed policy. Discussing Israel's faults and wrong actions can be part of campus debate, as should be discussions of all nations, cultures, and societies. The red herring of censorship is not at issue. Israel-bashing, demonization, double standards, hateful language, anti-Semitic images, and obsession with Israel more than any other country are signs, indicators, and alarms that something other than debate and honest criticism are at work. Universities cannot pretend that calling for the destruction of Israel with the use of Nazi images is part of normal academic discourse. If they do, they are being untruthful with themselves. Perhaps, they are afraid to admit the failure up to this point to have appropriately addressed the issue. It is better to remedy the problem now, rather than compound it through the inability to admit more should have been done before. The rejection of anti-Semitism and anti-Israelism on campus is an act of moral courage.

Exposing anti-Semitism and anti-Israelism includes the willingness to judge ideas: not all ideas are good or of equal worth. Universities should celebrate cultural differences with the ability to discern right and wrong across cultural boundaries. Not all cultural practices are good, and not all are equal in their contributions to the benefit of the human family. Moral strength means celebrating good teaching that helps students think, analyze, and distinguish sound ideas from suspect ones. It means teaching, not preaching; exploration and rigorous examination, not propaganda. This includes anti-Israel propaganda, which cannot be framed as merely a clash of cultural ideas.

One may read our analysis with puzzlement. After all, some characterize the "Israel debate" as merely part of the free exchange of ideas. Clearly, faculty who support Israel can be found on college campuses all over America. Students rally on behalf of Israel, books are published that support Israel, and so on. Anti-Israelism does not signal the absence of pro-Israelism. Indeed, this is often the rationale, or excuse, for anti-Semitism and anti-Israelism in higher education. Advocates of free speech may say that clearly opposing forces can speak on campus and do. The presence of pro-Israel speakers, classes, faculty, or materials on campus, however, does not address the core issue.

Having a pro-Israel speaker does not erase an anti-Semitic diatribe from some other speaker. Good Israel talk does not balance bad Israel talk. Indeed, the balanced approach is a denial of the problem. Universities do not balance racism and sexism with "positive images" of blacks and women. They make it clear that racism and sexism do not belong on campus. Period. The same needs to be said and done about anti-Semitism and anti-Israelism—they have no place on campus. Period. Otherwise, universities should abolish their policies of zero tolerance for intimidation of students or hate speech. Why have them, when they are not applied uniformly? If hate speech against Jews is allowed as part of the balance of ideas on campus, then hate speech against all others should be afforded the same protected status in the name of freedom. Tolerate all racism or prohibit it. The truly civil university does not offer a cafeteria of selective protections.

Fears about the preservation of academic freedom have trumped academic responsibility. Anti-Israelism can flourish because the academy is afraid to confront this ideology and those who preach it for fear of going down some slippery slope that will infringe upon academic freedom. But other slippery slopes are just as profoundly damaging to the ideals of the university, including the failure to ensure both high quality and honest scholarship, adhere to principles of truth, preserve civil discourse, and provide freedom from intellectual intimidation. All of these affect academic freedom and define academic responsibility. All are tainted by anti-Semitic and anti-Israel ideology and expression on campus.

THE TRULY CIVIL UNIVERSITY DOES NOT OFFER A CAFETERIA OF SELECTIVE PROTECTIONS.

This volume is a call for reform in higher education. The university has all the structure, mechanisms, and values to address anti-Semitism and anti-Israelism on campus. Formal systems include peer review, evaluation of scholarship and teaching, committees for hearing student complaints, and disciplinary measures for inappropriate faculty or student behavior. These mechanisms are not fully deployed in the case of anti-Semitism and anti-Israelism.

They should be, however, because those who support higher education expect colleges to use the tools they have to keep their own house in order. When it comes to prejudice, propaganda in the guise of scholarship, or the failure to execute teaching responsibilities adequately, the full force of university controls should be exercised. This includes creating a normative environment that banishes anti-Semitism and anti-Israelism from the accepted values of the campus and disciplining those who violate those norms.

Campuses have informal guidelines that prohibit campus sexism, racism, and other forms of prejudice. Anti-Semitism and anti-Israelism have not been adequately constrained by these norms. University presidents, deans, faculty, trustees, and other stakeholders have not applied these norms to speak out firmly and consistently to condemn anti-Semitism and anti-Israelism.

Anti-Semitism and anti-Israelism on campus are symptoms of a much larger malaise. Reform is necessary to protect Jewish students, to be sure. Even more importantly, the failure to ensure the intellectual safety of Jewish students marks a corruption of the university as a civil institution. Colleges and universities should address anti-Semitism and anti-Israelism, not for the sake of the Jews, but for their own sake. The uncivil university must reclaim its civility.

CHAPTER TWO
DEFINING THE CIVIL UNIVERSITY

PURPOSES OF THE CIVIL UNIVERSITY

In its finest state, the university is a deeply moral enterprise, dedicated to improving the quality of human existence through the pursuit and dissemination of knowledge. Its impact on society cannot be overemphasized. Universities not only add knowledge to a community, but they also contribute to society by imparting moral (which is not to say necessarily religious) instruction to their students and serving as the training grounds for those future contributors to society. From scientific and medical advancements to contributions in literature, philosophy, and social sciences, the reach of university graduates into the society at large is incalculable and invaluable. As a result of their contributions, universities have been accorded a special status in society.

> For the three-plus centuries of American higher education, universities and colleges—both state-owned and private—have held a privileged position. With this special position have come responsibilities and expectations. As the country has grown and developed, the expectations that society holds for higher education have grown. When the first college was founded in 1636, two purposes were spelled out in its charter: to graduate enough "men of the cloth" to lead the colony's churches and to graduate "lettered gentlemen" able to lead the affairs of the colony. . . . These two purposes—education

for the workforce and for civic life—have remained the bedrock of public expectations to this day.[1]

This "privileged position" turns the university into a public trust, an institution devoted to developing good citizens for the well-being of all. In other words, the public trusts the university with its future, and in turn the university receives support from the public in many forms: government subsidies, grants, tax breaks, research contracts, as well as philanthropic contributions, extraordinary protections from the vicissitudes of politics, and even the right to regulate and police itself.

The public trust originates in the long-standing connection between American universities and the government.[2] In many cases, universities owe their very existence to federal legislation and federal funding, beginning with the land grant movement established by the Morrill Act of 1862.

> The land grant movement came in response to the rapid industrial and agricultural development of the United States that attained such momentum in the middle of the [19th] century. Universities were to assist this development through training that went beyond the creation of "gentlemen," and of teachers, preachers, lawyers, and doctors; through research related to the technical advance of farming and manufacturing; through service to many and ultimately to almost all of the economic and political segments of society. The land grant movement was also responsive to a growing democratic, even egalitarian and populist, trend in the nation. Pursuing this trend, higher education was to be open to all qualified young people from all walks of life. It was to serve less the perpetuation of an elite class and more the creation of a relatively classless society, with the doors of opportunity open to all through education.[3]

By making a university education available to all, the federal government created a kind of implied contract with institutions of higher learning that has deepened and broadened since 1862. The wide availability of a university education is a cornerstone of the American value system and a fundamental tenet of America's story of itself: anyone with drive can succeed in the United States. (Despite the morality tales circulated by high school guidance counselors and other well-meaning adults, most applicants to college receive an offer of admission. According to author James Twitchell, "There are about 2,500 four-year colleges in this country, and only about 100 of them refuse more applicants than they accept. Most schools accept 80 percent or more of those who apply. It's the rare student who can't get in somewhere.")[4]

In their book, *The Future of Higher Education*, Frank Newman, Lara Couturier, and Jamie Scurry attribute "[t]he success of American higher education [to] the broad social compact . . . —a widely shared understanding of what it is that higher education does for society and the support, privilege, and respect that society provides in return."[5] In addition, they believe that many Americans link the promise of a better life—the attainment of some version of the American dream—to a university education, which "[i]s perceived as imparting substantial personal benefits, both economic and social, especially among groups that have been historically disadvantaged and are still striving for equal opportunities in society."[6]

The two-way flow of benefits between institutions of higher learning and the public they serve are reflected in the tripartite mission of the civil university: to add knowledge to the wider community, to create moral citizens, and to provide the community with able and skillful members whose contributions improve the overall lot of society. To achieve their mission, universities should expect students to learn through a variety of disciplines, gaining both intellectual and social experiences that will make them better citizens. Students are to adhere to rules of honest performance and intellectual diversity with a broad base of ideas, courses, and disciplines. They are also to learn enough to prepare them for fruitful contributions to the society of which they are a part. Nearly every commencement speech is filled with noble exhortations for graduating seniors to go out and be productive citizens who help improve the quality of human existence.

Over time, universities have reached out to an increasingly broad segment of the American people. "[Universities] have been steadily expanded from preparation of young men for leadership in the community to preparation of a broad share of the population for participation in the workforce and civic life; from polishing the elite to providing widespread social mobility; from generating scholarship aimed at supporting certain beliefs to supporting unfettered, evidence-based debate about social issues as well as wide-ranging and trustworthy research essential to modern society."[7]

For the last century, most four-year colleges in the United States have offered a "liberal education," which, according to Stanley Katz, Princeton

University professor and President Emeritus of the American Council of Learned Societies, trains students to think broadly and to become contributing members of society: "The association of colleges and universities currently defines liberal education as: 'a philosophy of education that empowers individuals, liberates the mind from ignorance, and cultivates social responsibility. Characterized by challenging encounters with important issues, and more a way of studying than specific content, liberal education can occur at all types of colleges and universities.'"[8]

Most students want—cherish—a true liberal education. According to a 2004 survey of incoming freshman conducted by the Higher Education Research Institute at the University of California, Los Angeles, most students attend college for the chance to improve their financial prospects. Students rank "training for a specific career" (75 percent), "to be able to get a better job" (72 percent), and "to be able to make more money" (70 percent) as important reasons for deciding to go to college. The economic motivations for attending college have become more important over time. Twenty years ago, only one-third of students stated that they were attending college in order to get a job; today, nearly three-quarters are motivated by such goals.

Career and economic success, however, are not the only motivations for attending college. Almost 77 percent list "to learn more about things that interest me," 65 percent "to gain a general education and appreciation of ideas," and 52 percent to "find my purpose in life." Career issues are strong, but aspiration and learning also matter. About 41 percent even say that they want college to help them to be "a more cultured person." Students expect when they attend college to be influenced in who they are and how they lead their lives.[9]

Yet, some universities seem unable to resolve what they may perceive as the conflicting pressures exerted by students for vocational training and the heartfelt sentiments of their mission statements. Few, if any, mission statements mention power, money, and prestige as goals of a university education. Ross Gregory Douthat described these dueling aspects of his pedigree education in *Privilege: Harvard and the Education of the Ruling Class*.

> But in the wider, institutional culture of Harvard, such academic idealism is regarded as a quaint curiosity at best. It's all very well for the drones and the bookworms and the people who want to be profes-

sors themselves, the attitude goes, but for the rest of us, there's no reason to let such noble pursuits get in the way of the *real* business of Harvard, which is understood to be the pursuit of success, and the personal connections from which such success has always flowed. At its crudest, a Harvard education is a four-year scramble to ingratiate oneself—with professors who write recommendations; with employers who offer internships and lucrative post-college positions; and with the pundits and poets and politicians who flock to Harvard to speak and debate and hobnob with students.[10]

While Douthat's experience at Harvard cannot represent the experiences of all students at all liberal colleges, his view is indicative of the university's muddled sense of its own mission. Students can learn to think, analyze, and form honest, well-conceived opinions, at the same time that recruiters for investment banks, the United States government, and other employers are setting up brochure-filled tables along campus pathways. There is an important place for career training and employment help at the university. But these cannot supercede the other parts of the school's mission. Without simultaneously teaching students to think and to develop a strong sense of morals, American universities would be graduating class after class of Faustian clones. Who wants to live in *that* America, no matter how prosperous?

WITHOUT TEACHING STUDENTS TO THINK AND TO DEVELOP A STRONG SENSE OF MORALS, AMERICAN UNIVERSITIES WOULD BE GRADUATING CLASS AFTER CLASS OF FAUSTIAN CLONES.

The mission of the civil university remains the same whether the university is designated "public" or "private." While public institutions are the creations of government and are subject to the incumbent restrictions and regulations (and perks, such as the ability of its employees to join public sector unions) not applied to private universities, the independent status of private universities is something of a myth. Their designation as *non-profit* corporations is telling: non-profit status is given to entities that serve the public good in some way, like hospitals, museums, social service agencies, and so on. Because of the financial support, both in actual dollars as well as in tax subsidies, given by the public sector to *all* universities, whatever their designation, *all* universities are deeply entwined with the public and therefore must serve the public. Indeed, there is no completely "private" university.

In April 2005, Robert J. Birgeneau, incoming chancellor of the University of California, Berkeley, recognized in his inaugural address the obligation of all institutions of higher learning to fulfill their end of this social contract:

> We must clarify what is "public" in the public nature of the University. If we had enough financial resources to fund ourselves in every respect without any funds from public revenues and we were able to do everything we do today but as a private entity, would we have achieved Berkeley's mission? I say emphatically no. At the core of our mission is our commitment to fulfill the public trust and to bequeath to subsequent generations educational opportunities that extend the public good.[11]

ALL UNIVERSITIES ARE DEEPLY ENTWINED WITH THE PUBLIC AND THEREFORE MUST SERVE THE PUBLIC. INDEED, THERE IS NO COMPLETELY "PRIVATE" UNIVERSITY.

While most people understand that universities add knowledge to the community through research, teaching, and the open exchange of ideas in an intellectual marketplace, fewer think about the moral and ethical impact of a university education on its students. In addition to skills and knowledge, universities transfer beliefs and worldviews to young adults. This happens at a time in life when individuals are particularly open and vulnerable to ideas and influences. It is during college, when many students are exposed to people unlike themselves for the first time, that students form and re-form opinions about other religious, racial, and ethnic groups. Identity formation takes place between the ages of 18 and 25, just as it does through childhood and adolescence. Indeed as marriage and career are delayed, adolescence may last well into a person's twenties. Students are taking longer to finish their college education, taking time off either before they enter colleges and universities or in the middle of their college years, and more individuals are obtaining graduate degrees. Therefore, the time of influence for universities is not only the ages of 18 to 22 but increasingly between the ages of 18 and 30. Even more than the media and perhaps as much as their parents, universities may affect a student's beliefs about race, religion, and other essential societal issues for a lifetime.

Colleges and universities train future leaders in media, government, academia, health care, law, and other professions in the United States. One cannot be a leader in any of the important realms of society without accreditation at either the undergraduate or graduate level (except for entrepreneurs who are fortunate in business despite, or because of, their lack of a college degree). As a result, along with religious organizations, few institutions in society are more important in shaping the moral fabric and beliefs of America than colleges and universities.

Another role of colleges and universities is to train and enlighten participating citizens. Democracy depends upon an informed citizenry steeped in the values and history of the nation's founding principles. The civil university, in preparing graduating students to be fruitful members of civil society, should graduate students who know and appreciate the philosophical tenets of democracy and the values of American society. At the same time, students should learn about other cultures and traditions around the world. It is important for good citizens to be capable of societal criticism and to be able to analyze the strengths and weaknesses of American institutions and ideologies. (Whether the focus also should be on the strengths and not the weaknesses is a fundamental issue worth exploring.)

The reach of universities goes far beyond the borders of their campuses. Universities provide intellectual content to the American public. Professors often appear as talking heads on news shows discussing crime rates, racial politics, the economy, and a host of other issues relating to both national and international concerns. Representatives from local universities are often commentators during elections. Law school professors often become celebrities during trials of interest to the American public. Universities provide experts for the print and the electronic media. A book or article may spark controversy and debate, and an academic can travel the media circuit discussing his latest theory or findings. Entrepreneurial academics are especially adept at serving as experts, lecturing the general public with their worldview.

Universities also serve as a nexus among institutions. For example, higher education has historically been steeped within religious movements. Now-secular universities, like Harvard, continue to maintain a divinity school to train religious leaders. Connections between universities and government are profound (look at all the presidents and presidential candidates that come from Yale University). Elementary and secondary school teachers, as well as school administrators, are trained in the nation's universities.

Higher education also has an enormous impact on the wage-earning capacity of its graduates. A college education is a ticket to greater economic prosperity for those who are able to attain a degree. Universities help create an economic elite, and what they teach therefore helps shape the entrepreneurial engines of America and fuel movement into the middle and upper classes of our society.

Universities have been contributing to the public good for over half a century by partnering with federal, state, and local governments on a vast array of research projects, evaluations, professions, and studies. Clark Kerr, in his book, *The Uses of the University*, tracks the history of this partnership to the middle of the 20th century. "[F]ederal support of scientific research [began] during World War II. The wartime laboratories that were the forerunners of such continuing government-financed research centers as the Lincoln Laboratory at the Massachusetts Institute of Technology, the Argonne at the University of Chicago, and the Lawrence Radiation Laboratory at the University of California, Berkeley, opened a new age. The major universities were enlisted in national defense and in scientific and technological development as never before. (In World War I the universities had only been a source of raw recruits.)"[12] In addition, university faculty are used to assess a variety of civic services, from transportation needs in American cities and the availability of health care to the rise and fall of crime rates around the country. Vast amounts of research money flow into the universities with the expectation that technical expertise will help solve or address public sector problems.

> PROFESSORS AND STUDENTS ALIKE SHOULD OBJECTIVELY PURSUE THE TRUTH, FREE OF IDEOLOGICAL BIAS IN BOTH RESEARCH AND TEACHING.

DRIVING VALUES OF THE CIVIL UNIVERSITY

In its ideal state, the civil university achieves its fine and far-reaching educational and social goals by adhering to a strong set of values. In fact, the image of the ideal university among the American public is that of a place of honest and rigorous scholarship, unimpeachable ethics, academic freedom, and diversity of every sort. If the reach of the university is as broad and long-lasting as it seems, then the upholding of these values is imperative for the civil university to maintain its civility.

The first, and perhaps the highest, value governing the ideal university is honest scholarship. That is to say, professors and students alike should objectively pursue the truth, free of ideological bias in both research and teaching. In an era when some campuses seem to require monolithic thinking to fit in, Harvard University history professor Stephan Thernstrom questions the wisdom that a community must be united in its ideology to remain united as a community. He asks,

> Is Harvard University really a "community" that requires ideological conformity? The First Baptist Church of Peoria is such a community, with a common conception of God and how best to worship Him. Possibly Bob Jones University is such a community. But no great university can retain its greatness if it attempts to enforce the equivalent of a religious creed on its members. What really holds the members of the Harvard "community" together is much more limited: It is— or at least it used to be—a common commitment to pursue the truth through disciplined scholarship, and a faith that freedom of inquiry is the best means to arrive at the truth.[13]

Without fear from reprisal, suppression, or other consequences, challenges to the old order, surely one of the great contributions of the university to the public, stand little chance of emerging. Gil Troy, professor of history at McGill University, implores his colleagues to create an environment where the truth becomes the only predictable outcome of scholarship. "We need classrooms that are safe testing grounds for ideas, both new and old. We need campuses encouraging students and colleagues to experiment boldly, rigorously, honestly, creatively, systematically, and, as much as possible, apolitically."[14]

The search for the truth—whatever the outcome of that search— should govern all scholars of the civil university, as evidenced by the statement of professional ethics of the American Association of University Professors: "[Professors'] primary responsibility to their subject is to seek and to state the truth as they see it. To this end professors devote their energies to developing and improving their scholarly competence. They accept the obligation to exercise critical self-discipline and judgment in using, extending, and transmitting knowledge. They practice intellectual honesty. Although professors may follow subsidiary interests, these interests should never seriously hamper or compromise their freedom of inquiry."[15]

Honest scholarship includes rigorous research. First, it is expected that the highest standards of research will be used, subject to ongoing peer review. Second, research should be cutting edge, moving forward the frontiers of knowledge. Third, it is expected that research should be interesting and understandable, not only to other academics but to the public at large. The marketplace of ideas should help our understanding of the world and societies around us. If academics write and speak only to each other, the public is not well served. Pursuit of knowledge and moral values are entwined, and making higher education a moral enterprise. Conducting unbiased, objective research is not detached from nor antithetical to issues of moral concern.

In writing about the teaching of moral values on campus, George Dennis O'Brien, former president of Bucknell University and the University of Rochester, notes that

> [t]here are at least three places where ethics lurks about the quad. First, moral intent—broad and vague—is often proclaimed in the institution's official prose. It is the perennial theme of commencement oratory as properly educated graduates are sent forth to reform a tired old world. Second, whatever the cloudy cultural hope of commencement oratory, there is a highly specific and rigid ethic implicit in the institutional research ideology, which defines the contemporary university. This internal research university ethic is as powerful as it is often unacknowledged and underdeveloped. . . . Finally . . . contemporary students abound in ethical enthusiasms for various liberations—the more notable the research institution, the more notable the crusade.[16]

IF ACADEMICS WRITE AND SPEAK ONLY TO EACH OTHER, THE PUBLIC IS NOT WELL SERVED.

Part of the ethical environment on campus involves the honest and fair exchange of ideas. Universities should be places free of intimidation of speakers, shouting and booing, name-calling, or presenting only one side in difficult debates. But not all ideas are equal. Colleges and universities should not be homes to lectures about the genetic inferiority of blacks, scientific debates on whether or not the earth is flat or round, or other subjects where scientific or other moral judgments have rendered such discussions obsolete. The civil university not only prohibits prejudice and bigotry on campus but also opens the minds of those students who may arrive with such beliefs. The civil university welcomes legitimate debate on, say, the origins of life on earth, whether democracy is achievable or desirable in the Arab world, or the usefulness of DNA as a legal tool.

Honest scholarship can only be pursued when professors and students enjoy true academic freedom, which is not the freedom to say whatever one wishes without regard for the rigors of research or the love of the truth. Academic freedom is the ability to pursue a line of inquiry to its furthest reaches without hindrance of ideology, politics, or outside influences, including those emanating from the administration, the government, or industry. In other words, academic freedom means the ability to examine unpopular ideas despite their unpopularity. One university declared that

> ACADEMIC FREEDOM IS NOT THE FREEDOM TO SAY OR WRITE ANYTHING WITHOUT BOUNDARIES.

> [a]cademic freedom, which endows members of the university with the right to hold, express and teach any views they deem fit, and to research and publish their findings without restraint, is widely recognized as essential to the pursuit of knowledge. In order to flourish, university life needs to be an environment where people are prepared to search for the truth, wherever it may lead and whomever it may offend. Intellectual and scientific breakthroughs inevitably challenge the prevailing order, which is why those who make them frequently face repression and the attention of the censor.[17]

Of all the values at the civil university, professors guard academic freedom most closely. Academic freedom is essential, but it is also subject to the bounds of peer reviews, including assessment of scholars from disciplines outside one's own. Academic freedom includes adhering to standards of research set by fields of inquiry and accepted disciplines. Teaching and research must be grounded in knowledge and previous work. Academic freedom is not the freedom to say or write anything without boundaries. Intellectual responsibility is part of academic freedom.

Research methods must be ethical, which is why, for example, universities have human subjects review standards. Publishing in peer review journals means that some work is considered more worthy, sophisticated, or correct than other work. Research cannot be falsified, nor conclusions drawn that are not supported by data. All of these constrain what faculty may do or say. Academic freedom is not a license for irresponsibility, unethical, or incorrect research or teaching. Moreover, it should not be used as a shield from criticism, cheapening the value of the open and unfettered pursuit of knowledge. Faculty have to be careful not always to invoke the right to academic freedom as a defense against criticism from the non-academic world. Lee Bollinger, president of Columbia University, argues strongly for maintaining the wall between the academy and the "secular" world. "The risk in joining the public sphere," he writes, "is that we jeopardize the scholarly ethos. We therefore need to maintain the line between the differing roles—that of the scholar professional and that of the citizen. The last thing we want to do is to turn the campus into a political convention."[18] The academy should welcome the views of the outside world, because universities can learn from those outside their walls, as well as from those within.

Academic freedom extends beyond just the classroom, lecture hall, and laboratory into the hiring of professors and the offers of tenure. The civil university should not try to create political counterbalances, because it should promote and protect academic freedom regardless of ideology. Indeed, President Bollinger rightly believes that the trend to hire professors from different ends of the political spectrum is misguided. "We should not accept the idea that the remedy for lapses is to add more professors with different political points of view, as some would have us do. The notion of a 'balanced curriculum,' in which students can, in effect, select and compensate for bias, sacrifices the essential norm of what we are supposed to be about in a university. It also risks polarization, with 'liberal' students taking courses from 'liberal' professors and 'conservatives' taking classes from 'conservative' professors."[19]

Others argue correctly that even the appearance of bias would be a violation of the university's commitment to protect academic freedom. Ames et al. note: "The issue of potential bias (whether on the basis of ideology, gender, or religiosity) strikes at the heart of the academic enterprise. If scholars face discrimination on the basis of ideology, gender, religiosity, or any other characteristic not directly related to the profession, this would constitute a major problem, a problem requiring immediate attention and rectification."[20]

CAMPUS STAKEHOLDERS

All members of the university community, both internal and external, are bound by a system of checks and balances in which every stakeholder has a specific role to play to keep the community strong. Perhaps the most visible member of the internal community at a university is its president, who, among many other practical obligations, must provide moral leadership to the university community as well as to the outside world. Classics scholar Victor Davis Hanson describes the ideal role of the university president: "Their first allegiance ought to be to honesty and truth, not campus orthodoxy masquerading as intellectual bravery amid a supposedly reactionary society."[21] Furthermore, university presidents must be willing to use their position to promote the values of the civil university to society at large. One analyst writes, "In a world addicted to sound bites, instant analyses, and fast-paced rhetorical responses, the disciplined insights and deliberative approaches that college presidents can bring to public discussion are hardly democratic luxuries. College presidents can and must use their professional stature to promote the unhurried consideration of large questions. Their willingness to speak out on moral issues can remind us all of the essential nature of idealism."[22]

While university presidents are the most visible administrators (and often the main spokespeople for the college in fundraising, government, community, and other circles), they alone do not hold the responsibility for providing moral guidance to the campus. Provosts, deans, and other members of the administration have an obligation to be good stewards, to address student concerns promptly and fairly, and to enforce university policies and regulations consistently. In addition, administrators must ensure the financial health of the university by setting and adhering to budgets, aiding in fundraising, and working toward the university's vision for its own future.

Faculty, in addition to respecting, supporting, and modeling the values of honest and rigorous scholarship, academic freedom, and diversity of thought, should also strive to be excellent teachers. First and foremost, the university is a teaching institution, entrusted with both transferring knowledge and helping its students learn to think. Faculty must respect the policies and ethics set by the administration, and adhere to a code of professionalism that both sets an example for students and contributes to the general well-being of all members of the university community. Second, the university is a research institution, although tenure decisions in many colleges emphasize research accomplishments far more than teaching skills.

University trustees must fulfill their fiduciary duty to the university by working with the administration and faculty to ensure the long-term health of the institution. They are charged with monitoring the performance of the president, helping to oversee the fiscal state of the university, ensuring that the mission of the institution is upheld, and providing thoughtful and apolitical review of tenure recommendations from the faculty. Trustees are almost invisible to the students and many of the faculty; yet, they play a critical oversight role that helps create the best possible learning and working environment for both.

Students, too, have a responsibility as members of the public trust. No one is obliged to attend university. Those who do choose to go commit themselves to being good university citizens. If a student violates the code of ethics or otherwise disobeys university regulations, he or she may be disciplined or expelled. In turn, students may expect to receive what they pay for: a useful, enlightening education that will help them along whatever path they pursue upon graduation.

After all, teaching is a fee-for-service enterprise, where students pay substantial sums to purchase a college or higher degree. Students are entitled to the goods and services that they shop for and buy, and what they expect is to be prepared for a career. A private university tuition costs an average of $20,000 per year and can reach as much as $36,000.[23] Americans are willing to pay such sums because education, more and more, is viewed as a service that provides a tangible good.

PUBLIC STAKEHOLDERS

Since the university is a public trust, representatives of the public should have clear and vital responsibilities (and expectations) of the university. Without their active participation, the public aspect of the public trust would suffer. Alumni, as most alums would attest, have the obligation to donate money to the university to support the current generation of students, as they were supported when they were students. Alumni should serve on committees, such as those on admissions and policy, when asked, and provide vocal and visible leadership to other alumni in their own regions. Most importantly, alumni have a responsibility to continue their social contract with the university by being good campus citizens, by advocating for positive change, for unbiased leaders, for diversity of thought and action. Alumni owe their alma mater much more than loan payments and donations; they have an ethical debt to use their education for the greater good.

Alumni often become donors, sometimes major donors, to universities. Philanthropy has long played a fundamental role in the development of higher education in the United States.[24] Prior to 1900, fundraising had been a sporadic and often difficult matter for even the most successful of institutions. After the turn of the century, this picture was altered by developments at Yale and Harvard. The Yale Alumni Fund, which had been started in 1891 in order to collect small contributions, began receiving gifts in such volume that a separate endowment fund was created in addition to the annual donation given to the university. At this same juncture, the Harvard class of 1880, on the occasion of the twenty-fifth anniversary of its graduation, gave $100,000 to the university. Every subsequent class would give at least as much. Substantial gifts thus became for the first time a recurrent and dependable source of income.[25]

Such endowments have been long sought after in higher education—and large gifts have been the prize that university presidents have coveted for almost 300 years:

> From the time of the establishment of the Hollis Professorship of Divinity at Harvard (1721), it was gifts, and particularly gifts permanently preserved as endowments, that permitted American colleges to do things that were not strictly encompassed in the education of undergraduates. In the nineteenth century, the true research institutes of American colleges—the observatories and the museums—were established in this way.[26]

The best research universities, from their inception, have relied on this model for their very existence. As Roger Geiger noted, "it was the burgeoning philanthropy for higher education that had launched the bold experiments [of emphasizing graduate studies] at Johns Hopkins, Clark, and Chicago. To university presidents of this era it was axiomatic that research needed its own, specifically earmarked funds if it were to flourish."[27]

The university could not survive in its current state without being one of the most successful fundraising machines in history. As David Kirp noted, "It is important not to romanticize academe, not to slip into nostalgia for a time that never really was. Dollars have always greased the wheels of American higher education; were it otherwise, the term 'legacy' would not have a meaning specific to universities."[28]

Alumni give regularly to yearly capital campaigns. Wealthy alumni often give large gifts earmarked for specific departments, programs, or facility developments. Major donors often give gifts ranging from $1 million to more than $300 million. The Institute for Jewish & Community Research's study of mega-giving shows that in 2001, nearly half of all gifts over $1 million go to institutions of higher education, which annually receives combined gifts in excess of $6 billion in mega-gifts.[29] Gifts can come in the form of cash, securities, art, patents, and land.

These enormous contributions deepen the university's obligations to the public, because philanthropy is subsidized by the public sector. Philanthropic dollars are tax deductible. Capital gains taxes are lost to the public coffers when appreciated assets such as stocks or real estate are donated. Charitable giving may also lower a household tax bracket. All of these tax subsidies are an accepted (and desirable) part of the partnership between the public sector and the non-profit sector, including higher education.

Philanthropists who give to universities do so because they believe they are contributing to the public good. Their gifts—and the non-profit status of the university—imply that donors are supporting a public service, and in turn the university must be accountable to those donors by adhering to its own values, enforcing its own regulations, and spending the money as it was intended.[30] No university is obliged to accept a gift with strings that are deemed unacceptable. Minimally, the university should be straightforward in how a gift will be utilized, no matter the size of the donation. To do otherwise would be to violate the ethics of the civil university.

If the university is to remain so privileged both in terms of support from government and philanthropy (even though there is a nascent protest movement against the university's protected status), then its obligations to the public should guide its every move. Every stakeholder—both internal, such as faculty, trustees, administration, and students, and external, including alumni, philanthropists, government at all levels, and the public at large—must fulfill its part in ensuring the university's mission, or the public trust will be broken. It is the responsibility of all who benefit from the university, which means it is the responsibility of all who live in

American society, to insist that the civil university's values of unbiased scholarship, academic freedom, and diversity of thought and person be rigorously defended on every campus.

Chapter Three

The Emergence of the Uncivil University

The Lingering Legacy of the Sixties

Three unrelated but interconnected systemic trends have merged on campus in what can only be described as a "perfect storm" that has undermined the civil university. The first is the continuing legacy of the 1960s on campus culture. The second is an impressive level of fiscal inattention, which creates some bureaucratic quagmires. And the third is the abdication of moral leadership by many entrusted with the university's well-being.

The legacy of the 1960s is the primary determinant of contemporary campus culture. Over the past four decades, professors trained in the protest culture of the 1960s and 1970s have come to dominate both the classroom and the back rooms of the universities. That is to say, most of the older generation of professors still teaching attended college during those tumultuous years when the university was the epicenter of the quaking of American society; subsequent generations of graduate students have been trained by those same professors. It is logical, then, to expect the politics of that era in the form of a certain hegemony of thought would show up in the content taught in lecture halls as well as in tenure decisions.

The most obvious example of this ideological tilt is the political narrowness of the faculty, exemplified by the high number of registered Democrats as opposed to Republicans. While the country as a whole is generally split between the two parties, within the walls of the university, Republicans—and conservatives—are substantially underrepresented among the faculty. If one assumes that a certain percentage of the students who graduate from college hold conservative political views, register with the Republican party, and contribute to the red side of the fabled "red state/blue state" division in America, then it would seem odd that their professors would so overwhelmingly represent only one party.

The political imbalance on college campuses can sometimes be quantified by looking at federal data on campaign contributions by faculty members and other employees. For example, in 2004, faculty members and other employees from the University of North Carolina, Chapel Hill, gave far more to Democrats running for national office than to Republican candidates. "According to the federal data, about 80 or so University of North Carolina employees have given about $40,000 to the Kerry campaign, and about 20 university employees have given about $18,000 to Bowles. . . . Democrats got 93 percent of the contributions from University of North Carolina employees, by dollar value. In terms of the number of contributions, 97 percent have gone to Democrats."[1]

THE LEGACY OF THE 1960S IS THE PRIMARY DETERMINANT OF CONTEMPORARY CAMPUS CULTURE.

At Duke University, employee donations also favored Democrats: "In dollar value, democratic candidates and PACs got 86 percent of the take. Looking at the number of donations, Democrats got 89 percent of the contributions from Duke employees. . . . Although Durham [is] well known as being left-leaning, donations from other residents haven't favored Democrats to the same extent that the campus contributions have."[2]

Other studies corroborate the finding that colleges and universities tend to be populated by faculty who politically identify themselves as Democratic, especially in fields like sociology, anthropology, and history.[3] These are the faculty who most directly interpret America's and the world's civic narrative. "The mono-mindedness on campus is actually deeper than even these data indicate . . . and likely to deteriorate in the future. Why? Because the few Republicans who do exist on campus are mostly older faculty. Among full professors at Berkeley and Stanford, the ratio of Democrats to Republicans is 7:1. But among younger untenured assistant and associate profess-sors [sic] it's a ridiculous 31:1. Among the rising generation of professors, in other words, Republicans are almost extinct."[4]

As a result, students who identify as Republicans or who hold conservative views and the conservative movement even may feel marginalized on some college campuses. A federal investigation was prompted in February 2004 by an incident at the University of North Carolina involving a student chastened by a professor for his conservative beliefs. The Department of Education's Office of Civil Rights found that the professor did harass the student. The president of the University of North Carolina's College Republicans said, "It's just ridiculous that there are no conservatives. To me, it's kind of ironic. On the one hand, the university is for affirmative action and wants intellectual diversity at the university. But they don't have [conservative] professors, so what kind of diversity is that?"[5]

William Pilger, the pseudonym of an assistant professor of classics in an unidentified Southern university, wrote an op-ed in the *Chronicle of Higher Education* in which he discussed his clandestine political affiliation. His account could have been written by an academic of a different political persuasion during the McCarthy era. "Last year," Pilger wrote, "it was different. My advocacy on behalf of the conservative students gradually became more public. Nowadays there is much more at risk for me: the respect of colleagues, students' perception of my openness to all thoughtful ideas, and, not least, the long-term career repercussions of marching to the beat of a different drummer—in this case one that weighs several tons and has a trunk.

"You see, I am a Republican. And strive though I may to conform, to be in the academic in-group, I cannot."[6]

One may argue that in a sea of conservative trends in American society it is a good idea to have some institutions, including higher education, that retain their liberal culture. On the other hand, one could argue more appropriately, that colleges and universities should have no ideology whatsoever. Unfortunately, it is the overwhelming imbalance in favor of liberals on campus that may encourage ideologically biased scholarship to prevail as a by-product of spoken or tacit peer pressure. To counteract that tendency, higher education should not be reformed by conservative belief systems, or anything else. While some conservatives are seeking to provide ideological balance to the prevailing liberal culture of colleges and universities, the entire system would be better off if ideologies were not balanced but, rather, absent.

The question of ideology is so profound that it may be even affecting tenure decisions. Are faculty selected and promoted based solely on the merit of their research and their teaching? Or do politics and ideology play a role? Is it conceivable that some faculty are not hired in a department because they do not present themselves within some pervasive ideological standard, or are not promoted because they think and write differently than the prevailing culture? This may be a shameful truth in higher education, and one that requires much more inquiry and research.

THE ENTIRE SYSTEM WOULD BE BETTER OFF IF IDEOLOGIES WERE NOT BALANCED BUT, RATHER, ABSENT.

As part of the ideological legacy of the 1960s, the contemporary university retains the protest culture that once defined higher education—and shaped world history for the final third of the 20th century. Protest culture is not the same thing as the explosion of outrage and rebellion that marked the social movements of the 1960s on college campuses. Today, protest has become an end as much as a means. What the protest is *for* matters less than protesting *about* something. Indeed, the protest culture is a combination of angst and energy, wanting something to be different (whatever it is) with less regard for the actual purpose. Institutionalized protest can claim any mission at any moment, the fad, controversy, or outrage of the day.

Protest culture fashions an amalgam of causes that may or may not be related. For example, a protest rally against the war in Iraq may include advocates for gay and lesbian rights, saving the environment, and abortion rights, to name a few. The only connection between the causes is the activism around them. The protest culture includes students who are at a time of life when they are thinking about their identities and most apt to want to redefine the world. They are naturally drawn to what they believe to be injustices and wrongs to be righted. The protest culture also exhibits itself among faculty who place less emphasis on the search for truth and emphasize instead the challenge of existing norms.

The legacy of the 1960s relishes bashing conventional wisdom for the sake of the criticism, not necessarily to add to our knowledge to find better ways of understanding the universe or the human condition.

The protest culture has enshrined the canon of free speech as a synonym for controversy and pushing boundaries. Yet, free speech is not exactly free.

FREE SPEECH = POLITICAL CORRECTNESS

Ironically, while the constitutional guarantee of free speech was meant to protect unpopular views, on many campuses free speech may safeguard largely those with whom the majority campus community agrees. "There have been hundreds of incidents of the theft and destruction of college newspapers by some groups, on campus and off, who feel they are expressing their freedom of speech by suppressing access to speech with which they disagree in the paper. Even the mayor of Berkeley, California, felt free to confiscate copies of a student newspaper that opposed his election. And less than a dozen have yet been arrested or even investigated and disciplined by any college administration to date."[7]

Political correctness can lead to a self-censoring milieu that is more stifling than anything Senator Joseph McCarthy might have imagined. For example, when President Lawrence Summers raised a question about why women are less represented in the sciences, he was so roundly criticized that he was forced to apologize, significant numbers of faculty voted no confidence about his leadership, and it created an enormous brouhaha about whether or not he was a gender bigot. Certainly, accepted scientific knowledge should prohibit faculty from teaching a course about why the earth is flat. On the other hand, there is still some debate about gender differences in the choice of career, including a body of literature suggesting that social rather than biological determinants are largely at play. But President Summers was merely posing a question, not advocating a position. The kind of thought censorship that the president of Harvard University was forced to endorse is a perfect indicator of the level of thought control that now occurs in higher education.

> POLITICAL CORRECTNESS CAN LEAD TO A SELF CENSORING MILIEU THAT IS MORE STIFLING THAN ANYTHING SENATOR JOSEPH MCCARTHY MIGHT HAVE IMAGINED.

This kind of political correctness is dampening academic discourse. Gil Troy wrote,

Studying history should cultivate critical thought, depth, and perspective, not sloganeering or aping the latest academic trends. Whatever happened to "a free marketplace of ideas" and "freedom for the
thoughts we hate"? [sic] When did our desire to be political mission-
aries upstage our mission as educators? We need to be vigilant and
consistent, attacking abuses regardless of the perpetrators' politics.
Violence to silence speakers, professorial pressure for students to
embrace political positions, collegial censure of mavericks, must end,
whether the speakers, students, or professors are liberals or conservatives.[8]

Violence, intimidation, and censure are all the most uncivil of tactics in an
environment designed to cherish free interchange.

Political correctness can create an intellectually uninteresting environment, perhaps as damaging to the purpose of universities as the abrogation of academic freedom. "These same universities often shut out, or
look away from, arguments that do not support these beliefs. The result is
not 'neo-Stalinist' monoliths [. . . b]ut it is universities that are boring, provincial, shut in."[9] Of course, a thousand flowers bloom on campus, and a
multitude of ideas abound, but prevailing ideas may overcome less politically correct doctrine.

The political correctness of the university lessens the exchange of
ideas. In his book *Restoring Free Speech and Liberty on Campus*, Donald Alexander Downs critiques

[t]he threats to free speech and civil liberty that have sprung up on
America's campuses following the wave of so-called progressive
reforms instituted in the late 1980s and the 1990s. The most important reforms included speech codes, broad antiharassment [sic]
codes, orientation programs dedicated to promoting an ideology of
sensitivity, and new procedures and pressures in the adjudication of
student and faculty misconduct. Although these measures were
laudably designed to foster civility, tolerance, and respect for racial
and cultural diversity, they too often had illiberal consequences.
Rather than improving the campus climate, the new policies often
provided tools for moral bullies to enforce an ideological orthodoxy
that undermines the intellectual freedom and intellectual diversity
that are the hallmarks of great universities.[10]

Political correctness allows students and faculty to prohibit others
from speaking. Universities should be bastions of civil discourse. Breaches

of this value should be as frightening to the faculty and the university community as a whole as imagined intrusions on academic freedom. The heart and soul of the university are violated by the destruction of information and the intimidation of speakers. These are the antithesis of free speech.

In *The Shadow University: The Betrayal of Liberty on America's Campuses*, Alan Charles Kors and Harvey Silverglate make a good case that the internal mechanisms of the university often fail at protecting students from ideologies, retaliatory preferences, and oddly informed codes about free speech and harassment that often result in the censorship and the harassment they were supposed to prevent. They document such cases at the University of Pennsylvania and elsewhere, arguing that "sunshine is the best disinfectant" for an ailing system.[11]

CONFUSING FREE SPEECH AND ACADEMIC FREEDOM

When it is not being invoked as part of a protest on campus, free speech is most often used interchangeably with academic freedom, one of the primary values of the civil university. While academic freedom and free speech are not equivalent, they have shared a similar fate in the university. That is, academic freedom has been subverted on campus. It has become an excuse for shoddy scholarship, irresponsible teaching and public commentary, and low-level performance. Academic freedom has evolved from protection against political influence to job security—an employment contract rather than an intellectual contract. As a result, many faculty are isolated from the normal kinds of checks and balances that market forces provide for excellence in performance. Faculty utilize largely self-regulating processes that sometimes succeed and sometimes do not.

Academic freedom has come to mean "hands off"—no institution, individual, or group has the right to monitor, question, challenge, or influence what goes on inside the walls of academe. Professors and administrators who engage in or defend inappropriate academic behavior will often hide behind the right of academic freedom. For example, in response to being implicated by a faculty panel investigating charges of intimidation of Jewish students by pro-Palestinian professors at Columbia University, Columbia professor Joseph Massad said, "I feel chilled by this. I don't know what to do in the classroom anymore. I can't censor myself. And I will fight back. These are, in my opinion, forces of darkness, and I and the majority of the faculty will not let them take over. . . . I am simply an entry point for right-wing forces that want to destroy academic freedom. . . . My crime is not only that I'm Palestinian. What galls them most is that I'm a pro-Jewish Palestinian critic of Zionism."[12]

ACADEMIC FREEDOM HAS EVOLVED FROM PROTECTION AGAINST POLITICAL INFLUENCE TO JOB SECURITY—AN EMPLOYMENT CONTRACT RATHER THAN AN INTELLECTUAL CONTRACT.

Outside influences are seen to be *de facto* threats to academic freedom. No matter what faculties say or do, no one has the right to step into the ivory tower. Attempts to scrutinize faculty bring cries about repressive assaults on academic freedom, and references to police states or even the Inquisition, a time of religiously inspired torture and murder. "The head of the New York Civil Liberties Union said she fears that Columbia's investigation into complaints by students against anti-Israel scholars will 'turn into an inquisition into the political views of professors.' Donna Lieberman, executive director of the New York State affiliate of the ACLU, also urged Columbia in a statement last week not to allow critics outside the university to 'interfere with academic freedom.'"[13]

The misuse of academic freedom permits faculty to inject their own personal belief systems and ideology into their research and into the classroom. Some students complain that professors are preaching rather than teaching and bringing their own beliefs into the classroom. It is not that students enter college without opinions; rather, they have a broad range of opinions reflecting the depth and breadth of opinion in the country, not just those found inside the walls of campus. Freshmen do not come into college with an overwhelming liberal or conservative belief system. While 57 percent believe that same sex couples should have the right to legal marital status, only 33 percent believe that the death penalty should be abolished. Fifty-four percent say abortion should be legal, a bare majority, and 50 percent believe affirmative action should be abolished. More than half, 58 percent, "believe there is too much concern in the courts for criminals." In a sign of how traditional most college freshmen are their two most important objectives are "raising a family" (75 percent) and "being very well off financially" (74 percent) as opposed to improving their understanding of other cultures, cited by 43 percent, a significant minority.[14]

A science professor may use the classroom as a forum to talk about the United States' foreign policy, and a professor of French literature may object to the way women are treated on campus. These ideological skirmishes, however, are nothing compared to scholarship being politically driven, sabotaging an objective search for facts or truth. Even journalism has some rules about separating news from opinion pieces (although it is also becoming more difficult to determine news from opinion in both the electronic and the print media, as journalists often report what they think rather than what they find). Students should not be subjected to ideology parading as objectivity and certainly not in the name of academic freedom.

While academic freedom has been used as a catchall phrase to thwart oversights and accountability, it "was never intended to be a license for sorry work habits; it concerns the freedom to teach in the classroom in one's area of expertise, within the general standards set for students at a college."[15] Those standards include the pursuit of truth through objective research, scholarship and teaching that is free of bias. Scholarship should be guided by open inquiry. This is not to say that scholarship and moral purpose have no connection. The university is steeped in the tradition of pursuing truth for moral purposes, given the religious foundations of many private universities, especially the elite institutions.

But neither scholarship nor the classroom are supposed to be platforms for personal views that interfere with objective inquiry or honest and civil discourse. Those that taint their findings or their conclusions with what they believe rather than what they find are considered antithetical to the purpose of scholarship. Individual faculty members who promote propaganda do not always feel that they must hide behind assertions that they are not pushing their own worldview. In fact, quite the opposite, they are very proud of this approach, and believe the purpose of education is to teach their particular ideas: "There is no historian in the world who is objective. I am not as interested in what happened as in how people see what's happened.[...] Indeed the struggle is about ideology, not about facts. Who knows what facts are? We try to convince as many people as we can that our interpretation of the facts is the correct one, and we do it because of ideological reasons, not because we are truth seekers."[16]

The loss of objectivity in scholarship has become so acceptable as to be enshrined in some universities. "In 2003 the University of California's Academic Assembly did away with the distinction between 'interested' and 'disinterested' scholarship by a 45–3 vote. As Berkeley law professor Robert Post explained, 'the old statement of principles was so outlandishly disconnected to what university teaching is now that it made no sense to think about it that way.' The reality, as Professor Post recognized, is that many professors now literally profess. Far from teaching the mechanics of knowledge, they are in fact preachers of sorts, spreading a gospel akin to that of Howard Dean."[17]

One of the basic tenets of academic freedom is appropriate oversight. There is little evidence that scholarship is being monitored sufficiently, in terms either of quality or bias, within the university. Indeed, many attempts to provide outside review are stiff-armed by charges of intrusion on academic freedom. For example, H.R. 609, the College Access and Opportunity Act of 2005, would provide oversight of funding for area studies, particularly Middle East Studies.[18] Colleges and universities have pulled out their lobbying stops in order to prevent this legislation. What could be more absurd than taking federal money for a whole variety of purposes including Middle East Studies and arguing that the federal government has no right to provide oversight? The National Science Foundation, for example, regularly reviews its grants. This is an accepted norm for outside funding.

THE LOSS OF OBJECTIVITY IN SCHOLARSHIP HAS BECOME SO ACCEPTABLE AS TO BE ENSHRINED IN SOME UNIVERSITIES.

The limits on adequate audits or oversight within the campus walls stem in large part from the power of the faculty. In his inaugural address as the incoming president of Williams College in 1873, Paul Ansel Chadbourne declared that "[p]rofessors are sometimes spoken of as working for the college. They are the college."[19] This granting of nearly absolute power to the faculty diminishes the health of the university and renders meaningless the system of checks and balances among all the stakeholders who should be ensuring the long-term vitality of the institution.

In *All the Essential Half-Truths about Higher Education*, George Dennis O'Brien argues that the faculty are the universities—but only if there is a different kind of faculty—one that is truly committed beyond its own narrow self interests. "'The faculty *is* the university'—but the faculty that is the institution is a faculty engaged in 'distinguished service' to *institutional* mission, not just distinguished service to *disciplinary* mission. Creation of such a cadre of faculty suggests not only different promotion polices but also different patterns of 'faculty formation.'"[20]

It is administrative weakness—a fear of their own faculty—that has allowed biased professors too much latitude to spread propaganda without fear of censure and, as was documented in the film *Columbia Unbecoming* regarding anti-Semitic and anti-Israel professors, to intimidate students with whom they disagree. Had the administrators at Columbia University addressed the student complaints, the documentary might never have been made. But the administrators were afraid of faculty backlash. The *New York Times* placed responsibility for the public relations debacle squarely on President Lee Bollinger. "It is generally felt that animosity toward Mr. Bollinger would be more subdued were it not for the snowballing disputes that began with the charges by the pro-Israel students against the pro-Palestinian professors. Many at Columbia seemed piqued at what they felt was Mr. Bollinger's tardy and timid handling of the issue, which contributed to its becoming a protracted matter that saturated the university with sour publicity."[21]

It is not that professors cannot have opinions. Faculty should be allowed to be wrong, even to be publicly stupid, but when they do, as in the case of Ward Churchill, what does it say about those who hire him and promote him and those like him? The tenure system, intended to protect academic freedom, not academic dishonesty, has become the screen behind which unprofessional professors like Churchill can hide. Education historian Diane Ravitch wonders, "How did a man with such hateful views win tenure at the University of Colorado? This question goes to the heart of the academic enterprise. Does a university have a responsibility to make certain that the men and women who are hired and promoted on its faculty are well qualified, base their academic work on evidence and reason, and express themselves with civility?"[22]

Ravitch, herself a research professor at New York University who has expressed controversial and unpopular views, understands that even on campus, free speech has its limits. "Much as the university claims to defend free speech without regard to its content, there are clearly limits and boundaries. It is hard to imagine any great university hiring a historian who dressed in Nazi garb and wrote an obsequious biography of Adolf Hitler. It is hard to imagine a great university granting tenure to someone who advocated the forced sterilization of certain races or of people with below average intelligence. It is impossible to imagine a university biology department hiring a professor who endorsed the literal truth of the biblical story of Creation and denied evolution."[23]

For some observers of the university system, tenure is considered so problematic that they call for abolishing a system that may no longer be a real bulwark protecting academic freedom:

> The primary practical effect of tenure is to make universities almost ungovernable. Those ostensibly in charge—presidents and trustees—come and go; the faculty remains, serene and untouchable. This helps to explain some of the dysfunctions that mar big-time universities, such as the overemphasis on publishing unintelligible articles and the under-emphasis on teaching undergraduates. Armies of junior faculty and graduate-student drudges have been enlisted to assume the bulk of the teaching load because most of the tenured grandees think that instructing budding stockbrokers and middle managers is beneath them. And there is almost nothing that administrators can do about it because mere laziness is no grounds for removing someone with a lifetime employment guarantee.[24]

John M. McCardell Jr., former president of Middlebury College, argues that tenure is an outdated concept:

> [T]enure is a great solution to the problems of the 1940's, when the faculty was mostly male and academic freedom was at genuine risk. Why must institutions make a judgment that has lifetime consequences after a mere six or seven years? Publication may take longer in some fields than in others, and familial obligations frequently interrupt careers. Why not a system of contracts of varying length, including lifetime for the most valuable colleagues, that acknowledges the realities of academic life in the 21st century?
>
> Moreover, when most tenure documents were originally adopted, faculty members had little protection. Today, almost every negative tenure decision is appealed. Appeals not upheld internally are taken to court. Few if any of these appeals have as their basis a denial of academic freedom.[25]

Perhaps tenure is the villain in the system's malfunctions, but perhaps not. Within the university, the tenure system, not surprisingly, has its passionate supporters. Tenure has its usefulness and is not likely the source of much of the university's problems. Any bureaucracy often finds power vested in those who are the most stable, long-term employees. Even without tenure, faculty will still accrue the most seniority in the system, compared to the students or trustees. Some mid-level positions in the administration, in the provost's office, or development department will have similar staying power, but faculty would still be the most organized and entrenched, even without tenure.

How tenure decisions are made should be of more concern than whether or not the tenure system is a good one. In a letter to the editor of the *New York Times*, written by three Columbia University professors in response to the *Times* article, "The Clash of Ideas at Columbia," the professors—one a former provost of Columbia—wrote to clarify to outsiders exactly how the tenure system works. "Columbia does not operate in the way you describe. Individual departments do not have the 'power to appoint and promote faculty,' and therefore cannot have that power 'wrested away' from them. The tenure review process is carefully designed to exclude a candidate's department from wielding any power over the final tenure decisions."[26]

An ideal system, it would seem, but untrue. There is a tenure review process, but departments wield tremendous power because that is where initial decisions are made. The dean and provost often consent to department decisions. Trustees sign off almost automatically. While departmental recommendations are sometimes overturned at administrative levels, deans and provosts do not complete most of the evaluations on which decisions are made. They do convene outside university review committees and seek objective review beyond the department. Individual departments are hardly all powerful, but neither are they bystanders in the tenure process.

The tenure system often seems under attack as protecting "incompetent" professors. Professors of economics and authors of *Faulty Towers: Tenure and the Structure of Higher Education*, Ryan Amacher and Roger Meiners, argue that abolishing tenure would not solve the problem. They lay blame instead on structural problems within the university, including the need for more trustee oversight and more accountability for faculty and administrators. "Critics of higher education have good reason to be disturbed by some of the foolishness observed in colleges, but the focus on tenure is misplaced. That tenure appears to protect incompetent professors is merely a symptom of structural defects that limit competition. 'Reforming' tenure without addressing the structural defects will not result in improvements. Instead reform should aim to bring stronger trustee oversight and involvement in universities, more choice for students, more accountability for faculty and administrators, and more competition among our universities by removing many of the bureaucratic constraints they now face."[27] Even if the tenure system were abolished, systems for accountability and oversight would have to be strengthened (or developed). Appropriate management of faculty is at issue, not tenure.

Certainly, the faculty have become the most powerful stakeholders in higher education, and they exert perhaps too much control over the campus. They make decisions about curriculum, who should be hired and promoted within the department, student requirements, acceptable scholarship, and a whole range of activities that empower them. Their endurance both in terms of their longevity compared to other stakeholders and the firewall of academic freedom gives them enormous bureaucratic position. It is from this position of strength that the myth that the university *is* the faculty has evolved. Certainly, it is in the faculty's best interest to continue to promote this myth. While lip service may be given to the idea that the purpose of higher education is to serve the students, or to provide benefit to the overall society, or to champion academic freedom, faculty in their hearts believe that the university belongs to them, and the bureaucratic structure endorses this feeling. This feeling of control can lead to an abuse of power.

THE MISUSE OF MULTICULTURALISM

Part of university gospel preaches the religion of "multiculturalism." Just as academic freedom has been subverted into a focus on free speech and honest scholarship sometimes has given way to bias, the diversity of thought and people that once thrived in the civil university has devolved from its noble purpose of knowledge and respect about a variety of cultures and societies within America and around the world to celebrating and protecting racial and ethnic isolation rather than interaction.

Rob Reich, in *Bridging Liberalism and Multiculturalism in American Education*, distinguishes between "*descriptive* multiculturalism, [which] denot[es] the demographic coexistence of various cultures within a single society; and *normative* multiculturalism, [which] denot[es] a moral ideal or specific political agenda."[28] Furthermore, Reich proposes a reasonable and healthy definition of multiculturalism, one which fits into the values of the civil university.

> For the purposes of this work, I understand the term *multiculturalism* to represent a theory or position that emphasizes diversity over sameness, recognition of difference over homogenizing similarity, the particular over the universal, the group over the individual, race and ethnicity over, say, class and gender, and cultural identification rather than cultural affiliation. I understand most people to use the phrase *multicultural education* to represent an approach to education that emphasizes learning about and celebrating a child's home culture, learning about and recognizing the cultures of others, an expanded curriculum that incorporates contributions of minority groups, and an expanded repertoire of pedagogical strategies designed to reach students of diverse cultural backgrounds.[29]

In many cases, multiculturalism has become the defense of racial and ethnic isolation, and even physical and intellectual segregation. College campuses may have college dorms specifically for one racial or ethnic group.[30] Intellectual pursuit may be framed through gender or racial lenses that actually inhibit open and honest intellectual discourse. Colleges and universities may be more interested in the percentages of certain racial and ethnic groups on their campus than in how well they actually learn from one another.

While higher education theoretically embraces the idea of learning about world cultures, many colleges and universities have abandoned the most fundamental way of learning about another people, which is the basic language requirement that places value on American college students learning at least one language other than English. For all the politics of race and ethnicity, American college graduates remain among the most uneducated in the world when it comes to speaking some other tongue other than their own. While we promote multiculturalism, our curriculum requirements are remarkably provincial. Are colleges suggesting that there is little value in requiring their American

MULTICULTURALISM HAS BECOME THE DEFENSE OF RACIAL AND ETHNIC ISOLATION, AND EVEN PHYSICAL AND INTELLECTUAL SEGREGATION.

students to be able to converse in a language other than their own with people from around the world, or are we afraid that our students are not intelligent enough to learn another language at all?

The perversion of diversity into the politics of race, gender, and ethnicity is another legacy of the 1960s. Multiculturalism has been converted from the celebration of difference, and how different nationalities, ethnicities, races, and cultures can learn from each other, into a divisive and stifling political correctness. Multiculturalism centers more on sensitivity than sensibility, rights as opposed to responsibility or justice, and language control rather than learning. Multiculturalism is the antithesis of real diversity, and of enlightening interchange and cross-fertilization from many cultures.

Furthermore, embracing multiculturalism sometimes has been reduced to embracing intellectual pigeonholing, which means that only black people can teach about black society, Jews about Jews, or individuals of Arab and Muslim descent can teach about the Middle East.[31] What could possibly be more horrific in terms of perverting the purpose of multiculturalism than the notion that scholarship has to be based on one's race, ethnicity, or gender in order to be legitimate? This is partially due to the sad legacy of Saidism, the paradigm put forward by Edward Said, that led to the ideological poisoning of Middle East Study centers and departments all over academe.

Sometimes misplaced emphasis on multiculturalism results in an intellectual scam, as in the case of Ward Churchill, a Colorado professor without a Ph.D. who called 9/11 victims "Little Eichmanns who may have deserved punishment for their participation in what went on in the sterile sanctuary of the twin towers." In an article for the *National Review*, Victor Davis Hanson wrote:

> Churchill, it turns out, has no Ph.D., although it is the terminal degree required under normal circumstances at all such major research universities. Few, other than poets, novelists, and artists, are ever hired for tenure-track positions without it. Churchill probably also lied in claiming American Indian ancestry, thereby gaining entrée to favorable hiring and tenure considerations.
>
> The disturbing story went on for days, as accounts of former Weather Underground ties, a past trip to Libya to cultivate dictator Muammar Qaddafi, and several prior arrests surfaced about Churchill . . . The $114,032-a-year Churchill may have distorted his Vietnam-

era military service, and routinely misrepresented scholarly texts to fit his own particular revisionism.

In other words, Ward Churchill's plight gives us a glimpse into the strange world of the contemporary postmodern university of tenured ideologues, where professed identity politics, ethnic or gender chauvinism, and a disbelief in empiricism allow a con man to bully his way to guaranteed lifetime employment, and a handsome salary, and the right to say anything at all, no matter how inflammatory.[32]

UNCHECKED BUREAUCRACY

The misuses of academic freedom and multiculturalism deriving from the stale legacy of the 1960s are allowed to flourish in part because of the bureaucratic sprawl of the contemporary university. As university bureaucracy has grown, concerns about money, prestige, and image sometimes supercede actual learning and research content. In the *U.S. News and World Report* annual guide to American universities, the editors focus upon input criteria, especially financial factors, and nothing about the range or quality of the teaching curriculum. (Higher education is loathe to actually embrace output measures). Andrew Delbanco, Julian Clarence Levi Professor in the Humanities at Columbia University, complains that learning seems secondary at the two Ivy League universities where he has taught. "Yet one hears comparatively little discussion of what students ought to learn once they get there and why they are going at all. Over my own nearly quarter-century as a faculty member (four years at Harvard, nineteen years at Columbia), I have discovered that the question of what undergraduate education should be all about is almost taboo."[33]

A large part of the problem is the lure of money. As author David Kirp observes in *Shakespeare, Einstein, and the Bottom Line: The Marketing of Higher Education*, "Ever since Harvard College and the College of William and Mary opened their doors over three centuries ago, money has been a pressing concern."[34] Although universities enjoy non-profit status (and all of the associated perks thereof), they are insatiable gluttons devouring billions of dollars each year in the pursuit of their goals. Derek Bok, former president of Harvard University, likens universities to

> compulsive gamblers and exiled royalty: there is never enough money to satisfy their desires. Faculty and students are forever developing

new interests and ambitions, most of which cost money. The prices of books and journals rise relentlessly. Better and more costly technology and scientific apparatus constantly appear and must be acquired to stay at the cutting edge. Presidents and deans are anxious to satisfy as many of these needs as they can, for their reputation depends on pleasing the faculty, preserving the standing of the institution, and building a legacy through the development of new programs.

The need for money, therefore, does not merely occur now and then in the wake of some ill-considered decision on the part of state officials to cut university budgets. It is a chronic condition of American universities, a condition inherent in the very nature of an institution forever competing for the best students and faculty.[35]

Furthermore, as a number of observers have noted, the for-profit sector of higher education is growing. As the university has evolved from an incubator preparing young men for society into a (more) unabashed vocational advancement program, a number of new for-profit degree-granting institutions have emerged, putting even more financial pressure on the not-for-profit institutions. Moreover, it raises questions about why the public sector subsidizes higher education, especially if they are not adequately serving the public good.

Is survival really the best that the public universities can manage? Unless they are contributing to the social good, it isn't clear that they *deserve* public subsidies. If higher education is simply serving "customers," then those customers, rather than the taxpayer, should be paying the bills. If public universities really "mean business," as the president of the University of California has asserted, then why shouldn't the government rely on schools like DeVry, which is a business, to do the teaching? After all, as Dennis Keller says, "public universities aren't as driven to be customer-centered."[36]

And yet, individual colleges and universities often resist cooperation, efficiencies, and economies of scale to make them run better. Bok warns that the development of ideal models for improvement, such as increasing teaching loads, may or may not really improve the quality of education, or even much improve the bottom line. Other reforms, however, are necessary.

The need for economic reform in higher education was pointed out eloquently by Alison Bernstein, vice president for the Knowledge, Creativity, and Freedom Program at the Ford Foundation. She notes:

Paradoxically, the university as an institution has often been remarkably resistant to innovation and change. As many visionary leaders who have aspired to wide-scale reform are aware, large bureaucracies, political minefields, and pockets of well-entrenched faculty can act as tough barriers to institutional change. Even in times of budget cuts, rather than reshaping and rethinking the core mission of the university—and what programs are necessary to accomplish that mission—institutional leaders often simply downsize current programs proportionately. In essence, they tread water, hoping to maintain all or most services until markets bounce back.[37]

She goes on to say, "While budget cuts are always a hardship, they also represent an opportunity. Few resources force institutional leaders to revise strategies and create change. The impetus for change can be used either to scale down programs that already exist, or to restructure the broader curriculum and institutional structures around the core mission."[38] Of course, having too much money can also be a problem for the university, reinforcing inefficient and even wasteful practices.

Universities, for all of their oft stated desire for separation from the "secular" world, remain firmly entrenched in the outside economy. Still, the university system, with the exception of a few elite institutions, is in financial stress or on the verge. Tuition costs continue to rise far beyond inflation rates, physical plants need constant feeding and repair, the cost of research continues to go up. All of these very real needs are indicators of why the university keeps clamoring for more money to pay their bills, compete with other campuses, and attract more prestigious scholars. Plus, the simple fact is that university life is expensive. In their book, *The Future of Higher Education*, Frank Newman, Lara Couturier, and Jamie Scurry lay out the seven most important market forces pressuring higher education:

- Public, private, and for-profit institutions alike are competing to attract students, in ways and with an intensity never seen before, using financial aid, advertising, and campus amenities.

- Traditional universities are more focused on developing new revenues than ever before, including starting for-profit ventures that blur the once sacrosanct dividing line between for-profit and nonprofit.

- There has been huge growth in the number of for-profit universities and colleges, the degrees they give, and the acceptance of their degrees by students and employers.

- Thousands of virtual programs are growing rapidly, altering the way many students attend college and how classes are delivered as new forms emerge.

- Corporate universities and certificate programs are widespread, in some fields becoming the preparation preferred by employers.

- New organizational forms are emerging, such as those at the British Open University or the University of Phoenix, that rely heavily on technology and challenge the hegemony of the traditional faculty and the academic discipline-oriented college or university.

- For the first time, higher education has gone global. Even the degree structure of ancient European universities is changing to make them more competitive.[39]

The harshest critics of higher education believe it is a system that may financially implode. The hunger for money, combined with the inefficient use of the billions that universities do receive, may lead to unimaginable instability that has not been seen in the not-for-profit world. But the drive for resources without a moral compass lies at the core of the uncivil university. As O'Brien asks in *All the Essential Half-Truths about Higher Education*, "If the twin crises of the modern university are morals and money, is the public paying a lot for the demoralization of the young?"[40]

Charles Sykes, research fellow at the Wisconsin Policy Research Institute, found that the "modern university [is] distinguished by costs that are zooming out of control; curriculums that look like they were designed by a game show host; nonexistent advising programs; lectures of droning, mind-numbing dullness often to 1,000 or more semi-anonymous undergraduates herded into dilapidated, ill-lighted lecture halls; teaching assistants who can't speak understandable English; and the product of this all, a generation of expensively credentialed college graduates who might not be able to locate England on a map."[41]

The mad search for money and its negative impact on the quality of a college education are self-inflicted conditions caused by the university's refusal to take a hard look at itself. The university is in denial about its own internal ills and continuously seeks to shift the blame elsewhere. Self-examination to resolve these problems is rare. If the university refuses to improve its own financial model, for example, how can it be expected to remedy more intangible ills, like biased scholarship and uncivil behavior?

Sykes lays the responsibility for this state of affairs at the feet of the faculty, who, he believes, have perpetrated "one of society's most outrageous and elaborate frauds. It is replete with the pieties, arcane rituals, rites of passage, and dogmas of a secular faith. It also has an intimidating and mysterious argot (best described as 'profspeak') and a system of perks and privileges that would put the most hidebound bureaucrat to shame. Ultimately, the academic culture represents a sort of modern-day alchemy in which mumbo-jumbo is transformed into gold, or, in this case, into research grants, consulting contracts, sabbaticals, and inflated salaries."[42]

While Sykes is hyperbolic in his outrage, the system as a whole requires some retooling. Government at all levels has gone through a restructuring process, the private sector continues to do so, and many non-governmental organizations (NGOs) have been forced to restructure. Colleges and universities have not, because of the unique dedication of their alumni and donors, because it is a decentralized system, and because the myth of the ivory tower is so widespread. The economics of higher education are not as rigorously examined as they should be. If the university were operated more like a for-profit business (like the businesses it actually operates), it would be forced to become more efficient, because it would be accountable in ways that its trustees rarely require. Whole departments might be consolidated at fewer campuses across the country, and redundancies in the nationwide academic system might be eliminated.

University system-wide reorganization might even lead, for example, to the closure of many colleges and universities, simply because they are not managing their resources well. Other institutions might be better off merged, especially since technology now allows more sharing of resources. Entrenched faculty, the provincialism of each institution, and a failure of self-regulation results from the abdication of responsibilities of so many stakeholders.

As Newman et al. note, the need for efficiency is not a luxury but rather an obligation for the university.

As stewards of the public trust and investment, state colleges and universities are obligated to spend public funds in a way that most effectively responds to public needs. Private universities and colleges are similarly obligated to their donors, to their students, and to the public that accords them many subsidies and exemption from taxes. This requires turning an eye to cost and efficiency. Recent projects have demonstrated that there can be substantial cost savings through interinstitutional and interdepartmental collaboration in purchasing, library materials, technology infrastructure, and more. Similarly, savings are made possible by expanding the use of outsourcing beyond the bookstore and food service to such tasks as maintenance of technology infrastructure. All of these tasks remain largely unaddressed at most institutions.[43]

The niche system of offering doctorates in esoterica is yet another example of inefficiency, albeit not a new one. Observers more than a century ago bemoaned the trend toward so many advanced degrees with such limited scope. "In 'The PhD Octopus,' the Harvard philosopher William James penned the most celebrated condemnation of alleged Germanic tendencies toward pedantry and overspecialisation in American graduate studies. A substantial number of humanists defended an ideal of liberal culture against the growing trend toward specialised erudition."[44]

The effects of razor-thin scholarly enquiry are twofold: First, overspecialization is expensive, because the more narrow a scholar's focus, the more scholars are needed to represent a range of ideas in a particular field. Second, overspecialization has led to scholarship accessible only to others who manage to squeeze themselves into the same academic crevice. While no one is suggesting that scholars write only shallow works published as mass market paperbacks, members of the academy have a responsibility to disseminate knowledge outside of themselves. In speaking only to each other, they are disregarding one of the primary values of the civil university.

The greatest challenge to creating cost reforms in the university comes not from the administration or the trustees, both groups charged with the financial health of the institution, but from the faculty, which protests nearly any reorganization as an intrusion into their protected realm, their academic freedom. Yet, "[t]eaching and learning do matter. Higher education has hidden teaching and learning under a veil of secrecy, suggesting that what goes on in the classroom is too sacred for scrutiny. Institutions now need to do more than provide the opportunity and resources that allow learning; they must take responsibility for learning."[45]

RALLYING AROUND ACADEMIC FREEDOM—SOMETIMES

These cries of academic freedom and the need for independence and autonomy have not kept faculty from fully engaging with the private sector—while simultaneously being worried that higher education is too driven by market forces. "Rather like the child who, after murdering his parents, asks for leniency because he's an orphan, universities grown plump feeding at the commercial trough now complain that they've been victimized by the market. This contention of victimization is, of course, a central part of the modern Higher Ed, Inc., brand. The next words you'll hear will be 'Please give. We desperately need your support!' "[46]

Jennifer Washburn, in *University Inc.: The Corporate Corruption of Higher Education*, analyzes the increasing ties between business and the academy, especially in industry-sponsored research that comes with all kinds of restrictions. Certainly where profits are at stake, as opposed to intellectual quality and diversity, higher education is less absolute in its demand for freedom from outside influences. Washburn argues that "economic growth and academic scholarship need not be in conflict. But if the two are going to be compatible, academic entrepreneurship needs to be radically reconceived."[47]

Universities partner with private enterprise to develop new products. Indeed, increasing numbers of patents are issued to universities in conjunction with business. This is especially true in the areas of scientific and medical research. Universities also manage public sector facilities, such as the Livermore Science Lab at the University of California, Berkeley. Chancellor Robert Birgeneau recognized that "[a]s a public university, we expect that our major support should and will come from the state and federal governments. However, we also recognize that we have important relationships with society as a whole, most especially with the business sector."[48]

Colleges and universities find themselves involved in a range of businesses, only some of which are inextricably linked to the university's research function. In addition to real estate, universities generate profits from hospitals, sports, financial investment, and public institution management. Universities generate enormous revenue through these business activities. A university with a good-sized campus, some extra land, maybe a hospital and a few other business activities, could be the envy of many private corporations.

College sport programs, especially football and basketball, have the potential to make a university well-off. Top programs not only attract large gifts from philanthropists, but they generate profits in the same way as professional sports teams, except college teams do not have to pay their players. Profits come from ticket sales, the marketing of team apparel, television contracts (though this money does not go directly to any one university), and related sports training camps offered to the public. Moreover, top sports teams add visibility and prestige to the university, increasing donations and even the number of students who want to attend.[49]

Patent development is another source of revenue. Another source of wealth is development of patents. It is logical that technological, scientific and other discoveries would be made in a place where so much research and development occurs. Universities hold the rights to an array of very valuable products, from drugs to computer applications to medical equipment. Universities may enter into profit-making arrangements with companies for which they develop products.[50]

While the corporate influence on college campuses is huge, it is not necessarily a detriment to higher education that the private sector is so actively involved. This debate goes on in higher education all the time. What is problematic is that faculty willingly participate in research sponsored by corporations, sign all kinds of agreements on how they will do their research and how their research will be used, and then hypocritically complain about the outside influence of government, trustees, or alumni.

The firewall that faculty has erected against outside scrutiny and regulation is largely self-selecting and self-serving. In reality, many faculty are engaged in a variety of ways with the society at large, but seem to forget their outstretched hands when they are claiming status as a protected class of people. Faculty serve as consultants to a wide variety of institutions and are increasingly involved in profit-making enterprises. College professors can be seen regularly in the media, they are often the talking heads and media stars about subjects as widespread as crime, family structure, and foreign policy. They often appear on shows that have ideo-

logical frameworks in which they enthusiastically and actively participate. Clearly, faculty want a moat around academic freedom, but only on
their own terms and when it suits them.

ABDICATION OF MORAL LEADERSHIP

The final front creating the perfect storm of mission failure at the
American university is the abdication of leadership by too many alumni,
donors, trustees, and administrators. Their roles and responsibilities
should be unambiguous and therefore their
failure to execute them with honor all the   FACULTY WANT A MOAT
more egregious. Administrators are to pro-   AROUND ACADEMIC
vide both competent management and, at   FREEDOM, BUT ONLY ON
the higher levels of authority, moral leader-   THEIR OWN TERMS AND
ship that helps fulfill the purpose of the   WHEN IT SUITS THEM.
institution. Alumni are expected to provide
financial support, volunteer hours, and to help represent the institution to
the larger society. Donors, both individual and corporate, are expected to
contribute to the financial needs of colleges and universities and offer
advice and guidance. Trustees are obligated to provide fiduciary oversight
of the institution to make key decisions in terms of the mission of the
organization, and to help in the financial health of each college and university. Higher education depends upon the execution of everyone's
responsibilities in the fullest and most efficient manner.

Faculty and administrators have a great moral responsibility. Faculty
who know that intimidation of students violates the ethical construct of
their profession should speak out. Yet, we often see the opposite, faculty
rallying around the cause of academic freedom to thwart investigation of
such cases, even when it is necessary—and helpful to the overall health of
the institution. The university would fare much better if faculty did not
automatically support egregious violations of academic standards by
invoking the cloak of academic freedom. But the opposite is usually the
case. In the process, they cheapen the meaning of academic freedom.

For example, a typical response to accountability comes from Jonathan Cole, a former provost at Columbia University. He views the challenges to Professor Joseph Massad as an "attack"—both a personal
attack and an assault on academic freedom. Indeed, his comments refer
to the outside world—both the media and concerned NGOs, almost as

Southern authorities referred to civil rights activists in the 1960s as "outside agitators." He wants the university to settle its own controversies, thank you: "There are few matters on which universities must stand on absolute principle. Academic freedom is one of them. If we fail to defend this core value, then we jeopardize the global preeminence of our universities in the production and transmission of new knowledge in the sciences, in the arts, indeed in every field of inquiry. Whenever academic freedom is under fire, we must rise to its defense with courage—and without compromise."[51]

Trustees have abdicated too much of their fiduciary responsibility, especially in the realm of tenure decisions. Trustees need to be more accountable in making other stakeholders more accountable. Because they are unpaid volunteers, expectations are low, "[b]ut, unlike compensated boards of corporations, where members also face liability for failing in their duties, college board members are providing charity with almost no chance of liability for miserable decisions."[52] For the most part, tenure decisions are rubber-stamped by nearly every board of trustees or regents in any college or university throughout the United States. Once the process goes through the department, dean, provost, president, or chancellor, boards of trustees tend to believe that they would be interfering with academic freedom if they were to pay more serious attention to the lifetime contracts that they award. The failure of trustees to be more judicious in their role in granting tenure is just one of the many areas that college trustees could be more effective. Of course, trustees are threatened with the specter of violating academic freedom were they to become more involved. This is the great intimidation game played by the faculty that works so successfully.

Alumni are, in large part, the unsuspecting players in the failure of the university. They are rarely used for purposes other than annual campaigns, designated giving, or volunteer roles that are designed to increase their giving. They are used to gain access to other donors. Rarely are alumni utilized in any way that helps set policy in a serious way or utilizes their academic training. Alumni could play a major role in helping to set the mission of the university, but are mostly kept at arm's length in that realm.

Some donors to higher education could be classified as among the most irresponsible philanthropists in America. Donor control and intent have become increasingly the norm in philanthropy. Donors want to know where their money is going, what it will be used for and to have specific outcomes. Donors demand accountability when they give their money away. Higher education offers the illusion of donor control and intent by offering naming opportunities for professorships, programs, and buildings. Yet nearly all monies within the university budget are fungible, and dollars that go for one purpose free up dollars for something else. Moreover, donors are told they cannot be involved in personnel decisions, curriculum, or other aspects of university life for which their money is given. In practically no other realm of American philanthropy are donors so often told to give their money and shut up, or otherwise they will be violating the core mission of the institution. Some donors do protest: "An increasing number of philanthropists are getting concerned about how they give to higher education, including some who want their money back."[53] For the most part, they are unsuccessful. Instead, academic freedom is used as a lever to prevent responsible philanthropy from both individuals and foundations.

ACADEMIC FREEDOM IS USED AS A LEVER TO PREVENT RESPONSIBLE PHILANTHROPY FROM BOTH INDIVIDUALS AND FOUNDATIONS.

Faculty have established their position with great skill, while other stakeholders have done a less thorough job in playing their appropriate roles in the system of higher education. Administrators are often weak, sometimes decent managers, fundraisers, and bureaucratic executors, but very often lack leadership skills. They may not set the appropriate moral tone for the institution, especially provosts and presidents.

Over thirty years ago, the Carnegie Commission on Higher Education characterized the position of college presidents as almost powerless, and little has changed that view today. "The presidency is an illusion. Important aspects of the role seem to disappear on close examination. In particular, decision-making in the university seems to result extensively from a process that decouples problems and choices and makes the president's role more commonly sporadic and symbolic than significant. Compared to the heroic expectations he and others might have, the president has modest control over the events of college life. The contributions he makes can easily be swamped by outside events or the diffuse qualities of university decision-making."[54]

Still, the office is not without its power to set a moral tone, to inform and lead, to administer well, and to help define and refine the mission of the institution. In the end, university presidents are not all-powerful, but neither are they powerless. As the public head of the university, they have a moral obligation to—and one assumes, a professional interest in—assuming the role of genuine, not titular, leadership. University presidents "enjoy the perquisites and prestige of the office. They enjoy its excitement, at least when things go well. They announce important events. They appear at important symbolic functions. They report to people. They accept and thrive on their own importance. It would be remarkable if they did not. Presidents even occasionally recite that 'the buck stops here' with a finality that suggests the cliché is an observation about power and authority rather than a proclamation of administrative style and ideology."[55]

Yet far too often, the president, like the alumni, the donors, and the trustees, simply gives in to the myth of the university as a Neverland where the faculty does not need to grow up. They "solicit an understanding of the limits to their control. They regret the tendency of students, legislators, and community leaders to assume that a president has the power to do whatever he chooses simply because he is president. They plead the countervailing power of other groups in the college or the notable complexities of causality in large organizations."[56] They often fail to provide moral leadership, trusting in a system that continues to betray its own community by elevating ideology and unlived ideals so that the university remains out of reach of real reform.

One can toss the blame for the failures of the American university all around—from the legacy of the 1960s on campus to the inefficiency of the bureaucracy to the abdication of leadership by the primary stakeholders, all leading to the confusion of purpose and mission. But the entirety of responsibility lies in the combination of all of these. If the campus truly protected academic freedom and free speech, if the university were run more efficiently, if tenure decisions were based on real academics and monitored by the trustees, if the administration provided real and public leadership, even in the face of unpopular decisions . . . if all of these stakeholders lived up to the ideals of the civil university, then the perfect storm would never gel and certainly anti-Semitism and anti-Israelism would not be allowed to be part of campus life.

THE HOSTILITY OF THE INTELLECTUAL LEFT TOWARD ISRAEL

Add the marriage of the left and higher education into this mix, which creates a comfortable environment for anti-Semitism and anti-Israelism on campus. Martin Kramer writes, "As the students of the 1960s became the junior faculty of the 1970s, the academic center moved leftward."[57] Caroline Glick further explains that many professors today developed their politics "during the 1960s, when Third World revolutionaries were all the rage. While mainstream liberals outside the university moved on from this, the universities, as if stuck in a vat of formaldehyde, remained frozen in time."[58] Hostility toward Israel is regarded as activism in the same vein as anti-Vietnam war protests, anti-apartheid boycotts and other past causes. Indeed, the anti-establishment of the 1960s has largely become the establishment on campuses today, and anti-Israelism is part of the menu.

The university and the left now seem interchangeable, inseparable. The anti-Israel movement is a significant beneficiary of this climate on campus. Idealized Palestinians, for many professors, are the modern-day revolutionaries, and therefore heroes of the ongoing "fight" against global oppression. The activism of today's faculty continues to make the case for "revolution" against the oppressor—whoever it is. They have championed the distrust of the powerful, whether it is big business or the military. This worldview has had an important impact on how Israel was once viewed and how that image has changed.

In a scathing critique, analyst Jim Piereson has labeled higher education "The Left University." He distinguishes the "left" university from the "liberal" university, referring not to political balance, but rather to the liberal character of higher education. "The effort to restore these ideals on campus is thus something that both conservatives and liberals should applaud. The left university should not be replaced by the right university. It should be replaced by the real university, dedicated to liberal education and higher learning."[59]

Anti-Israelism is deeply embedded in the ideology of the left, which tends to embrace the designated underdog. The economically disadvantaged are seen as the intentional by-product of insensitive elites, or at the minimum, the powerful do not care about the poor. "Victims" are deemed righteous, not by their own behavior, but rather by the disparity of power between themselves and their "oppressors." The greater the disparity, the more the perceived underdog garners support and the more the powerful elicit disdain. Palestinians are now the left's most treasured victim. They are viewed to be fiercely fighting oppression.

ANTI-ISRAELISM IS DEEPLY EMBEDDED IN THE IDEOLOGY OF THE LEFT.

As a result, anti-Israelism is part and parcel of the litany of causes embraced by the left (some of them quite worthwhile). An anti-Israel rally attracts all kinds of organizations from the left. For example, in 2003, approximately 200 people gathered at the University of Wisconsin, Madison, Library Mall to protest "Israeli occupation of disputed Middle East Territories." The protest was sponsored and organized by the International Socialist Organization, the Palestinian Right to Return Coalition, and co-sponsored by Alternative Palestinian Agenda, Jews for Equal Justice, Jewish Voices against the Occupation, the Madison Area Peace Coalition, U.S. Out Now, Solidarity, and Left Turn.[60]

It would be wrong to label the collective thoughts of the left as a cohesive ideology, since much of the current agenda is reactive, what should *not* be done, rather than what *should* be done. The left has overrun true liberalism, giving way to clichés. True liberalism embraces individual rights, civil liberties, and private property. Liberalism champions progress and reform. This is not what the left is today. The left now purveys the politics of race, in which anti-Israelism has become embedded in a racial paradigm of righting the wrongs of colonialism. Coupling anti-Israelism with promoting racial justice has been a clever way of branding Israel as the world's most notorious racial villain. This accounting has great currency on college campuses. The politics of race are particularly odd when condemning Jews and Israel, since Jews are the most multicultural people in world history.[61] Moreover, Israel is one of the most multicultural societies in the world, having drawn its citizens from over 100 countries. A significant proportion of the population (about 40 percent) consists of Asian, Arab, and African Jews. The representation of Israel as "white" oppressors would not pass a fact check in an introductory course in anthropology, sociology, or political science. But the left does not rely on facts.

Anti-Israel rhetoric from the left also focuses on Jews as a religious group, and how wrong it is for Israel to be a theocratic state devoted solely to Judaism. These "facts" are also wrong. First, Israel is a country where a number of religious groups practice their own religions, including Islam and Christianity (with state-enforced protection). Second, and just as important, Jews are not only a religious group but an ethnic group, a nationality, a tribe, and a people. Significant numbers of Jews list their culture and ethnicity before their religion when asked about their racial, ethnic, or religious identity in social science surveys.[62] Israel is a homeland for the Jewish people, not just those who practice the Jewish religion. The left embraces the right of people to have their own nation state, except Jews. Anti-Zionism, from the left, is not just a protest against the idea of the Jewish state, it is a protest against the idea of Jewish peoplehood.

Earl Raab points out that much of today's anti-Israelism emanates from the radical left. This hatred of Israel does not exclusively stem from anti-Semitism, but also includes the demonization of America and the West as well. Raab explores the motivations of "some of the leftist pundits and public intellectuals whose vocal prejudice against Israel derives mainly from their ideology—that is, the Palestinians are Third World victims of the First World imperialist team of America and Israel."[63] In this way, anti-Israelism from the left can be arguably closely related to anti-Americanism, as well as anti-Semitism. Over time, coming full circle, anti-Americanism endorses and devolves into anti-Semitism.

There was a time when Israel was embraced by the left. Following the establishment of the state of Israel, many on the left saw the Israeli story as one of a struggle against all odds, with enemies on all sides. Israelis used to fit the prototype of the struggling underdog, and in the narrative of the Arab-Israeli conflict were supported for their role as such. Israel was the Cinderella story of the world. Impoverished Jews, emerging from the horrors of the Holocaust, were attempting to re-establish themselves in their homeland. As a presidential candidate, John F. Kennedy stated to the Zionist Organization of America's New York convention in 1960 that "Israel was not created in order to disappear—Israel will endure and flourish. It is the child of hope and the home of the brave. It can neither be broken by adversity nor demoralized by success. It carries the shield of democracy and it honors the sword of freedom."[64]

The portrayal of Israel as the "oppressor," and the Palestinians as the "oppressed," has become fixed in the rhetoric of the left. This viewpoint has also remained entrenched despite the fact that Israel was founded upon the socialist ethics espoused by many on the left, and that, today, Israel is the Middle East's only democracy, and perhaps the only country in the Middle East in which liberal values of freedom of speech and the press, religious freedom, and feminism are championed. In contrast, the Arab world generally is actively opposed to women's and minority rights. Indeed, in March 2004 Human Rights Watch issued a report documenting the fact that Egyptian police continue to arrest and "to routinely torture men suspected of homosexual conduct."[65]

To understand the connection between leftism and anti-Israelism, one must situate the discussion within the context of a broader political history. Nissan Ratzlav-Katz writes in an article entitled, "They Were Victims Once: When the American Left Turned on Israel," "June 1967 was ... the month that the self-described 'progressive' left in America began abandoning Israel. . . . Liberals like victims. . . . Jews, or the Jewish state, refusing to act the part of the victim are unwelcome among leftist intellectuals."[66]

Many observers have noted that when Israel successfully defeated the Arab armies in the Six Day War, the Jewish state was transfigured in the eyes of the left from a biblical David to a monstrous Goliath. In the intervening decades, this portrayal of Israel has largely become entrenched and is today the prevailing attitude among many outspoken liberal professors. According to Earl Raab, the sector of the left-wing that espouses this anti-Israel position "may be a minority of the liberal population, but it is particularly vocal and influential because it has a special impact . . . on college campuses."[67]

The 1967 war began a shift that has continued, perhaps even accelerating over time. After Israel secured a victory over the Arab states through a preemptive strike, securing enough land to quadruple its land area and effectively expand its military capabilities, the intellectual left began to reevaluate its perception of Israel. No longer could Israel be viewed as the champion of the weak. Edward Said, the late Columbia English professor who was a pioneer of contemporary intellectual anti-Israelism, proclaimed that "today it is Palestine not Israel that is the progressive cause."[68] Suddenly, Israelis were no longer the underdog and embracing of the Palestinian cause had begun.

Although three all-out wars—in 1948, 1967, and 1973—were waged by Arab countries and a state of semi-bellicosity or outright hostility continues to exist with the majority of them, it is politically savvy for the Arab majority to demur from their involvement in the continuing Middle

East conflict. Framed as such, the powerful Israelis are paired up against a people with no military, no leadership, and no power. Gradually, the Palestinians became the darling of the left and the threat to Israel from its neighbors conveniently disappeared. The War of 1973, when the Arab armies launched a surprise attack on Yom Kippur, Judaism's holiest day, might have reversed the shift begun in 1967. Israeli forces suffered heavy losses and the Jewish state's survival was at risk. Yet the young nation's ability to rally only reinforced the idea that Israel had become a military superpower.

The Arab-Israel conflict was changed into the Palestinian-Israeli conflict. Israel, the beleaguered nation was now cast as the bully. A Brown University student and anti-Israel contributor to various publications, Chris Shortsleeve, writes, "Calling the conflict Zionist-Arab rather than Zionist-Palestinian effectively hides who this conflict really involves. . . . Most of the conflict has specifically involved the Palestinians, and not the broader Arab world."[69]

As the left saw it, the difficulties of occupation cemented Israel's place among the nations on the wrong side of the power equation. In 1987, the first Palestinian Intifada erupted and scenes of Israeli soldiers facing Palestinian youths became proof positive for many that Israel was the oppressor. A permanent state of hostility and open war that continued to exist between Israel and Syria, Iran, Iraq, Libya, Saudi Arabia, and other Arab states became completely overshadowed by the Palestinian plight. Israel's security concerns became obsolete, because the Palestinians, as such a powerless people, could not possibly threaten the Jewish state.

This view overshadows the geopolitical reality of the region. Do none of the hostile Arab nations or Iran pose a threat to Israel? Certainly, the war tactics have changed to endorse and support terrorism, which has a devastating effect on Israel's psyche and economy. Huge proportions of Israel's gross domestic product go for defense. Israel is still in a state of siege, as it has been since Arab countries first declared war upon it. Why is this all lost on the left?

And especially the left on campus? It would seem that the university has not specifically sought to be a center of anti-Semitic and anti-Israel activity in the United States, yet the combined fronts of campus protest culture, fiscal inattention, and abdication of leadership have swirled together to create a perfect storm of incivility in which anti-Semitism and anti-Israelism can thrive. What is unique about these ideologies that have allowed them to persist for so many years (or, for so many centuries, in the case of anti-Semitism)? To understand how the particular ills of the uncivil university are made manifest on campus, it is essential to understand the nature of anti-Semitism and anti-Israelism as ideologies.

CHAPTER FOUR

THE PERSISTENT PREJUDICE

ANTI-SEMITIC IDEOLOGY

Anti-Semitism on college campuses is by no means a new phenomenon. The Jewish success story in America, as swift and widespread as it has been, was impeded by quotas that limited the number of Jews that could attend, or serve as faculty at many colleges and universities, especially the elite institutions.[1] Because Jewish culture traditionally placed so much emphasis on education, Jews were eager to fully participate in America's higher education opportunities, and these educational barriers were particularly onerous. Jews gravitated toward both college and advanced degrees in medicine, law, and other professions. Some universities, reflecting contemporary societal anti-Semitism that did not begin to dissipate until the 1950s and 1960s, feared being inundated by Jews. Quotas were designed to ensure that Jews did not matriculate or teach beyond an arbitrary percentage set by each individual college.

Charles Lindbergh's "philosophy" about Jews in the United States, was mirrored in the quotas limiting Jews in higher education. According to James Freedman, former president of Dartmouth College, "Charles A. Lindbergh confided to his journal in 1939, 'A few Jews add strength and character to a country, but too many create chaos.'"[2] Jewish sensitivity about quotas partially derives from this unpleasant history of anti-Semitism.

Twentieth century discrimination against Jews continued a long history in American higher education. Many of the great universities were founded as religious institutions, steeped in the tradition of various Christian denominations. Jews attended as outsiders in a campus milieu that was dominated by Christian theology, purpose, and culture.[3] Relationships between Jews and Christians in America were hardly as overwhelmingly positive as they are today, and Jewish students (if admitted at all) faced anti-Semitism inside the walls of academe as well as on the outside. Anti-Semitism was part and parcel of Christian teaching and behavior, and permeated the experience of Jews at many of the "best" colleges and universities in the United States. All of this seemed to be in the past. It was unexpected that anti-Semitism would surface again in higher education.

Some analysts are beginning to take note of the high levels of anti-Semitism and anti-Israelism on today's college campuses:

> Legislators and public officials are also taking a look at possible actions in response to growing concerns about trends on campus. Thus, in response to concerns that anti-Semitic acts on campus have been fueled by Middle Eastern Studies programs receiving federal support, Congress is now considering legislation to strengthen oversight of such grants—and to strip institutions of support where such abuses are found. And, responding to similar concerns, the U.S. Commission on Civil Rights recently announced that it will look into the scandal of campus anti-Semitism.
>
> At the same time, some philanthropists have begun to see a connection between anti-Americanism on campus and other pathologies, particularly anti-Semitism, anti-Israelism, racial separatism, and hostility to business. They are surely right to see a connection among these malignancies, and right also to see that they need to be attacked as strands of a broad ideology that has found a home in the left university. Such donors, once they are in the field, will bring a new urgency to the challenge of dislodging this orthodoxy from the academy.[4]

Anti-Semitism is not new to the campus, because it is not new to the United States. While Jews have enjoyed more freedom, security, and access in the United States than any other society in recent history (or perhaps ever), the American Jewish experience has not been free of anti-Semitism. Until the post–World War II era, Jews were limited in the neighborhoods in which they could live. Restrictive covenants, endorsed and enforced by the federal government, banned where Jews and blacks could buy a home.

Certain corporations did not hire Jews and some businesses limited how far Jews could go within the corporate structure. Anti-Semitism was more widespread in both newspapers and radio (Henry Ford and Father Coughlin). Many Jews did not feel safe wandering outside of their own neighborhoods, fearing physical violence.[5]

Until the last two generations, large percentages of Americans held anti-Semitic views. Positive perceptions of Jews have been steadily growing over the last forty years, while negative perceptions of Jews declined precipitously following the Great Depression and World War II. As the Holocaust was unfolding, levels of anti-Semitism in the United States were rising as well. The safety and security that American Jews take for granted today were much more precarious seventy years ago.[6]

Anti-Semitism in the United States is part of an evolving tradition, a persistent and pernicious prejudice that has the ability to transcend time and place.[7] An ancient hatred that has been transplanted to hundreds of cultures, societies, and nations over the centuries, Jew-hating, Jew-bashing, and Jew-blaming are stereotypes that have the ability to be adapted seemingly anywhere, anytime. Jews are whatever anybody wants them to be, but always, the outsider, the stranger. Jews are "other"—people who are not like me, a group that is external to my group. Jews have beliefs, values, and behaviors that are foreign, mysterious, and destructive. Yehuda Bauer notes "anti-Semitism is a cultural phenomenon rather than an expression of prejudice. Prejudice would be a more individual expression of hatred or distaste for a group. Anti-Semitism forms as cultures develop reasons for attacking, expelling or exterminating Jews."[8]

Because Jews are mythical, their images and stereotypes are even contradictory. The Nazis labeled Jews as sub-human, an inferior race that because of their intelligence managed to wield disproportionate power. One stereotype about Jews is that they stick together too much; yet another stereotype is that Jews try to push into social circles or communities

ANTI-SEMITISM IS A PERSISTENT AND PERNICIOUS PREJUDICE THAT HAS THE ABILITY TO TRANSCEND TIME AND PLACE.

where they do not "belong." Still another stereotype holds that Jews are so industrious that they advance to everyone else's disadvantage, but they do so only because they are shady in their business practices. The contradictions in anti-Semitism are explained well by historian Paul Johnson:

Asked to explain why they hate Jews, anti-Semites contradict them-selves. Jews are always showing off; they are hermetic and secretive. They will not assimilate; they assimilate only too well. They are too religious; they are too materialistic, and a threat to religion. They are uncultured; they have too much culture. They avoid manual work; they work too hard. They are miserly; they are ostentatious spenders. They are inveterate capitalists; they are born Communists. And so on. In all its myriad manifestations, the language of anti-Semitism through the ages is a dictionary of non-sequiturs and antonyms, a thesaurus of illogic and inconsistency.[9]

Anti-Semitic ideology and myths are so powerful that anti-Semitism exists where Jews do not even live. Studies have shown for example, that anti-Semitic attitudes in Japan are quite high, with an almost complete absence of a Jewish population.[10] The myth of the Jews and the ideology of anti-Semitism serve the purpose of Jews being a lightning rod for a host of attitudes, feelings, and beliefs. For the Japanese, anti-Semitism is linked to anti-Westernism and anti-Americanism. High levels of anti-Semitism among some segments of the black commu-nity are linked to anger and resentment about whites. Xenophobia in Europe about the grow-ing Muslim, Arab, African, and Asian popula-tions can be expressed through singling out Jews, who represent all of the foreigners that are "taking over" native cul-tures. Even if there were no more Jews in the world, anti-Semitic myth would persist. So entrenched is the idea of Jews upon which anti-Semi-tism is nourished and transformed again and again, that Jews would have to be invented even if there were no Jews.

JEWS WOULD HAVE TO
BE INVENTED EVEN IF
THERE WERE NO JEWS.

ATTITUDES AND BEHAVIOR

There are two ways to think about anti-Semitism. First, anti-Semitism is a set of attitudes and beliefs, including stereotypes about Jews. Opin-ions may be formed through information absorbed from family, friends, community, or the media. Attitudes and beliefs are important indi-cators about the relationship that an individual, group, or society may have with Jews.

Second, attitudes and beliefs may be expressed through behavior—actions against individual Jews, institutions, or the community as a whole. It is behavior that is the ultimate concern of Jews or any group in dealing with stereotypes and prejudice. How people act, what they do, both individually and institutionally, matters the most. Behaviors can include discriminatory practices in housing, employment, or education, exclusions from participation in certain institutions such as country clubs or other social organizations, or physical harm, violence to individuals or property, even murder. Individuals and institutions may be anti-Semitic but never act upon it. Anti-Semitic belief and behavior are linked. The higher the levels of anti-Semitic opinion and belief, the more likely anti-Semitic activity and behavior are likely to be, although the exact connections between belief and behavior are not completely understood.

For the most part, anti-Semitic behavior is strictly limited in contemporary America. Legislation, police enforcement, and social norms have emerged against violence against individuals because of their race or religion. Discriminatory behavior against Jews in every sector of American society is now rare. In their everyday lives, Jews are, for the most part, safe and secure in America.

Still, polling data show that anti-Semitic beliefs continue to persist in the United States. Significant proportions of Americans hold at least one or two anti-Semitic stereotypes: Jews have too much power, control the media, and are more loyal to Israel than to the United States (basically a charge of treason). About 10 to 20 percent of the American population is significantly anti-Semitic, in terms of attitudes and beliefs, depen-ding on the scale one uses to evaluate how Americans think and feel about Jews.[11]

Certain facts, however, are indisputable. First, anti-Semitic attitudes and beliefs persist across a broad spectrum of American society. The stereotypes of Jews have not disappeared, despite the removal of discriminatory barriers. Second, data show that philo-Semitism has increased over the years; that is, growing numbers of Americans hold positive attitudes about Jews.

MOST AMERICANS SEE JEWS AS CO-RELIGIONISTS, GOOD AMERICAN CITIZENS, AND HAVE OVERALL GOOD FEELINGS ABOUT JEWS.

Most Americans see Jews as co-religionists, good American citizens, and have overall good feelings about Jews (or at least neutral feelings). Indeed, one could safely argue that Americans as a whole are more philo-Semitic than they are anti-Semitic. While it would be absurd to say that anti-Semitism has disappeared in America, it is even more absurd to argue that

Americans do not feel differently about Jews today than they did seventy years ago, or that Jews are not significantly more integrated into America.

No one could reasonably argue that anti-Semitic beliefs in this country keep Jews from positions of authority, influence, and power in American business, government, or nonprofits. Jews are disproportionately represented in the House of Representatives and Senate of the United States, the Supreme Court, and in every presidential administration of the past forty years. Jews serve as board members and trustees of museums, symphonies, and universities. They are captains of industry in practically every important realm of American business. A political barrier was broken when Joseph Lieberman, a Jewish senator from Connecticut, was nominated as the Democratic vice presidential candidate in 2000. A majority of Americans voted for the Gore/Lieberman ticket, with Lieberman's Judaism being common knowledge. It is still unclear whether a Jew could be nominated for and win the presidency; the core group of anti-Semites in this country could be large enough to defeat a Jewish candidate. Yet, sometime in the not-too-distant future, the possibility of a Jewish presidential candidate is quite real.

Philo-Semitism has partially derived from changes in the teachings and preachings of various Christian churches.[12] Certainly, Vatican II in 1965 and the reappraisal of the role of Jews in the death of Jesus began a warming of the relationship between Jews and Catholics that continues to this day. John Paul II's vociferous condemnations of anti-Semitism broke new ground. His approach to Judaism has been continued by his successor, Benedict XVI. A variety of churches, including Lutherans, Presbyterians and Episcopalians, have condemned anti-Semitism as antithetical to the teachings of their denominations and to Christianity as a whole.

The Catholic Church led the way through Vatican II when it declared that "in her rejection of every persecution against any man, the Church, mindful of the patrimony she shares with the Jews and moved not by political reasons but by the Gospel's spiritual love, decries hatred, persecutions, displays of anti-Semitism, directed against Jews at any time and by anyone."[13] The teachings of Vatican II were reaffirmed over and over again by Pope John Paul II. He noted in 1986 that "the Jewish religion is not 'extrinsic' to us but, in a certain way, is 'intrinsic' to our own religion. With Judaism therefore, we have a relationship, which we do not have with any other religion. You [the Jews] are our dearly beloved brothers, and, in a certain way, we could say that you are our elder brothers."[14]

On August 19th, 2005, Pope Benedict XVI visited the Cologne synagogue and stated, "Today I too wish to reaffirm that I intend to continue on the path to improve relations and friendships with the Jewish people following the decisive lead by John Paul II." He noted that progress had been made "but much more remains to be done."[15]

The Catholic Church has not been alone in stating its rejection of anti-Semitism (although many denominations did so years later than the Catholic Church). The Episcopal Church, at its general convention in July 1988, declared, "We call upon the churches we represent to denounce anti-Semitism, no matter what its origin, as absolutely irreconcilable with the profession and practice of the Christian faith. Anti-Semitism is sin against God and human life." The Episcopal Church was repeating the declaration of the World Council of Churches assembly from its first meeting in Amsterdam in 1948. They went on to say that "those who live where there is a history of prejudice and persecution of the Jews can serve the whole Church by revealing that danger whenever it is recognized."[16]

Similar statements against anti-Semitism have been passed by the Presbyterian Church and others over the past 40 years. Current Christian theology has placed itself squarely in opposition to anti-Semitic rhetoric and behavior. The driving force behind this volume echoes the command of the Episcopal Church—that the society as a whole is served by revealing the danger of anti-Semitism wherever it is recognized.

In the United States, Christianity and Judaism have been linked to such a degree that America is often called a "Judeo-Christian" culture, noting the bond between Christianity and Judaism rather than emphasizing the differences.[17] More and more, Jews are no longer considered "incomplete Christians" or "anti-Christians," as Christians in America have labeled them in the past.

Philo-Semitism also flows from the thorough integration of Jews into American society. Jews live in neighborhoods with Christians, go to work with Christians, attend schools with Christians. Increasingly, Jews and Christians marry one another, so that extended families throughout America include both Jewish and Christian relatives. Like so many trends in America, the growth of philo-Semitism, alongside persistent anti-Semitism, indicates a society where opposite views are held by significant parts of the population.[18]

Anti-Semitic behavior, while curtailed, has not disappeared, just as anti-Semitic attitudes, while they have declined, are still a reality. The United States Air Force Academy recently dealt with anti-Semitic activities in the form of overly aggressive proselytizing to the point of intimidation of Jews, and others who did not hold certain Christian beliefs.[19] A number of websites representing a variety of anti-Semitic groups from both the right and the left have mushroomed. Hate groups still create and disseminate anti-Semitic literature. Occasionally, physical violence against Jews still occurs, including the murder of a Jewish doctor in Connecticut, and shooting attacks upon Jewish institutions in Los Angeles that resulted in injuries.[20] Of course, hate crimes take place against other groups in the United States as well. Brutal murders of blacks, transsexuals, Asians, and others have occurred over the same decade in which a small number of Jews were attacked. While racial and ethnic relationships in America are vastly improved, prejudice and bigotry remain.

ANTI-SEMITISM GROWING AROUND THE WORLD

Although anti-Semitism in the United States has diminished, other parts of the world have seen a continuation or a resurgence of higher levels of anti-Semitism.[21] Anti-Semitic beliefs are more widespread in Europe, and anti-Semitic activities in terms of violence against individuals and desecrations of synagogues and Jewish cemeteries are rising in a number of countries throughout Europe. Anti-Semitism persists through a number of right wing groups, including neo-Nazis, and as discussed, anti-Israelism is embedded in the rhetoric of the left.

According to a report conducted by Tel Aviv University's Stephen Roth Institute for the Study of Contemporary Anti-Semitism and Racism, the World Jewish Congress, and the Anti-Defamation League, there has been a substantial increase in anti-Semitic incidents worldwide.[22] The study states that 2004 marked the highest record of anti-Semitic incidents since 1989. "Anti-Semitic violence had risen by dozens of percent, especially in physical assaults, the report said. The highest number of such incidents was recorded in France, Britain, Canada, and Russia, mainly due to immigrant absorption problems, financial or social difficulties, and prejudice."[23]

Certain anti-Semitic stereotypes remain in Latin America (particularly the charge of deicide—that Jews were responsible for the death of Jesus).[24] One of the worst anti-Semitic acts in the last ten years took place in Argentina— the bombing of the Jewish community building, which killed almost a hundred people.[25] However, neither Europe nor Latin America is the geographic home of the most virulent anti-Semitism in the world.[26] This dishonor belongs to the Middle East, concentrated in Arab countries and Iran.

OTHER PARTS OF THE WORLD HAVE SEEN A CONTINUATION OR A RESURGENCE OF HIGHER LEVELS OF ANTI-SEMITISM.

The campaign against the Jews in the Middle East is remarkably ugly.[27] Arab countries organized and some continue to employ an economic boycott of Israel.[28] State-endorsed television in Egypt recently broadcast a version of the Protocols of the Elders of Zion, a scandalous diatribe against Jews. Moreover, Jews have been targeted and murdered in terrorist attacks in Tunisia and Kenya, organized by Al-Qaeda, the Saudi Arabian-spawned terrorist group. Textbooks in the Palestinian areas of Gaza and the West Bank are filled with virulent anti-Jewish language. Palestinian newspapers regularly report on the "blood libel" charge originated by Christian anti-Semites which claims that Jews use blood from children for Jewish religious rituals.[29]

One Arab reformer who grew up in Lebanon, has decried the constant barrage of anti-Israel propaganda she heard as a child:

> But let me begin by talking about my experience growing up in Lebanon where doctrinal hatred of Jews and Israel was ever present. From television programs, to national songs, hourly radio newscasts and newspapers, our citizens were fed a steady diet of lies poisoning our attitudes towards the Jews. *Israel-Aaesrael*, Israel is the devil. Al-*Yahud shayateen*, The Jews are evil. *Sarakou Al-Ard Al Arabiyah.* They stole Arab land. *Al Wakt al wahid allazi yassir endana salam huwa lamma naqtul kul al yahud wa narmihum bil bahr*, The only time we'll have peace in the Middle East is when we kill all the Jews and drive them into the sea. Every time Israel was mentioned it was attached to the phrase, *Al adew al Israeli.* The Israeli enemy. . . .
> My country and others saw nothing wrong with practicing this form of mind abuse. Of taking a generation hostage, molding them into misguided weapons; some willing to be martyred in the name

of Islam or Palestinian nationalism. It's a form of mental child abuse taking place in every Arab country.[30]

This anti-Semitism is not new, of course. Much of the Arab world aligned with Hitler during World War II and adopted Nazi ideology about the Jews. Today, few Jews remain in Arab lands, nearly all of them forcibly expelled after the creation of Israel. Arab countries have achieved what Hitler set out to do: to make their countries *"Judenrein"*—free of Jews.[31] Official Arab propaganda in some countries advocates openly and proudly the goal of wiping Jews off the face of the earth.

Some Arab nations use any forum, event, or medium to espouse anti-Israelism, even converting a dialogue on social and economic programs with Latin America into a political platform to condemn Israel. For example, a Brazilian summit between South American and Arab leaders in May, 2005, that was meant to promote economic, cultural, scientific, and political cooperation ended with the signing of a declaration that urged Israel to abandon Palestinian territory. The forum was condemned by Brazilian Jewish leaders for not sticking to economic and cultural issues. The declaration also implied that terrorism was justified against Israeli citizens. In response, the Brazilian Jewish leaders issued a "No to Terror" manifesto criticizing the summit for not adhering to its economic/cultural agenda, seeking to differentiate between "good and bad terrorism," and for supporting "armed movements aimed at harming civilians." The summit was additionally used to denounce U.S. economic sanctions against Syria.[32]

Of course, not every Arab or Muslim is anti-Semitic, and not every Muslim state is actively promoting anti-Semitism. Some Arab countries like Jordan, are attempting to improve relations with Israel. It would be only another form of prejudice to claim that every member of some other group was a bigot. Nevertheless, anti-Semitism in much of the Arab world has become institutionalized, in the same way that church-sponsored anti-Semitism plagued Europe for so long and the government sanctioned, endorsed, or enacted anti-Semitic acts as it did in Nazi Germany.

It would also be inaccurate to say that Arab and Muslim anti-Semitism is the result of the establishment in the state of Israel. While Arabs and Jews have enjoyed decent relationships over the centuries in certain places and times (such as Yemen or Spain), Jews were often second-class citizens in Muslim countries (as were Christians). Claiming that anti-Semitism derives from the existence of the state of Israel and somehow would be ameliorated if Israeli policies were different, or even more radically, if the Jewish state did not exist, is a distortion of history. These assertions gloss over the problematic historical relationship that Islam, particularly in Arabia, has had with other religious groups.

The Fusion of Anti-Semitism and Anti-Israelism

Traditional anti-Semitism and anti-Israelism have become entwined. Anti-Israel rhetoric now serves as a substitute for anti-Jewish rhetoric. The ideology and myth of the Jews has been transfigured into the ideology and myth of Israel. Much of the traditional language of anti-Semitism and the core stereotypical beliefs about Jews have been off-loaded onto Israel.

Indeed, anti-Israelism serves as a wonderful cloak for anti-Semitism, which is no longer socially acceptable in some segments of society. For others, anti-Semitism and anti-Israelism are part and parcel of the same belief system, and there are no social norms constraining either.

> THE TRADITIONAL LANGUAGE OF ANTI-SEMITISM AND THE CORE STEREOTYPICAL BELIEFS ABOUT JEWS HAVE BEEN OFF-LOADED ONTO ISRAEL.

In an op-ed entitled, "New Laban and New Nephi," Yasir Kaheil, a Utah State graduate student, argues that Judaism itself is to blame for the violence in the Middle East. It shows the blending of traditional anti-Semitism with anti-Israelism. He writes, "I have always believed that if you pick any Israeli by random and ask him, 'What is your favorite thing to do?' He'd say, 'Making up stories.' [...] Mothers have always warned their children about not to tell lies, because it's not good policy. In regard to Israelis attempting to steal Palestinian land we hear the lies and propaganda again and again, because maybe if they say it enough times they, and the world, will believe it."[33] Kaheil draws from traditional anti-Jewish canards in using Jewish scripture against the Jewish people.

> It is not a mystery of why Israelis don't respect other religions when they read in the holy book of Talmud the following "great" verses:
> - "Just the Jews are humans, the non-Jews are not humans, but cattle," Kerithuth 6b, page 78 Jebhammoth 61,

- "The birth rate of non-Jews has to be suppressed massively,"
  Zohar 11, 4b,
- "The non-Jews have been created to serve the Jews as slaves,"
  Midrasch Talpioth 225,
- "The non-Jews have to be avoided even more than sick pigs,"
  Orach Chalim 57, 6a.

One should keep in mind that talmud [sic] is Hebrew for "to learn."[34]

This column drew two letters of protest for its "vile tone"[35] and described the article as "bigoted," "inflammatory," and "anti-Semitic."[36] The quotes Kaheil includes are drawn from a fraudulent 1912 Russian text that has been widely disseminated on numerous anti-Israel sites throughout the Middle East.

A definitional disclaimer and caution is essential: criticism of particular Israeli governmental policies or actions is legitimate. Criticism of Israeli policies is not *de facto* anti-Israel nor anti-Semitic. However, both anti-Semites and anti-Israelists have become particularly adept in claiming that they are the victims of the Jews if they criticize Israel, no matter what they say or how they say it. They argue that Jews and supporters of Israel complain that *any* criticism of Israel is anti-Semitic. "If you are critical of Israel, in any way shape or form," argues Nubar Hovsepian, the Middle East Center Associate Director for Development at the University of Pennsylvania, "you risk being labeled as anti-Semitic and therefore dismissed."[37] They completely turn the tables, pointing out that Jews are hiding behind charges of anti-Semitism to silence critics of Israel. This charge is a great deflector and has to be examined for what it is: a way to use the image of normal political or social discourse as a shield while promoting prejudice.

Criticizing Israel is not anti-Semitic. Criticizing only Israel certainly embodies anti-Israelism and often has tinges of anti-Semitism. In some cases, legitimate criticism of Israel will cross the line into anti-Semitism. The following, from an editorial in the *Coastal Post*, a consistently anti-Semitic and anti-Israel conspiracy newspaper in liberal Marin County, California, is an example of this crossover. Israel is labeled a military expansionist and violent colonizer, and the behavior of campus Zionist organizations is likened to McCarthyism:

> The military expansionism of Zionist Israel has occupied the media
> for well over half a century. . . . Sharon's campaign of both covert and

violent colonization is condemned around the globe. . . . Beginning sometime in late 2001 . . . on some campuses, Zionist organizations have attempted to stifle criticism of Israel and its fascist behavior just as Senator Joseph R. McCarthy in his anti-Communist campaign during the Nixon Administration tried to stifle criticism and control public discussion, employing character assassination, innuendo with threats of political, economic, and even judicial retaliation.[38]

Israel is a democratic state with a free press and opposing political parties and views. Its policies and actions are openly debated and criticized within Israeli society. In the same way that Americans question U.S. policies on every social and political issue one can imagine, so it is true of Israeli society. Should Israel have settlements in the West Bank? Should Israel build a security barrier? Should Israel engage in preemptive strikes against terrorists? These are all legitimate questions for internal and international debate. Israel advocates themselves are critics of some Israeli government policies.

However, it is the music, the tone, as well as the words and the context used to discuss Israel that characterizes anti-Israelism. Are the policies of Israel questioned, debated, and criticized more often, or sometimes singled out as compared to other societies? Is a passionate Israel critic outraged about the military policies of Israel, but not of Iran or North Korea? Is criticism aimed at Israel about human rights violations from an individual or group that has no concern for repression in Cuba or Burma, or the abrogation of a free press in Russia? What if someone is obsessed with the Israeli treatment of Palestinians but has nothing to say about the horrors that occur in Sudan? Is a group passionate about the social status of Palestinians, but is oblivious about the untouchables in India or the lack of women's rights in Saudi Arabia and Iran? It is the double standard and hypocrisy that together distinguish anti-Israelism from legitimate questions about Israeli government policies.

Most of all, perhaps, anti-Israelism is revealed through the attack on Israel's sovereignty as a Jewish state, especially when the legitimacy of no other nation state on the earth other than Israel is questioned. No political movement suggests that Australia, Canada, New Zealand, or the United States have no right to exist as nation states. We hear no claims that Kuwait and Iraq, creations of post-colonial European imagination, have no right to exist. Only Israel is targeted as a Jewish state. Are all groups allowed a nation state except Jews? This points to both anti-Semitism and anti-Israelism.

The new anti-Semitism is anti-Israelism, attacking Israel and Israelis with the same symbolic fury previously reserved for the idea of the Jew. Expressed under the veneer of political criticism and human rights advocacy, Israel has become another caricatured version of the hated Jew. With this new anti-Semitism, Jews outside of Israel are also implicated since they advocate for a Jewish state. Those who support Israel are dismissed as tools of the all-powerful Zionists.

A connection between anti-Semitism and anti-Israelism often can be identified by looking at networks and philosophical influences. For example, the website for University of Birmingham, United Kingdom, lecturer Sue Blackwell, who called for the boycotts of Israeli universities, contains a link to a website owned by an anti-Semitic neo-Nazi activist who promotes Holocaust denial and anti-Semitic conspiracy theories.[39]

Anti-Semitism in the form of anti-Israelism attempts to legitimate prejudice by referring to Israel rather than Jews, transforming traditional bigotry into supposedly progressive, political advocacy. Groups who support Israel also become targets. For example, neo-con is used nearly synonymously with "Jew" as a way to attack Jewish officials in the United States government. They are accused of sacrificing American interests for those of a foreign power, namely Israel, typical of the anti-Semitic stereotype to charge that Jews are more loyal to Israel than to the United States. In France, the "new communitarian intellectuals" has become a phrase used to attack French Jewish social commentators and journalists.[40] Jews or their allies who work in support of Israel are now identified as a cabal that is determined to undermine the civilized world's interests.

While anti-Semitism has morphed into anti-Israelism, it retains the classic dimensions of anti-Semitism. Anti-Semites, in the guise of anti-Israelists, will always declare that they are not anti-Semites, just critics of Israel's policies. Whatever they are, they will deny that they are anti-Semitic or anti-Israel:

> Let's call this "conceptual" or "neo-antisemitism."[sic] This variant lacks the eliminationism [sic] of the classical type, but it is rife with its most ancient motifs: greed, manipulation, worship of false gods, sheer evil. What is new? It is the projection of old fantasies on two

new targets: Israel and America. Indeed, the United States is an anti-Semitic fantasy come true, the Protocols of the Elders of Zion in living color. Don't Jews, their first loyalty to Israel, control the Congress, the Pentagon, the banks, the universities, and the media? This time, the conspirator is not "world Jewry," but Israel. Having captured the "hyperpower," Jews *qua* Israelis finally do rule the world. It is Israel as the Über-Jew, and America as its slave.[41]

Historically, for example, Jews were responsible for both communism and capitalism, even though they were opposing economic systems. Now, Israel is accused of trying to rid the Jewish state of all Palestinians while at the same time designing an apartheid system to ensure that Palestinians remain slave laborers in perpetuity. The current campaign against Israel and the Jewish people is reminiscent of historical attacks against the Jews. The rhetoric is severe—calling for mass expulsion and murder. These are not mere words. While the Jewish state has faced similar situations throughout its existence, the fervor of the current campaign is unusual in its widespread influence, diversification of tactics, and masking of intent. Israel is faced with violent terrorist attacks against its citizens in Israel and overseas. It sustains decidedly one-sided criticism and condemnation from the United Nations, and, in the case of the United Nations Conference Against Racism at Durban, rampant anti-Semitism under United Nations auspices.[42]

The Arab campaign against Israel and the Jews in the United Nations is sometimes justified as an expression of the cultural values of those trying to destroy the Jewish state or murder Jews. For the internationalists who support a growing authority and legitimacy of the United Nations, anti-Israelism would seem to be unacceptable, since the creation of the Jewish homeland was endorsed by nearly every country in the United Nations at the time.

Singling out Israel has been a hobby in the United Nations in the past thirty years or so.[43] There have been more resolutions condemning Israel in the United Nations than resolutions criticizing all other nations combined in its sixty-year history. The United Nations is attempting to redress these wrongs and hopefully is beginning to move away from its open hostility to Israel and Jews.[44]

As noted in one op-ed, the need for reform in the United Nations vis-à-vis Israel is essential:

The paradox is that while it created Israel in the tragic aftermath of the Holocaust, the UN has become an international instrument for isolating the Jewish state in the community of nations. As a recent study by the American Jewish International Relations Institute documents, permanent UN agencies—including the Division for Palestinian Rights of the Secretariat, the Committee on the Exercise of the Inalienable Rights of the Palestinians, and the Special Committee to Investigate Israeli Practices affecting the Human Rights of the Palestinian People—exist only to argue the Palestinian cause and disseminated criticism of Israel.

Millions of dollars are squandered annually in what is essentially a propaganda operation. But worse than the economic waste is the fact this blatant bias only makes it harder for Israel and the Palestinians to do the hard work of making peace.[45]

While necessary, the reform of the United Nations is by no means certain.

The transference of stereotypes about Jews to Israel is common among the anti-Semitic/anti-Israel bigots. Not only do Jews control the instruments of power in American society, such as the banks and media, but the Israel lobby controls Congress. It was the Israel lobby, and the Jewish neo-cons that took the United States to war in Iraq, not for the originally stated reason (to deal with weapons of mass destruction) or the commonly stated rationale today (to bring democracy to the Middle East and fight terrorism) but rather to protect the interests of Jews and Israel. It should make no difference whatsoever that the Israeli government was (and is) far more concerned with Iran than Iraq. But logic and truth rarely play a role when it comes to anti-Semitism and anti-Israelism.

Some analysts draw subtle distinctions between anti-Semitism and anti-Israelism. Tamir Sorek, a Cornell sociology professor who taught a Palestinian-Israeli conflict course was quoted defining the differences between anti-Semitism and anti-Israelism in a *Cornell Daily Sun* newspaper article:

"Anti-Semitism, or I think it would be more accurate to say, anti-Jewish positions and expressions—it's something that exists and we know it. There is also what I can call anti-Israelism. This is another category. This is the perception of Israel as a unified and homogenous power of evil, and the source of all evil in the Middle East. This is academically ridiculous but it is not anti-Semitism. It is not against Jews as Jews," Sorek said. "And there is a third category, which is criticism of Israel. The public discourse and the public debate over these

subjects tend to ignore the differences between these categories."
Sorek said that the lines separating these three distinct categories
tended to get blurred.[46]

A recent poll among Europeans showed that Israel was considered
among the greatest threats to world peace[47]—more than Russia with its
vast nuclear arsenal, a destabilized Pakistan that also possesses nuclear
weapons, aggressive militaristic states such as North Korea, the burgeoning overpopulated countries, and so on. One anti-Israelist said that "Israel
is an aggressor, imperialistic in its aims and has become, for many, the
greatest threat to global stability."[48]

Why is Israel, with its six million people and a geographic area the
size of New Jersey, considered such a great threat to world peace by so
many Europeans?[49] Could this have something to do with Jews? Or do
these Europeans buy the story that all would be well in the Middle East if
only the Palestinian-Israeli "problem" were solved? Or are the Arab
threats of terrorism or restricting oil flow so daunting that Israel is fin-
gered as the destabilizing factor out of fear? The focus on Israel disregards
the poverty in Egypt, the radical Wahabi extremism in Saudi Arabia, and
the theocracy in Iran.

In sum, what is anti-Israelism? It is the United Nations passing resolutions that say Zionism equals racism (later rescinded) that was promoted by nation-states with some of the worst human rights records in
the world, overseen by a former Nazi secretary general.[50] Anti-Israelism is
the multitude of United Nations resolutions that target Israel but never the
Arab states that sponsor such resolutions. Anti-Israelism is attacking Jewish nationalism as the only movement considered unacceptable in the
world—that all other peoples deserve a nation-state, including the Palestinians, but not the Jews. Anti-Israelism focuses on human rights violations in Israel (which do exist as they do in the United States and all
nations) but turns a blind eye to most egregious human rights violations
that take place in countries all over the world. We will know that anti-
Israelism is diminishing when there is an appropriate focus on the rights
of women in Arab countries, the criminal justice system in Saudi Arabia, and
the abrogation of the free press in Egypt, just to name a few examples.

Anti-Israelism is the Presbyterian Church adopting a resolution calling for divestment from Israel, somehow equating Israel with South
Africa, the only other country to be targeted for a divestment campaign.[51]

How is it that the Presbyterian Church is officially more interested in the human rights issues of the Palestinians as opposed to the repression of women throughout the Arab world, the murder of female babies in China as a solution to overpopulation, the mass murders in Sudan, the slave trade of North Africa, or the repression of untouchables in India? The focus on Israel smacks of hypocrisy, double standards, and a kind of nation-state bigotry that is unimaginable for leadership representing one of the more liberal Protestant denominations in the United States (which simultaneously condemns all forms of prejudice, including anti-Semitism).

Anti-Israelism is the condemnation of terrorist attacks against civilians all over the world, but the legitimizing of terrorist attacks against Israeli citizens. Anti-Israelism is attributing the problems of the world to Israel, and that if somehow the Palestinian-Israeli issue were resolved, then all of the problems that exist in the Arab world that emanate from repressive regimes, including poverty, abuse of human rights, and abrogation of individual freedoms, would be solved. Anti-Israelism is the exclusion of the Jewish state from regional economic associations and exclusion from United Nations committees.[52] Anti-Israelism is the attempted academic boycott that occurred among some British scholars to restrict work with Israeli professors and scientists. Anti-Israelism is the Arab boycott against doing business with Israel and the companies, including some in the United States, that support it. Anti-Israelism is the divestment campaign on college campuses, in religious denominations, and among other institutions, the unsubtle attempt to link Israel with the apartheid practices of South Africa. Anti-Israelism is the vilification and demonization of Israelis and Jews that portray Israeli soldiers as brutes without concern for life, that Israelis are racists, using the language that Israelis are the new Nazis, that Israeli soldiers are baby killers, and that no army is more brutal or repressive than the Israelis. Anti-Israelism is anti-Semitism rewrapped and repackaged. It reflects the ancient myths about Jews—their power, their sinister behavior, and their ability to control the world.

There are only fourteen million Jews in the world out of a population of more than five billion.[53] If one listens to the rhetoric of the anti-Semites and the anti-Israelists (and now the anti-American voices as well), one can only assume that there are hundreds of millions of Jews in the world controlling government, controlling the banks, controlling the media, and who are poised to reap the profits from everybody else's distress. There

are fifty Arabs in the Middle East for every Jew. In a world with over a billion Muslims, it is remarkable that the fourteen million Jews in the world
are able to wreak such havoc, to have such absolute control on the reigns
of power, and to be the focus of so much attention.

This is why the traditional anti-Semitic stereotypes about Jewish control of power centers, including the banks and the media but also, of
course, Hollywood, play such an important role in understanding contemporary anti-Semitism and anti-Israelism. Because the United States is
the most powerful country in the world, it is essential that anti-Israelism
and contemporary anti-Semitism include charges of American Jews controlling the United States government through its Israel lobbies: through
its distorted media, through mythical Jewish financial power, buttressed
by government influence wherever necessary, and so on. It is no accident
that the United States is referred to as the big Satan, and Israel is the little
Satan, and that they are both said to be manifestations of the decadent
power and control of Jews.

Anti-Israelism is often linked with anti-Americanism. Paul Johnson
links the mentality of anti-Semitism to anti-Americanism:

> Americans are excessively religious; they are excessively materialis-
> tic. They are vulgar money-grubbers; they are vulgar spenders. They
> hate culture; they are pushy in promoting their own culture. They
> are aggressive and reckless; they are cowardly. They are stupid; they
> are exceptionally cunning. They are uneducated; they subordinate
> everything in life to the goal of sending their children to universities.
> They build soulless megalopolises; they are rural imbeciles. As with
> anti-Semitism, this litany of contradictory complaints is fleshed out
> with demonic caricatures.[54]

The popular refrain in the Arab world is that America's image problem in the Middle East is supposedly driven by America's support of
Israel.[55] Of course, anti-American sentiments are high in some parts of
Latin America, Western Europe, and Asia. Is this because America supports Israel? Or, have America, Israel, and the Jews all become synony-
mous with unbridled power, lack of appropriate morals, purveyors of war,
and so on?

The elevation of Israel into the status of a world dominating power
continues today. While critics of Israel used to claim that the Jewish state
was more or less a U.S. protectorate, if not the 51st state, today it is not

uncommon to hear that it is in fact the United States that is a pawn of Israel. In an article entitled "Road Map or Road Kill?," for *The Nation*, Rashid Khalidi, the head of the MEALAC department of Columbia University wrote that "Sharonistas who dominate the Bush Administration continue to prevail, as they have in nearly every Washington showdown since September 2001.[56]

What does it mean that a professor at an Ivy League university would use the bully pulpit of his academic appointment to spout such a claim? Khalidi is by far not the only professor to exploit his or her position in the name of a political cause. Anti-Semitism and anti-Israelism are more than mere ideologies or political positions: they are twin expressions of institutionalized prejudice. They have become, in some cases, pervasive on the campuses of many American universities, the strongest indication of how much civility has been discarded in contemporary higher education. In the following chapters, we examine incident after incident of mis-information, like that of Khalidi, intimidation, and plain bad scholarship, all in the service of supporting a particular and nefarious ideology. These chapters illustrate, through a close examination of anti-Semitism and anti-Israelism on campus, just how much damage the perfect storm has wrought in the American university.

Chapter Five

Ideology and Propaganda

Targeting Jewish Students and Israel Advocates

Larry Mahler, a Jewish student in his senior year at the University of California, Irvine, lamented, "It's hard to be openly proud and celebrate my heritage. I feel uncomfortable and feel [other students] won't accept my Judaism to the same extent they accept other cultures and religions."[1] A sophomore at Northwestern University, Hillary Levun stated that "[a]s a Jewish girl, it made me feel unsafe and insecure about my place at Northwestern. I think it's absolutely disgraceful that I have to worry about hatred for my culture being expressed in places of residence. As a fairly progressive campus I feel that it's a major setback for our integrity and morale."[2]

These voices of Jewish students tell the story of how the university has failed, permitting a converging rise of anti-Semitism and anti-Israelism on college campuses that marginalizes Jewish students. It is a case study of higher education losing its way, violating its own norms, and abandoning its own values. Anti-Semitism and anti-Israelism in higher education highlight how academic freedom is misused, promoting a perverted form of diversity, and how politicized scholarship subverts honest research.

In the age of celebrating multiculturalism as a pillar of academic life, could there be anything more disappointing than Jewish students being made to feel uncomfortable, even ashamed about their religion, ethnicity, and culture? The progressive university was supposed to have left behind the legacy of anti-Semitism that plagued higher education in America for most of its history. In an institution devoted to the exploration of ideas in a civil atmosphere, how is it that those who support Israel are branded as racists? Yet Jewish students and other campus citizens are subjected to intellectual ostracism and intimidation for their culture and religious beliefs.[3]

IN THE AGE OF CELEBRATING MULTI-CULTURALISM, COULD THERE BE ANYTHING MORE DISAPPOINTING THAN JEWISH STUDENTS BEING MADE TO FEEL ASHAMED ABOUT THEIR RELIGION, ETHNICITY, AND CULTURE?

Jewish students increasingly have been reporting a significant level of alienation and intimidation for their views and their identities. Kenneth L. Marcus, now the staff director for the United States Commission on Civil Rights, speaking of a complaint filed against the University of California, Irvine, over claims of anti-Jewish harassment, stated, "I'm certainly praying that there will not be more of these cases, but my sense is this is going on, and there will be."[4]

There is, perhaps, no greater barometer of academic freedom (and civility) on campus than the level of freedom from intellectual harassment. While students should be challenged and presented with competing views, no student (or faculty) should be intimidated, harassed, or physically threatened. Yet there are today too many stories of Jewish students who feel, either for fear of a bad grade, social exclusion, or even physical harm, that they cannot reveal their Judaism and that they certainly cannot openly state their position should they be a supporter of Israel.

Jewish students have expressed that, in certain classes, they may avoid expressing their opinion to evade the possibility of confrontation or humiliation. Others who have been bold enough to contradict an anti-Israel argument made by a student or a professor tell stories of being verbally and emotionally attacked in an effort to de-legitimize and silence their opinion. For example, Columbia student "LS" reports, "I took a class with [Professor] George Saliba [as we discussed the Palestinian–Israeli conflict, he] sort of drew me outside the classroom and told me to walk with him on his way out. . . . He said, 'You have no voice in this debate. . . . See, you have green eyes,' he said, 'You're not a Semite. . . . You have no claim to the land of Israel.'"[5] (Saliba has denied ever making the statement.)

Other Jewish students feel as if their point of view is simply not respected. As a result, self-censorship takes place. Discussion is cut off before it begins. How can we measure the silence? The position professors take out of the classroom can affect what students may or may not say in the classroom. The general level of comfort in a class is dependent largely upon the feeling that the professor is fair-minded. How do Jewish students feel about attending a class taught by Central Connecticut State University physics professor Dr. Sadanand Nanjundiah, who wrote that "the U.S. Congress is but the Washington branch of the Israeli Knesset." Nanjundiah also wrote, "The sheer arrogance with which the Israeli lobby operates in the U.S., making or breaking Congressional careers through its largesse and/or its anti-Semitic baiting of anyone who questions the policies of the current Israeli regime, is truly breathtaking and unparalleled in democratic society."[6] Or, what about Georgetown professor Hisham Sharabi, who was quoted in the *Lebanon Daily Star* saying to Balamand University students and faculty that, "Jews are getting ready to take control of us and the Americans have entered the region to possess the oil resources and redraw the geopolitical map of the Arab world."[7] A professor's conduct both in and out of the classroom contributes to the environment in which students are supposed to learn, and when a particular professor chooses to openly attack a constituency within the student body, how can any student feel comfortable?

What if students are attacked by name? And what if the names are singled out because they are Jewish names? Yale assistant professor of genetics Mazin Qumsiyeh, who is also the co-founder of the group "Palestinian Right of Return Coalition," made many Jewish students feel targeted when he obtained a list of students whom he labeled a "pro-war cabal" and circulated their names. The "pro-war cabal" was no more than the Yale pro-Israel student membership list.[8] Qumsiyeh claims not to have known this; however, explanations for how he obtained the list and why he thought it was appropriate to label each student a war monger are absent. Prejudice is the likely answer, and coming from a professor all the more disturbing.

Intimidation leading to self-censorship is accompanied by the outright exclusion of Jewish students and representatives. If there are no Jewish students, there is no need to shut them up. Speaking as a guest lecturer at the University of Texas, Austin, in March, 2002, Palestinian journalist Munah Hamzeh said she would not continue until two pro-Israel students left: "I will not speak with members of Texans for Israel in the audience." They were asked to leave the meeting, which was sponsored by the Palestine Solidarity Committee. Co-Chairman Saeed Moody said that, while the event was not restricted to members only, "this was for pro-Palestine members who want to actively promote our views." Bob Jensen, an associate professor, said he did not intervene because it was not his place to step in on a student-organized event.[9]

Likewise, pro-Israel Jewish students reported being excluded from a Jewish-Arab discussion group at the University of Chicago. To ensure a "safe and friendly" environment, students who were deemed too "right wing" were not invited. Despite the exclusion, a university dean attended the event.[10] At the University of California, Berkeley, in February, 2002, Jewish campus representatives attending the annual divestment conference organized by Students for Justice in Palestine were harassed and excluded from parts of the conference.[11] What other scenario on campus would legitimize the exclusion of students from university sponsored events? What would happen if homosexual students were banned from campus gatherings, or those who support women's rights in Iran were banned from a lecture hall?

Jewish students also have found themselves targets of other students who seek to intimidate supporters of Israel. A student at the University of California, Berkeley, reported having endured intense anti-Semitism while campaigning for a student government office. "People spit on me and said 'Zionist' and kept on walking. I was spit on a couple of times. I was called a conservative Zionist bastard, a f**king Jew. . . . There was another girl helping me out who happened to be Catholic, and a guy said, 'Hey, are you a Jew girl?'"[12]

Some campuses, in many ways, have become hostile environments for Jews and has lead to some questioning if the negative experience is worth the benefit. David Weinberg, an 18-year-old freshman at University of California, Berkeley, told the *Colorado Daily*, "It's ironic that this is the home of the Free Speech Movement, and there is no free speech on this campus. This has been the most frightening year of my life. I have definitely questioned whether coming here was the right decision, and a lot of students should not come here."[13] Weinberg's worries may seem unwarranted to some, but considering the violence that has erupted at some of the more extreme campuses, his concern is real.

A spate of harassment and violence erupted at the University of California, Berkeley, in 2001. In December of that year, a member of Chabad, a Jewish religious group, was assaulted on campus on the way to the Chabad house.[14] Then during spring break of 2002, the Hillel window was smashed and graffiti stating, "F**k the Jews," was painted on the building.[15] Later, during a Simchat Torah celebration, a Jewish participant was assaulted close to campus.[16] These incidents all happened on one campus, over the course of a short period of time, highlighting how quickly campuses transform from verbal to physical hostility.

The signs exist all over the country. More often than not, the first signs of growing intimidation are anonymous. At the University of Chicago, in a campus dorm, a Jewish student put up a sign publicizing a pro-Israel rally on campus. It was defaced with the words, "F**k Zionists, F**k the Israeli pigs."[17] In 2002, at the University of Colorado, swastikas were drawn on a religious structure utilized by Jewish student groups.[18] At the University of Wisconsin, Madison, someone scrawled the messages, "Kill the Jews" and "Make it snow Jewish ash" in a classroom.[19]

The phrase, "the writing is on the wall," has no better application than on American college campuses today. Anti-Semites in the midst of the campus anti-Israel movement do little to hide their contempt for Jews and their vitriol leaches out for the entire campus community to see, if they choose to look. None should be surprised that the extremes of the University of California, Berkeley, can also be found on other campuses.

While any one student is responsible for his or her own actions, and accountable as such, faculty are another matter. If a professor intimidates a student, he or she must be dealt with through appropriate university mechanisms. However, in the bigger picture, what is important is the general climate of hostility and political incorrectness that many Jewish students face. If the result of campus anti-Israelism is that significant numbers of

IT IS NOT JUST STUDENTS WHO FEEL INTIMIDATED BY CAMPUS ANTI-ISRAELISM, BUT ALSO FACULTY.

Jewish students feel that they must keep their mouths shut, then the collective faculty have a serious breach in the overall decorum and appropriate behavior of their peers.

Moreover, it is not just students who feel intimidated by campus anti-Israelism, but also faculty themselves. One faculty member describes what is almost indescribable. Laurie Zoloth, former professor of Jewish Studies at San Francisco State University, depicted the hostile climate on her campus in a widely circulated e-mail. "I cannot fully express what it feels like to walk across campus daily, past maps of the Middle East that do not include Israel, past posters of cans of soup with labels on them of drops of blood and dead babies, labeled 'canned Palestinian children meat, slaughtered according to Jewish rites under American license,' past poster after poster calling out 'Zionism = racism,' and 'Jews = Nazis.' This is not civic discourse, this is not free speech, this is the Weimar republic with brown shirts it cannot control."[20]

ANTI-SEMITISM AND ANTI-ISRAELISM AT HOME ON CAMPUS

Higher education is a fertile home for anti-Semitism and anti-Israelism for a variety of reasons. First, campuses have been targeted by anti-Israel groups as an arena for the anti-Israel agenda. Those who are committed to anti-Israelism hope to capture the hearts and minds of young people in America's educational systems. Arab World and Islamic Resources (AWAIR), an Arab-American advocacy group that promotes anti-Israel propaganda, makes clear in its mission statement, "Recognizing that no work is of greater importance than the preparation of our young people for their roles as thoughtful and informed citizens of the twenty-first century, and recognizing, too, that U.S. involvement with the Arab World and with the wider world of Islam is certain to remain close for many years, AWAIR's goal is to increase awareness and understanding of this world region and this world faith through educational outreach."[21] The *Arab World Studies Notebook* also says, "We hold that preparing our young people for their roles as thoughtful, informed citizens of the next century is our most important work."[22]

Second, universities are complex bureaucracies. There are a multitude of decision-makers, which include presidents, trustees, faculty, provosts, deans, associate deans, vice presidents for this, and associate vice presidents for that. Like New Orleans and the rest of the Gulf Coast following the devastation of Hurricane Katrina, the victims of that horrible tragedy were less beleaguered by conspiracy than they were by incompetence. Governments at all levels failed, most of all in their ability or willingness to communicate with one another to ensure appropriate action. Anti-Semitism and anti-Israelism flourish on college campuses partially because of the paralysis of bureaucracy in dealing with student complaints, monitoring conferences and events, and so on. Everyone is in charge, so no one is in charge. Anyone who has been inside higher education knows that many colleges and universities are wrapped more in red tape than green ivy.

MANY COLLEGES AND UNIVERSITIES ARE WRAPPED MORE IN RED TAPE THAN GREEN IVY.

Third, higher education is conducive to anti-Semitism and anti-Israelism because many of the stakeholders abdicate responsibility. Trustees do not want to interfere for fear of violating academic freedom. Faculty do not want to appear overzealous criticizing other faculty. Most university presidents, provosts, and deans look for stasis and avoid issues that rock the boat.

Fourth, universities are a fertile environment for anti-Semitism and anti-Israelism because activists with the most energy and loudest voices often capture organizational mechanisms. People in the middle tend to be disenfranchised by the activists who are most committed to a particular agenda. Research performed by the Institute for Jewish & Community Research revealed that, in fact, most professors do not hold negative views regarding Israel.[23] Anti-Semites and anti-Israelists triumph on campus not because of their large numbers, but because of the willingness of the few to pursue their agenda. Those who may disagree with them tend to be silent, busy, or indifferent. The same phenomenon is seen in contemporary American politics in both the Republican and Democratic parties, and a number of NGOs, including the Presbyterian Church. The vast majority of Presbyterians are neither anti-Semitic nor anti-Israel. Yet, a few activists were able to capture the institutional decision-making processes to pass anti-Israel resolutions. This phenomenon is widespread on campuses as well.

Fifth, the ideology of anti-Semitism and anti-Israelism fits within the larger campus themes that include anti-war, (violence is never justified, war is bad, there is no just cause), anti-West, anti-American (Europe and America are powerful and bad, Brazil and Algeria are good), white people are bad, all other people are good, power is bad, weakness is honorable. These themes appear over and over again in the anti-Semitic, anti-Israel framework.

It is not surprising, therefore, that anti-Semitism and anti-Israelism have found their way into America's educational systems, partly from forces outside the university and partly from within. Like the United Nations, the campus has developed into a comfortable home for anti-Israelists. Moreover, it is a platform from which one can reach a large audience, not only of students, but also of the many millions of Americans, and people around the world, who regard the American university as the incubator of change and the leader in intellectual thought.

Some observers argue that levels of anti-Semitism and anti-Israelism can be measured primarily by the number of events, the shrillness of the rhetoric, or the most egregious expressions of either to take place in colleges and universities. Because both anti-Semitism and anti-Israelism are myths and ideologies, and have become blended in both rhetoric and activity, they exist beyond mere measurement of incidences and the most visible expressions. These belief systems, as they have in the past, take root in particular groups and institutions and express themselves in different ways over time, but they are there, more or less dormant, more or less active.

NO INSTITUTION OF HIGHER LEARNING SHOULD ALLOW JEWISH STUDENTS TO BE INTIMIDATED OR ATTACKED, OR PRO-ISRAEL SPEAKERS TO BE PHYSICALLY THREATENED.

The following analysis shows that the "Israel debate" is not a true intellectual debate at all, but rather a failure of the university community at all levels to properly protect its highest ideals. No institution of higher learning should allow Jewish students to be intimidated or attacked, or pro-Israel speakers to be so physically threatened that they cannot safely visit a campus. Such an environment is antithetical to the mission of America's universities. While we have, unfortunately, come to expect this kind of atmosphere from Wahhabi extremists from Saudi Arabia or in the official dogma of Iran's dictatorial mullahs, this kind of propaganda has no place on campuses.

Anti-Semitism and anti-Israelism on campus ideology has four primary components. First, Jewish nationalism is characterized as racism. Because "Zionism=racism," Jews do not deserve to have a nation-state in Israel. Second, the Holocaust is not a Jewish historical experience, but rather a Palestinian one. Third, violence against Israelis is justified, even terrorism, and Americans cannot judge such actions by Western moral standards. Fourth, Jews and Israel control America, the American government, and U.S. foreign policy.

ZIONISM = RACISM: ISRAEL DOES NOT BELONG TO THE JEWS

The unique set of issues that Israel, Palestinians, and other Middle Eastern nations face are framed on campus to fit within the politics of race and inequality. Palestinians are portrayed as poor and brown, while Israelis as rich and white. Israelis are colonists; Palestinians are indigenous. These labels tap into the well of racial politics on campus. The Palestinian narrative attempts to replicate the civil rights history of African Americans, the struggle for economic success of Mexican Americans, or the historical geographic segregation of Native Americans. Competing claims of nationalism between Palestinians and Jews are rarely evaluated on equal grounds. Jewish nationalism is somehow a form of white supremacy while Palestinian nationalism, though it often calls for expulsion of the Jews, is regarded as legitimate self-determination.

The double standards that plague Jews and Israelis in relation to Palestinians (and to most other peoples for that matter) are exemplified in the campus reaction to Jewish nationalism. While one may debate the idea of a Kurdish state between Iraq, Turkey, and Syria, the discussion will tend to focus upon political considerations and feasibility. Those who reject the idea will not, however, do so because of a fundamental denial of Kurdish nationalism. The same could be said for most any people.

The Palestinian cause is different: embraced as representative of the struggle against colonialism, white supremacism, economic exploitation, and nearly all other forms of oppression. However, for Palestinians to effectively play the part of the ultimate victim and inherit the legacy of black South Africans in carrying the flag of resistance, there must also exist an ultimate white oppressor. If Palestinians are indigenous revolutionaries, then Israelis are counter-revolutionaries. If Palestinians are economically disadvantaged, then Israelis are capitalist exploiters. If Palestinian nationalism is righteous, then Jewish nationalism is sinful.

Campuses are incubators of national and global movements and proudly promote social justice. Issues of racial equality, rejecting colonialism, and advocacy for human rights are part of campus lore and can spark sporadic protest. If there is a social issue based on these core campus concerns, then chances are it will be adopted by the protest culture of American colleges and universities. However, this protest culture no longer has clearly defined core inspirational causes for which to fight. The desire for social justice is still there, but the objectives are fuzzy. How to achieve racial equality or protect human rights seems elusive. Current causes do not have the sting, passion, or clarity of the anti-Vietnam protests, the fight for civil rights, or the war on poverty. This has left a vacuum that anti-Israelists have been too willing to fill by imitating the 1960s framework. David A. Harris, of the American Jewish Committee, explains that, "[Anti-Israelists'] claims that Israel is a 'colonialist, racist, occupying' power find a receptive ear among the sometimes overlapping anti-globalization crowd, other minority communities, human rights activists, the far—and sometimes, not so far—left, and the America-can-do-no-right believers."[24] Israel fills a niche.

Those who ascribe to a "progressive" ideology have easily adopted this framework. Brown University alum, Sarah McDermott, wrote in the campus paper, "If progressives have an anti-Israel bias, it is for good reason. Zionism, liberal Zionism included, is discriminatory by definition, and is used as a tool of colonialism and imperialism. It is, therefore, incompatible with progressive politics."[25]

There is more than one, in many ways contradictory, disparaging view of Jewish nationalism (just as Jewish stereotypes are contradictory). One attack on Jewish nationalism questions or denies the existence of a Jewish people, and thus the need for any Jewish state. How can Jews really be a people if they have been separated for so long? Columbia University professor Joseph Massad exemplifies this position by asserting the idea that "European Jews are descendents of the ancient Hebrews is 'preposterous,' 'absurd,' and even somehow 'anti-Semitic.'"[26] Aren't they just citizens of their most recent country of origin? Utah State graduate student, Yasir Kaheil, in response to a Yemeni Israeli, wrote: "Mr. Serbin, a 'Yemeni Jew' sounds to me more correct than 'Israeli.' If for some reason the Yemeni government denied you as a 'Yemeni citizen' then, it's an issue between you and them, why don't you discuss that with them? . . . The only solution that I can think of for this Israeli/Palestinian issue is for all of the Israelis to go back to where they came from. Mr. Serbin, I believe you are from Yemen, why not go back to your country?"[27] Why didn't all Jews go back home after World War II? The radical black Muslim speaker, Imam Malik of Masjid Al-Islam, also known by various versions of Amir Abdel Malik Ali, speaking at San Francisco State University, declared that Israelis should return "to Germany, to Poland to Russia. The Germans should hook y'all up. You should go back to Germany."[28] Jews that have emigrated to Israel are alternately regarded as either self-appointed victims or rabid ideologues, neither of which have a right to their own country. But Israel is the only Jewish state in the world, and it resides on the only land Jews have a connection to, one that has lasted thousands of years. Rejecting Israel is to reject Jewish nationalism, for such a thing does not exist—and never will—without the land to which it is tied.

"Zionism is racism." "Israel is a European colony." "Israel is apartheid." All of these canards are commonly promoted on campus today. Israel is whatever racial politics tend to despise. The assertion that Jewish nationalism, or Zionism, is racism is not indigenous to college campuses. It was the United Nations that first gave this idea credence around the world, with a resolution that was ultimately repealed.[29] However, today, it is on campus that the Zionism = racism prejudice remains.

At a panel discussion entitled "Crisis in Palestine," University of Hawaii ethnic studies professor Ibrahim Aoude proclaimed, "There is no legal basis for the state of Israel. Israel is a colonial project, and no colonial project has a legal basis for existence." He continued, saying that "[w]hether it's suicide bombing or Israel military; against the Palestinians in the West Bank, we think the source of this violence is the occupation, and we are working to end that." Regarding the "occupation," he proclaimed, "[I]t's so heinous, it's so palpably wrong, even if there weren't suicide bombings, just the Israel occupation alone day-to-day is a war crime."[30]

With professors so passionate in their attacks on Jewish nationalism, it is not surprising that students often parrot them. A frequent columnist for Wayne State University's *South End* newspaper wrote in 2003, "[C]olonialism is embodied in the Zionist project. Part of the reason why settlers have disproportionate influence is because they are the full expression of Zionism. It's a relationship where both parties use one another; the settlers use Tel Aviv to achieve their millennial ends while Tel Aviv uses settlers to achieve their empire."[31]

Israelis are not only World War II fascists, they are also portrayed as pre-20th century colonialists. Israel is cast on campus as a country of European white men, who suppress Palestinians because they are poor, brown, Muslim, indigenous, or all of these. Israel is the last holdover of a colonial era long since passed. It is, in fact, the equal of the worst of all colonizers, past and present. Brenda Abdelall wrote in the *Michigan Daily*, "As the ghettos of Palestine continue to expand . . . we find ourselves in a society eerily reminiscent of South Africa during apartheid."[32] An op-ed in the *Brown Daily Herald* included the assertion that "[c]olonialism is not 'the occupation' but the entire institutionalization of apartheid in Palestine."[33]

Poet Tom Paulin, who has been invited to speak on various campuses, increasingly so as his remarks have become more vehemently anti-Semitic and anti-Israel, stated, "I never believed that Israel had the right to exist at all." Paulin continued, "In my view the European culture carries a very heavy responsibility for the creation of Israel."[34] Once accepting Israel as a colonial project, one superimposes all the negative imagery of white colonial Europe onto a nation created from the hated rejects of Europe and the Arab world: the refugees from the Holocaust and pogroms as well as homeless Jewish exiles from Arab lands. Franz Julio wrote in the San Francisco State University Golden Gater, "We must all admit that Jewish nationalism—Zionism—is responsible for the deaths and human-rights abuses of thousands of Palestinians."[35]

Precisely because Jewish nationalism was once embraced on campus and supported as a shining example of self-determination and freedom, it is now attacked as an unnatural and unacceptable notion. What were once lauded as Israel's great successes, the development of the land, absorption of refugees, the defense of their freedom, have all been turned around. Instead of Israelis being pioneers, they are settler land thieves; instead of providing a safe haven for persecuted Jews, Israel endorses racial superiority and separation; instead of defenders of their pursuit of freedom, Israelis are new age conquistadors with no limit to their hunger for land.

Zionism, or Jewish self-determination, is lumped together with the only nationalistic movements rejected on campus—fascist nationalist movements and their remnants. Franz Julio continued, "Unfortunately, blind nationalism usually leads to a false perception of supremacy over others and an ethnocentric perception of infallibility. Chauvinistic nationalist movements eventually become oppressors themselves. Zionism is no exception. It's a form of extreme religious and ethnic nationalism supported by the state of Israel and internationalist Zionist pressure groups."[36]

Jewish nationalism is thus equated with Jewish international conspiracy charges. The hegemony of Jews takes on a new form. Rather than being Europe's rejects, Jews represent European power: "Zionist Jewish colonialism and its commitment to European white supremacy in Jewish guise."[37] In a letter to the editor of *Commentary* magazine, a speaker at the Duke divestment conference and Yale University professor, Mazin Qumsiyeh, compared Israel to South Africa and fascist Europe. Zionism is "a 'diseased' ideology of ethnocentric nationalism and racism that we are familiar with from South African apartheid and European fascism."[38]

Anti-Israelists make exaggerated claims to convince students and other faculty that they have been misled and even lied to about not only the history of Israel, but also the fundamental principals that guide it. Massad repeated the declaration of Yasser Arafat in an article he wrote for *Al-Ahram Weekly*. "Zionism is a racist movement that discriminates against Jews themselves and allies itself with colonialism; Israel is a racist state . . . and Israel is a settler colony intent on territorial expansion."[39] Colonialism, Zionism, and Jewish nationalism become interchangeable.

RATHER THAN BEING EUROPE'S REJECTS, JEWS REPRESENT EUROPEAN POWER.

These themes can even be the focus of campus-wide events. The University of California, San Diego, annually hosted an event titled, "Anti-Zionism Week," until the name was changed to, "From Oppression to Liberation" Week, (though the content remained the same). Just up the road, at the University of California, Irvine, "Zionism Awareness Week"[40] has been a forum through which to berate Israel and delegitimize Jewish nationalism. Imagine a university-sponsored event attacking the national movement of another people. Would the university even entertain the idea of an anti-Kurdish rally? Not likely.

Many students of color may be susceptible to the image of Palestinians as the new racially oppressed victim. It is not difficult to make this jump, for the promotion of Palestinians as such becomes part of the lore of the politics of race in the university. Unfortunately, the popularity of radical black Muslim speakers on campus has only added fuel to this fire. For over a decade, preceding the current anti-Israel push, black Muslims on campus introduced consistent anti-Semitic propaganda.

Then Nation of Islam spokesman, Khalid Abdul Muhammad, spoke to an audience at Kean College in 1993, declaring:

> Who are the slumlords in the Black community? The so-called Jew . . . Who is it sucking our blood in the Black community? A white imposter Arab and a white imposter Jew. Right in the Black community, sucking our blood on a daily and consistent basis . . . You see everybody always talk about Hitler exterminating six million Jews. That's right. But don't nobody ever ask what did they do to Hitler? What did they do to them folks? They went in there, in Germany, the way they do everywhere they go, and they supplanted, they usurped.[41]

Opening for Muhammad on February 23, 1994, at Howard University, Malik Zulu Shabazz led the audience in a chillingly anti-Semitic chant:

> Shabazz: "Who caught Nat Turner and killed Nat Turner?"
>   Audience: "Jews"
>   S: "Who is it that controls the Federal Reserve? Who?"
>   A: "Jews"
>   S: "Who is it that set up the Hon. Marcus Garvey and the Justice Department and the judges that sent him to prison?"
>   A: "Jews"
>   S: "Who? Who?"
>   A: "Jews"[42]

Shabazz, at another rally, specifically singled out Jews in the audience. Audience member Noa Zilbering, a Jewish faculty member, said of the speech, "It was the most terrifying thing I ever experienced."[43] Zilbering explained how Shabazz asked the few Jews in the audience of over one hundred to identify themselves and then asked who among them believed in Jesus. When none of the Jews raised their hands, he replied, "See, how can we accept you?"[44] Nation of Islam speakers lace their speeches about black empowerment with anti-Semitic sentiments. Jews, as is the case in traditional anti-Semitism, provide a convenient scapegoat.

Anti-Semitism among radical black Muslims is nothing new, but one change that has occurred has been an increased interest in international events and hostility toward Israel. At a University of California, Irvine, event in 2005 held by the Muslim Student Union and slated as the "Desperation of the Zionist Lobby," speaker Amir Abdel Malik Ali effectively called for the termination of a Jewish state. "Two-state solution is off the table. No. One state. And check this out! One state . . . majority rules. One state . . . majority rules."[45] In 2001, at a Muslim Student Association conference at the University of California, Los Angeles, cleric Muhammad-al-Asi stated, "Israel is as racist as apartheid could ever be . . . you can take a Jew out of the ghetto, but you can't take the ghetto out of the Jew."[46] At another rally held in Wheeler Hall on the University of California, Berkeley, campus, Ali directly implicated Israel in the 9/11 attacks. "The Israelis knew about and were 'in-control' of 9/11," and it "was staged to give an excuse to wage war against Muslims around the world."[47]

Ali, an imam linked to the Masjid Al Islam mosque in Oakland and a graduate of San Francisco State University, continued with a tirade against Zionists, making clear that he only limits his criticism to Zionists in order to avoid being labeled an anti-Semite. "The Zionist Jews done really messed up. I'm talking about the Zionist Jews, not all Jews, not the Jews who are down with us—because not all Jews are Zionists. I have to say that, otherwise I'll get called an anti-Semite."[48]

These speakers have played a significant role in bringing home the supposed racism of Israel/Zionism and linking it directly to racism experienced by an American student of color. In 1997, Khalid Abdul Muhammad declared, "Our entertainers, our basketball players, our football players, our track stars, our baseball players, our entertainers and athletes are in the palm of the white Zionist Jew's hand. . . ."[49]

Nation of Islam speakers can be particularly divisive on campus. For many students of color, their teachings on self-empowerment and community organizing hold significant appeal. In celebration of Black History Month, Amir Abdel Malik Ali presented a lecture entitled "The Legacy of Malcolm X" to a diverse crowd, sponsored by the Muslim Students Association, the African American Achievers Club, the Cultural Affairs Club, La Raza Unida, the Polynesian Club, the Native American Study Organization, Filipinos for Education, Art, Culture and Empowerment, and the

Psychology Club.[50] One student attendee, Hasani Gomez, commented, "What I receive from the message is a sense of motivation and inspiration to take what has gone on in the past and applying it to people today."[51] The history of Malcolm X, a popular figure on campus, is generally tied to that of the Nation of Islam, despite his eventual break with the movement. The anti-Semitism embedded within much of the Nation of Islam's, and other organizations,' teachings is secondary in the minds of most students on campus, especially those of color.

The campaign against Jewish nationalism recycles typical anti-Jewish stereotypes, including that Jews are controlling, conspiratorial, and without morals. Jews are crafty, untrustworthy, and aggressive. These age-old anti-Semitic ideas are unacceptable in normative campus discourse. But this changes if the focus is Israel. Professor Norton Mezvinsky, of Central Connecticut State University, has been quoted stating that Jews believe "the blood of non-Jews has no intrinsic value," and that this allows Jews to consider that the killing of non-Jews does "not constitute murder according to the Jewish religion." In addition, he is quoted stating that, "the killing of innocent Arabs for reasons of revenge is a Jewish virtue."[52]

One can openly declare that the Jewish state is not to be trusted, that its aims are to militarily, economically, and socially dominate not just the Palestinians, but the entire Middle East. Senior Fadi Haidar, a senior at the University of Houston, wrote:

> Israel has never believed in peace, because peace would mean an end to its project in the Middle East. For those of you who are not well informed of the history of that part of the world, the Israeli project is based on three basic goals: First, the establishment of a nation that extends from the Euphrates to the Nile; second, the possession of all Middle Eastern precious resources including oil and water; and third, an immense exodus of Arab citizens toward inner deserts or their being employed in low-level jobs.
>
> Moreover, Israel does not want peace because its leaders believe their country is stronger with enemies at its border rather than friends, since it can keep on getting $8 billion in aid from the American government every year.[53]

Israel, the Jewish state, is portrayed here as war-mongering, founded upon a "project" designed to conquer Egypt, Syria, Lebanon, Jordan, Iraq, and Saudi Arabia. The goals of the Jewish state are to control the resources and subjugate Arabs to suit Jewish needs, whether this means expulsion or pseudo-slavery. Moreover, Israel will never accept peace, if only to retain the precious money that the U.S. provides, very much echoing traditional stereotypes of Jews who would do anything for money, even keep their own people in a perpetual state of war. Likewise, Juan Cole, president of the Middle East Studies Association and University of Michigan professor wrote on his internet blog, "Israel's policies toward the West Bank are unparalleled in the contemporary world. . . . There are no other countries that insist on occupying a people whom they do not wish to absorb, but only to steal from."[54] The assertion that Israel maintains its position in the West Bank for the purpose of theft is a reflection of long-held stereotypes of Jews being greedy. It is clever to play on old anti-Semitic canards and attempt to convince readers that the conflict between Palestinians and Israelis is due to nothing more than Jewish greed.

The fusion of anti-Semitism and anti-Israelism inevitably takes one beyond the borders of Israel and implicates any Israel supporter, group of supporters, and Judaism as a religion. In the University of Massachusetts' student *Daily Collegian*, a letter was published by emeritus professor of mathematics Helen Cullen, who wrote, "Judaism and the Jewish identity are offensive to most human beings and will always cause trouble between the Jews and the rest of the human race."[55] Though individual Jews who reject Israel are lauded by anti-Israelists and used as shields against accusations of anti-Semitism, Jews as a group find themselves accused of being part of an aggressive, domineering, untrustworthy, subversive "cabal."

ISRAELIS ARE PERPETRATING GENOCIDE

If Jewish nationalism is rooted in racism, colonialism, and exploitation, it follows, then, that Israel, its citizens and its supporters must be brutal aggressors, actively endorsing and committing crimes against humanity. This includes genocide, ethnic cleansing, and references to a new "holocaust," among others. Anti-Israelists freely make claims of Israel perpetrating the grossest violations of human rights and international law. Israel is an expansionist state carrying out ethnic cleansing and genocide on a helpless, innocent victim. Christopher Neal wrote in the University of California, Los Angeles, *Daily Bruin*, "Israel is systematically killing and imprisoning a whole people. An entire group of human beings is seen as less than equal."[56]

The reference to "systematic killing" is intentionally reminiscent of the Nazi extermination plan for Europe's Jews. Israelis have been assigned the identity of the worst of the world's oppressors, practicing the world's worst crimes. Emory University senior Farzad Masroor wrote, "The racist dehumanization of the Palestinians is part and parcel of the Arab–Israeli conflict. [. . . S]uch dehumanization was necessary to conceive and fulfill the widely supported Zionist expulsion plan of the Palestinian population."[57]

Genocide, ever since the Holocaust in which six million Jews were murdered at the hands of Nazis and collaborating regimes, has been considered the most heinous crime humans can commit. It refers to deliberate actions undertaken for the specific purpose of destroying an entire religious, ethnic, racial, or national group. The accusation of genocide should be used sparingly, because to dilute its meaning would be to disarm it of its power. Indeed, the world has been very slow to declare genocide as it unfolds (too slow even when it is appropriate), such as is the case in Sudan today, or was the case in Rwanda where the intervention came entirely too late.

However, the accusation of genocide is used freely against Israel. University of Illinois professor of International Law Francis Boyle equates Israel with Nazi Germany in an article entitled "The International Laws of Belligerent Occupation." "The paradigmatic example of a 'crime against humanity' is what Hitler and the Nazis did to the Jewish People. This is where the concept of crime against humanity came from. And this is what the U.N. Human Rights commission determined that Israel is currently doing to the Palestinian People: Crimes against humanity. Legally, just like what Hitler and the Nazis did to the Jews." He continued, explaining that "Israeli Prime Minister Ariel Sharon is what international lawyers call a genocidaire—one who has already committed genocide in the past."[58] The propensity of Israelis to carry out such crimes is presumed and asserted often. Washington Square News columnist Charlie Beckerman posited, "What if Sharon decides that the best way to defend his country is some nice, old fashioned genocide?"[59]

Israel and its political leaders are under constant suspicion, presumed to be planning or conspiring to carry out heinous acts against the Palestinians. Sharon is regularly likened to Hitler, Israeli soldiers to Nazi Gestapo officers. In a letter to the editor entitled, "There is a Long History

of Sharon's 'Racism,'" Julie A. Belz, an assistant professor of applied lin-
guistics and German at Penn State, claims that Sharon is a "Judeo-Nazi,"
and that Israel is a brutal occupying force that "creates mass graves and
dumps Palestinian bodies into them," and "prevents the Red Cross from
delivering food, water, and medicine to wounded Palestinians." She
argues further that people are not aware that "American tax dollars have
paid for these atrocities."[60] This particular abuse of Holocaust imagery is
among the most disturbing aspects of the anti-Israel ideology on campus.

EVOLVING ANTI-SEMITISM: HOLOCAUST DENIAL

Branding Israelis murderers, guilty of genocide is a difficult claim to
make of a community decimated by the Holocaust. That is, however, unless
the impact, the legacy, or even the validity of the Holocaust can be successfully challenged. It is according to this paradigm that images of Israelis as
brutal "genocidaires," committing crimes of Holocaust proportion, are
rooted in a fundamental denial of the Holocaust, and rely upon the industry that has turned Holocaust denial into a pursuit of fraudulent history.

Holocaust denial has become an anti-Semitic industry, based on the
absurd claim Jews did not experience mass murder during World War II
at the hands of the Nazis, that somehow the Holocaust is the fabrication of
super powerful Jews who control the media. Holocaust denial and Holocaust revisionism are particularly insidious. Holocaust revisionism is
representative of a uniquely pseudo-academic form of anti-Semitism.
Revisionists attempt to prove, through the fake social and physical scientific methods, that the Holocaust either never occurred, or that if it did
occur, it was not the genocidal tragedy of the documented historical proportions. What is important to recognize is that revisionists use, albeit
erroneously, what appear to be academic methods to support their claims.
The purpose of this effort is precisely to frame their work as legitimate
historical review in order to gain entry to academic circles. Revisionists
rarely resemble their less savvy counterparts who desecrate Jewish cemeteries, yell anti-Semitic epithets, or author material on the grand Jewish
conspiracy. Yet their work is arguably more destructive because it attacks
Jews as anti-Israelists do—by pretending to be something other than they
are. By framing their work as a pursuit of academic truth, revisionists
attempt to sidestep the real nature of their bigotry. "'Revisionists' depart

from the conclusion that the Holocaust did not occur and work backwards through the facts to adapt them to a preordained conclusion. Put another way, they reverse the proper methodology . . . thus turning the proper historical method of investigation on its head."[61]

Holocaust denial and revisionism have spread across the world. In Europe, a mix of denial, guilt, and prejudice has led to a healthy revisionist movement that has produced books, articles, and conferences challenging the truths of the Holocaust. In 1950, Germany's Frederick Meinecke authored one of the earliest pieces, *The German Catastrophe*, calling into question the veracity of the Holocaust. In 1964, *The Drama of European Jews* was introduced by French writer Paul Rassinier. American Arthur Butz's *The Hoax of the 21st Century: The Case Against the Presumed Extermination of European Jewry* was published in 1976 and ushered in David Irving's infamous *Hitler's War* in 1977.

In 1994, David Irving sued both Penguin Books UK and Emory University's professor of Modern Jewish and Holocaust Studies Deborah Lipstadt for libel, claiming they had defamed him by calling him a Holocaust denier in Lipstadt's book, *Denying the Holocaust: The Growing Assault on Truth and Memory*. Lipstadt is a scholar who has investigated Holocaust denial groups. The defendants were exonerated while Irving was found by the court to have deliberately misstated history. In the court's summary judgment, Justice Charles Gray said, "I have found that, in numerous respects, Irving has misstated historical evidence; adopted positions which run counter to the weight of the evidence; given credence to unreliable evidence and disregarded or dismissed credible evidence."[62]

The Middle East was a growth market for imported European Holocaust revisionism but recently has become the primary exporter to the rest of the world. For example, current Palestinian Prime Minister Mahmoud Abbas wrote his dissertation in Russia entitled, "The Other Side: The Secret Relations Between Nazism and the Leadership of the Zionist Movement," which was later published in a book in Arabic.[63] Abbas included statements of Holocaust denial such as: "Having more victims meant greater rights and stronger privilege to join the negotiation table for dividing the spoils of war once it was over. However, since Zionism was not a fighting partner—suffering victims in a battle—it had no escape but to offer up human beings, under any name, to raise the number of victims, which they could then boast of at the moment of accounting." Abbas further posited "[i]t seems that the interest of the Zionist movement . . . is to inflate this figure so that their gains will be greater. This led them to emphasize this figure in order to gain the solidarity of international public opinion with Zionism. Many scholars have debated the figure of six million and reached stunning conclusions—fixing the number of Jewish victims at only a few hundred thousand."[64]

Holocaust denial is one of many anti-Semitic enterprises that takes advantage of a penetrable and easily influenced environment on college campuses to gain support for otherwise unacceptable positions. According to Lipstadt, "their strategy was profoundly simple: place ads in college newspapers, where the culture of academic freedom and the inexperience of student journalists would make it easier for their ideas to appear."[65]

The Holocaust-revisionist Institute for Historical Review has made efforts in the past to promote its cause specifically on campuses through media project director, Bradley Smith, who leads the Committee for Open Debate on the Holocaust. In the spring of 1991, Smith submitted a full-page paid advertisement to the *Daily Northwestern* of Northwestern University. The newspaper printed the ad, with the headline, "THE HOLO-CAUST STORY: How Much is False? The Case for Open Debate."[66] Since then, various other campuses have been targeted for propaganda. In the late 1990s, at Dartmouth, the University of Maine at Farmington, and Salisbury State University, Bradley Smith advertisements denying the Holocaust were printed. The Ohio State University *Lantern* refused to accept an ad that claimed the Holocaust never occurred but, instead, it ran the ad on the editorial page as opinion, still giving weight to its legitimacy.[67]

Denial of the Holocaust should fall outside the boundaries of acceptable discourse on campus. One would be hard-pressed to find a course seriously entertaining the subject in an American college. The university, however, does not exist only within the classroom. Revisionists and deniers have found ways to inject their position into the campus culture, despite having little influence within the formal curriculum.

DENIAL OF THE HOLOCAUST SHOULD FALL OUTSIDE THE BOUNDARIES OF ACCEPTABLE DISCOURSE ON CAMPUS.

The United States is home to both survivors of the Holocaust and American soldiers who witnessed the liberation of Nazi concentration camps. It seems almost absurd that anyone in America would even attempt to deny the truth concerning the Holocaust, especially at a university. While campuses should be places to challenge ideas, some areas do not warrant reexamination, reconsideration or any other form of evaluation. One can discuss the causes of the Civil War, not if the Civil War occurred. Likewise, there are no serious attempts to revise the accepted truth that the United States enslaved millions of Africans. Some things are true, some are false, regardless of how they are presented. Over six million Jews were murdered. Yet somehow neither respect for truth and integrity nor for saving human dignity prevents claims refuting the Holocaust from sometimes being circulated on campus. Holocaust denial should be denied—always.

Part of the reversal of Israel's fortune on campus has entailed the hijacking of some aspects of Jewish identity. Just as Israel was once an example of the underdog overcoming adversity, so too the Holocaust produced world sympathy for victimized European Jewry. In the same way Israeli history has been rewritten to delegitimize it, so has Jewish history been reworked so that the Holocaust becomes a Palestinian experience, not a Jewish one at all. This allows for the Palestinians to be classified as the ultimate victims of an Israeli imposed holocaust. Anti-Semitism and anti-Israelism even deny Jews their history. Jews are not Jews, Palestinians are the real Jews. The Holocaust is, in fact, a Palestinian legacy.

This most bizarre and clever distortion reverses identities. The Holocaust is not a Jewish legacy after all. Professor of Latino Studies at Columbia University Nicholas De Genova proclaimed at a rally that "the heritage of the Holocaust belongs to the Palestinian people. The State of Israel has no claim to the heritage of the Holocaust."[68] Such a declaration would seem ridiculous, but is part of a comprehensive revision that attempts to rob Jews of their history. In this looking glass world, the Holocaust is nothing more than a manifestation of man's worst evils and Jews who died by the millions (if they died at all) were simply victims of war along with everyone else. This dispossession of Jewish experience is constructed partially to challenge the necessity of a Jewish state by dismissing the history of violent anti-Semitism.

ANTI-ISRAEL IDEOLOGY ASSERTS THAT THE HOLOCAUST IS, IN FACT, A PALESTINIAN LEGACY.

As a result, Jewish students and professors, who even may have had family who perished at the hands of the Nazis, must tolerate seeing and hearing equations between Israel and Nazi Germany, between

Adolf Hitler and Ariel Sharon or other Israeli leaders. Comparisons are regularly made between Palestinian refugees and Jewish concentration camp inmates. Images such as the numbers tattooed on Jews, the rounding up of civilians in the middle of the night, and the utter disregard for life are used on campus to intensify the descriptions of Palestinian refugee camps.

During the Holocaust, Jews had tracking numbers tattooed on their forearm by the Nazis to aid in their systematic extermination. Fadi Kiblawi, president of Students Allied for Freedom and Equality at the University of Michigan, claimed in the *Michigan Daily* that Israeli troops have tattooed identification numbers on the foreheads and arms of Palestinians.[69] The assertion, however absurd, evokes the desired emotional response. And it is the image that is important, not the truth. If everyday students can be made to consider that Palestinians could face such horrible treatment, then certainly it would follow that Israelis are the Nazi perpetrators.

Palestinian villages and cities are likened to concentration camps, where Jews were forcibly transferred into slave labor, and murdered. The world had never seen anything like what the Nazis built to exterminate Europe's Jews, nor has anyone since. Joseph Stalin's mass murders, and genocide in Cambodia and Rwanda are reminders that not only Jews have been targeted for slaughter. The mechanization and planned structure of the Nazi death camps remains (thus far) unrepeated in human history. Yet Palestinian municipalities, the same ones in which journalists reside, in which families are raised, in which business is conducted, somehow are equated with the horrors of the Nazi death camps. New York University student Mingyou Cheo wrote, "The sense of injustice and racism is undeniable once you've experienced it. It's like you're in a huge prison or concentration camp."[70]

If the Palestinian experience is equal to that of Jews during the Holocaust, then certainly it can also be likened to that of any other communities that have suffered genocidal attacks. Ghaith Mahmood wrote in the *Daily Bruin*, "[T]he mass graves being built in the West Bank . . . eerily parallel a scene out of the genocide in Bosnia. Witnessing the Israeli army rounding up all the men in Palestinian villages . . . and then branding them with identification numbers brings back horrific images of a concentration camp somewhere in Auschwitz."[71]

The hijacking of the Jewish Holocaust experience transforms the swastika into a symbol of Palestinian suffering. Today, students walking to class may find themselves passing signs, banners, or posters bearing a swastika, a caricature of a uniformed SS officer, or Hitler himself used in direct reference to Israel and Israelis. In the dichotomy of the oppressed and the oppressor, if the Palestinians are the real Jews, then it follows that Israelis are the real Nazis.

At the University of California, Berkeley, in April 2002, while Jews commemorated Holocaust Remembrance Day by reading the names of victims aloud, members of the Students for Justice in Palestine staged a protest, carrying signs that stated, "Holocaust or not, everyone must be accountable for their actions," and, "Israel lovers are the Nazis of our time."[72] At the same university, following the cancellation of a speech by former Israeli Prime Minister Benjamin Netanyahu (because of the threat of violence), a student wrote, "In terms of tactics, the Israeli Defense Force is comparable to the Nazi regime."[73] The university has become a place where a Jew can be labeled a Nazi for supporting Israel.

Jews are depicted as even worse than the Nazis, because Jews should know better, because Jews learned nothing from their own experience. This assertion reverses the claim that the Holocaust was not a Jewish experience (typical of anti-Semitic contradictions). Anti-Israelists argue that Jews should be more just in their treatment of Palestinians precisely because Jews experienced the Holocaust. Nazis knew no better. They were simply misguided and subject to the evils of the human condition. Jews, on the other hand, who are either citizens of Israel or its supporters, are re-committing the crime done to them with full knowledge of the pain of oppression, and worse, against an even weaker victim, the Palestinians. "[T]he people of Israel, who know the most brutal of oppressions, have become the oppressor."[74] Subooshi Hasan, a senior, wrote, "Houses are broken into; men are rounded up, stripped and handcuffed; and numbers are serialized on their arms. This is not 1945 Nazi Germany, although Nazis did perpetrate such acts against the Jews and anyone they considered 'threatening.' This is 2002 Palestine and the aggressors are the Israeli army. Isn't it surprising how the United Nations gave the present-day land of Israel as a means to atone for what had happened in Nazi Germany?"[75] Even though this depiction is fictional, the scenario of the victim turned oppressor is alluring.

According to a student at the University of California, Berkeley, Joseph Anderson, Zionists missed the lessons Jews could have learned from their oppression and instead practice "Israeli apartheid." He explains how Jews have monopolized "real" pain through what he calls "victim's psychological identification reaction," and, therefore, cannot realize the brutality of their current actions. Those who "were once victims of long-term severe abuse and brutality (as European Jews were under Nazism and European anti-Semitism) often go on to abuse and brutalize others." He grounds this in the idea that Zionists harbor the "false belief that no one else . . . has ever really suffered what the victims have suffered."[76] Anderson, albeit with the trappings of academic discourse, accuses Jews of being incapable of recognizing right from wrong.

One of the primary purposes of superimposing the Nazi extermination of Jews upon the Palestinians is to erode one of the fundamental purposes of Israel. Israel was supported in its creation, for many, because Nazi Germany demonstrated once and for all that Jews required a national home. Immediately after World War II, Jewish refugees needed somewhere where they would no longer be subject to the whims of nations that did not want them. If Jews can be successfully denied the legacy of the Holocaust, what need is there for a state to protect them?

TERRORISM AGAINST ISRAEL IS LEGITIMATE

Americans do not tolerate or excuse terrorist acts, especially in the wake of 9/11. Americans consider acts of violence against civilians deplorable. Yet policies of terrorism, even targeting children, are tactics employed by the Palestinian Authority and organizations such as Hamas and Islamic Jihad (designated terrorist organizations by the American government). In order to garner campus support for Palestinians, it is, therefore necessary to provide a rationale for Palestinian terrorism. This excuse comes in the form of a distorted cultural relativism, attempting to "contextualize" murder, as opposed to adhering to universal definitions of good and evil. Some reason that one can criticize cultures deemed similar to one's own, but cannot judge societies we do not comprehend. Palestinian terrorism cannot be judged because we, as Americans, are unable to really understand their culture or their experience.

The cultural relativists divide the world into two basic groups: those who are like us and those who are not. One might presume the first of these groups would benefit from such a label and, conversely, the second would not. Yet on campus, in a perfect Catch-22, it is the opposite. Acts deemed deplorable by the West cannot be judged by Western standards. Criticism and judgment are viewed as both insensitive or uninformed. How can a Westerner judge the actions of those in the developing world, when their respective experiences are so disparate? Herein lies a fundamental contradiction. The more contemptible an act is in the West, the more foreign to the West it is as well. Therefore, the more contemptible the action, the less capable Westerners are of comprehending it, and ultimately judging it. This scenario plays both ways, and non-Westerners would be equally incapable of judging Western actions. However, the reality is that cultural relativists seem to restrict criticism to the West, not from the other direction.

Admittedly, this framework sometimes has legitimate applications. Presuming that Japanese businesspeople and American businesspeople can interpret what the other is saying by evaluating the other's actions according to their own cultural norms is folly. Determining that a culture is backward solely based on one's lack of familiarity with that culture is not only wrong but also can be dangerous. However, relativism run amuck has led to the absolution of some of the most objectionable practices around the world. Female genital mutilation, arranged marriages for girls as young as six years old, the drowning of baby girls at birth, and suicide bombings are all foreign and unquestionably wrong in the West. Yet each, to varying degrees of effort, is defended under the banner of accepting diverse cultural practices or not understanding them.

As a result, Israeli lives seem to have less worth than Palestinian lives. Professor M. Shahid Alam wrote in *Al-Ahram*, an Egyptian weekly, that Israel has carried out "ethnic cleansing" of Palestinians and are turning their living conditions into "concentration camps." He condoned suicide bombings, writing that "resistance is a Palestinian right . . . dispossession is implemented by force, and it follows that resistance to the coloniser must also be violent."[77] During "Israeli Apartheid Week" at the University of Toronto, terrorism was deemed a legitimate activity. "When one Jewish student asked for either speaker to denounce the killing of civilians and children, the answer was as follows: 'Terrorism will end when apartheid ends.' This left the impression that the speaker does indeed fully endorse terrorism against Israel and other democracies, including the United

States. Underscoring the radical agenda of the one-sided event, that same week, flyers appeared across campus with the logo of the Al Aqsa Martyrs Brigade, the Fatah-affiliated terror group responsible for the murder of countless Israeli civilians."[78] Do we want to be teaching students that terrorism, as long as it is against certain groups, is legitimate?

Many students and professors alike go to great lengths to justify crimes committed by Palestinians. It should be more difficult to press the case for the Palestinians as the unjust victims of indiscriminate violence when American students see Palestinians periodically appearing on the news, having blown themselves, and as many Israelis as they can, to pieces. Some even glorify suicide bombers, painting them as freedom fighters. Becoming a murderer can elevate one to an even higher level of victimhood; suicide bombers are *forced* to act inhumanely as a result of Israeli oppression. At Kent State University, associate professor of history Julio Cesar Pino wrote a poem in the *Kent Stater* on April 15, 2002, titled, "Singing out prayer for a youth martyr," in which he praised a female suicide bomber.

> You are not a terrorist, Ayat. The real terrorists are those who some 100 years ago hijacked a beautiful religion and transformed it into a real estate venture. Glancing around the world, they saw in Palestine "a land without a people, for a people without a land," as their spokesmen and women chant ad nauseam. The Zion of the concertina wire, F-16 bomber death planes and tank crews collecting skulls and shedding martyrs' blood. The birthplace of your ancestor, and mine, the Palestinian pacifist Joshua ben Josef, is now a battle zone— with Christians, Muslims and peace-loving Jews trapped inside Bethlehem. . . .
>
> Your last cry, by gesture rather than the spoken word, was "Stop, thief! This is not your land and we are a people." I can assure you, Ayat, that the whole world stopped to listen. Even the numbskull who parades as president of the United States heard you, and, following the text written for him by his handlers, expressed astonishment at how a teenager could perpetrate such an act. Simply, it is pronounced "justice" and spelled C-O-U-R-A-G-E.[79]

The annual Divestment Conference, an event held for the promotion of a drive to divest university funds from companies doing business with Israel, was first held at the University of California, Berkeley, then the University of Michigan, Ohio University, and Duke University. The conference steadfastly refuses to criticize suicide bombings. The conference organizers endorse the principle of refusing to even comment on Palestinian violence because it is, simply, not their place to do so. Yet at these same conferences demonization of Israel is commonplace, focusing on Israeli "violence."

While committed anti-Israelists intentionally depict Palestinian terrorism in a manner that helps make their case, others accept this framework for different reasons. The tenets of cultural relativism do not specifically justify terrorism, however, neither do they justify taking a stance against terrorism. The campus community may feel comfortable criticizing the Israeli government and/or military, as if it were their own, while at the same time they feel daunted in evaluating Palestinian actions. This double standard exemplifies the inherent problem with a worldview in which the other is excused for their actions.

There are those that do address the issue of Palestinian terrorism; however, they quickly turn the discussion toward what they view as the instigating cause: Israel. At a University of California, Irvine, forum titled "Stop and Listen," Muslim Student Union Vice President Zohib Ghani stated that, "Suicide bombers are a symptom of the problem. Resistance is a symptom of oppression."[80] Ghani simply glosses over suicide bombing as a direct function of oppression. Could Palestinians resist what they define as oppression through various means that do not include mass murder? The vast majority do. But redirecting the discussion to Israeli oppression avoids taking any ethical position on Palestinian terrorism.

Likewise, Wayne State University student Salah O. Ahmed wrote in the South End student newspaper that, "while it's necessary to condemn the practice [of suicide bombing], it's a mistake to view it as anything but one side of a coin."[81] When the murderers are Palestinians, it seems two wrongs do make a right. Moreover, equating suicide bombings with Israeli occupation represents a remarkable double standard. Though Israel goes to great lengths to avoid civilian casualties, its actions are, nevertheless, compared to mass murder. In a letter to the editor entitled, "Let's Be Reasonable," Utah State student Ashraf Shaqadan argues, "If suicide attacks are brutal acts carried out by few individuals in the recent years, many more vicious acts such as assassination and kidnapping of civilians, demolition of homes . . . are committed by the mighty Israeli 'forces'—not individuals. . . . The suicide bombings," he concludes, "are the symptom of a more dangerous disease that includes grave human rights abuses. . . . It's the Israeli occupation that provokes the suicide bombings."[82]

The only valid comparisons to suicide bombings would be to the isolated cases of Jewish extremists who have committed acts of terror against Palestinians. Yet when such acts do occur, Israelis do not make the same efforts to excuse the motivations, especially not by Israeli officials or pro-Israel advocates. Prime Minister of Israel Ariel Sharon strongly condemned a Jewish extremist who was guilty of a heinous attack on Israeli Arabs. "A reprehensible act by a bloodthirsty Jewish terrorist who sought to attack innocent Israeli citizens."[83] Israelis know it is wrong and say so, with rare exception. Terrorism deserves nothing but condemnation, whether committed by Jews, by Palestinians, or by any other people.

For some on campus, the more difficult the conditions in which Palestinians live, the more dissonance campus citizens experience, and the easier it becomes to accept a different moral baseline. Shaya Mohajer wrote in the *New University*, "At some point, subjugated, voiceless peoples will take up arms (often weapons as crude as rocks) against soldiers who have invaded their streets and will try to resist."[84] Helpless Palestinians are therefore not subject to civilized norms. Moreover, it is a common tactic to confuse discussions of terrorism with other forms of conflict: suicide bombings become no different than rock throwing, both unavoidable symptoms of Israeli oppression.

In the wake of a bombing that killed scores at a Passover celebration, a Jewish holy day, University of Georgia history professor Eve Troutt Powell, explained that suicide bombings are the "result of hopelessness . . . (and) anger at the current situation. There are many people who feel their lives don't count as much to the world."[85] Directly following what was one of the worst Palestinian terrorist attacks, Powell reminds her campus that Palestinians are unique and deserve special consideration due to their hardships.

The inherent problem of defending murderers often leads terror apologists to contradict themselves in attempting to craft what they view as an acceptable justification for terrorism. At a University of Chicago pro-Palestinian rally, a member of the Arab Student Union's executive board stated that "suicide bombings are absolutely wrong. . . . But the suicide bombings cannot be understood through the simple lens of terrorists and anti-terrorists. They must understood [sic] as a direct product of the brutal Israeli occupation and the resulting lack of any hope among the [P]alestinian people."[86]

If, indeed, the speaker believed that suicide bombings are "absolutely wrong," there would be no need to qualify the statement by referring to Israeli brutality and Palestinian hopelessness. These topics serve to try to blur the moral standards by which Palestinians are judged. The first statement is only offered to appeal to Americans' core feelings about suicide bombing, providing legitimacy to the statement, though the speaker quickly backtracks, redefining "absolute." In a similar statement, Mohamad Bydon wrote in *The Dartmouth* that, while he can "see no possible justification for terrorism," suicide bombing can be defended because "most movements of national liberation resorted quite heavily on an armed struggle that utilized guerrilla or terrorist tactics."[87] Again, if there is "no possible justification for terrorism," Bydon need not have continued. However, he did and moved on to defend what he claimed was unjustifiable by arguing that terror is an often-necessary tool of resistance.

An icon of resistance and the leader of a movement often likened to that of the Palestinians, Nelson Mandela, showed moral leadership by guiding the African National Congress to adhere to accepted norms of behavior, lest the international community reject the bid for self-determination.[88] He made concerted efforts to restrict violence against civilian targets, despite pressure and, some argued, justification for Palestinian-style terrorism. The reasons for such control were not only to encourage international support, but also to build internal stability and leadership. Rules of engagement require enforcement and Nelson Mandela's African National Congress accepted these boundaries (though some violated them), battling among the different rival factions to secure a unified and civilized stance regarding terrorism. The result was success, both internationally and nationally.

In contrast, the Palestinians have no unified stance regarding tactics to achieve a nation-state, and, most importantly, seemingly little concern that their most egregious acts will harm their cause. As a result, Palestinians, absolved of responsibility, are not held accountable for their actions. This lack of accountability for internationally recognized standards goes far beyond the campus. Arafat was rewarded for his leadership of a terrorist organization first when, in 1994, he was permitted to return to Israel and previously was invited to speak at the United Nations General Assembly soon after the Palestinian Liberation Organization massacred Israeli athletes at the Munich Olympics (which did not even warrant a delay in the games).[89]

Today, Palestinian terrorists need not worry too much about the effect that a bus bomb, a mortar rocket, or sniper attack that kills civilians will have on campus opinion. Certainly, there is a negative reaction in general American society. However, the academic arguments do not support the instincts of everyday Americans. American sensibilities are dead wrong. Notre Dame University philosophy professor James Sterba, in a comparison of Palestinian terrorism to Allied bombing campaigns during World War II, explained, "The Palestinians have no comparable support from anyone. It is under these circumstances that a moral justification for Palestinian suicide bombers against Israeli civilians emerges."[90]

Certainly, there are many people on campus, students and professors alike, who openly condemn terrorism and proclaim that suicide bombings are never acceptable, under any circumstances. However, many stop short of naming Palestinians as those who carry out such acts. The act of terrorism or the general phenomenon is criticized: the terror, not the terrorist. Apologists for Palestinian terrorism do not necessarily claim that the killing of civilians is right, but rather, that one cannot say that it is wrong for another to do so. Therefore, it has become off limits to talk about *Palestinian* terrorism, even though one may condemn terrorism in general. Fault does not lie with an individual, or even the organizations that dispatch snipers and suicide bombers. If fault lies anywhere, it is squarely upon Israel and the occupation. Even while condemning terrorism, Palestinian terrorism is justified.

While nearly every Palestinian casualty of violence is regarded as a victim, regardless of the circumstances of his or her death or injury, the label of victim for Israelis is applied selectively, and sometimes not at all. When the death tolls are announced by Palestinian groups, or provided to other organizations, they regularly fail to make any distinction between armed militants and civilians, even including those terrorists Israel has killed and some who have killed themselves along with busloads of Israelis.[91]

The explanation for such double standards lies in the basic assertion that Israel, by virtue of its military strength or because they are illegitimate occupiers, is always at fault. Palestinians as a people are victims. Even one who straps a bomb to him or herself, was a victim first. Conversely, Israeli children who are killed by terrorists are caught up in this unfortunate conflict not so much as victims but as by-products, an inevitable result of occupation. Or worse, as deserving death for their complicity. Tom Paulin stated that he believed "[Brooklyn-born Jewish settlers] should be shot dead. I think they are Nazis, racists, I feel nothing but hatred for them."[92]

Israeli casualties may be elderly women within the green line, in Gaza or in the West Bank. They may be border police or Israel Defense Forces soldiers. Yet these distinctions are blurred on campus. Whether an Israeli soldier is killed in combat, a border policeman is knifed at a checkpoint, a settler is shot by a sniper, or a student is blown up at school, the reaction will often be the same. They "deserved it," to varying degrees. Perhaps the death of an Israeli infant evokes temporary feelings of sympathy. Massive suicide bombings will also tend to shake up the balance of concern for a brief time. The next time a Palestinian terrorist commits murder, the excuses will begin again.

The devaluation of Israeli (and Jewish) lives relates to violence outside of Israel as well. When Israelis are targeted by various terrorist groups while traveling outside Israel, the response on campus is similarly muted, even though Palestinian victims as terrorists are not directly part of the story. Israelis become the target of "justified" anger by nearly anyone, anywhere, anytime. They become the quintessential enemy of peace, and therefore of the world. Until Israel stops its "apartheid" practices, Israeli citizens everywhere, anytime, are fair game.

JEWS CONTROL AMERICA

Brian Avery, an activist for the International Solidarity Movement, which sends students to Israel so "if some of these foreign volunteers get shot or even killed, then the international media will sit up and take notice," wrote in the *Wall Street Journal*, that both George W. Bush and John Kerry are, "on auction to the Jewish lobby."[93]

One of the core arguments of anti-Israelists has been that Israel is not the friend Americans believe it to be. Indeed, it is quite the opposite. It is a leech on America, draining American tax dollars, engendering anti-Americanism around the world. Penn State student Tyler Bitten, in a letter to the editor entitled, "Military Aid to Israel Should Be Ended Soon," argues that

Arab anger toward the United States is justified by its support of Israel. "Its [sic] ironic that a religious state founded by a group that has been persecuted so much would do the same to others. Calling their occupation and invasion of Palestine 'self-defense' is a further insult to our intelligence. I am sick and tired of my tax dollars going to fund the military of a religious state that occupies and oppresses others. The United States should have nothing to do with this policy of human dispossession [...]. The only real way to end the violence is to stop all military aid to Israel and become a neutral third party."[94] America enters wars "because of Israel," and involves itself in Middle East volatility on Israel's behalf. More alarmingly, Israel is accused of conspiring to control America and use its power to serve the purposes of Zionist expansion and oppression of Arabs. Israel and Jewish lobbies are at the bottom of these efforts, thus labeling every American Jewish supporter of Israel as a co-conspirator (or even traitor).

While serving as president of Arab Students United, New York University student Nadeen Aljijakli distributed, via email, an article by former Ku Klux Klan member David Duke claiming that the primary reason we are suffering from terrorism in the U.S. is because our government policy is completely subordinated to a foreign power: "Israel and the efforts of worldwide Jewish Supremacism."[95] Aljijakli, when informed of the author's racist history, suggested that she would not have chosen the article had she known, but nevertheless agreed with the arguments put forth.

The idea that Israel or Jews are controlling governments is nothing new. Accusations of dual loyalty are part of anti-Semitic lore. One hopefully expects something different within academe. University of Georgia student Adam Gobin wrote in the *Red and Black* about Jewish influence in America, "Not only does the Israeli lobby control legislation . . . but it also controls the media giants."[96] His language is typical of old anti-Semitic lies, altered to name Israel or Israelis rather than Jews, thus shielding against charges of anti-Semitism. Similarly, substitute "pro-Israel factions" with Jews in the following statement. "I am outraged that my government is the largest . . . supporter of Israel. . . . Mr. Bush is afraid to [cut off support for Israel] because, as his father learned in 1992, certain pro-Israel factions are friends he doesn't want to lose."[97] The author implies that Jews who did not like his foreign policy orchestrated the senior Bush's defeat in 1992. While it is certainly possible that American Jews may not like any particular president's foreign policy and choose not to donate money to nor vote for a second term, it is dangerous to posit that America's six million Jews have conspiratorial control over America's democratic process.

Some do not shy away from making accusations directly about Jews. The University of Illinois student paper, the *Daily Illini*, printed an opinion piece by Washington resident Ariel Sinovsky titled, "Jews Manipulate America." Sinovsky writes:

> The Jews, master salesmen that they are, have been able to persuade Americans that it is in American interests to support Israeli oppression of Palestinians. . . . Too often defective foreign policy has been promoted as something in the interest of American people while in reality it was done to satisfy the desires of Jewish oligarchs. . . . The President should act immediately to deal with this threat. First, separate Jews from all government advisory positions and give them one year fully paid sabbatical. . . . Jewish ability to promote their desires, disguised, as being in the interest of the American people, one day will evaporate. Then the Jews might face another Holocaust.[98]

The outrage of this article, surprisingly, lies not in the content only, although its bigotry is obvious and disgusting. The headline, which seems to support the anti-Semitic vitriol that runs through the entire article, was likely created by an editor, not the author. The student newspaper chose to run an anti-Semitic opinion piece, and moreover, contributed to it with the headline, "Jews Manipulate America." The title itself, regardless of article content, has a strong anti-Semitic effect. The editors were free to title the article "anti-Semite Expresses His Bigotry," or, "Anti-Semitism Diminishes Palestinian Cause." However, they did not. In such a case, the content of the article, the decision to print the article, and the headline of the article all represent some level of anti-Semitism, intentional or not.

Accusations of conspiracy have plagued Jews throughout history. Professor M. Shahid Alam wrote in the Egyptian weekly, *Al-Ahram*, that Israel, "could only emerge as the bastard child of imperialist powers, and it could only come into existence by displacing the greater part of the Palestinian population, by incorporating them into an apartheid state, or through some combination of the two. In addition, once created, Israel could only survive as a militarist, expansionist, and hegemonic state, constantly at war with its neighbors." He then explains that, "Jews, as junior partners of the imperialist powers, would seek to deepen the Orientalist project in the service of Western power." The current landscape of Middle East Studies is now divided, Alam explains, into "one camp, consisting mostly of Christians and Muslims, [which] has laboured to bring greater objectivity to their study of Islam and Islamic societies. . . . The second camp, now led mostly by Jews, has reverted to Orientalism's original mission of subordinating knowledge to Western power, now filtered through the prism of Zionist interests." These Jews "work to incite a civilisational war between Islam and the West."[99]

Conspiracy theories, however, are not for everyone. Most people realize that coordination among a disparate people over long periods of time to attain specific goals is near impossible. More often than not, conspiracy is better explained by much simpler and less sinister forces. For these non-conspirators, arguments focus largely upon convincing Americans that it is Israel that terrorists hate, not America. At the University of California, San Diego, Sarah Kaiksow wrote in the *Guardian*, "I would argue that Israel creates so much anti-American sentiment the world over that we are shooting ourselves in the foot by letting Israel do whatever it wants without [sic] impunity."[100]

This argument appeals to a very basic concern for Americans: their own security. If Americans can be convinced that their safety is in jeopardy because of Israel, they also can be convinced to alter, even to end the relationship. In an op-ed entitled "U.S. Must Learn From Israel, React Responsibly," University of Wisconsin, Madison, student Jonathan Linder argues that Israel's approach to terror has been unsuccessful and implies that it has fostered Arab hatred of America. "The Palestinians see American-made weapons killing their people, their civilians, their innocent victims, their mothers and fathers and loved ones, all of whom are faceless to us. Hate for America and Americans based on this is not justifiable or even truly understandable, but it could have played a role in what happened Tuesday."[101]

Some have compounded the idea that America is threatened because of Israel with the assertion that it is threatened directly by Israel, and the Jews, as well. In 2002, Santa Rosa Junior College's student newspaper, *The*

Oak Leaf, published an opinion article by civil engineering student Kevin McGuire titled, "Is Anti-Semitism Ever the Result of Jewish Behavior?" McGuire writes:

> Israel is the largest and most dangerous terrorist organization in the world. . . . The Zionist Jews believe they are the "chosen people" of god and that the world was given to them and is their possession. The Zionist Jews want to establish a Jewish holy land with no non-Jews present. . . . This attitude of racial hatred and genocide is also reflected in the Torah. . . . In closing, A [sic] 1998 quote from Osama bin Laden: "So we tell the Americans as people, and we tell the mothers of soldiers and American mothers in general that if they value their lives and the lives of their children, to find a nationalist government that will look after their interests and not the interests of the Jews."[102]

JEWS BRING IT ON THEMSELVES. THIS CHARGE IS TYPICAL OF BIGOTS AND RACISTS—THE VICTIMIZED GROUP IS SOMEHOW RESPONSIBLE FOR THOSE WHO HATE THEM.

This piece asserts what anti-Semites have always contended—Jews bring it on themselves. This charge is typical of bigots and racists—the victimized group is somehow responsible for those who hate them. Such clear anti-Semitism immediately set off a rancorous debate about how and why such an article was printed. The ensuing turmoil led to some campus and community anger directed at the newspaper editor who was culpable, and even more so the faculty advisor who failed to inform the editor of her right to refuse opinion articles that contained hateful language. The faculty advisor refused to publicly discuss the incident. However, this is not the first problem for the *The Oak Leaf*. The college paid a $45,000 settlement over claims of sexual harassment that arose when male students posted anatomically explicit and derogatory remarks about two women on campus on a men-only bulletin board created by the journalism department.[103] Lack of oversight seems to be a recurring theme.

If the threat to America's security is not convincing enough, complicity is also added to the mixture, by repeatedly reminding the campus community of the aid Israel receives from America and the violent, racist uses of that money. "[As a U.S. citizen] you contribute to the bullets used to kill Palestinian children. . . . As Americans you support the closures of schools and the disconnection of electricity of whole towns."[104] These approaches rely on an appeal to the basic dignity and goodness of Americans. However, at the root of efforts to distance the United States from Israel are much more forceful and insidious assertions about Israeli conspiracy, Israeli control over the United States government and economy, and American domination of the Middle East through proxy, namely Israel. All are designed to disrupt the American-Israeli relationship, to rally Americans to reject Israel as an ally.

A widespread ideology has the potential for harm; belief systems can have real impact over time. It is dangerous to ignore the rhetoric of Al Qaeda, the racist rantings of the Aryan Nations, or Kim Jong Il of North Korea, as it was to ignore the psychosis of Hitler about his desire to kill Jews. Ideology and rhetoric have meaning, and their expressions have real effects on individuals' lives. Ignoring anti-Semitism and anti-Israelism on campus, or dismissing them as insignificant, limited in scope, or claiming that the bigots do not really mean what they say, are all forms of denial. Anti-Semitism and anti-Israelism are dangerous belief systems, especially on college campuses, where they should be so unwelcome.

CHAPTER SIX

UNCIVIL POLITICS AND CAMPUS MISCONDUCT

The ideology of anti-Semitism and anti-Israelism expresses itself through a number of venues and behaviors on campus. Middle East Studies centers and institutes have become notorious for their anti-Israel bias. Specific efforts such as the campaign for universities not to invest in Israel have been launched. Anti-Israel propaganda can be found all over the campus, both inside and outside the classroom.

MIDDLE EAST STUDIES AND ORIENTALISM

Middle East Studies programs are at the forefront of the anti-Israel movement and engage in anti-Semitic behavior. Faculty members, primarily from fields related to the Middle East but also from other disciplines, have unabashedly politicized their classrooms, one day teaching that the Israelis are committing war crimes, another speaking at a rally to incite opposition to Israeli "apartheid." They author diatribes against Israel, the United States, and the West through campus, national, and international media, saving some of the most objectionable statements for Middle Eastern media. Perhaps they hope no one will translate their most egregious rhetoric into English.[1]

The field of Middle East Studies has become dominated by a specific political outlook that situates the world, and everyone in it according to a narrow agenda. Poor scholarship, both due to errors of commission and omission, plague the work of Middle East Studies faculty, including revisionism in rewriting the history of Israel and Jews. As a result, some students and faculty have found that they are marginalized because of their religion, nationality, or political beliefs. Students can be made to feel as if their views are invalid, or even bigoted. Some have reported being directly harassed by professors. Pro-Israel faculty have, in the instances where they have chosen to counter the many claims made against Israel, found themselves sometimes in the academic hinterlands. Certainly not all professors in Middle East Studies are anti-Israel, nor have all those who have criticized Israel done so inappropriately. But the anti-Israelists have successfully silenced many dissenters and dominate the field.

Institutionalized academic anti-Israelism did not develop overnight, or even over the past decade. Along with the shift to the left discussed earlier, an overhaul in Middle East Studies began in the late 1970s that deconstructed nearly all established scholarship about the region. Columbia English professor Edward Said initiated this revolution when he wrote a scathing critique of Middle East Studies in 1978 titled *Orientalism*. Said indicted "virtually all previous Western scholarship on the region as ill conceived and racist."[2] Said successfully played into the politics of race, leveling the most loaded charge he could make.

The ideas in *Orientalism* were quickly embraced and transported from Said's literary discipline and adapted by the social sciences. Franklin Foer explains: "Middle East scholars took Said's argument and transposed it to political science. Terrorism and fundamentalism were suddenly racist, reductionist concepts."[3] In American institutions, concrete changes occurred. Martin Kramer wrote, "*Orientalism* not only overturned bookshelves, it overturned chairs. It became a manifesto of affirmative action for Arab and Muslim scholars and established a negative predisposition toward American (and imported European) scholars. In 1971, only 3.2 percent of Middle East area specialists had been born in the region."[4] In 1992 MESA's president, "Our membership has changed over the years, and possibly half is now of Middle Eastern heritage."[5]

Orientalism was, or is, in effect, according to Said, a construct of the Western mind, which is totally incapable of grasping the reality and complexity of the Middle East. Middle Eastern culture is categorized, stereotyped, and demonized. Said's argument included the assertion that "only

Muslim and Arab scholars could escape orientalism's limitations," an academically limiting and racially discriminatory notion in itself.[6] Respected experts in Middle East Studies such as Bernard Lewis were discredited over time by Said's paradigm. In one of the most intellectually dishonest movements in modern academic history, the least experienced, least talented scholar of Middle Eastern origin was considered more capable than the most established scholars of Western origin. This led directly to an ideological shift in Middle East Studies departments. Kramer explains that the field of Middle East Studies was "cut off from the American mainstream by the influx into faculty ranks of ideological radicals. . . ."[7]

MIDDLE EAST STUDIES PROGRAMS ARE AT THE FOREFRONT OF THE ANTI-ISRAEL MOVEMENT AND ENGAGE IN ANTI-SEMITIC BEHAVIOR.

An entirely new worldview accompanied the influx of Saidian scholars into North American Middle East Studies, dismissing any notion of an Islamic threat, reflexively criticizing American foreign policy and, most importantly, "situat[ing] the Palestinians in a much wider context. They were but the latest victims of a deep-seated prejudice against the Arabs, Islam and the East."[8] Said himself described the evolution of Middle East Studies in the United States as "a story of cultural opposition to Western domination."[9] The opposition zeroed in on one unifying factor, the Palestinians, which is not surprising considering Edward Said's Palestinian heritage. Middle East Studies became a political tool, and it became "acceptable, even expected, for scholars to spell out their own political commitments as a preface to anything they wrote or did."[10]

Alongside the glorification of the Palestinian cause was the demonization of Israel. Said anointed Palestinians as indigenous peoples defending their homes, Israelis as European colonizers. Each was descriptively forced into narrow roles of the strong and the weak, with externally defined identities superimposed. Thus, both Jews and Palestinians who did not fit into the narrow mold were marginalized. Palestinians (or other Arabs and/or Muslims) who reject the dominant socio-political view of the Middle East, if even found within academia, are few and generally ostracized in the Middle East debate. Likewise, progressive Jews, who once were more aligned with Palestinian causes searching for solutions to the conflict, have found themselves unwelcome if they are not ideological clones of Saidism.

The comprehensive worldview that places Palestinians at the forefront of struggle and Israelis at the center of oppression does not sustain itself without the façade of intellectual legitimacy. There is a highly active academic leadership that crafts the various arguments against Israeli's right to exist. Middle East Studies, both in terms of institutions and centers, as well as departments and individual professors, lead the charge. Professors can use literature, poetry, and social science to write, teach, and protest about Israel. Books, papers, and editorials are published, speeches are made, petitions are drafted, and classes are taught by faculty members who seek to isolate and delegitimize Israel. Middle East Studies is their ideological home, whether they are part of that field or not. Harvard Yiddish professor Ruth Wisse writes of anti-Israelism, "Universities have allowed Middle East departments to disseminate anti-Israel propaganda, . . . representing violations of intellectual honesty and academic impartiality."[11] Of course, some Middle East centers are better than others; not all faculty are propagandists, and good scholars can be found. But the overall quality and objectivity are problematic.

Middle East Studies are, and always have been, something of a politicized field, even if it was not as extreme as it is today. Its roots lie within area studies, designed for practical political application. Middle East Studies centers were created specifically to better understand the different peoples that America was increasingly encountering, largely as a result of engagement with and containment of worldwide Soviet influence. Funding, initially provided through the National Defense Education Act of 1958, has fluctuated based primarily on the rise or fall of political interest in the region. Therefore, the discipline has always been responsive to political currents.[12]

SCHOLARSHIP ON THE MIDDLE EAST TODAY HAS BECOME A PLATFORM FROM WHICH TO FIGHT PERCEIVED WESTERN DOMINATION AND TO ABSOLVE THE ARAB WORLD OF WRONGDOING.

Scholarship on the Middle East today has become a platform from which to fight perceived Western domination and to absolve the Arab world of wrongdoing. It is also an attempt to ascribe blame specifically to the United States for any and all of the political, cultural, and social problems ongoing in the Middle East, especially in the Arab world. The ideology outlined by Said has sunk its roots deep into Middle East scholarship, and advancement in the field has become dependent upon adherence to an anti-American, anti-Israel agenda. Franklin Foer, senior editor of the *New Republic Online,* recounts a conversation with a tenured professor who wanted to remain anonymous but admitted, "'You don't get tenure by praising American policy,'" while Marius Deeb, professor of Middle East politics at Johns Hopkins University, lamented, "There's a uniformity, and sometimes one gets frustrated with the taboos. For instance, one can't publicly disagree with the statement that Lebanese Hezbollah is a resistance movement."[13]

Middle East scholarship tends to absolve the existing cultures, and political or religious leadership for any of the widespread problems in the region. Low levels of employment, poverty, oppression of women, political violence, lack of many basic rights, and other pathologies plague most Middle Eastern nations. Ostensibly, these are the topics professors devoted to the region should be focused upon. However, insightful analyses are rare, borrowing from a long history in the Middle East of blaming the outsider. The prolific and widely respected historian Bernard Lewis writes, in his analysis of the Middle East entitled, *What Went Wrong?,* that "meanwhile the blame game—the Turks, the Mongols, the imperialists, the Jews, the Americans—continues, and shows little sign of abating. For the governments, at once oppressive and ineffectual, that rule much of the Middle East, this game serves a useful, indeed an essential purpose—to explain the poverty that they have failed to alleviate and to justify the tyranny that they have intensified. In this way they seek to deflect the mounting anger of their unhappy subjects against other, outer targets."[14]

Middle East Studies faculty largely fail to acknowledge this abdication of responsibility for all things wrong in the Arab or Muslim world that is at the core of the conflicts in the region. Prominent Arab scholar, Fouad Ajami, author of the *Dream Palace of the Arabs,* is an exception. He writes in *U.S. News and World Report* about the connection between the situation in Israel and that in Afghanistan, explaining, "It is a linkage born out of the abdication of political responsibility, out of the victimology that excuses the terror against civilians by pleading the 'special conditions' of the Arab world and the imagined hurts inflicted on it by the West. This is an Arab world now gripped in poisonous rage."[15]

The refusal to engage in self-evaluation by many Middle Eastern political leaders, religious leaders, and journalists has been adopted by

Middle East scholars and has largely hindered their ability to analyze events in the region objectively. For example, while American faculty rush to the defense of academic freedom in the United States, little was said about the attempt to lynch the president of a Palestinian University in Gaza. The *Jerusalem Post* reported, "The largest Palestinian university in the Gaza Strip was shut down after hundreds of Fatah-affiliated students tried to lynch the institution's president. . . . Nijem, who was appointed just last week, was forced to hide for nearly three hours as the students tried, unsuccessfully, to break down the door of his office."[16]

If good scholarship depends upon debate, refining arguments through responding to appropriate critique, then it would follow that a field characterized by a dominant worldview finds good scholarship suffering. Bernard Lewis writes, "It is painful for a Middle East specialist to admit the fact, but it is nevertheless inescapable. Professional advancement in Middle East Studies can be achieved with knowledge and skill well below what is normally required in other more developed fields or more frequented disciplines, where standards are established and maintained by a large number of competent professionals over long periods."[17]

The system for ensuring high academic standards, rigorous research, and unbiased inquiry has failed in Middle East Studies. For some, the most damaging effect of the politicization of the field has been the lowering of academic standards. Brandeis University president Jehuda Reinharz stated, "My problem is not the anti-Zionism or even that many of them are anti-American, but that they are third-rate. The quality of the people [in Middle East Studies] is unlike any of the qualities we expect in any other field."[18]

Middle East Studies faculty often make generalized, misleading, or outright false statements in order to help shape their arguments against Israel and the United States. University of Michigan professor Juan Cole stated that, "much of the Arab world has a formal peace treaty with Israel,"[19] though only Egypt and Jordan have signed formal peace treaties. Cole also claimed that "Saddam Hussein never gave any real support to the Palestinian cause, and he did not pay suicide bombers to blow themselves up."[20] It has been widely substantiated that Saddam has paid the families of Palestinian bombers $25,000, the families of other "martyrs" $10,000, with over $30 million paid in total.[21]

Middle East Studies at Columbia University serves as an excellent example of what is wrong in the field throughout the academy. The anti-Israel bias in its Middle East and Asian Languages and Cultures (MEALAC) department and related fields has created nothing short of an academic scandal. Students complained of ideological harassment, marginalization, and intimidation. The university failed to properly hear their grievances and many faculty rallied by closing ranks around academic freedom to respond to the charges against the individual instructors. The list of signatories to the Columbia/Barnard petition for divestment from Israel provided below illustrates the ideological uniformity and hostility toward Israel characteristic of the MEALAC:[22]

- Nadia Abu El-Haj, anthropology, Barnard
- Lila Abu-Lughod, anthropology and women's studies
- Samir Awad, MEALAC
- Gil Anidjar, MEALAC
- Janaki Bakhle, MEALAC
- Zainab Bahrani, art history and archaeology
- Elliot Cola, MEALAC
- Elaine Combs-Schilling, anthropology
- Marc Nichanian, MEALAC
- Hamid Dabashi, MEALAC
- Joseph Massad, MEALAC
- Brinkley Messick, anthropology
- Frances Pritchett, MEALAC
- George Saliba, MEALAC
- Nader Sohrabi, MEALAC
- Marc van de Mieroop, MEALAC

This type of groupthink dominates Columbia's MEALAC department. During a ceremony for the John Jay Professional Achievement Awards, one recipient, John Corigliano, composer and Columbia alum, explained his success in music. "I wasn't discouraged by any kind of fundamentalist 'there is only one way' kind of composing. I say this because . . . there has been an enormous, enormous amount of publicity about . . . the anti-Israel policy in these [Middle East Studies departments]. And one can say that of the department of Middle Eastern languages and cultures at Columbia, that that's true here."[23]

Professor of Iranian Studies and MEALAC department chair Hamid Dabashi was quoted after September 11 expressing doubt about bin Laden's responsibility for the attacks. The campus newspaper, quoted him saying that Zionism is "a ghastly racist ideology," and condemning the "Israeli slaughter of innocent Palestinians in Jenin."[24] Joseph Massad, writing in *Al-Ahram Weekly*, a Cairo-based Arabic paper used by some professors to express more controversial ideas, clearly endorsed a one-state solution in which the Jewish identity of Israel would be lost.[25] Rashid Khalidi, in acceptance of the Edward Said Chair in Middle East Studies, explained his reasons were predicated on the political exposure or, "better access to the news media," he would obtain at Columbia.[26] Columbia assistant professor of anthropology Nicholas De Genova was quoted as saying, "the state of Israel has no claim to the Holocaust," and he wished "a million Mogadishus" on American troops. [Note: Though Americans suffered losses, more than 1,000 Somalis were killed in that operation.] One can only wonder about the objectivity and quality of the rest of their research and teaching.

Columbia is a sorry example of a potentially productive program gone awfully wrong. However, it is not alone. Professors from a variety of fields prone to propaganda and hostile toward both Israel and America can be found throughout academe. Harvard professor Nur O. Yalman wrote in the *Harvard Crimson* on September 21, 2001, that September 11 was "an act of blood revenge," and "there had been too much murder going on in Israel and the West Bank for no extreme reprisals to take place."[27]

While certain universities and departments within universities are worse or better than others, the influence of anti-Israelists in Middle East Studies is widespread. The Middle East Studies Association of North America, the representative body of professors and departments nationwide, boasts a membership of 2,600 professors from departments of hundreds of universities. Then President R. Stephen Humphreys, in explaining the Middle East Studies Association of North America's clear disregard for all the elements in the Middle East that led to September 11, admitted, "Middle East studies probably should have taken terrorism more seriously," but qualified his statement by claiming that "our field was blindsided by September 11, but so was the FBI, CIA, and everybody else who's supposed to know about this stuff."[28] Humphries neglected to recognize, however, that those responsible for "dealing with this stuff," relied on accurate scholarly support from this government funded system. Fifteen federally funded Title VI Centers for Middle East Studies at Harvard, Yale, Princeton, Pennsylvania, Berkeley, Chicago, Santa Barbara and others are supported to provide "expertise." They are funded by the Department of Defense because of the importance of their work to national security. They are supposed to help government from being blindsided from this "stuff."[29]

In an act of paranoid anti-Israelism, a petition was signed by more than 1,000 academics "warning against Israel's possible 'ethnic cleansing' of Palestinians in the 'fog of [the Iraq] war.'" It read: "We urge our government to communicate clearly to the government of Israel that the expulsion of people according to race, religion, or nationality would constitute crimes against humanity and will not be tolerated."[30]

Anti-Israel professors are perhaps most unsavory when in the classroom, addressing rooms full of students who deserve to be taught by unbiased scholars. The fact is that anti-Israel courses and course material pervade study on the Middle East, as well as various other disciplines. There are certain courses that stand out above the rest as particularly egregious examples of scholarly malfeasance. These courses violate rights of students to an education free of propaganda. A sophomore from Amherst College wondered about certain faculty, "There comes a point when you wonder are you fostering a discussion or are you promoting an opinion you want students to embrace or even parrot?"[31]

Some anti-Israel courses are identifiable by subject, such as the course, "The Politics and Poetics of Palestinian Resistance," instructed by Snehal Shingavi, a graduate student at the University of California, Berkeley, while other, seemingly non-partisan courses, such as "Palestinian and Israeli Politics and Societies" at Columbia, are actually forums for the political bias of the individual faculty member, in this case, Joseph Massad. Shingavi, founder of Students for Justice in Palestine, following the lead of Edward Said, introduced his course through the English department. In this manner, Shingavi avoided much of the political tension in Middle East Studies, and succeeded in having his course description go through without adequate review by the department and administration. The course description is below:

> Since the inception of the *Intifada* in September 2000, Palestinians have been fighting for their right to exist. The brutal Israeli military occupation of Palestine, an occupation that has been ongoing since

1948, has systematically displaced, killed, and maimed millions of Palestinian people. And yet, from under the brutal weight of the occupation, Palestinians have produced their own culture and poetry of resistance. This class will examine the history of the Palestinian resistance and the way that it is narrated by Palestinians in order to produce an understanding of the Intifada. . . . This class takes as its starting point the right of Palestinians to fight for their own self-determination. Conservative thinkers are encouraged to seek other sections.[32]

This course description reflects a variety of problems. First, it expressly intends to cover the "politics" of the conflict, yet as an English course, taught by an English graduate student, has no mandate to do so. Second, in the first line it expressly asserts that all of modern day Israel is "occupied," rather than just the West Bank and Gaza Strip, thus rejecting Israel's right to exist. Third, without commenting in any form on the methods of resistance, this University of California, Berkeley, course openly condones Palestinian violence that overwhelmingly targets Israeli civilian populations. Fourth, this course description excludes "conservative thinkers." This last stipulation (and only this component of the course) drew widespread attention and criticism. The university objected to the overt discrimination of students based on racial, religious, ethnic, or political differences. While the course description was amended, only the part about "conservative thinkers" was omitted and the content of the course remained untouched.

Professor Joseph Massad has come under intense scrutiny for the ways his anti-Israel ideology affects his teaching and relationship to students. Students assert that they are subject to Massad's own vehemently anti-Israel views. A fellow anti-Israelist in Massad's class stated, "I agree with Massad's stance, and I am glad to be able to take a class where the professor isn't afraid to condemn a country for chronic flouting of United Nations resolutions and international law. At the same time, the lack of zionist [sic] voices in the . . . reading list and the strict guidelines on paper topics (they steer you toward making Massad's own points) make this class not as thought-provoking as it should be."[33] Another of Massad's students was less accepting of the bias in the class. "This was possibly the most offended I've ever been. Massad does not even pretend to give the entire picture, he states that on the first day. . . . I worry about the people who enter the class with little to no knowledge of the topic and form their opinions based on Massad's lectures and assigned readings. . . . The class is taught unethically, and should be renamed 'Why Palestinians Hate Israel.' "[34]

Massad's class, though lacking Shingavi's clearly stated anti-Israelism in the course description, is, in a way, more insidious because it draws students searching for a balanced viewpoint. Massad's course is billed as the Palestinian-Israeli Conflict 101 but is an advanced course in anti-Israelism, clearly intending to encourage students to be part of the campaign against Israel. First-year Columbia student Ariel Beery wrote of Massad's class in the *Columbia Spectator*, "[in] the syllabus for his class, . . . he bluntly states, 'the purpose of the course is not to provide a "balanced" coverage of the views of both sides, but rather to provide a thorough yet critical historical overview of the Zionist–Palestinian conflict to familiarize undergraduates with the background to the current situation from a critical perspective.' "[35]

The promulgation of anti-Israelism in the classroom does not only occur in those classes covering the Israel-Palestine conflict, but also in those without the intellectual rationale to address the subject. At Harvard, student Jordana R. Lewis wrote of Foreign Cultures 17, a required core curriculum course, in the *Harvard Crimson*, "The material from Foreign Cultures 17 is not quite propaganda, but it comes close." Guest speakers in the class "spit venom at the state of Israel," she reported. "Considerable damage is done when a class . . . is fed one point of view disguised as historical truth. And, responsibility for this damage extends to the University's highest levels, especially when that class is part of the Core program, sanctioned by the College as fundamental knowledge."[36]

Sometimes anti-Israelism seeps into the most improbable classrooms. Required courses to fulfill general or major requirements are unavoidable. Students must take these courses and if, in order to do so, they must enroll in an anti-Israel course, a student may, in effect, be forced to endure what they consider indoctrination or open hostility. When a course is necessary to advance in a student's chosen field, they may find that their field of study and their own religious identity are unnecessarily at odds.

For example, in an interview with the Institute for Jewish & Community Research, cognitive science major and University of California, Berkeley, student Matar Davis, spoke of problematic materials she encountered there in her statistics class as a freshman student in the fall of 2003. The class name was "Probability and Statistics," taught by Professor Charles J. Stone, and it was an entry level class required for a number of majors. In the appendix of the instructor's supplement packet was a reprinted article from the *Guardian*, a local Bay Area progressive newspaper, titled, "Action Against Israelis and Apartheid Blocked Regularly: U.S. Veto," which contained a selective list of United Nations resolutions vetoed by the U.S. since 1972, mostly involving issues regarding perceived human rights violations by Israel. The article attempts to indict the United States and Israel by throwing in one example each of the United States vetoing a recommended arms embargo to South Africa, a trade embargo with Cuba, and a renewal of the peacekeeping mission to Bosnia. Matar said that the appendix was never even used in class.

NEGLECT IN MONITORING THE QUALITY OF SCHOLAR-SHIP AND IN CURBING PERSONAL BIAS HAS ALLOWED ANTI-ISRAEL PROFESSORS TO HAVE ALMOST FREE REIGN.

On the final exam for the class, there was an exercise that stood out to Matar:

> On the final exam, there was a European survey or poll presented on how Israel is the greatest threat to world peace. The problem was he didn't present all of the details that went into this poll. I knew that there were problems with the poll from reading about it and discussing it with friends. He presented the poll as a dumbed-down version. Considering that it was presented in a diluted format, you had to choose the answer that the poll was valid based on what was presented, as opposed to being based on what I actually knew. The message going away was that Israel is the greatest threat to world peace. This was a freshman class. As a freshman, you don't have a filter yet on what professors are teaching, it's before you get jaded, everything the professors present at that point is sort of like gold.[37]

The neglect in monitoring the quality of scholarship and curb personal bias has allowed anti-Israel professors to have almost free reign to develop and promote a one-sided, hostile view of Israel and couch it within the broader context of racism, oppression, and inequality that are so appealing to students on campus. Although the genesis of the anti-Israel position among Middle East Studies faculty has been developing over decades, only recently have students, faculty, and a few administrators begun to address the imbalance. Thus far, it has been difficult to redress these issues within the university system. The influence of anti-Israel faculty, both in the volume of their collective voice and the unity of their numbers, intimidates many administrators, especially when the flag of academic freedom is raised.

As a result, some students have gone outside the university. Jewish students at Columbia agreed to appear in a video entitled *Columbia Unbecoming* to describe their experiences.[38] The video was used as a catalyst to force the administration to investigate the claims that Jewish students were being intimidated. An investigation took place; however, it lacked focus and its conclusions were vague. Fierce resistance by Columbia professors effectively limited the investigation. Some feel the final report was a "whitewash," but the university did admit its student grievance processes needed an overhaul.[39]

The debate about Middle East Studies bias has focused upon the politicization of the study of Israel and the marginalization of Jewish students. These issues are, however, symptoms of a larger problem, the effects of which can create similarly disturbing experiences for other students as well. Israel may well be the ultimate target of much of the intellectual dishonesty in the field of Middle East Studies, but in this process, a comprehensive worldview is promoted to support anti-Israel positions. Issues of oppression, racism, slavery, and genocide around the world are downplayed to maintain focus upon Israel. In particular, societal problems in Arab and Muslim countries are glossed over to provide the basis for a black and white comparison between the victimhood of the Arabs and the brutality of the Israelis. While Jews have taken the brunt of what some have called the "Palestinianization" of Middle East Studies, they are not the only casualties of this historical revisionism. Americans and the West are also branded as international aggressors and the source of the problems in the Middle East.

The Arab and Muslim voice is presented on campus as almost exclusively anti-Israel, anti-American, and pro-Palestinian. This is not, however, because all Muslim and Arabs on campus share a uniform vision, but rather, because dissenting Arab and Muslim voices have been ridiculed and even muzzled. A Kuwaiti student at Foothill College turned in his political science final exam essay lauding the Constitution of the United States as a progressive document that has helped to spread freedom throughout the world. The student, Ahmad Al-Qloushi, claims that his professor not only failed him, but in fact also told him, "'Your views are irrational.' He called me naïve for believing in the greatness of this country and told me, 'America is not God's gift to the world. You need regular psychotherapy.'"[40] Intellectual integrity is assaulted, and anti-American ideology is part of that attack.

Al-Qloushi had personal reasons to be pro-American. His point of view comes from having grown up in the Middle East, seeing his country taken over by Iraq, his family imprisoned, and witnessing the subsequent intervention by America to free his nation. No one could reasonably assert that his opinion is invalid, especially since he was writing from his own worldview.

While dissenting Arabs and Muslims can be ridiculed for their opinions, there are many others who have found that issues important to them are simply ignored. Middle East Studies departments often encompass study on lands that stretch into Asia, as well as North Africa. When the efforts of the faculty are focused upon one country (Israel) that involves less than 1 percent of the land, the people they are entrusted to study and teach about, including entire countries, fall through the cracks. A Sudanese refugee, Daoud Salih, spoke at Columbia University concerning criticism of the Middle East Asian Languages and Cultures Department at that institution. He openly lamented the fact that ethnic cleansing occurring in Sudan, at the hands of an extremist Islamist government, has been largely overlooked,[41] or intentionally minimized by the faculty supposed to teach about the region.

Irshad Manji, a Muslim born in North Africa and raised in Canada, writes in her book, *The Trouble With Islam*, of what she regards as a tribalistic, conflict-oriented, Arab narrative of Islam that dominates the Muslim world, and thereby the Middle East and Middle East Studies. She calls this repressive tradition, "Foundamentalism," whereby the "founders" of the religion impose their orthodoxy on the world's more than one billion Muslims, thus suppressing parallel narratives and marginalizing non-Arab Muslims (as well as Arabs who reject the party line). After she challenged a Muslim Student Association member as to why there are differences in the practice of Islam, such as in Pakistan, the student replied, "Because Pakistanis are not real Muslims. They're converts. Islam was revealed to the Arabs."[42] The dominant Arab story of opposition to the West and struggle against invaders has become a mantra in Middle East Studies, with Israel and the United States cast as the villains.

THE INTIMIDATION OF PRO-ISRAEL FACULTY

In order for the campus to be a haven for anti-Israel intellectuals, those who would either disagree with the political position or protest the ideological uniformity must be marginalized. This process occurs on a number of levels. The first is the most obvious: swell the ranks with like-minded professors and overwhelm the debate. It is important to note that the pro-Israel or anti-Israel voices do not line up precisely along religious, national, or ethnic lines. Not all Arab or Muslim faculty are anti-Israel, nor do they necessarily participate in the anti-Israel propaganda of many Middle East programs. On the other hand, some Jewish faculty are decidedly anti-Israel, and are often used as examples by the anti-Israelists as proof that their position is a widespread, commonly held belief (even among Jews). Still, most Jewish faculty are not anti-Israel.

Yet, the intense hostility toward Israel, and those who support Israel, displayed by a minority of professors has not only intimidated students in the classroom but has also succeeded in creating an atmosphere of risk for faculty who choose to respond to the frequent attacks leveled against Israel on campus. In an environment where a segment of the student and faculty ranks have unified against any and all support of Israel, an individual faculty member is vulnerable to attack if he or she chooses to speak out against the politically correct culture. The attacks are not physical, but they do not have to be.

Social and professional isolation can be a very real threat for faculty members. Success in academia is tied to a community of intellectuals and the interchange of ideas and information. Acceptance by other faculty is very important, especially those in the same department who can weigh in on issues of course assignment and tenure. Pro-Israel professors who have chosen to speak out, and even those who are not pro-Israel but have made statements that could be construed as such, can face isolation for their views. This danger is increasingly acute where it concerns professors who are members of a department in which vocal anti-Israel professors dominate.

Professor of history Robert David "KC" Johnson, from City University of New York, Brooklyn College, was denied tenure despite the fact that many well respected colleagues in his field regarded his work to be stellar. "A talented historian and remarkable teacher is being told that Brooklyn College has no room for him because academic freedom is a scarce commodity there, limited to those with tenure or those who subscribe to the proper ideology du jour."[43] An investigation into his tenure review revealed that the decision was made by members of his department who cited reasons such as "uncollegial behavior" for his denial of tenure. Johnson, on the other hand, claimed that those in his department simply did not like his views and, therefore, actively sought to obstruct his academic career. Specifically, he pointed to an incident when he disagreed with his fellow department members regarding the Middle East and that since then, he had been isolated and rejected by his peers. "It all started with the teach-in," he said.[44] Professor Johnson's case is unique in that his admirers forced further inquiry into the decision and in the end City University of New York chancellor Matthew Goldstein overturned the decision. Despite the reversal of Johnson's tenure rejection (a rare act of courage by trustees regarding tenure), the incident carried with it a clear warning to other professors, especially those whose reputation in their field may not be widely recognized enough to save them from a similar attack to what Professor Johnson experienced.

A part-time professor at DePaul University is fighting for his job of fifteen years. Professor Thomas Klocek is reportedly widely liked by students, his course often full. He has been accused of harassment by members of Students for Justice in Palestine and United Muslims Moving Ahead. The story told by the accusers is that Klocek approached their table set up to distribute materials and engaged them in conversation which is described as "a racist encounter," in which Klocek made "derogatory and racist comments." Klocek maintains that he, in no way, acted in an inappropriate manner. Rather, he claims to have engaged in legitimate debate, pointing out that there was more than one side to the story they presented. He challenged the students on a variety of issues, according to him, without any hint of hostility or degradation. According to accounts, he objected to the Students for Justice in Palestine comparing Israelis to Nazis. He responded by suggesting that, "although most Muslims are not terrorists, most of today's terrorists are Muslims."[45] Did the professor shout? Intimidate? Make racist statements? Or, in the surreal world of multiculturalism turned upside down, is it truly racist to contend that a form of political terrorism involves primarily Muslims? If he did behave unprofessionally, then he should go through channels of disciplinary review, and be dealt with if found responsible for engaging with students inappropriately. Whose side of the story is true will come to light, but it is secondary to the issue of the administration's response.

The DePaul University administration adopted the students' claims as truth and suspended Klocek, completely disregarding Klocek's statements to the contrary and therefore, also his reputation and devotion to the university. Susanne Dumbleton, dean of the DePaul School for New Learning in which Klocek teaches, distanced herself from Klocek in the campus paper, *The DePaulia*, stating that he, "is a part-time faculty member whom the university contracts for individual courses. He has no further responsibilities . . . at this time."[46] Moreover, it appears that the administration failed to pursue proper avenues for the suspension of a professor, including a hearing, which Klocek was denied. Dean Dumbleton defended her actions by saying, "No student anywhere should ever have to be concerned that they will be verbally attacked for their religious belief or ethnicity."[47] And, while he is technically suspended with pay, as a part-time professor, he is paid according to his course load, which, after suspension, is none. The administration's procedure will most likely receive wide attention as Klocek has retained a lawyer and states he intends to sue the university. Just to add another twist, DePaul University invited Ward Churchill, the University of Colorado professor who called 9/11 victims "little Eichmanns," to lecture at the university.

Sadly, there are Jewish professors who have found they simply cannot tolerate the anti-Semitism they experience and leave their university. Professor Laurie Zoloth of San Francisco State University, after having witnessed a mob protest against a Jewish student peace rally, was appalled by the absence of faculty speaking out against such bigotry. She wrote, "Counter demonstrators poured into the plaza, screaming at the Jews to 'Get out or we will kill you' and 'Hitler did not finish the job.' I turned to the police and to every administrator I could find and asked them to remove the counter demonstrators from the plaza, to maintain the separation of 100 feet that we had been promised. The police told me that they had been told not to arrest anyone." She lamented the fact that "the police could do nothing more than surround the Jewish students and community members who were now trapped in a corner of the plaza, grouped under the flags of Israel, while an angry, out of control mob, literally chanting for our deaths, surrounded us. . . . There was no safe way out of the Plaza. We had to be marched back to the Hillel House under armed San Francisco police guard, and we had to have a police guard remain outside Hillel."[48] After attempting to shed light on what she regarded as a hostile environment for Jews at San Francisco State University, she moved to Northwestern University.[49] San Francisco State University president Robert Corrigan has condemned anti-Semitism on his campus. As dissenting professors leave, universities lose some of the intellectual diversity that they cherish.

THE INTIMIDATION OF PRO-ISRAEL SPEAKERS

If pro-Israel views are discouraged within the campus community, the student body, or the faculty ranks, pro-Israel advocates can be openly attacked when they come to speak about the Middle East. Protests and even small-scale riots have taken place in response to the arrival of pro-Israel speakers on campus. Both the speakers and the attendees have been demeaned, insulted, and even physically threatened. Speakers have had to cancel their appearances at a number of universities as a result of security concerns generated from the level of hostility from the protesters. Even Natan Sharansky, who spent years fighting for human rights in the Soviet Union, has been "pie-ed" in the face, and more disturbingly, "[t]wo years ago, the visit of Israeli official Natan Sharansky to Boston University to defend Israel was greeted with a bomb threat that nearly forced the cancellation of his lecture."[50]

Israeli statesmen, regardless of their political party, have been demonized on campus. When they arrive for speaking engagements, they may find that the hostility present on campus prevents them from speaking. Former Israeli Prime Minister Ehud Barak was vigorously protested and vilified as a war criminal at the University of California, Berkeley, despite the fact that he had centered his administration on peace-making. Likewise, in Canada, Concordia University, "the site of violent clashes two years ago that scuttled a speech by former Israeli leader Benjamin Netanyahu, has turned down a request by a Jewish students' group to have Mr. Barak deliver a lecture," thus, "igniting a storm over whether the institution is curbing free speech in the name of keeping peace on its politically fractious campus."[51]

These incidents of the prevention of free speech stand in stark contrast to an event that took place at Colorado College in 2002, when Hanan Ashrawi, the former spokeswoman for and colleague of Yasser Arafat, was invited to campus to give a keynote speech at a symposium honoring the first anniversary for the 9/11 terrorist attacks. Colorado Governor Bill Owens commented, "It's outrageous to be bringing this woman, who has done so much to divide the Middle East and has applauded terrorism."[52] Ashrawi delivered her address amid non-violent protests consisting mainly of "scattered boos [and] hand-held signs."[53] At the same time, we would argue that scattered boos for Ashrawi are inappropriate and that she has the right to speak.

Daniel Pipes, a critic of Islamic radicalism, has been denied access to a number of campuses and, when allowed to speak, has been accosted by mobs of angry protesters who, in the process of silencing him, accuse Pipes of attempting to abrogate free speech and curb academic freedom. University of Wisconsin, Madison, graduate student Mohammed Abed argued that Pipes' appearance at his campus was of little benefit to anyone, "How is the normal American on the street being benefited by coming in and listening to this xenophobic bulls**t."[54]

The protesters seem unaware or unconcerned that they are engaging in the very practice of which they accuse Pipes. The campaign to silence Pipes has been solely politically motivated, rather than based on the merits of his scholarship. Therefore, the attacks on Pipes constitute an attempt to eliminate the ideas of a dissenter, the most classic denial of free speech. While on the one hand attacking his website as "McCarthyist," Pipes' detractors are, on the other hand, actively working to impose speech restrictions on Pipes by protesting, interrupting, and interfering with the pre-sentation of his views on campus. Pipes' detractors have gone so far as to brand him a "racist." Anti-Israelists attempted to deny him access to York University using this tactic. Margaret Wente wrote in the *Toronto Globe and Mail* of the protesters, "'No free speech for racists,' they argued, as if Dr. Pipes were another Ernst Zundel. The university's Centre for International and Security Studies disinvited Dr. Pipes to a meeting with students because it was 'uneasy' about him. The York University Faculty Association wrote a letter to its members accusing Dr. Pipes of being 'committed to a racist agenda.'"[55]

The hypocrisy on campus regarding Israeli speakers is most obvious by comparing the anti-Semitic and anti-Israel speakers that have been invited to campus and how clearly they cross the boundaries of civil discourse. Poet Tom Paulin, invited on various occasions to speak at Harvard University, Columbia University, and others, as noted earlier, has expressed a desire to have all West Bank settlers shot.[56] Meanwhile, even those Israeli speakers who do come to campus under protest and endure the insulting onslaught by protesters, maintain a high level of civility and even applaud protesters for exercising their democratically ensured right to express themselves, something the protesters actively try to deny the speaker. A glaring example of the double standard applied against pro-Israel speakers occurred at the Rochester Institute of Technology:

> Students at the Rochester Institute of Technology have been protesting an upcoming lecture, mandatory for some seniors, by pro-Israel Middle East expert Daniel Pipes, while public concerns have not been voiced over another speech, part of the same series, by Ali Mazrui, a professor accused of ties to organizations supporting terrorism. . . . Dr. Ali Mazrui, who has repeatedly made anti-Israel comments, spoke at an Islamic extremist institution and is accused of ties to groups supporting terrorism, has escaped student criticism.[57]

In the face of open discrimination against pro-Israel representatives, the issue of balance concerning the Middle East debate on campus certainly has been raised. Jewish community leaders, among others, has asked for redress from lecture series, teach-ins, and other events geared toward Middle East education that have excluded voices that sometimes represent contrasting views. However, the response has been to invite Jewish or Israeli speakers who could hardly be considered pro-Israel. A tiny number of Jewish scholars are also anti-Israelists, and these scholars have found that they are in increasing demand by the anti-Israel camp. Even though they are rare, they are frequently cited by propagandists to demonstrate that they themselves are not anti-Semitic. How could they be? Jews agree with them.[58] Fringe Jewish activists and intellectuals such as Norman Finkelstein and Joel Beinin, among others, who claim to support Israel (but advocate for extreme anti-Israel claims) are invited to provide a false appearance of intellectual balance. They present a minority opinion of the Jewish community as the dominant viewpoint.

Stanford professor of Middle East history Joel Beinin attended, in solidarity, a memorial for "Al Nakba," or the "Catastrophe," as Palestinians refer to the creation of Israel. Yael Ben-zvi, a student member of the organizing group for the event, Coalition for Justice in Israel/Palestine, explained "[Nakba is] the word . . . used to refer to the devastation of Palestinian society and the dispossession of the Palestinian people resulting from the ethnic cleansing conducted by Zionist forces during 1947–48."[59]

Boycotting of Israeli Scholars

Marginalization of those who speak on behalf of Israel has proliferated in Europe so far as to lead to attempted discrimination against all Israelis, or at least Jewish Israelis. A boycott of Israeli scholars, research, and students has been advocated. This includes refusal to publish scholarly papers, invitations to academic conferences, and keeping Israelis off scholarly journal reviews. The boycott, initiated in England and promoted throughout Europe, initially was directed at limiting European Union funding of Israeli academic projects. The boycott ultimately became a far larger endeavor, one that, though never delineated completely, was intended to impede Israeli scholars in almost every meaningful sphere of academia. Israeli scholars from a wide number of disciplines have had their work rejected by dint of its Israeli origin, graduate students have been rejected for having served in the Israeli army (as all Israeli males over the age of eighteen do), and some Israeli scholars have even been removed from editorial boards for simply being Israeli. As a movement, the boycott has failed up to now, bringing a storm of protest from many academics (bravely) for the attack on academic freedom the boycott represents. But like the divestment campaign, it is not dead and its continued existence is a minor victory for anti-Israelists, especially if it spreads to the United States.

Professors Stephen and Hillary Rose, the husband and wife professors of, respectively, Open University and Bradford University who started the boycott with a letter to the London newspaper *The Guardian*, articulated the boycott as a form of economic sanctions against Israeli academic institutions: "Odd though it may appear, many national and European cultural and research institutions . . . regard Israel as a European state for the purposes of awarding grants and contracts. Would it not therefore be timely if at both national and European level a moratorium was called upon any further such support unless and until Israel abides by United Nations resolutions and opens serious peace negotiations with the Palestinians?"[60]

The actual form of the boycott, however, was far less focused than this initial call might have suggested. Indeed, a month later, one of the most vocal proponents of the boycott, Professor Mona Baker, head of the Centre for Translation and Intercultural Studies at the University of Manchester, and owner and publisher of *The Translator* and *Translation Studies Abstracts* informed two Israeli professors, Professor Gideon Toury and Dr. Miriam Schlesinger, both of whom were on the advisory board of journals owned and edited by her, that she was asking for their resignations. When they refused, she simply fired them. Dr. Schlesinger was a former chairperson for Amnesty International in Israel and part of a protest group that delivered supplies to Palestinian towns in defiance of Israeli blockades, and Professor Toury was one of the leading Hebrew translators in the world.[61]

Though the boycott had called for targeting institutions rather than individuals, Baker explained that such distinctions are essentially meaningless. "I am boycotting Israeli institutions through their representatives, rather than Israelis as nationals. I don't know how else you can boycott an institution (in the abstract)."[62]

Some who had initially signed the boycott petition, which, with a mirror petition in France, had drawn over 700 signatures, were mortified at the direction the boycott had taken. Dr. Stephen Howe, a signatory to the initial boycott petition, wrote, "I find [Baker's firing of two Israeli scholars] morally and politically unacceptable and contrary to the letter and the spirit of the statement I had endorsed."[63] Calling academic freedom an "abstraction" and concerns over its limitations "exaggerated," the Roses seemed to tacitly endorse the path chosen by Baker.[64]

Israeli scholars were also marginalized in their attempts to publish in international journals. Of the 1,000 odd papers sent out by Israeli researchers and scholars about twenty-five editors returned them unopened because they originated in Israel. "Numerically, that is not a lot," said Professor Paul Singer, a physicist of the Haifa-based Technion Israel Institute of Technology. "On the other hand, in the past we never received negative responses of this kind."[65] Dr. Oren Yiftachel, a prominent academic dissident who has been critical of Israel in the past, had a paper sent to the politically left-wing journal *Political Geography*—co-written with a Palestinian professor, Dr. Assad Ghanem—returned unopened with a note saying that the journal was not accepting submissions from Israel. The paper described Israel as "'a state dedicated to the expansion and control of one ethnic group;' the paper concluded that such societies 'cannot be classified as democracies in a substantive sense.'" Nonetheless, the paper was reviewed only after *Political Geography* informed him that it might be persuaded to publish if he included a comparison between his homeland and apartheid South Africa in his article.[66]

Most prominently, Amit Duvshani, a graduate of Tel Aviv University who was interested in pursuing a doctorate in genetics from Oxford University, was surprised to find his application rejected by Professor Andrew Wilkie on the grounds that there was "no way would I take on somebody who had served in the Israeli army." Wilkie added that he had "a huge problem with the way that the Israelis take the moral high ground from their appalling treatment in the Holocaust, and then inflict gross human rights abuses on the Palestinians because [the Palestinians] wish to live in their own country."[67] Wilkie apologized, and was suspended for two months.

The cumulative effect of the boycott is difficult to quantify. According to Colin Blakemore, an Oxford University professor of physiology, who was not affiliated with the boycott: "I do not know of any British academic who has been to a conference in Israel in the last six months." Moreover, according to John Levy of the Academic Study Group on Israel and the Middle East, "There is a palpable slowing down of academic activity."[68] The effect of the psychological and economic toll of the intifada is enormous alone, but the boycott's effectiveness cannot be—and indeed, is not—measured by the number of papers rejected, graduate students turned down, or editors fired by dint of their national origin. "I am certainly worried," said Dr. Toury. "Not because of the boycott itself but because it may get bigger and bigger so that people will not be invited to conferences or lectures, or periodicals will be judged not on merit, but the identity of the place where the author lives."[69]

Mona Baker, in yet another attempt to hijack the Holocaust, actually says that the failure of the boycott is similar to Europeans not taking more action against the genocide of the Jews. She comments, "I am convinced that long after this is all over, as it was with the Jews in the Holocaust, people will start admitting that they should have done something, that it was deplorable and that academia was cowardly if it hadn't moved on this."[70]

Thus far, the Israeli academic boycott has not reached American universities. But trends in academia tend to cross international borders. The boycott denotes a marked escalation both in respect to tactics and philosophy. As Harvard professor Stephen Greenblatt, president of the Modern Language Association of America noted, "An attack on cultural cooperation, with a particular group singled out for collective punishment, violates the essential spirit of scholarly freedom and the pursuit of truth. Such an act is intellectually and morally bankrupt."[71] Though Stephen and Hillary Rose dismissed such concerns, the infringement upon academic discourse and the blatant discriminatory standards of the boycotters have effectively "upped the ante" in the ideological battles in universities.

DIVESTMENT

Divestment and the apartheid accusation have become central aspects of the anti-Israel movement on campus. It is centered in the claim that Israel is currently and always has been an apartheid power over the Palestinian population. From this, one can then superimpose the model of protest used to topple apartheid South Africa upon the Israeli-Arab conflict. In doing so, "those who would hold the state of Israel to a standard different from any other sovereign state, create an environment that makes constructive dialogue almost impossible."[72] The idea of divestment was first vocalized by law professor Francis Boyle of the University of Illinois at Champagne-Urbana, who, not altogether coincidentally, was also a legal advisor to the Palestine Liberation Organization during its days as a recognized terrorist group. He writes of the divestment campaign, "I issued a call for the establishment of a nationwide campaign of divestment/disinvestment against Israel, which I later put on the Internet. In response thereto, the Students for Justice in Palestine of the University of California, Berkeley, launched a divestment campaign against Israel there. . . . This grassroots movement is taking off!"[73] Rapidly, efforts to compare Israel to apartheid South Africa materialized in student newspapers, Middle East Studies departments, and other forums. The University of California, Berkeley, submitted the first petitions for divestment. Boyle's University of Illinois followed shortly. Soon after came Harvard University, the Massachusetts Institute of Technology, and the University of Pennsylvania, followed by the University of Texas, the University of Chicago, the University of Michigan, Princeton University, the University of California, Los Angeles, Duke University, the University of Florida, Yale University, New York University, and many others.

A number of university leaders have spoken out against the immorality of the divestment campaign, including some who accurately exposed its anti-Semitic underpinnings. Harvard President Lawrence H. Summers' address at morning prayers on September 17, 2002, addressed the anti-Semitic undertones of the campaign to divest from Israel. Summers stated, "Serious and thoughtful people are advocating and taking actions that are anti-Semitic in their effect if not their intent." He elaborated, "Some here at Harvard and some at universities across the country have called for the university to single out Israel among all nations as the lone country where it is inappropriate for any part of the university's endowment to be invested. I hasten to say the university has categorically rejected this suggestion."[74]

Other university presidents followed suit. Columbia President Lee Bollinger issued a statement exclaiming, "As President of Columbia . . . I want to state clearly that I will not lend any support to this proposal. The petition alleges human rights abuses and compares Israel to South Africa at the time of apartheid, an analogy I believe is both grotesque and offensive."[75] Barnard President Judith Shapiro stated, "I am issuing this statement to make clear my opposition to a divestment demand that singles out one country in an unsupportable way."[76] Duke President Nannerl O. Keohane was more equivocal, saying that a policy of divestiture "is too blunt an instrument to use in a situation where there are good arguments to be made about responsibility and complicity on both sides."[77] Even for a president who suggests that Israel is partially at fault, divestment was too extreme.

Divestment, as a goal, has failed in academia—thus far. However, some have debated if this was ever the true goal of the campaign. Harvard law professor Alan Dershowitz states, "Divestiture is really not the goal. It's a campaign to miseducate and misinform the next generation. It's a variation of (Nazi propaganda minister Joseph) Goebbels' Big Lie. If you repeat something often enough, it will be true."[78] Indeed, while no administration has seriously entertained the idea of pulling funds from companies that do business with Israel, the "Israel debate" that it sparked on campuses has given anti-Israelists exposure like never before to spread historical inaccuracies. Samuel G. Freedman writes, "Its true goal is not the two-state solution. . . . No, a close reading of the divestment movement's own literature indicates a tolerance for terrorism and an ultimate goal of undermining Israel as a Jewish state."[79] The conference organizers maintain a controversial stance on terrorism that validates some of Freedman's accusations. The conference website declares, "It is not our place to dictate the strategies or tactics adopted by the Palestinian people in their struggle for liberation."[80] Many divestment petitions clearly identify the full return of refugees as a key demand, thus endorsing the elimination of Israel as a Jewish state. At the University of Florida, the student group leading the divestment drive is named Nakba '48, a clear reference to Israel's creation as their ultimate focus. Thomas L. Friedman summed up the critique of the divestment campaign in an editorial for the *New York Times*, writing that, "Singling out Israel for opprobrium and international sanction—out of all proportion to any other party in the Middle East—is anti-Semitic, and not saying so is dishonest."[81]

The divestment campaign, though unsuccessful financially, has played a significant role in normalizing anti-Israelism on campus. In the long run, this may prove just as damaging as any actual pulling of funds would have been. Moreover, it has spread far beyond the campus. The divestment campaign, legitimized on campus, even as it was defeated, has been picked up by the Presbyterian Church,[82] considered by the Anglican Church, and a variety of organizations large and small. Higher education has served its purpose as an incubator of ideas for the general society. This ideal did not, however, include disseminating morally bankrupt ideas that even the university rejects.

THE DIVESTMENT CAMPAIGN HAS PLAYED A SIGNIFICANT ROLE IN NORMALIZING ANTI-ISRAELISM AS AN IDEOLOGY ON CAMPUS.

Conferences, Protests, Propaganda, and Campus Media

Students and faculty alike, in addition to the classroom experience, participate in and are exposed to a wide variety of informal educational (and not so educational) activities intended to supplement and enrich one's campus experience. The campus community finds symposia, conferences, films, and exposure to a variety of printed information all the time. A host of experiences inform and influence students and others. Walk on a campus and someone will offer pamphlets, flyers, and bumper stickers. Lunchtime speakers will be encountered making their address from atop a podium on stage or a milk carton on the quad. Rallies, protests, and demonstrations occur anytime, with propagandists chanting slogans, performing sensationalist street theater, or attempting to actively disrupt classes. Campuses are alive with a vast array of activities and images.

The anti-Israel campaign on campus has relied heavily on the daily campus expressions outside the classroom. Pamphlets that utilize anti-Semitic language circulate about Israeli abuses. Speakers visit campuses across the United States, with the primary purpose of delegitimizing Israel, and in some cases, demonizing Jews as well. Conferences and teach-ins present often biased panels of speakers, misleadingly offered as balanced debates. Texts, whether one page or many pages, are churned out by pro-Palestinian groups and presented as factual literature to students, who are often unfamiliar with the propaganda purpose of such materials.

Conferences and Teach-ins

Forums, conferences, lecture series, speeches, and events are held on college campuses under a variety of auspices that include legitimate (although harsh) criticism of Israel, to events that promote hatred toward Jews. In a variety of fields, such campus events are valuable additions or alternatives to traditional classroom experiences. However, anti-Israel topics, speakers that espouse anti-Israel views and sometimes wholesale anti-Semitism often appear on campus podiums.[83] Referring to former New Jersey Poet Laureate, Amiri Baraka:

> It was not Baraka's ranting which upset me most. Having read his work, I was thoroughly prepared for whatever was bound to come out of his mouth. It was the response he received from my fellow Yalies that shocked me. Following a reading of his notorious poem "Somebody Blew Up America," the puerile verses of which are now well known to the Yale community, Baraka launched into a paranoid tirade. As he cited "evidence" of Israeli complicity in the World Trade Center attacks, many Yale students vigorously nodded their heads in approval and erupted into cheering. At the end of the event, the crowd leapt to its feet to give the former poet laureate of New Jersey a rousing standing ovation.[84]

These speakers, whether brought to campus for their views on Israel or not, have become recently popular and in demand due to the notoriety they received from their anti-Israelism. As such, they are part of the overall anti-Israel lecture team visiting campuses. The co-sponsorship with other student groups helps lend support and legitimacy to anti-Semitic and anti-Israel speakers. Zahi Daumi, an associate professor of cell and molecular physiology at Pennsylvania State University, and co-founder of Al-Awda, the coalition for the Palestinian Right of Return, put on a presentation as part of a weeklong series of protests against Israel. The two-hour session, attended by over 100 people, argued for a Palestinian right of return, and that Israeli occupation had created a sense of hopelessness among Palestinians. The presentation was sponsored by the Coalition for Justice in Palestine, "a group created by the Muslim Student Association, the Black Caucus, and the Arab Union Society."[85]

The University of Pennsylvania Muslim Student Association celebrated "Islam Awareness Week" by inviting "Reverend" William W. Baker, "a former chairman of a racist and anti-Semitic organization, the Populist Party," to speak on October 9, 2002. Baker is the founder of Christians and Muslims for Peace and has a history of racism and anti-Semitism. In 1983, speaking before the Christian Patriot Defense League in Missouri, Baker expressed "his disgust at traveling to New York City, getting off the plane to meet 'pushy, belligerent American Jews.'" Five thousand dollars, partially in university funds, were used to sponsor the week-long event.[86] At the University of Toronto, "Israeli Apartheid Week" was organized by the Arab Students' Collective, which included "lectures about the roots of what the students call Israel's ethnic cleansing and segregation of Palestinians." A member of the student group, Hazem Jamjoum, stated, "We're trying to educate people on the fact that Israel is an apartheid state and not simply a military occupier of the Gaza."[87]

IN THE MOST EXTREME CASES, WHICH ARE NOT ALTOGETHER UNCOMMON, A SPEAKER WILL UNABASHEDLY PROMOTE HATRED TOWARD JEWS.

In the most extreme cases, which are not altogether uncommon, a speaker will actively promote hatred toward Jews. These events can be called speakers forums, resembling as much as they can, official university-sponsored counterparts, or they can be called "teach-ins," at which the speakers attempt to "teach" students outside the restrictions of the classroom. At a teach-in, professor of Iranian studies Hamid Dabashi, head of the department of Middle Eastern and Asian Languages and Cultures at Columbia University, explained the purpose of a teach-in. "We just get angrier and angrier. But this is where the blessed thing called 'teach-in' comes in handy. Tonight, we think for ourselves. Revenge of the nerdy 'A' students against the stupid 'C' students with their stupid fingers on the trigger."[88]

It is within the university-sanctioned, yet the insufficiently monitored environment of "teach-ins" that the anti-American and anti-Israel attitudes of some professors are most fully expressed. At the same event, professor of anthropology and Latino studies Nicholas De Genova was quoted at a rally declaring that "U.S. patriotism is inseparable from imperial warfare and white supremacy." He said, "U.S. flags are the emblem of the invading war machine in Iraq today. They are the emblem of the occupying power. The only true heroes are those who find ways that help defeat the U.S. military."[89] Such comments led to community outrage, yet dissent was relatively absent when the same professor asserted that "The heritage of the victims of the Holocaust belongs to the Palestinian people. The state of Israel has no legitimate claim to the heritage of the Holocaust."[90]

The Second Palestinian Solidarity Conference held at the University of Michigan in 2002 featured speakers such as Sami al-Arian, the Florida State University professor once quoted as saying, "Let us damn Israel . . . until death," at a public forum, and currently charged by federal authorities on terrorism charges.[91] Conferences are some of the more organized of the anti-Israel activities. They are preplanned, advertised, and sponsored, sometimes by the university. Events include such examples as a Palestinian film festival, an Intifada Week, or a national divestment conference. The content of each varies significantly. However, they are often embroiled in some sort of controversy. For example, Jewish students felt compelled to file a lawsuit against the University of Michigan over the anti-Semitic speakers invited to the Second Divestment Conference. At the University of Chicago, the April, 2002, Palestine Film Festival's logo was a map representing all of Israel as occupied Palestine. During the festival's opening statement, the Film Festival's director, remarked, "After all, $4 billion dollars of our tax money annually have

"U.S. PATRIOTISM IS INSEPARABLE FROM IMPERIAL WARFARE AND WHITE SUPREMACY."

bankrolled atrocities committed by the Israeli forces, like the recent massacre in Jenin—the horrific details of which are just now being uncovered. 'Gaza Strip' was also shown at Drew University."[92]

Conferences, lectures, and teach-ins can occur ad hoc at any time and any place on campus, whether in a hall as a formal engagement held by an interest group or in a corner of the "quad," with no sponsorship. They can take the guise of academic panels, discussions, or even art shows.[93] Generally, the less supervised the event is, the more blatant the attacks against Israel and America. The irony of the flood of anti-Israel lecturers on campus is that this form of informal education is generally the realm of the marginalized voices in the university system. However, because Middle East Studies and related fields are inundated with anti-Israel professors, they are far from marginalized on campus. Nonetheless, they feel the need to influence students outside of the classrooms that they already control.

The question is whether the students understand the separation, or simply regard the words of their professor as legitimate, inside or outside the classroom. Undoubtedly some do, especially when university facilities are utilized, such as is the case for both Palestinian Solidarity conferences at the University of California, Berkeley, one at the University of Michigan, and another at Rutgers University. By tacitly endorsing anti-Israel or anti-American events and allowing university space to be used for these purposes, administrations seem to put the university stamp of approval on the content as an accepted part of university discourse.

Protests, Rallies, and Guerrilla Theater

Anti-Israel protests and rallies are a primary vehicle for expressing anti-Israel behavior and rhetoric on campus. Some of the most disturbing acts of anti-Semitism and anti-Israelism on campus have been displayed at such protests. Anti-Israel protests and rallies vary in form and intensity. Sometimes they are simple gatherings of people holding signs and chanting slogans. Other protests have included hate speech, physical harassment, and other forms of intimidation. Examples of campus protests include the following:

- Guerrilla theater consists of acting out some sort of sensational improvisational event on campus. For example, at the University of California, Berkeley, on February 7, 2002, an anti-Israel demonstration was held on the steps of Sproul Hall where a skit was performed featuring a student dressed up as Israeli Prime Minister Ariel Sharon stomping on a cardboard "Palestinian village" to show "what house demolitions are really like."[94] Theatrical protests commonly include "checkpoints" set up at major thoroughfares on campus forcing students to pass through a limited area where protesters act as Israel Defense Forces soldiers, harassing students as they pass. At the University of Michigan on March 10, 2002, to protest a pro-Israel conference taking place on campus, Students Allied for Freedom and Equality, acting as Israel Defense Forces soldiers armed with cardboard machine guns and sirens, refused to let a "Palestinian ambulance" through a mock checkpoint.[95] At the University of Maryland, College Park, representatives of the Muslim Student Association and Organization of Arab Students set up a mock checkpoint and labeled a courtyard "Occupied Territory," designating one path for "Palestinians" and another for "Israelis."[96]

- Occupations are held on university property by taking over a building and prohibiting access, using human force or chains. Students for Justice in Palestine at the University of California, Berkeley, has twice occupied Wheeler Hall. Serious violations of university rules, including prohibiting access, chaining doors, and assaulting a police officer, led to arrests.[97] However, a university conduct review ended in acquittal, which invited the second building takeover. University chancellor Robert Berdahl stated, "The interruption of academic activities [is] a serious problem. [SJP's] occupation of Wheeler seriously compromised [students'] ability to take exams."[98]

- Walkouts are a traditional form of protest that have also been employed in the anti-Israel campaign. In April, students at George Mason University held a walkout and sit-in. The event was advertised with flyers depicting a dead baby. Walkouts are infrequent, largely because professors are requested to allow or encourage students to attend rallies during class time, thus rendering the disruptive goal of a walkout ineffective. One professor who encouraged his students to walk out replied to inquiries, "I am a part-time faculty member with a heavy political involvement. I am not the person you should be talking to."[99]

- Protests against Israel, held under the auspices of commemorating Palestinian casualties, including terrorists, are organized to coincide with Holocaust Remembrance Day. In a protest of Holocaust Remembrance Day on April 10, 2002, pro-Palestinian students at the University of Michigan, Ann Arbor, stood on the steps of the Michigan Union with gags in their mouths and their hands tied to symbolize Palestinian suffering.[100] At the University of Colorado, Boulder, during Holocaust Awareness Week, Jewish students reported a "wave of anti-Israel graffiti" chalked in some areas of the campus. One chalking read, "Zionazis."[101] Hillel and the Anti-Defamation League jointly called upon the university leadership to issue a strong statement calling for the cessation of "provocative activity which is creating an atmosphere of fear and intimidation among Jewish students at the university."[102] On April 10, 2002, the Washington Square News featured an article about a vigil held by the New York University Students for Justice in Palestine and the Arab Students United to mark the 54th anniversary of the death of 100 Palestinians in the village, Deir Yassin. The article about the Palestinian vigil features a footnote at the end that points out, "In addition to being the anniversary of the Deir Yassin attacks, yesterday was the Jewish holiday of Yom HaShoa, Holocaust Remembrance Day."[103]

- Commemorations of al-Nakba, the "great catastrophe," are held on Israeli Independence Day, claiming Israeli independence constitutes a crime against the Palestinian people. On April 16, 2002, at a protest against Israeli Independence Day at the University of Michigan, students carried signs that read, "Stop the Killing: End the Occupation," and "U of M: Divest from Israeli Occupation." Saying they were "inspired" by the "massacre [in] Jenin," students staged a mock funeral, carrying four stretchers draped with Palestinian and Israeli flags representing the victims of the Israeli occupation in the West Bank.[104] At New York University on April 18, 2002, speaking at a pro-Palestinian rally held on Israeli Independence Day, Art Miller, member of the Arab American Anti-Discrimination Committee, said of Israeli checkpoints, "The sense of injustice and racism is undeniable once you've experienced it. It's like you're in a huge prison or concentration camp."[105] Members of TorchPAC, New York University's pro-Israel group, were upset because the university issued a permit to Arab Students United allowing them to conduct the protest on Israeli Independence Day, at the specific location that TorchPAC had been advertising as the setting for a pro-Israel rally. On April 18, a major rally against "Israeli occupation" was held at Dartmouth.[106] At the University of Colorado, Boulder, the Coalition for Justice in Palestine and the Colorado Campaign for Middle East Peace in Denver sponsored a pro-Palestinian event on April 17. The event involved Denver "peace activists" sharing their "first-hand accounts of the Israeli-Palestinian violence," and the plight of the Palestinians.[107]

- Mob protest has occurred repeatedly in order to intimidate other students or effectively deny guest speakers the right to appear. The most notorious of these protests occurred at San Francisco State University. A peace rally organized by Hillel was accosted by a substantial mob of hostile counter-protesters, requiring police protection to evacuate the Hillel students. The Hillel rally organizer, a senior computer science major, was quoted as saying, "They tore down our flags and stomped on them, and they cornered us, and they were screaming that Hitler should have finished the job."[108] The University of California, Berkeley, and Concordia University both were forced to cancel speeches by former Israeli Prime Minister Benjamin Netanyahu due to security concerns created by the mob protest.[109] Daniel Pipes is routinely protested, and requires heavy security and entrance through the back door to ensure his safety.[110] In April, 2002, Shimon Shetreet, deputy mayor of Jerusalem, was protested during a talk at Tulane University.[111]

Rallies, protests, and guerrilla theater are sensational, eye-catching, and for some, just plain "trendy." Certainly, some protesters believe strongly in their cause, but often, the ranks of protesters are filled with those seeking something other than the professed cause of the event. Undoubtedly, there are those who are simply "raging against the machine," regardless of the particular focus. However, while some may attend a protest for a myriad of unrelated reasons, they are easily coalesced against Israel. These open displays of anti-Israelism are the greatest recruitment tool available to the anti-Israel campaign. Protesters are loud, proud, assertive, and for some, cool—the essence of what they believe universities are supposed to represent. The anti-Israel movement has worked hard and successfully to present its cause as a righteous movement, rooted in basic ideals of equality, freedom, and justice.

Propaganda Literature

Propaganda literature regularly includes rally/protest announcements, printed lists of accusations against Israel, historically inaccurate timelines, "informational booklets," divestment explanations, compilations of victim accounts, political action pamphlets, maps detailing "occupied" Palestine, Frequently Asked Questions, and other such materials. In addition, on various campuses, handouts have openly promoted lies and slanderous accusations that unquestionably cross over into blatant anti-Semitism. The following materials were collected on various Northern California campuses during the 2002–03 academic year.

The University of California divestment campaign's "Frequently Asked Questions" pamphlet created by Students for Justice in Palestine poses a series of questions, including, "What is the UC's relationship to Israel?" "What is Divestment?" "Why should the UC divest?" "Doesn't Israel need the money?" and "Isn't the conflict in the Middle East complicated? Aren't both sides committing violence?" The answers include, "The blood of Palestinian people should not be spilled for profits," "The majority of national conflicts in the Middle East have been initiated by Israel," and, "[The conflict] is not really complicated." This type of pamphlet is a staple of the anti-Israel campaign. It is aimed at those who do not have much knowledge about the Middle East and provides simple answers that appeal to a student's sense of equality and justice.

A flyer by Stop Our Silence on Palestine from the University of California, Berkeley, is titled, "Anti-Semitism is wrong." The explanation following, however, has little to do with condemning anti-Semitism. It points to the "injustice and unthinkable brutality that is going on in the Middle East," and manipulates a famous Holocaust quote by claiming, "It is time to stop saying, 'They came for the Palestinians . . . and I did nothing.'" The usage of Holocaust imagery, including the appropriation of Jewish suffering has been discussed earlier. This flyer exemplifies both. The term anti-Semitism is redefined as prejudice against all Semites, including Arabs.

Anti-Semitism has always described anti-Jewish bigotry, and changing the application of the term does not change the act that it describes. Coupled with the last line on the flyer—replacing "Jews" with "Palestinians" in a quote about the Holocaust—the intent of the flyer is clearly to supplant Jews as victims of genocide and discrimination.

Another flyer by the same organization claims U.S. money is "being used against an indigenous civilian population. . . . There are children with eyes shot out, limbs destroyed. . . . The amount of terrorism by Israel dwarfs that of its opponents." This flyer is largely sensationalist. However, such materials may be some students' primary source of information, and what is obviously false to some is readily accepted by others.

No Justice No Peace authored a flyer designed for a "checkpoint" demonstration. On one side it reads, "TRY BEING A PALESTINIAN FOR A DAY. Go to the Checkpoint at Sather Gate." On the reverse, it reads, "The Palestinian Daily Experience Apartheid? Wasn't that South Africa? What is happening in the Gaza Strip and the West Bank could describe events in South Africa." The text is designed to be both intriguing and provocative. Unlike many anti-Israel materials, it does not make bold claims, but instead simply alludes to them. The reason is that this text is designed simply as a primer so that when the student does go to see the mock checkpoint, they are ready to hear that Israel is apartheid reincarnated.

Protest flyers created by the Justice in Palestine Coalition call for a national day of protest on the anniversary of the Sabra and Shatila massacre committed by Lebanese guerrillas against Palestinians. It reads in large type, "Free Palestine" across the top and "No More U.S. Israeli Crimes of Occupation." Below, it reads, "Support Palestinian People's Right of Return," "Stop U.S. Aid to Israel," "Divest from Israel Now," and "No New War on Iraq." Interestingly, an identical flyer for the same protest advertises a "Stop the War on Iraq Before It Starts" rally in the headline. However, below it identifies the day as, "Free Palestine—National Day of Protest." The lower lines are identical to the other flyer, except that "No New War on Iraq" comes first and the three Palestine-related demands follow. These flyers exemplify the arbitrary litany of causes of a protest and co-opting of activist energy, particularly concerning the anti-war movement.

While anti-Israel literature proliferates on campus, some materials promote unadulterated anti-Semitism. At San Francisco State University, the Muslim Student Union circulated flyers depicting a can labeled "Palestinian Baby Meat." Written across the can was the phrase, "Manufactured in Israel under U.S. license." This is an unveiled restatement of the ancient blood libel that first arose in Europe. Like so much of European anti-Semitism, it is now proliferating in the Middle East. The root lies in an accusation that Jews bake bread with the blood of gentile children, a lie created to justify the persecution and murder of Jews. Surprising to some, it has now arrived at North American universities.

Campus Media

Campus media provide visible outlets for the arguments and accusations of the anti-Israel movement. Campus media include university-issued campus news, independent student publications, satirical reviews, and others. Many campuses have a university subsidized student newspaper. The publications reach a large number of readers on campus. Students, charged with much of the operational and editorial responsibilities, often publish poor reporting, diatribes, and hate speech in the mistaken belief that they are upholding freedom of speech. Moreover, the general anti-Israel trend within some international media are reflected in student media. Student media are ideal for the promotion of anti-Israelism and even anti-Semitism.[112]

Although university administrators and journalism faculty (or other faculty involved in student media) generally distance themselves from taking responsibility for newspaper content and staffing, they are intimately involved in the management or oversight of student newspapers. There are few universal standards for the operation of university newspapers. Methods of governance vary depending on the university, creating differing degrees of independence for the students. Faculty members often have supervisory influence over the newspaper and may even comprise part of media boards that choose the editor-in-chief of the newspaper. The editor-in-chief is the student in charge of the newspaper, and he/she is supposed to determine the content and staffing. It is understood that student newspapers are to maintain editorial independence, but can they really maintain independence when students are so intertwined with faculty and administrators?

Faculty and administrative influence on newspaper staff and story production manifests itself in many ways. The editor-in-chief may have regular or sporadic meetings with the media board, assistant dean, chancellor, or even a university president. The composition of media boards, also known as newspaper publication or advisory boards, differs by institution. They may consist of any combination of school officials, including the chancellor's staff, university presidents or vice presidents, deans, outside media professionals, student government representatives, or newspaper staff. Sometimes there is not a formal student voice on these boards, and meetings are closed to the student journalists.

In an online Associated Collegiate Press forum, a student from Northwestern (Louisiana) State University wrote about closed meetings and the media board at his school, "The Media Board meets openly but closes to all students and possibly community members . . . to discuss and vote on the editors and radio manager. Advisers and some other faculty have remained in the room to also discuss the candidates. The vote is not released, nor, as far as I know, is it public record."[113]

In addition to advisory boards, there often is a professor who plays the role of "publisher" or "faculty advisor" of the campus paper. These professors may even have an office in the "newsroom." They help set the political tone because they make or approve of staffing decisions and guide the newspaper's department editors. They also serve as the liaison to journalism departments. Students often receive credit and grades from this professor for their internships at the paper. The influence of faculty "advisors" can foster an environment that tolerates and sometimes promotes flawed and problematic student journalism practices on controversial subjects such as Israel. Consider the following editorial statement. "Because this is a land of freedoms, the right of those who would see the Israelis driven into the sea . . . must be fiercely protected."[114]

In the case of Arizona State University's *State Press*, a slanderous article targeting Hasidic Jews in Israel was published at the urging of the director of the university's Walter Cronkite School of Journalism, Douglas Anderson, and the Director of Publications, Bruce Itule. The article, written by journalism student Mary Leigh Summerton, "told of a quadriplegic Jew being stoned to death at the Western Wall in broad daylight by a mob of Hasidic Jews because he desecrated the Sabbath by using an electric wheelchair." Initially, the article was accepted as partial fulfillment of requirements for a journalism class that Anderson and Itule co-taught and then they recommended it for publication in the *State Press*. The journalism professors did not question the authenticity or truthfulness of this hard-to-believe account, although it included no dates or names and the story had never been mentioned in the general press.[115]

Student newspapers are frequent platforms for anti-Israel professors. In the University of Massachusetts' student *Daily Collegian*, a letter was published by emeritus professor of mathematics Helen Cullen, who wrote, "Judaism and the Jewish identity are offensive to most human beings and will always cause trouble between the Jews and the rest of the human race."[116] At Kent State University's student newspaper, associate professor of history Julio Cesar Pino praised suicide bombers,[117] and in the University of Central Florida's *Central Florida Future*, visiting professor William James Martin justified the use of suicide bombers comparing the ideology of Israel's founding fathers to Hitler's theory of ethnic cleansing in *Mein Kampf*.[118] While anti-Israel and sometimes anti-Semitic sentiments proliferate within student media, colleges are capable of taking swift action if they feel the norms of civil discourse are violated. For example, an undergraduate at the University of North Carolina was removed from her position at the student newspaper when she called for racial profiling of Arabs.[119] The "norms of civil discourse" worked well in this case.

Editorial cartoons are also a realm of anti-Semitic expression in campus newspapers. Intent is sometimes hard to discern when it comes to art, especially intentionally socially provocative cartoons. For example, satire can often walk a thin line between promoting bigotry and ridiculing it. The *Brown Daily Herald* at Brown University published a cartoon that asks, "Who is an American?" then answers, "Some of them are 'Jew'-ish. This mysterious other lives in houses called 'dreidels' and poisons water supplies! But don't let the baby-eating scare you away from our horned friends . . . your children run much too fast!" Supposedly, the author, Greg Schilling, sincerely apologized and indicated he intentioned no anti-Semitism. Unfortunately, the satire may have been lost on many readers. The judgment of the paper in printing the cartoon is in question. However, the cartoonist is not likely to have intentionally promoted bigotry. (See "The Uncivil University Illustrated.")

Another article, published in the Texas A&M student newspaper, illustrates a split screen. On the left is an enormous Nazi soldier, identified by a swastika on his armband, bent over a decrepit victim, beating him or her with the date 1942 written above. On the right is the same soldier, but with a Star of David instead of a swastika, beating the same victim with the date 2002 above. The cartoonist presents Israelis as today's Nazis. (See "The Uncivil University Illustrated.")

Independent interest group newsmagazines circulated on campus are another prolific source for hate speech and incitement. Muslim newsmagazines like *Al-Talib* at the University of California, Los Angeles, and *Al-Kalima* at the University of California, Irvine, call Zionism the "forgotten apartheid" and promote Hamas and Hezbollah as legitimate and noteworthy resistance movements.[120]

The continued publication of these calumnies, and the ongoing intimidation, marginalization, and censorship of pro-Israel students and other scholars have turned the campus into a hostile environment not just for Jews, but for all who believe that the university should be free of political haranguing, biased scholarship, and the hegemony of a singular point of view. The many incidents recorded in this volume (and the many more uncovered during research and not reported here) show that the university has lost its way, but it is not irretrievably lost. Changes are already underfoot both within the university and among the other stakeholders who form part of the public trust, but much remains to be done. In the concluding chapter, we examine what is already being done to remedy the incivility of the contemporary university and offer ten recommendations on how to reclaim the campus as a truly public institution.

CHAPTER SEVEN

RECLAIMING THE CIVIL UNIVERSITY

Addressing campus anti-Semitism and anti-Israelism requires remedies internal to higher education as well as outside intervention when the university is unable or unwilling to take action. Ridding the campus of anti-Semitism and anti-Israelism involves efforts that reinvigorate the core values of higher education: preserving academic freedom, celebrating the benefits of diversity, and insuring high quality, honest scholarship.

The potential need for outside intervention indicates that universities are failing to appropriately self-regulate. Yet, the university has all the necessary structural mechanisms to address anti-Semitism and anti-Israelism on campus. Formal systems include peer review, evaluation of scholarship and teaching, committees for hearing student complaints, and disciplinary measures for inappropriate faculty or student behavior. Unfortunately, these procedures are not fully deployed in the case of anti-Semitism and anti-Israelism.

The failure to appropriately address anti-Semitic and anti-Israel bigotry is an indicator of a frightening breakdown in a number of university processes involving many stakeholders within higher education. Donors are not paying enough attention (including Jewish donors who give billions of dollars to higher education[1]). Trustees, often successful business leaders who are much more attentive in their entrepreneurial spheres, fail to appropriately execute their fiduciary duties both in the operations of the institution and the mission. Most of all, faculty and administrators exhibit unawareness, indifference, and sometimes even cowardice.

We do not cavalierly advocate for more public sector regulation of higher education. This would be a course of last resort. However, even though the university system fiercely resists outside oversight, higher education is legally, financially, and morally part of the public trust. Self-regulation is part of the agreement that universities have with the public sector. The failure to properly do so should rightly bring in outside corrective measures. If university faculty and administrators do not curb anti-Semitism and anti-Israelism (or any form of prejudice), this violation of the public trust should be handled by the other stakeholders in the university system. Government should not have to intervene to insure the moral behavior of colleges and universities. On the other hand, the public sector would be abdicating its fiduciary and moral responsibility to allow anti-Semitism and anti-Israelism to continue unchecked. If higher education does not solve this problem on its own, then federal and state governments should bring the full power of their financial, legal, and moral authority to bear on universities.

> THE UNIVERSITY HAS ALL THE STRUCTURAL MECHANISMS TO ADDRESS ANTI-SEMITISM AND ANTI-ISRAELISM. UNFORTUNATELY, THESE PROCEDURES ARE NOT FULLY DEPLOYED.

WHAT IS BEING DONE

The current relationship between higher education and the public sector is already being redefined. Legislators are attempting to reassert the need for intellectual diversity by introducing measures designed to track the use and effectiveness of monies provided for certain areas of higher education. For example, Republican representative Pete Hoekstra of Michigan led the introduction of House Resolution 3077, a bill to create oversight for the funding of higher education's most politicized field of study, area studies. This bill was always intended to become part of a much larger bill for the renewal of the Higher Education Act of 1965 and has been folded into House Resolution 609:

> There is established in the Department an independent International Higher Education Advisory Board (hereafter in this section referred

to as the "International Advisory Board"). The International Advisory Board shall provide advice, counsel and recommendations to the Secretary and the Congress on international education issues for higher education.[2]

"International education issues" refers specifically to Title VI programs. Title VI of the Higher Education Act allocates federal funding for the study of world regions, language, and international expertise, in an effort to provide the public and ultimately the federal government, with valuable, relevant knowledge about the world. It was created in the wake of challenges from Russia to American interests abroad and was expected to bolster national security through a partnership with academia. Middle East Studies departments fall under the larger umbrella of area studies and are partially dependent on Title VI monies for operating funds.

FEDERAL AND STATE GOVERNMENTS SHOULD BRING THE FULL POWER OF THEIR FINANCIAL, LEGAL, AND MORAL AUTHORITY TO BEAR ON UNIVERSITIES.

House Resolution 609 reaffirms the original intent of Title VI and ensures continued commitment by the federal government. In return, however, the federal government, recognizing the growing politicization of areas studies, and Middle East Studies in particular, requires that a new International Advisory Board be created to ensure that the original intent of Title VI is fulfilled. The bill does not introduce any new requirements upon the field of international and area studies, nor does it hinder academic work in the field by attempting to restrict it through government oversight. Rather, the fostering of reciprocity between academic centers and the federal government ensures the continuation of federal support for area studies.

The reality is that area studies, and, in a post-9/11 world, particularly Middle East Studies centers and programs, were not fulfilling their mandate. The Federal Bureau of Investigation reportedly has over 120,000 hours of pre-September 11th "terrorism-related" recordings that have yet to be translated, indicating a significant need for qualified translators.[3] Yet in an evaluation of America's anti-terror capabilities, *The 9/11 Commission Report: Final Report of the National Commission on Terrorist Attacks Upon the United States* revealed that only six undergraduate degrees in Arabic were earned in 2002.[4] The lack of return on federal investment calls into question the efficacy of continued federal funding for area studies.

Eliminating Title VI is out of the question, for now. Both the university and the federal government want to continue the partnership. The only option, then, is to reinforce federal support, even to increase it, but at the same time to set standards of qualification for these funds. Stanley Kurtz, a research fellow at the Hoover Institution, testifying before the House Subcommittee on Select Education, explains that

> Congress has significantly increased funding for Title VI since 9/11 in the interest of producing recruits for our defense and intelligence agencies who are well versed in the languages and cultures of regions with strategic importance to the United States. Representation by members of national security agencies such as Defense and NSA will assure that, no matter which party is in power, the minimum interests of these agencies in recruiting knowledgeable students are met.[5]

Additions to House Resolution 609, drawn largely from House Resolution 3077, are designed to save area studies funding, and, in many ways, give it increased power. The government, as the grantor, must derive some benefit from its investment. Through the institution of an advisory board, such positive gains are more likely, depending on the extent and quality of the oversight. Yet, many regard such oversight as unnecessary and unwelcome government intervention. In order to allay these fears, the bill explicitly states that, "Nothing in this title shall be construed to authorize the International Advisory Board to mandate, direct, or control an institution of higher education's specific instructional content, curriculum, or program of instruction."[6]

Nevertheless, faculty interest groups have fought the bill as if it entailed the elimination of Title VI funding altogether. Academia is united in urging legislators to reject the bill. The Organization for International Education, comprised of twenty-eight independent bodies, authored a memorandum, asserting that, "Many in the education community are concerned that this advisory board sets a precedent for Federal intervention in the conduct and content of higher education."[7]

The participating organizations are a who's who of academic related organizations, including the following:

- American Association of Community Colleges
- American Association of State Colleges and Universities

- American Council on Education
- American Councils for International Education
- American University of Beirut
- Association of International Business Education and Research
- Association of International Education Administrators
- The College Fund/United Negro College Fund
- Consortium of Social Science Associations
- Council of American Overseas Research Centers
- Council of Directors of National Foreign Language Resource Centers
- Council of National Resource Center Directors
- The Forum on Education Abroad
- Joint National Committee for Languages
- Middle East Studies Association
- National Association of Independent Colleges and Universities
- National Association of State Universities and Land-Grant Colleges
- National Humanities Alliance

The bill has been attacked as an assault on academic freedom, and the forces of the higher education industry reject outright the establishment of the oversight committee. Mark Smith, director of the American Association of University Professors, claims that there will be a "huge intimidating force over curriculum decisions" that impede academic freedom. Other faculty have taken this line of reasoning to the extreme. Nezar Alsayyad, chair of the Center for Middle East Studies at the University of California, Berkeley, made his position on the bill abundantly clear: "We get more money from the federal government. That does not mean we do what the government says. As academics, we have academic freedom. That's our God-given right."[8] Alsayyad's wholesale rejection is exemplified in his characterization of House Resolution 609 in the *Stanford Daily* as "a McCarthyist bill."[9]

Alsayyad, in his response to the bill, underscores the need for increased interaction between the government and the academic fields it funds. While academic freedom is designed to protect intellectual integrity, it is not God-given, but rather, university-ensured, and enforced by a system of checks and balances created by academics themselves.

Meanwhile, the Senate has created its own version of the Higher Education Act renewal. This bill is the result of compromise between the two heads of the Senate Committee on Health, Education, Labor, and Pensions. Instead of creating an advisory board to address concerns over Title VI funding, it introduces a number of other measures by which to monitor the effectiveness of federal money in providing qualified recruits for federal agencies. It also includes, at the forefront of the document, an assertion that institutions of higher education must promote intellectual diversity. One would presume that this simply states the obvious. However, just as the House bill has been fought by higher education lobbyists, the American Council on Education issued a statement outlining their concerns on the Senate Higher Education Act renewal: "We are extremely concerned about the bill's requirement that Title VI programs 'reflect diverse and balanced perspectives' with respect to applications made by institutions for funding, and institutional descriptions of such programs."[10]

Why would the American Council on Education feel the need to make such a statement, seemingly asserting that the organization does not support the reflection of "diverse and balanced perspectives" in academia? They fear it is an attempt by conservatives to counter-balance the liberal faculty.

Both the House and Senate versions of the Higher Education Act renewal are waiting to be approved. Following this, the two bills must be reconciled and made into one all-encompassing bill, along with all of the amendments that will certainly be added in the process. What will remain and what will be added is unknown, and there is always the possibility that the end result will be completely different from what is now being proposed.

Reform in higher education is not restricted to the provisions concerning Title VI of the Higher Education Act, or even federal funding. Similar attempts to reinforce the core principles of American higher education have been made at the state level. The General Assembly of Pennsylvania recently passed House Resolution 177 with a vote of 111 to 87. Also known as the Intellectual Diversity Bill, House Resolution 177 creates "a select committee to examine the academic atmosphere and the degree to which faculty have the opportunity to instruct and students have the opportunity to learn in an environment conducive to the pursuit of knowledge and truth."[11]

Republican senator Gibson Armstrong of Pennsylvania introduced the legislation, prompted, he said, by around fifty complaints by college students claiming discrimination over their political beliefs. The importance of state action to ensure intellectual diversity on campus derives from state public institutions of higher education. The bill asserts that both faculty and students should feel free from "the imposition of ideological orthodoxy." Students are to be graded solely based on "merit, without regard for ideological views."[12] This bill, again, seems only to repeat what everyone believes universities should be. Why is it that legislators believe that they must remind universities of their core mission?

Foundations and philanthropists are also beginning to take note of anti-Semitism and anti-Israelism on campus. For example, the Ford Foundation, among others, has taken notice of the decline of civil discourse on campus and the need to address anti-Semitism. In 2005, the foundation launched a $6.7 million initiative to understand and combat anti-Semitism, Islamophobia, and other forms of bigotry in the United States and Europe. Under this initiative is the foundation's "Difficult Dialogues" program, which aims to support efforts by colleges and universities to foster more inclusive campus environments, and to "engage effectively with the growing racial and ethnic diversity of their student bodies."[13] The foundation will award twenty-five grants of up to $100,000 to colleges and universities. Thus far, 136 institutions have been invited to submit proposals.

One philanthropist is attempting to create civil conversation in response to turmoil at Columbia University over charges of intimidation of pro-Israel students by professors. New England Patriots owner and Columbia alumnus Robert Kraft donated $1.5 million to the university to promote cross-cultural understanding and religious tolerance. The donation is reported to be going to programs that will create a more cohesive campus climate through such channels as dialogue groups.[14] Dialogue is useful. Students should learn how to speak respectfully with other students. Dialogue alone will not fix ideologically driven research or anti-Israel campaigns, but these programs are valuable as one method of improving civil discourse on campus.

Other philanthropists who give to higher education are taking a much more proactive role in how they give to colleges and universities. Prominent philanthropist Ronald S. Lauder, in an article entitled "A New Free Speech Movement, Starting with Alumni," wrote:

Thousands of alumni send money to their alma maters every year. They do so with fond memories of their time spent in colleges and gratitude for the training they received and for their achievements in life. But too often, their money goes to fund faculty who, at times, project views that are antithetical to the beliefs of these funders.

It's fine to donate money to your college. I can think of no better institutions in our country to be recipients of your philanthropy. But get to know your alumni association, follow the news at your college, do your homework, and don't be afraid to ask questions. The next time you fill out that check, make sure your money is designated to some place or someone whose viewpoints wouldn't make you cringe.[15]

While Lauder praises the intent of the giver, he rightly criticizes the practice of uneducated giving. In an effort to aid the university, philanthropists may very well be enabling a broken system to stumble along by continuing to provide funds that support deep dysfunctionality. Some are beginning to act more responsibly.

Some university presidents are also asserting moral leadership in condemning anti-Semitism and anti-Israelism. A 2002 letter originating from some current, former, and emeritus university presidents stated, "We are concerned that recent examples of classroom and on-campus debate have crossed the line into intimidation and hatred, neither of which have any place on university campuses. In the past few months, students who are Jewish or supporters of Israel's right to exist—Zionists—have received death threats and threats of violence. Property connected to Jewish organizations has been defaced or destroyed. Posters and websites displaying libelous information or images have been widely circulated, creating an atmosphere of intimidation."[16]

The letter, authored by a group of current or former presidents of Dartmouth, Howard, George Washington, Cornell, Notre Dame, and Brandeis, was circulated nationally in September–October 2002. The authors said their drafting of the letter was spurred by a series of incidents on campuses the previous spring in which Jewish students were targeted. They sought out others among their peers who would join them in signing the letter. During the process of gathering support for the letter from the leadership of other universities, the American Jewish Committee joined in the effort to distribute it to seek additional co-signers. "More than 300 university and college presidents" signed the letter described as

"College Presidents Decry Intimidation on Campuses." The letter advocates "academic integrity in two ways. We will maintain academic standards in the classroom and we will sustain an intimidation-free campus."[17]

However, not all major university presidents agreed:

> The Ivy League . . . was poorly represented: Brown University President Ruth Simmons was the only Ivy League president to sign the petition. Yale University President Richard Levin and the other Ivy League presidents declined to sign the statement. . . . "I just felt [that] while I am not out of sympathy with the people who wrote the letter, on the other hand we have to be mindful of all forms of discrimination and prejudice," said Levin, echoing the concerns of others over the statement's narrow scope. Levin said that, were he to take a position, he would prefer to do so individually. "I'm not a big fan of signing petitions." . . . Yale Muslim Students' Association president Sumeyya Ashraf '04 also said she supported Levin's decision. "If you're focusing on one minority group—it is quite a limiting petition."[18]

This objection is seemingly sound; the reality is absurd. Social norms on campus already hinder other kinds of racism and sexism. The letter is needed precisely because Jewish nationalism is excluded from these protective social norms. The failure of most university presidents to sign this document was a failure of moral courage and leadership.

While the vast majority of college and university presidents refused to sign the letter condemning anti-Semitism and anti-Israelism, 300 did step forward. And every day, decisions are made by presidents, deans, faculty, and other administrators to appropriately address these issues. Moral leadership and action are not absent, they are just less prevalent than their counterweights.

Individual universities also have shown moral leadership regarding anti-Semitism and anti-Israelism. For example, the president and board of trustees at Emory University allocated $25,000 to help cover a portion of the expenses Professor Deborah Lipstadt incurred for her defense against famed Holocaust denier David Irving, who had initiated a libel suit against her in the United Kingdom. Lipstadt wrote about Emory's response in *History on Trial: My Day in Court with David Irving*:

> Though Emory has a substantial population of Jewish students, few of its board members are Jews. The school is loosely associated with the Methodist Church. The board believed . . . that my case epito-

mized academic freedom and raised fundamental moral issues. They wanted to communicate a message that Emory stood squarely behind me. . . . Emory not only had given me the money, but had done so without my asking. . . . I slept well for the first time in weeks.[19]

Many examples of such leadership can be found. Unfortunately, they are not frequent enough.

University alumni have threatened to use their leverage to address anti-Semitism and anti-Israelism. For example, a number of Columbia alumni said they would withhold their contributions if the university does not address the anti-Israel bias in its Middle East Studies department. The strategy was cited in the *Jerusalem Post.* "In a shot across the bow of Columbia University, a group of Jewish Columbia alumni are warning the university that it had better remedy the anti-Israel atmosphere in its Middle East Studies department—or pay a price. A pair of Columbia alumni launched a letter-writing campaign last week threatening to withhold future financial support from the university until 'free speech' is restored to its classrooms."[20] For this tactic to work, however, a large number of alumni would have to follow through consistently with this action over time. They would also have to account for other donors who might actually increase their financial support to protect the "principle" of academic freedom.

The Jewish community has employed primarily two strategies to combat anti-Semitism and anti-Israelism. First, the Jewish communal approach has been focused on training Jewish students to be pro-Israel advocates, although some programs also target the general student body. In an op-ed for *Jewish Week*, Gary Rosenblatt wrote, "On the issue of campus activity, much of the focus of American Jewry during the last four years of the Palestinian suicide war on Israel has been on student protests and activities. Too little attention has been paid to what is taught every day in the classroom by professors who are respected as experts and who will still be teaching their one-sided views of the Mideast conflict long after the current crop of students have graduated and gone out into the world."[21]

Training Jewish students is worthwhile as a way to strengthen their identity as Jews or help them engage intelligently when encountering anti-Israelists. But teaching Jewish students to counter-punch the bigots will not begin to ameliorate the ideological root causes or expression of campus anti-Semitism and anti-Israelism. Moreover, it is unfair to expect Jewish students to bear the burden of combating entrenched ideology and uncivil behavior. If other stakeholders do not take up their respective responsibilities, Jewish students will continue to be subjected to a hostile environment. University administrators and faculty should mold an environment that does not require Jewish students to defend themselves against harassment or discrimination.

BUT TEACHING JEWISH STUDENTS TO COUNTER-PUNCH THE BIGOTS WILL NOT BEGIN TO AMELIORATE THE IDEOLOGICAL ROOT CAUSES OR EXPRESSION OF CAMPUS ANTI-SEMITISM AND ANTI-ISRAELISM.

Jewish communal organizations can also overestimate the value of teaching Jewish students now to be pro-Israel spokespeople. For example, a representative of one Israel advocacy organization noted that "students were unprepared to meet the challenges on campus last year, and they too often conceded the field to Israel's detractors. This year they are running circles around Israel's detractors." Another said, "The anti-Israel coalition seems to have abated somewhat. It was like a fever; it increased and went up to a crisis point last spring, but the fever has peaked and now it's come down."[22] Both observers fail to fully appreciate the systemic character of campus anti-Semitism and anti-Israelism.

Second, a number of communal activists and philanthropists have addressed the propaganda of Middle East Studies departments by creating Israel Studies programs and chairs as counterweights. Creating chairs of Israel Studies is a legitimate way to try to increase scholarship about Israel on campus in the same way that the university supports research and teaching about China, Brazil, or Algeria. But Israel chairs, or even the field of Israel Studies, are no antidote to anti-Semitism and anti-Israelism. First, Israel chairs can be filled with anti-Israeli propagandists. Donors do not control faculty positions. Second, Israel chairs cannot "balance" Middle East Studies departments.

Creating Israel chairs can be a problematic process, as in the case of Columbia University's search for its first chair of Israel Studies for the fall of 2006. The five-member search committee to permanently chair Israel Studies at Columbia includes two members who themselves are anti-Israel activists, Professor Rashid Khalidi and Professor Lila Abu-Lughoud.[23] Professor Khalidi was one of the professors at the center of the Columbia controversy concerning intimidation of Jewish students as documented in the film, *Columbia Unbecoming*.[24] Just as hiring in Middle East Studies is ideologically tainted, the process for hiring Israel Studies professors is also suspect. Finding unbiased faculty for Israel chairs has been less problematic at some universities.

The chair of the search committee, Professor Michael Stanislawski, who admitted to refraining from viewing *Columbia Unbecoming*, called the idea that Columbia was unfriendly to Jews or anti-Semitic a "calumny," in a *Columbia Spectator* interview. Expressing his disapproval for increasing the faculty's diversity of opinion by hiring additional professors to counter existing ones, he said, "We abhor the notion that some people have of 'balancing opinions.'"[25] Stanislawski also emphasized that the Israel Studies chair position is a political and not an academic appointment. We also abhor the idea of balancing opinion, as well as the refusal to acknowledge that Middle East Studies departments are themselves politically slanted.

While programs to combat anti-Israel bias are directed at educating and empowering students, the need for professors themselves to address anti-Israelism is obvious. A group of professors has organized a conference scheduled to take place as this volume goes to press that will, according to conference chair Philip Carl Salzman, "challenge the theoretical foundations that leads people to misconceptions about Israel." The conference organizers aim to address the ideology of post-colonialism, which they say leads to the demonization of Israel. The conference is sponsored by the 600-member Scholars for Peace in the Middle East, a group devoted to discrediting anti-Israel propaganda in academia.[26]

THE JEWISH COMMUNITY NEEDS TO BE PART OF A BROADER COALITION THAT WILL TAKE CORRECTIVE MEASURES.

Other approaches are also underway. The American Jewish Committee started a fund in partnership with the American Society of the University of Haifa to combat boycott actions against Israeli institutions. The fund was created in response to the decision by Britain's Association of University Teachers to sever ties with Haifa and Bar-Ilan universities (later reversed). "The fund will help Israeli institutions injured by academic boycotts use legal means against such actions and press for apologies."[27]

These kinds of political actions, unfortunately, are necessary but not sufficient. The Jewish community should actively combat anti-Semitism and anti-Israelism. But Jewish communal efforts alone will not address the fundamental core issues of the uncivil university. The Jewish community needs to be part of a broader coalition that will take corrective measures, not only to defend Israel, but to reassert what higher education should be about. Faculty, alumni, trustees, students, parents, and all other stakeholders must begin the arduous drive to reclaim the liberal university—de-politicizing classes, devoting itself to civil discourse, and embracing pluralism.

RECOMMENDATIONS

The methods for universities to eliminate anti-Semitism and anti-Israelism as part of accepted campus culture are summarized in the following recommendations.

1. More internal review of Middle East Studies departments, centers, and institutes is critical. Committees of scholars should be established, both from within the individual institutions as well as from other universities to review the level of scholarship, quality of teaching, and objectivity of this discipline. This process should be ongoing until it is clear that these departments and institutes conform to norms of quality and honest scholarship and teaching. All tenure decisions for this field should be made outside the departments. At the same time, appropriate public sector oversight of these federally funded programs should be instituted in the same ways that the National Science Foundation, the National Institutes of Health, and other public grant-making institutions operate.

2. Faculty who harass, intimidate, or discriminate against students because they are Jewish, Israeli, or supporters of Israel should be disciplined. Reprimand, censure, removal from teaching duties, and terminating employment are all appropriate, depending on the seriousness of the breach of academic conduct, and the frequency of its re-occurrence from any particular faculty member. Because bigotry should have zero tolerance, repeat breaches of this basic pillar of academic integrity are grounds for firing both un-tenured and tenured faculty members. Indeed, such discrimination should be identified in faculty handbooks as legal cause for

removing a tenured faculty member. In the meantime, Jewish students who are subject to harassment and discrimination should file complaints to the Office for Civil Rights, U.S. Department of Education, as students at the University of California, Irvine, have already done.

3. More seminars, workshops, symposia, lectures, and other campus activities are needed to educate the campus community about anti-Semitism and anti-Israelism. This subject also should be integrated into appropriate curricula, courses, and syllabi.

4. Colleges should establish appropriate rules about civil discourse: prohibiting shouting down speakers, physical threats, and using racial and ethnic slurs. Civil discourse also excludes advocating physical harm or even murder because of someone's racial, ethnic, or national background. These codes of conduct should be well publicized and included in student and faculty handbooks. Breach of conduct should require reprimand, suspension, expulsion, and termination for students and faculty. We are not suggesting that students do not have the right to advocate for support of Palestinian causes, or to protest Israeli government policies. But they must do so within the established norms of racial and ethnic discourse on campus. Stereotypes about Jews should be forbidden. Bigoted images of Israelis should be unacceptable.

Or, conversely, if campuses want to abandon speech codes, and stop regulating hate speech or promoting consciousness and sensitivity about race, gender, ethnicity, and nationality, then let a thousand diatribes, insults, and demeaning interactions bloom. If free speech is so valued, then let it be free. But universities cannot regulate speech through both formal structures and informal norms and ignore anti-Israelism.

5. University funds should not be used to sponsor racist speakers or events through student organizations, events, newspapers, or any activity subsidized with university dollars. Appropriate administrative and faculty oversight of student organizations are required, and administrative oversight of faculty, for example, who invite outside speakers, is necessary. If student organizations sponsor

inappropriate speakers or events, they should be put on proba-
tion, have their funds restricted, or be disbanded if they persist.

6. The cultural norms of the campus need to change over time, so
   that anti-Semitism and anti-Israelism are as unacceptable as other
   forms of prejudice on campus. This requires moral leadership,
   especially from university presidents, chancellors, and others in
   positions of moral authority. They need to speak out firmly, consistently, and passionately about this bigotry. Few have followed
   the lead of President Lawrence Summers of Harvard University
   or President Robert Corrigan of San Francisco State University in
   doing so.

7. University trustees should become more involved on a number of
   levels. First, they need to take more responsibility when granting
   tenure. Trustees, in deference to academic freedom, do not exercise their fiduciary obligations when they rubber-stamp tenure
   decisions made by the faculty and administration. Lifetime contracts should not be awarded without more trustee consideration.
   Corporate and NGO boards are being challenged to be more
   responsible in their oversight duties. College trustees should not
   be excused from this national trend. They also need to be more
   informed and attentive to what is being taught on campus. Trustees should not be intimidated into believing that they are interfering with academic freedom if they behave like a real board and
   less like the adjunct fundraising department (their only purpose
   being to give and solicit donations).

8. Donors and alumni need to demand more accountability when
   they make gifts to higher education, both to help make universities be more efficiently managed organizations, and to help guide
   the educational mission. Donor intent is a key element in the
   American philanthropic system. Part of the contract between philanthropists and recipient institutions is that donors have something to say about how their money is used. Donations also give
   philanthropists the right to have a say in the operation of the organizations, especially for those who give large gifts. Higher education is perhaps the only NGO system where donors are told that

their giving offers them few rights to fundamentally influence the institution: write the check and keep quiet. Hands-off (in the name of academic freedom) is the general guideline. Naming chairs or designating dollars for a particular program provide the illusion of donor control, but most monies are fungible. In a system built around "budget relief," resources are moved around as needed: more resources in one area frees up money for some other purpose. But donors are not supposed to tamper with the intellectual component of the university. Collectively, donors should hold both faculty and administrators accountable for dealing with the issue of anti-Semitism and anti-Israelism on campus.

9. The public sector should continue to press for accountability as well. The story of the Solomon Amendment is an excellent example. Congress was correct to pass the Solomon Amendment to halt all federal funding to colleges and universities that prohibit military recruiters from coming to their campuses.[28] It is absurd for the grantee (higher education) to tell the grantor (the federal government) what policies must be followed by the armed services in order for universities to take the money that they are given. Whether one agrees or not with the "don't ask, don't tell" policy of the military is irrelevant. Congress has the right to set conditions on dollars it allocates to higher education. Universities have the right to refuse the funds if they do not agree with the conditions. They cannot take the funds and simultaneously set the conditions for taking them.

10. The Jewish community, including Jewish trustees, donors, faculty, students, alumni, and community organizations, needs to take more innovative action, in cooperation with other religious, ethnic, racial, and national groups, to address anti-Semitism and anti-Israelism. Anti-Semitism and anti-Israelism are closely linked with anti-Americanism. Addressing campus anti-Semitism and anti-Israelism needs to be a Jewish community priority. Relatively few resources currently are devoted to this purpose, given the magnitude of the problem. Increasing numbers of Americans attend college. More education and reduced prejudice have always been linked. It would be most unfortunate if a college education

led to increased anti-Semitism and anti-Israelism. The current approaches of the Jewish community need critical evaluation, both in terms of focus and scope.

RECLAIMING THE CIVIL UNIVERSITY

Social norms in society are as important as the rule of law. Civilizations exist through a combination of restraint by public authority, self-restraint, and restraint through social approval and disapproval. The politics of multiculturalism on campus abhor prejudice based on culture, sexual identity, ethnicity, gender, race, religion, and nationality. Yet, the ideological assault on Jewish nationalism is embedded in the ideology of the left, and as mystifying as it may be, the left sees no contradiction between its espousal of racial and ethnic equality and its prejudice against Jewish national identity. Because the university has become a home to rhetoric from the left, this hypocrisy has been successfully transplanted to higher education.

Changing campus norms can help reclaim a civil institution. Students or faculty who interrupt debates and lectures should be suspended or put on leave. Those who use violent messages or advocate violence should be expelled. Faculty who publish shoddy research should not be promoted. A faculty member who intimidates students or evaluates them on the basis of belief (the professor's or the student's) should be censured—and fired if they persist. Departments that discriminate on the basis of ideology either in terms of hiring or promotion should be put in receivership or shut down.

Societal support for higher education is grounded in the belief that democracy is reinforced by a good liberal arts education. Stanley N. Katz, director of Princeton University's Center for Arts and Cultural Policy Studies, warned of the need to reform higher education: "A great deal is at stake for undergraduate education, and for the country. If we believe, as so many of the founders of liberal education did, that the vitality of American democracy depends upon the kind of liberal education undergraduates receive, we need to put the reimagination of liberal education near the top of our agenda for education in our research universities."[29]

Americans cherish their institutions of higher education and are rightfully proud of their quality and world leadership. Students from around the United States and the rest of the globe make great sacrifices to study at

American universities, and they generally graduate well-positioned for successful careers and poised to make important contributions to society. The "something amiss in higher education" is not education itself, but rather the inappropriate politics that colors too much of campus life. The solution is not to balance one biased ideology with another but rather to eliminate politics altogether, except as a tool to teach students (and many faculty) to think for themselves.

Without essential reforms, the academy risks further and further separation from the public that nurtures it and whom it serves. "What is at stake is our future," according to Brigitte Gabriel, a Lebanese-born Arab reformer, "the students of today who will become tomorrow's leaders. If their minds are poisoned with irrational hatred and the hate is not combatted and eliminated, then academic freedom and free speech in an open marketplace of competitive ideas is dead."[30]

The stream of goodwill directed toward the university is not endless. It must be renewed through the visible efforts of the stakeholders to take more responsibility for ensuring the safety and well-being of all members of the university community. The campus must reform not because the specific ideologies of anti-Semitism and anti-Israelism exist, but rather because any public institution that fosters expressions of hate is in need of drastic change. Anti-Semitism and anti-Israelism have found a harbor on campus, but they need not remain welcome there. It took four decades for the uncivil university to reach this point. It should not take another forty years in this desert for the civil university to find its way home once more.

Chapter Eight

CONCLUSION TO THE REVISED EDITION

Higher education is one of America's greatest institutions. It embodies some of the fundamental aspects of our culture that make much of what the American people have created in this country so unique. Among these is the belief that an informed citizenry is an essential component of a thriving democracy. Another is a cherished commitment to meritocracy. Undergraduate and graduate degrees are gateways to economic advancement, regardless of the individual's or family's starting point. A third is part of our holding fast to freedom of ideas. We constitutionally protect freedom of expression to ensure open transfer of ideas and a spirited public debate. The unrestrained pursuit and transmission of ideas for the advancement of individual and social ability is central to higher education's mission in helping to create and shape an informed and ethical American citizenry. Do universities today reflect these ideals?

The relationship between colleges and universities and American society is reciprocal. Academia should be as much a reflection of the American society in which it was built and nurtured as American society is a reflection of the achievements of colleges and universities. Just as academia plays a role in helping American society to thrive and grow, so too does the general society play a key role in insuring a healthy university culture.

Reminders of the interdependence of higher education and the general society in which it has flourished are a necessity. For both those inside and outside academia, it is too easy, even desirable to believe that when we have created something so great it will remain so forever. In the case of colleges and universities, our tendency toward complacency is fed by higher education's demands for insularity, self-regulation, and self-evaluation. Indeed, universities pride themselves on their independence. They have taken the freedom to pursue ideas, labeled it "academic freedom," and transformed it into a catch-all phrase that really means "everyone keep out." The message is clear to all other segments of American society; students may attend, philanthropists may contribute, and government may monitor (within limits) its bountiful grants. However, attempts to question, probe, and evaluate mission, structure, quality, or governance are seen as intrusions or potential infringements upon academic freedom. The relationship has become hardly reciprocal at all—universities do not believe they have very much to learn from the American public and its other institutions.

Over the past few decades, particularly, the university has isolated itself from everyday America. How do universities decide what are the subjects are taught? What are the building blocks of curriculum? How are faculty selected and promoted? How are ideas developed and disseminated? In these realms, the mechanisms built to protect academic freedom have been turned into walls of seclusion and little if any outside advice is heeded. To be sure, certain interactions have grown. College sports have become huge businesses, attracting millions of attending fans and major media audiences.[1] University hospitals are another major entrepreneurial activity that mixes with millions of Americans (and paying customers around the world).[2] Higher education is engaged in all kinds of contract research with the corporate world developing products. And universities regularly provide talking heads for radio, television, and other media about politics, crime, and a host of other subjects.

Where universities have become fortresses is in their core mission: teaching and research. It is within these walls that faculty and administrators can run amok. Faculty tend to promote like-minded colleagues and sometimes allow scholarship to become secondary to what they call collegiality, that is people who "fit" into the dominant social culture and ideological like-mindedness.

Administrators often abdicate their responsibilities to provide moral leadership. Buffeted by tenured faculty, unionized labor, consumer-minded students, and the never-ending search for more money, university presidents, provosts, and deans struggle to keep their heads above water. They are driven to be placating managers rather than voices of leadership. Trustees, who believe it is an honor to serve the institutions from which they graduated, or the community where the college is located, often act as onlookers or cheerleaders, but shy from their role as the tough business overseers they should be.

The defensiveness of university administrators about fiscal responsibility and of faculty to external critique of their work is as strong as ever. Faculty have responded with actions such as the creation of the Ad Hoc Committee to Defend the University, which states, "This is not just a question of academic autonomy . . . Many of the most vociferous campaigns targeting universities and their faculty have been launched by groups portraying themselves as defenders of Israel."[3] Administrators, for their part, have fought tooth and nail against federal requirements that cap the often inflated rates of university grant overhead.[4] Just as efforts are made to make the academy more accountable, more efforts are made from within to reinforce the isolation of the university.

If Americans were oblivious in the past to the abuses that can result from unresponsiveness to outside examination, they are less so today. The high cost of higher education and its never ending upward spiral has become increasingly irritating to students and parents, to say nothing of the state and federal legislators who provide billions to colleges and universities.[5] This is especially troublesome when considering the extraordinary wealth of some colleges and universities. Public officials are raising tough questions about the accumulating funds in endowments.[6] And much of American society takes issue with faculty and administrators when they seem "elitist," somehow above ordinary citizens. It makes it seem that universities are "out of touch." Or worse, when faculty and administrators violate basic rules of fairness, and are unapproachable for redress, it appears that universities have created an alternative universe to American values.

The Duke University lacrosse team fiasco that unfolded in 2006 is a perfect example. A group of white male Duke lacrosse players were accused of sexually assaulting one of two black female exotic dancers they had hired for a party. The alleged victim's accusation was the only evidence and questions about the credibility of the accuser surfaced almost immediately. Yet a criminally overzealous prosecutor, Michael Nifong, all but declared the lacrosse players guilty.[7]

The Duke administration failed abysmally to defend the students' rights to due process or to even respect due process itself. Instead of protecting its own students, the university engaged in the lynch mob frenzy. Worse, some faculty and administrators led the mob. No, they *were* the mob. Duke cancelled the highly successful lacrosse team's season, fired the coach, and suspended the students without even an indictment from the district attorney. The faculty, though wielding less power than the administration to punish the boys, was arguably more irresponsible and even malicious by waging a campaign of demonization against them. It was as if the university simply couldn't resist what they considered a "teachable moment" about race and privilege in America that had presented itself. Stuart Taylor Jr. and KC Johnson wrote in their book, *Until Proven Innocent*:

> Academic ideals used to include dispassionate analysis of evidence and respect for due process. No more. In the lacrosse case, Duke's faculty not only failed to stand up for procedural regularity, but a substantial faction of it gleefully joined the rush to judgment. Those professors also clung to that judgment even after a mountain of evidence had proved it wrong. The activists and others determined to fit the university even more tightly into the straitjacket of political correctness saw the lacrosse scandal as the opportunity of a lifetime. The affair provided a chance to exploit the assumed (and never questioned) victimization of black women to skewer privileged white males as much because of who they were as because of what they (allegedly) had done.[8]

The real teachable moment, of course, should have focused on constitutional rights, innocent until proven guilty, and not meting out collective punishments for individual behavior. All of these were trampled and lost in the dominant political culture of Duke, far more concerned about race and gender politics than truth. Most of all, the vast majority of faculty were silent, either believing in the mob activities of the faculty who went after the boys, or too afraid and cowardly to speak up against their activist colleagues.

The damage that was done to the reputation and psyche of the accused students was inexcusable and perhaps irreparable. The university's role in steamrolling these students shocked the American public. But they should not have been surprised. Most people simply do not know how bad it can be inside the academic walls when it comes to fair play and the prejudices that exist among college faculty.

Was the Duke scandal an isolated incident? Not by any means. There are, for example, numerous instances of universities violating constitutional law by attempting to silence certain categories of speech. The busy offices of the Foundation for Individual Rights in Education attest to the misuse of speech codes and attempts to circumscribe individual free speech. FIRE president Greg Lukianoff remarked that it was shocking at times how blatantly unconstitutional some actions defended by administrations can be.[9]

Administrative abuse often includes punishment of students for actions and statements that are merely contrary to campus politics. One student interviewed for a film entitled *Indoctrinate U*, a humorous yet scathing indictment of the university today, found himself being put into the same box in which the Duke lacrosse players were tossed. The white male student at California Polytechnic State University was posting literature for an upcoming talk by African American author Clarence Mason Weaver in the Multi-Cultural Center. The pamphlet included a photo of the author and the title of his book on black economic empowerment, *It's OK to Leave the Plantation*. When other students complained, the administration summoned him to explain his actions. The offense? He was charged with being "a suspicious white male passing out literature of an offensive racial nature."[10] The university found him guilty of disrupting a campus event and was ordered to send letters apologizing for his behavior, attend a racial sensitivity meeting, and meet with a university counselor. The student explained that, "the university claimed that the students were so offended by the content of the flier that they couldn't have a Bible study they had scheduled for later that night."[11] The university formulated an unrelated, but punishable offense because, like Duke, it fit well into a racial paradigm accepted on many campuses. The accused student, like the lacrosse players, has since sued the university.[12] The university settled the lawsuit.[13]

Such revelations about how irresponsible and damaging colleges and universities can be are a surprise for some. But should they be? Not if one has been following the growing body of literature that details the biases that have come to dominate faculty and dictate the tenor of campus culture. Studies of faculty, including two published by the Institute for Jewish & Community Research in 2006, show that there is a 3 to 1 disparity in favor of the political Left overall and a 6 to 1 disparity in social sciences and humanities.[14] These studies also showed that faculty hold high levels of prejudice against Evangelical Christians. What does this mean and why is it problematic? Opposing views, novel ideas, vigorous debate, and solidly defended arguments are all victims of a faculty that lacks the intellectual and political robustness that results from difference and competition. When too many think too similarly, the worst aspects of the dominant ideology seem to float to the top. The result is an unhealthy university.

Just as conservative thought has its negative outliers, so too does liberal/progressive thought. Equality, racial sensitivity, and equal opportunity are central concerns of all Americans. But as embraced by the Left on campus they can also be exaggerated as a disdain for those deemed privileged, one of the essential lessons learned in the Duke case.

Groupthink is negative in most situations, but it is poisonous to academia. It is important to emphasize that it is the groupthink, not the ideology itself that is so troubling. If conservative faculty dominated the campus to the extent that liberal faculty do, the effect would be equally destructive. Of course there is little chance of that in the near future, since only 17 percent of faculty identify as conservative.[15] Like minds simply do not challenge, vet, and provoke each other as they should, especially in a system that is so highly dependent upon peer review to authenticate and legitimate scholarship and conduct.

The consequences of a university drowning in its own chorus of like-sounding voices are many and far reaching. Some are immediate. The focus of this book, the lack of civility on campus, especially as it concerns discussion of the Middle East and Israel, is at the core of the erosion of the principles of higher education. Teaching and research about Israel have become a battleground between those who wish to restore the sacred parameters of dispassionate scholarship and intellectual honesty, and those who wish to remain committed to free speech that is not free at all.

Americans rely upon colleges and universities to be incubators of both ideas and civil discourse. When they fail, important opportunities are lost for which there is no substitute. Administrators lose true teachable moments by remaining passive in the face of bigotry. They help shape many students' understanding of tolerance and intolerance. Standards of objectivity are essential, and the loss of these standards threatens the intellectual health of the nation as a whole. Low quality scholarship also becomes self-perpetuating, as new, less qualified faculty find their way into tenured positions and instruct their own students. The long-term impact of a selectively tolerant and academically compromised system of higher education is devastating to our nation.

As colleges and universities travel down this path, Israel advocates will not be the only ones singled out for ostracism or intimidation. Groups unlucky enough to find themselves outside the good graces of the campus political orthodoxy can just as easily become one of academia's "whipping boys." Breaking the rules of fair play open up many opportunities for mischief.

A university not committed to its own ideals of tolerance, civility, and academic integrity is a university that builds a hostile environment. Inevitably, so long as the academy itself emphasizes politicized scholarship instead of quality scholarship, the campus will suffer, and not only from the effects of anti-Semitism and anti-Israelism. Jewish students are neither the only, nor perhaps even the most significant victims of the erosion of campus ideals. Rather, Jewish students, in a familiar role for Jews throughout history, are the "canary in the coal mine." Campus intolerance in the name of free speech or progressive orthodoxy most deeply wounds academia itself and, by extension, American society as a whole.

UNDERSTANDING FREE SPEECH AND THE FUTURE OF HIGHER EDUCATION

Our universities are not supposed to be so weak that they can be bent to the will of a minority of faculty and activists. But their stability is rooted in the empirical nature of the work performed within their walls. When this is subverted and biased scholarship is given a pass, the university loses its identity. Nearly half of all faculty today agree the university is a counterweight to the politics of the nation.[16] This perception inherently undermines the foundation of academia by making the relevance of scholarship and campus activity dependent upon the political currents of the day. While the American political system shifts regularly, academia does not. Certainly political activity will continue to be a strong part of campus life, but it cannot be the determining factor in the identity of the university.

Free speech advocates, including authors of this book, do not suggest shutting down debate about the Middle East, including discussions about Israel. But universities do not exert enough moral leadership or administrative oversight to combat the bigotries on their campuses. In the name of academic freedom and impartiality, they are either idle or inadequate in their responses to prejudice. In doing so, they are supporting an environment that is fundamentally inconsistent with the overall tone, rules of conduct, and moral positions against racial, ethnic, religious, gender, and sexual prejudice in higher education. Universities have set their own standards in dealing with tolerance, intolerance, and acceptable norms of speech and behavior. If enforced uniformly, they would not permit the kind of prejudice expressed against Israel and Jews on campus. They violate their own rules over and over again when it comes to anti-Israelism and anti-Semitism.

The UnCivil University delves into the disconnect between the realities of universities today and their own stated ideals established by their founders, by administrations, and by faculty over time. It also explores the history of anti-Semitism and provides a detailed case study of the current existence of anti-Semitism and anti-Israelism in higher education. The intent of the book is to educate the reader and to alert American society in general about its need to take an active approach to how we interact with our colleges and universities.

A recurring point made is that higher education in America is a "public trust." It is funded through tax dollars, given special exemptions, and in general, is fundamentally intertwined and dependent upon the public sector and private individual contributions. This means that the American public not only has the right, but the obligation to engage in the national effort to ensure the excellence of American institutions of higher education.

Higher education has made something of a fetish of "free speech" and "academic freedom," using them interchangeably as a rallying cry for non-interference into the life of the academy. Academic freedom is supposed to mean pursuit of knowledge and the exploration of ideas. Now, any outside attempt to monitor, regulate, or evaluate is characterized by the university community as an attack on free speech, or more commonly, as going down some slippery slope that *might* lead to interference with academic freedom. There is no question that the danger of over-zealous critics can be real—that some want to stop or circumscribe debate. What has been lost on the staunch defenders of free speech is that the limits being set inside the university are far more repressive than anyone on the outside is likely to achieve.

Calls for good scholarship, open debate, civil discourse, and greater economic and moral responsibility should not be dismissed as an assault on free speech. The deflection on the part of higher education is tantamount to running away from its own inconsistent, illogical, and uncivil behavior. A whole host of issues requires closer examination of the identity of higher education. Why do tuition hikes always outpace rates of inflation?[17] Why are there more administrators than instructors?[18] Why do universities have no payout rules for endowments?[19] Why do liberals outnumber conservatives by 3 to 1 and 6 to 1 in many disciplines?[20] How does the sports industry within higher education further the moral value of colleges and universities?[21] Why do Christian groups often meet so much resistance?[22] These and many more questions cannot be stiff-armed with charges of abrogating free speech.

Speech codes, and other behavioral modifications imposed by faculty and administrators suppress ideas, strive for intellectual and social uniformity, and push everyone to fit into the dominant political culture. The focus upon racial and gender identity is one area of expected conformity, liberal political advocacy is another. As we state elsewhere, liberalism is not the problem. Rather, a dominant political culture of *any* kind threatens the health of higher education. The one-sided political norms of the campus result in the stifling of thought and limit the richness of research and teaching. Universities have done to themselves what they say they fear the most: imposed political restrictions on speech, and more critically on ideas.

If anyone has any question about the extent of this censorship, look at the fate of Lawrence Summers, former president of Harvard University. If Harvard is the flagship of higher education, the standard for quality, then the sacking of Summers provides a perfect microcosm of how censorship works inside the academic community. Summers suggested that men and women might have different intellectual talents, proclivities, and skills as one factor to explain why more men than women are found in the sciences. Maybe it is utter nonsense, but maybe it is a subject worth discussion. His comments created such a firestorm that he eventually lost his job. He could not raise the question. It was not open for discussion. It was too offensive and insensitive. Could the Hoover FBI witch-hunt for communists be more intimidating and stifling than the Harvard faculty? Not likely. Harvard is the exemplar—certain ideas can be discussed, others cannot.

Anti-Israelism is an accepted ideology on many campuses and too often leaches into blatant anti-Semitism. Using hateful images of Jews somehow falls within the boundaries of accepted free speech. The real issue, of course, is that most faculty and administrators are attuned to the groupthink of gender politics, but anti-Israelism does not violate any of the sacred cows on campus. Universities will defend anti-Israel ideology and activism as protected by academic freedom because the political majority either agrees with its ideas, or does not care enough to object to it. Academic freedom is a wonderful cover when needed, and ignored when convenient.

Colleges and universities should be consistent: real free speech or uniformly enforced codes that make all offensive ideas and comments off-limits. We advocate the former—true free speech, but within the bounds of intellectual honesty and civility.

What colleges and universities have forgotten is that academic freedom is a means to an end, not an end itself. Academic freedom provides the platform and latitude to enrich American and world society. It comes with responsibilities and expectations.

Free speech is one type of cherished speech, but there are others. Intelligent speech is just as important, ideas of merit and weight, based in fact, and accumulated knowledge. Honest speech is essential. Telling lies and cloaking them in historical or scientific method is appalling. Manipulating or fabricating debate is unacceptable. Civil speech is critical, exchanging ideas in a safe environment. Bad manners, intellectual intimidation, and physical harassment have no place in higher education.

The defense of anti-Israelism on campus always focuses on free speech, the right of Israel critics to speak out. We endorse the idea of Israel critics speaking out. Abrogating free speech is not the solution to anti-Israelism.

Maintaining the standards of intelligent speech, honest speech, and civil speech, however, are equally important. The same standards of scholarship that apply to economics and physics should be maintained for

Middle East studies, for example. The same rigor that applies to analyzing Milton and Shakespeare should be enforced for Walt and Mersheimer, whose paper, "Israel Lobby" fails any true scholarly scrutiny. Civility would put an end to "Apartheid Week's" fake weapons on campus.

Certainly, some activity on campus today should be shut down according to campus rules, including restricting Jewish or pro-Israel student access to campus events, violently protesting the arrival of Israeli or other guest speakers, and spreading libelous accusations that verge on incitement. However, the great majority of anti-Israel activity on campus should not be prohibited, but rather should be met with strident and clear responses from administrators and faculty. The university community should speak out as to why many assertions circulating on campus are factually wrong, and why certain forms of dissent are improper and ineffective ways to communicate sound ideas. More restrictions are not the answer; more rigor, honesty, and civility are required. The abdication of responsibility, moral cowardice, and double standards plague higher education. They have created the world that they feared the most.

Epilogue to the Revised Edition

Overview

Three years have passed since the first edition of *The UnCivil University* was published in 2005. The subject of the research, anti-Semitism and anti-Israelism in higher education, has continued to be at the center of highly politicized, passionate, and often vitriolic debate on and off campus. The expression of anti-Semitism and anti-Israelism on campus continues. Certain developments, both positive and negative, have taken place since the release of the first edition that necessitate continued examination.

Given our documentation of the extent of anti-Israelism on campus, its ongoing expression should not come as a surprise. Anti-Israel ideology and anti-Semitism in its politically couched forms continue to be tolerated by too many university administrations and excused by too many faculty. Demonization of Israel, and oftentimes the Jewish state's Jewish (and more and more frequently non-Jewish) advocates remains an acceptable area of "study" in some of the nation's institutions of higher learning. Events dedicated to the slander of an entire nation and speakers who espouse hateful views of Jews persist on campus. The failure to adequately confront these bigotries amounts to implicit approval by the universities themselves.

Anti-Israelists have continued to take advantage of higher education's vulnerabilities: bureaucratic paralysis, a political culture that abhors conflict, and the perversion of the concept and meaning of free speech. As a result, anti-Israelists have achieved significant gains over the past few years, especially in the realm of language and historical revisionism. The publishing of books and papers accusing Israel and Jews of dual loyalty and apartheid are having a strong effect on the normalization of anti-Israel language.

There have been positive developments over the past few years as well. The observations we made in 2005, along with a wealth of other work that supports our findings, have invigorated the debate about the place of higher education in America.[1] The lack of university accountability has been challenged by concerned citizens, public officials, and by academics themselves. This includes issues of fiscal mismanagement, ideological, religious, and political bias and the ways that endowments are utilized.[2]

Some administrative heads, (though not nearly enough) have taken strong and brave stances against anti-Israelism and anti-Semitism on campus, re-asserting their oft-neglected role as true moral and ethical leaders in the campus community. Some university leaders also have encouraged civility by beginning to enforce standard university rules more uniformly. Groups that attempt to intimidate other students or others that want to hold meetings on campus property that exclude others because of their religious or political views are being called to task.

A variety of financial boycott schemes against Israel have died on the vine over the past few years. The United States Commission on Civil Rights and the United States State Department have both adopted some form of language recognizing the problem of contemporary academic or political anti-Semitism.[3] New student, faculty, and citizen groups have developed both from within and outside the Jewish community, calling for more honesty and rejection of bigotry disguised as debate or inquiry. These are all good trends.

As we have previously asserted, the increase or decrease of "background noise" on campus, the number, frequency, and volume of anti-Israel events or anti-Semitic incidents tell only a part of the story. The acceptance of anti-Israel ideology, the violation of accepted campus norms, and the export of anti-Israelism from the campus into the general society and onto the international stage are much more important trends and measures of campus anti-Israelism and anti-Semitism. They are also symptoms of the deeper malaise of the university. The quality of scholarship, the willingness of administrations to lead, the norms of political discussion—these are the phenomena by which we can gain insight not only into what the campus was like last year, or this year, but what it might be like five or ten years down the line. More importantly, it tells us how campus ideology might affect other parts of society.

In this revised edition of *The UnCivil University*, we revisit some of the themes explored in the original analysis of anti-Israelism and anti-Semitism in higher education. We also look at positive developments that demonstrate moral courage and administrative responsibility that is too often lacking among campus leadership. In addition, we detail a number of types of responses to anti-Semitism and anti-Israelism on campus, from the federal to the Jewish communal level.

We detailed a variety of kinds of incidents in the first edition of *The UnCivil University*. These selected incidents were illustrative, not exhaustive. Many more events were catalogued, but not included in the book. The same choice guides this edition, to include a sampling of issues that illustrate the campus climate rather than to create a compendium.

Continued Expression of Anti-Semitism and Anti-Israelism on Campus

If the University of California, Berkeley or Columbia University once exemplified the toxic combination of anti-Israel vitriol and lackadaisical administrative responses, it is the University of California, Irvine that carries the banner today. Irvine has come under so much criticism that a lawsuit was filed by the Zionist Organization of America against the university for breaching the civil rights of Jewish students. The suit was dismissed by the Department of Education's Office of Civil Rights for what largely amounted to a rejection based on technicalities. The substance of the complaint was not really addressed and many within the Irvine Jewish community, as well as members of the Senate Judiciary Committee claim the process was more of an exercise than an investigation.[4] Amid these questions, the Office for Civil Rights has reopened the Irvine case.[5]

Among the original complaints was that a rock was thrown at a Jewish student wearing an "everybody loves a Jewish boy" shirt by someone at the Muslim Student Union table. Another claims a student approached and said "F--k Israel," while lowering his pants to reveal a swastika tattooed on his body. One non-Jewish student remarked, "A lot of the administrators . . . don't really want to pay attention. They kind of just want to ignore the issue. They are afraid of it. . . . the anti-Semitism on campus sort of, you know, run amuk [sic]."[6]

Former Irvine student Reut Cohen has devoted a blog to cataloguing the instances of anti-Semitism at UC Irvine. The blog features a number of videos she took of anti-Israel demonstrations in which protesters can be heard calling for the destruction of Israel and expressing support for terror abroad:

> Our weapon, our jihad, our way of struggling in this country is with our tongues. We speak out, and we deflate their morale, and this is the best we can do right now. And our brothers and sisters on the other side of the world, they're handling business in their own way. May Allah give them strength.[7]

Despite the Department of Education, Office of Civil Rights investigation, (or because of its first failure to vigorously pursue the case) anti-Israelists at UC Irvine show no signs of moderating their anti-Israel activity. In fact, the consortium of protest groups at Irvine quickly followed up a recent event in 2007 titled "Holocaust in the Holy Land" with "Never Again? The Palestinian Holocaust." Featured speakers included Norman Finkelstein, the notorious Holocaust revisionist who is routinely featured on anti-Israel panels to deflect accusations of anti-Semitism because he is a Jew. Also present was Amir Abdel Malik Ali, who insinuated Jews were behind the September 11th attacks,[8] and Imam Mohammed al-Asi, who was quoted saying "You can take a Jew out of the ghetto, but you cannot take the ghetto out of the Jew" at UC Irvine in 2001.[9]

Administrative double standards have compounded the actions of overzealous anti-Israel protesters. For example, when an "apartheid wall," set up by the Muslim Student Union on campus was set on fire, the administration issued a public condemnation. However, when vandalism marred a Jewish structure with swastikas, university officials made no equivalent statement. Moreover, when a rally for tolerance was held, Jewish groups who asked to be included were denied. University officials, including Manuel N. Gómez, vice-chancellor of student affairs, attended and spoke at the rally.[10] He did not, however, address the very real problem that a tolerance event excluded willing participants; something the administration would normally not allow.

Sally Peterson, Dean of Students, sums up the university position fairly well by saying, "This is an issue of free speech. Hate speech is also protected speech. . . . There's no law against being a jerk, basically."[11] She is right of course, but misses the point. Campus free speech allows people to be "a jerk." At the same time, what about Ms. Peterson's responsibility to note the university's disapproval of what jerks say, not merely point out their right to say it. She and others have the opportunity to explain why the speaker is being a jerk. She can teach something instead of make excuses. Vice Chancellor Gómez added that, though hate speech may be present, he would not seek to curtail it, as "one person's hate speech is another person's education."[12] Gómez was recently quoted saying that his words had been distorted. According to the Jewish Journal, ". . . students are protected constitutionally when their speech causes discomfort and even emotional pain, as long as it doesn't incite violence."[13] He still misses the essential point about his own moral responsibility to say what is right and wrong, even in the absence of impending "violence." His lack of moral leadership is even offensive. In a nod to relativism, he simply claims there are two sides to every story; a poor approach to dealing with bigotry.

Anti-Israel students at the University of California, Irvine have not only succeeded in sometimes bullying Jewish students, and seemingly the administration as well, they have been accused of harassing the FBI on campus. An FBI agent followed a truck driven by a member of the UC Irvine Muslim Student Union on his way to take down a mock "apartheid wall" as the Israeli barrier against terrorism is called on campus. As reported, the student confronted the car and called over a number of other students who were also at the wall. At that point, according to FBI spokesperson Laura Eimiller, the FBI agent "blew his siren and used the car's public address system to warn the group. At that point it was clear that this was a law enforcement vehicle. At least one person threw or placed a cinder block under the law enforcement vehicle." Presumably the students attempted to either, one, detain the vehicle by obstructing its path or, two, harm the driver. Either way, it is clear that the students felt emboldened enough to obstruct a law enforcement vehicle and its occupant without fear of reprisal. Rightly so, too, because there was not even a university attempt to reprimand, much less charge any student with an unlawful act.[14] Perhaps they felt the charge was unsubstantiated, and could not find enough evidence.

On the other side of the country, Rutgers University played host to one of the Palestinian Solidarity Movement's annual anti-Israel extravaganzas in 2003 and has been in the news for a variety of anti-Israel and now anti-Semitic activities. Jewish students have reported menacing conversations outside their homes about "where the Jews live," windows being broken at a Jewish house, being called a "Kike" and seeing Nazi anti-Semitic caricatures placed over Hillel posters on campus. One student, Eytan Morgenstern, who wears a kippah, heard himself referred to as a "f—king Jew."[15] What does it mean when a university with 3,000 Jewish students fails to make some feel that they are safe?

Columbia University was previously the focus of a documentary film, *Columbia Unbecoming*, which focused criticism on Columbia's Middle East and South Asian Languages and Cultures Department for harassment against Jewish students.[16] An investigation into the department yielded a report that essentially whitewashed the problem. Almost every case reported by students was denied by the offending faculty and therefore dismissed by the administration, which conceded only that avenues for student complaints could be better.[17] Ignoring the problem, however, did not make it go away.

In November of 2007, a Jewish Columbia-Barnard University professor, Elizabeth Midlarsky, discovered a swastika spray-painted on her office door. This incident came following what she claims was a week of mailings to her and another colleague supporting Holocaust denial, containing literature also found on campus. Professor Midlarsky was quoted saying, "It's been a very strange month. Who would have thought that there'd be a swastika on a Jewish professor's door?"[18] Unfortunately, her incredulity is perhaps at odds with her own observations about anti-Semitism at Columbia, "There have been numerous occasions when one or more Jewish students came to me crying, upset." And in response to Columbia's hosting of Iranian President Mahmoud Ahmadinejad, "It underscores the openness at Columbia to speakers who are openly anti-Jewish."[19] The vandal also "X-ed" out the professor's name on her door. She has accepted police escort after dark.

While one might think that Columbia would make an attempt to curtail the animosity and hostility on campus, it has instead chosen to grant tenure to one of the more academically questionable and vocal Israel-obsessed scholars (which we distinguish from those engaging in legiti-

mate and well reasoned intellectual critiques of Israeli government policies). Nadia Abu El-Haj is a Palestinian American anthropologist who
writes on Israeli archeology and genomics and has devoted much of her
work to academic smearing of Israel. Alan F. Segal, a professor of religion
and Jewish studies at Barnard said that, "There is every reason in the world
to want her to have tenure, and only one reason against it—her work, I
believe it is not good enough."[20] Professor Elizabeth Midlarsky also
remarked about El-Haj, "Her scholarship is far from excellent. My understanding was that at Barnard only the best and brightest are tenured."[21] El-
Haj's tenure approval is disturbing on a number of counts. Not only is the
quality of her work considered highly questionable, she is yet another
political clone added to the ranks of anti-Israel faculty at Columbia.

Another New York campus underscores the erosion of tolerance on
campus toward Jews. In 2005, the Hunter College Palestinian Club posted
a sign showing the Star of David morphing into a swastika, and reading:
"History Repeats: Look What Hitler Taught Some of His Victims."[22] The
desecration of the Israeli flag and the Star of David by superimposing a
swastika upon it is a familiar feature of anti-Israel activities. It is not hard
to see how such symbols can open the door to openly hateful attacks.
When swastikas and Nazi comparisons are used on campus to condemn
Israel and Jews, and when the Holocaust is attacked as a false or fabricated
excuse for the establishment of Israel, it is easy to imagine that one person's hatred might be laid at the door, literally, of a professor published on
the Holocaust. Of course, free speech allows such expression and should.
On the other hand, what do campus administrators at Hunter College
teach about intolerance? Hold symposia? Special days on the use of hateful symbols? Or just reiterate the right of free speech?

Tolerating hateful "political" activity is a necessity, but the lack of
appropriate moral and intellectual counterweights can encourage religious intolerance. In Northern California, two sukkahs, which are strictly
religious Jewish symbols, on two campuses were vandalized over the
span of a couple of weeks in the spring of 2007. At the University of California, Davis, a sukkah was defaced with anti-Israel graffiti including,
"End Israeli Occupation" on a blank wall, and "Free Palestine" scrawled
across a sign wishing passersby a "Happy Sukkot." During the previous
week, a sukkah outside the Hillel house of San José State University was
set on fire.[23] Either anti-Israel activists find it appropriate to attack a reli-

gious symbol for political purposes, or the lowering of norms of religious tolerance on campus has invited open religious hatred to the campus. Either is unacceptable.

The lack of moral guidance in higher education often extends deeper, affecting campus organizations that play a large part in setting the tone of a campus, particularly university newspapers. A cartoon was published in an October 2007 edition of the University of Arizona at Tuscon newspaper the *Arizona Daily Wildcat* that promoted the stereotype of Jews being "cheap." The caption on the cartoon read, "Attention all crappy tipping Jews!!! Just because you're 'screwing' the server . . . does not mean that it's a mitzvah." Editorial decisions by campus newspapers on what to publish and how to frame what they do publish has been an ongoing issue, as noted in earlier chapters. Some seem to be the result of ignorance on the part of the author or artist, others are not so easily explained. But these excuses do not apply to the papers themselves when all content is reviewed, or is supposed to be.[24]

Editorials penned by the newspaper staff themselves can lead to serious concern about the management of student papers. In response to the Palestine Solidarity Movement Conference at Duke University in 2004, Phillip Kuiran, an editor for Duke's campus newspaper, *The Chronicle*, authored an op-ed entitled "The Jews." The article accused Jews of exploiting the events of the Holocaust to stifle political debate and detailing the "shocking overrepresentation" of Jews on college campuses. He wrote that, "what Jewish suffering—along with exorbitant Jewish privilege in the United States—amounts to is a stilted, one-dimensional conversation where Jews feel the overwhelming sense of entitlement not to be criticized or offended."[25]

Speaking of opposition to the Palestinian Solidarity Movement, Kurian wrote, "it is impossible to ignore the unprecedented outpouring of pro-Jewish, pro-Israeli support in defiance of free speech at Duke. Jewish alumni, faculty and staff have gone out of their way to lobby Duke to reject the PSM conference, mustering 92,000 signatures for their online petition . . ." What Kurian sees as a concerted effort to stifle free speech, others would characterize as exercising their own free speech to condemn what they find objectionable. His rejection of the opinions of thousands of concerned community members is unfortunately indicative of many responses to the efforts of the Jewish community and others to protest bigotry on campus. Oddly, Kurian, in effect, is calling for the denial of others' right to free speech. And his opposition to the Jewish community making their views known stands in stark contrast to his assertion that he "would probably let the Ku Klux Klan hold a conference on campus."[26] This double standard is too often applied. The Jewish communal response to anti-Semitism and shoddy scholarship on the Middle East has often been met with accusations of stifling academic freedom/freedom of speech. The hypocrisy of the argument is evident: the expression of distaste for occurrences on campus is an exercise of free speech itself.

There have been repeated instances of editorial boards and their faculty advisors not only being woefully unaware of what their paper is printing, but actually approving and adding to the bigotry of some pieces. Though the impact of hateful articles or cartoons on campus is important, what is also deeply disturbing is that campus papers can often be reflective of the culture in journalism departments at some schools. Journalism departments should be held to an even higher standard of excellence because they are responsible for turning out the future watchdogs of government and society in general. This function is integral to a viable and healthy democracy and requires an exceptional level of objectivity.

Newspapers have the right to print offensive items, though their decisions to do so also are open to critique. At the same time, universities have an obligation to teach when cartoons or other items are bigoted. Of course, just because something is offensive does not mean it is bigoted. But such discussions are more vital than merely crying "free speech" anytime a question of propriety is raised.

Though the incidents discussed here are by no means exhaustive, they serve to remind readers that the problems of anti-Semitism and anti-Israelism persist. Media interest, student reporting, global events, and other factors affect how much we hear, or don't hear about what is going on at colleges and universities almost as much as any real up tick or downturn in anti-Semitic or anti-Israel activity. What should be troublesome to all is that we continue to see egregious cases occur.

Pseudo-Intellectual Anti-Semitism—"The Israel Lobby"

John Mearsheimer, the R. Wendell Harrison Distinguished Service Professor of Political Science at the University of Chicago, and Stephen Walt, The Robert and Rene Belfer Professor of International Relations at the Kennedy School of Government at Harvard University coauthored in 2006 a paper titled, *The Israel Lobby and U.S. Foreign Policy*.[27] The paper's central thesis contends that, "the United States has been willing to set aside its own security in order to advance the interests of another state [Israel]." This position, the authors claim, is driven by a "loose coalition of individuals and organizations who actively work to steer U.S. foreign policy in a pro-Israel direction."

Walt and Mearsheimer's argument is a fancied up and academically couched age-old accusation against Jews of dual loyalty. The paper, originally commissioned by the *Atlantic Monthly*, demonstrated a distressingly low level of academic rigor. The magazine declined to publish it.[28] Harvard's Kennedy School of Government also removed its official logo from the paper, not wanting to put the status of its research reputation behind the Walt/Mearsheimer piece.[29] Despite the obvious politically motivated nature of the paper and its poor scholarship, it was published as a book in 2007 and Walt and Mearsheimer have enjoyed a level of celebrity status from this work, particularly among anti-Israel activist groups and even in the Arab world.[30]

Regardless of the questionable quality of the essay, the institutions the two faculty represent give the research ill-deserved weight and legitimacy. The professors' paper is used as evidence by anti-Israelists about Jewish control in Washington and an excuse for why most Americans support Israel.[31] Moreover, it plays upon a dangerous depiction of Jews as a power hungry and manipulative community. Yet the authors assert that their goal is to promote progress on the Middle East issue. Historian Walter Russel Mead notes that, "rarely in professional literature does one encounter such a gap between aspiration and performance as there is in The Israel Lobby."[32] The authors have failed to help at all.

Former President Jimmy Carter

Former president Jimmy Carter's book, *Palestine: Peace Not Apartheid*, is damaging on campuses for similar reasons: it is relied upon as important proof of the claims anti-Israelists make against Israel.[33] In his book, Carter lays the blame for the Israeli-Palestinian conflict directly at Israel's feet, writing that, "Israel's continued control and colonization of Palestinian land have been the primary obstacles to a comprehensive peace agreement in the Middle East."[34]

Intellectual criticism of the book has been widespread, just as it was against the Walt-Mearsheimer paper, and led to the resignation of fifteen protesting members of the Board of Councilors of the Carter Center: "We are deeply troubled by the President's comments and writings and are submitting the following letter of resignation to the Carter Center."[35] A host of reviewers have pointed to a variety of inaccuracies, many of which call into question either the veracity of the information in the book or the bias of the author himself. Dennis Ross, the lead negotiator at the Camp David negotiations in 2000, wrote in a *New York Times* op-ed, "Mr. Carter's presentation badly misrepresents the Middle East proposals advanced by President Bill Clinton in 2000, and in so doing undermines, in a small but important way, efforts to bring peace to the region." Ross specifically points out that Carter used maps Ross himself published and labeled them misleadingly, "perpetuating a myth about what was offered to justify the Arafat rejection of the peace agreement."[36]

Carter's actions following his book have reinforced the concerns of many. He has toured promoting his book while also attacking those who question its assertions. The impact of Carter's book on college campuses cannot be understated. He canonized the accusation of Israel as apartheid that was baptized on university campuses in 2000. And he has also given credence to the practice of misrepresenting history to suit political goals by engaging in it himself. Carter's book has led to speaking engagements at Brandeis University and Mansfield College, Oxford, as well as the receipt of the first Albert Schweitzer Humanitarian Award at Quinnipiac University in Hamden, Connecticut.[37]

Perhaps more disturbingly, Carter has reinserted himself into the Middle East conflict by unilaterally meeting with Hamas, an officially listed terrorist organization that the United States has deliberately attempted to marginalize in favor of the Palestinian Authority.[38] He returned from the meetings asserting that Hamas is a legitimate peace partner that would recognize Israel, while at the same time Hamas leader Khaled Meshaal rejected any such idea.[39] Either Carter is lying for Hamas to the West while Hamas tells the opposite to the Middle East, or Carter is shockingly unwilling to accept what Hamas itself declares. One way or the other, some damage is already done. It is consistent with the quality of his book.

No matter the absurdity of his actions, Carter is a former U.S. president and his use of the term "apartheid" in reference to Israel has legitimized the comparison and furthered the inherent condemnation more than any professor could have done. His book is referenced often by anti-Israelists who have been labeling Israel an apartheid colonizer for years.[40] He has played a significant role in normalizing slander against Israel, even if the factual accuracy of his arguments is refuted.

In the aftermath of the Lebanon War in 2006 and the revelation that a number of journalists' photos had been altered to show a more menacing and hostile Israel, a phrase began circulating on the internet, "fake but accurate," along with the tongue-in-cheek term, "truthiness," to refer to distorted information that, when exposed, is still defended as accurate.[41] Carter's book is a significant addition of the many pieces of anti-Israel propaganda that are far from reliable, but are relied upon nevertheless. It has considerable currency on campus because the words of a former president can paint an unfounded argument with a veneer of credibility.

Boycotts

It is also important, in analyzing the tenor of campuses and state of academia in America, to take some note of developments abroad. There have been, and continue to be, repeated attempts to institute academic boycotts against Israeli scholars and students, many of them originating in the United Kingdom. The institutional boycotts have yet to succeed and even produced important government action to counteract their effect.[42] Their impact, however, is not limited to their implementation, but how the debate about Israel is framed. The taint of illegitimacy lingers. Moreover, individual programs or scholars have been able to discriminate against some Israeli scholars. Israel is the lone target of academic boycotts. Neither the Sudan, Burma, China nor any other nation faces any real effort to boycott its scholars.

Language has been at the heart of many of the attacks against Israel in academia. If certain universally deplorable terms can be effectively linked to Israel, then the condemnation that these terms bring automatically transfers to Israel. Apartheid and Nazism are the two most frequently forwarded descriptors when criticizing Israel. Alan Dershowitz made the argument that the divestment campaign, which has been rejected as a university financial policy, was always more dangerous and more focused on the normalization of certain language and attitudes toward Israel.[43] The boycott, like divestment, is, in many ways, an attempt to superimpose the identity of apartheid South Africa onto modern day Israel. To a certain extent, this effort has been successful.

The most recent attempt to institute an academic boycott has been promoted by Britain's University and College Union (UCU) which bills itself as, "the largest trade union and professional association for academics, lecturers, trainers, researchers and academic-related staff working in further and higher education throughout the UK."[44] UCU voted to circulate and promote the Palestinian boycott against Israeli universities in 2007. However, the motion was put on hold when their lawyers informed them that such actions would be deemed discriminatory and therefore illegal.[45] Though the fact that the UCU allowed the boycott resolution to go as far as it did (and it is still simply on hold) is deplorable, it is likely that the vote was an example of how the processes of an organization can be hijacked by the most active and politicized members. UCU press officer, Dan Ashley, stated: "As I have made clear in the past, and as I reiterated on the floor of congress this morning, I do not believe a boycott is supported by the majority of UCU members, nor do I believe that members see it is a priority for the union."[46] Though the UCU likely already knew that a boycott would be illegal and that its members do not support it, the fact that it passed speaks volumes about how concerted efforts by the minority can effectively direct the course of action for a much larger body. It should be expected that similar attempts could continue abroad and at universities in the United States.

Campus tension rises and falls. One year may see a high level of protest and another a more subdued campus community. This tells us something about anti-Israelism on campus, but not everything. The Walt-Mearsheimer paper and Carter's book are more damaging than hundreds of conferences against Israel. Academic boycotts against Israel abroad give some insight into how the political culture of organizations can be utilized for anti-Israel prejudices. The question remains, which way is American academia heading?

ADMINISTRATIVE PROGRESS

There is ample evidence to support a pessimistic view of American higher education and its relationship to Israel and the Middle East conflict. But there is also evidence to the contrary. Although many American university administrators continue their flight from moral leadership in dealing with anti-Israelism, there have been some positive actions taken that illustrate how effectively, and sometimes easily, a university administration might impact the campus environment and academia in general. Two core areas of administrative action are discussed in this section: moral authority and faculty hiring and firing.

Moral Authority

Campuses will always have outliers. Incidents that test the limits of acceptability and tolerance are part of the life of academe. University administrators, presidents, provosts, deans, and others can take a leadership role either formally or informally in providing moral guidance. Of course, it is not their role alone. Faculty, alumni, and trustees must all do so. As in any organization, however, CEOs and other top managers set the tone.

The unwillingness of many administrators to play a leadership role has opened the door for much of the offensive behavior exhibited on campus today. Others have bucked the trend. It is important to continue to hold administrators accountable when they take the wrong stance or none at all in the face of violations of university rules, poor scholarship, and uncivil behavior. But it is equally important to recognize their successes. The actions of Lee Bollinger stand out, especially considering the fact that his university's Middle East and Asian Languages and Cultures department is among the most politicized in the country.

The World Leader's Forum at Columbia University invited Iranian President Mahmoud Ahmadinejad to speak on campus in September of 2007.[47] This invitation was widely criticized throughout the United States.[48] This is understandable, but it should be recognized that the invitation came from the university's faculty, which includes some of the nation's most active anti-Israel academics. Bollinger might have been able to block the invitation, though the power of the faculty should not be underestimated. He would have been soundly upbraided for abrogating free speech. The unhealthy distribution of power in the university means that the faculty could have called for and perhaps had his head, à la Lawrence Summers at Harvard. Bollinger chose not to engage in a battle about faculty rights, which would likely not have been fruitful. Instead he decided to express his condemnation of the Iranian president when he introduced him. The faculty who invited Ahmadinejad had their academic freedom. So did the university president. He chose to make the visit a "teachable moment."

Bollinger began by setting the tone of his remarks with, "Let's, then, be clear at the beginning, Mr. President you exhibit all the signs of a petty and cruel dictator." President Bollinger continued on to chastise the Iranian president for his oppression of scholars and activists, his denial of the Holocaust, his calls for the destruction of Israel, funding of terrorism, and nuclear aspirations. He ended with a statement that highlights the sensitive and difficult position presidents of universities such a Columbia find themselves in: "I am only a professor, who is also a university president, and today I feel all the weight of the modern civilized world yearning to express the revulsion at what you stand for. I only wish I could do better."[49]

The truth is that Bollinger was somewhat late to the game. His campus should never have insisted on the right to hear Ahmadinejad speak, not because they do not have the right to do so, but because they should have been demanding to hear from any one of the thousands of possible speakers who would have brought something meaningful and intelligent to Columbia. But Bollinger did nevertheless show up and reclaimed the moral authority so many university presidential offices have abdicated. Not since former Harvard president Lawrence Summers has a president so clearly exercised his power from the bully pulpit. Was Bollinger rude to his guest? Perhaps. Did he change Middle East politics? No. Did he teach the Columbia community and all those who covered the event about issues of right and wrong, good and bad, and the need to confront bigotry? He did.

And he did not stop there. In response to the proposed boycott of Israel by British University professors, Bollinger asserted that "if the British UCU is intent on pursuing its deeply misguided policy, then it should add Columbia to its boycott list, for we do not intend to draw distinctions between our mission and that of the universities you are seeking to punish. Boycott us, then, for we gladly stand together with our many colleagues in British, American and Israeli universities against such intellectually shoddy and politically biased attempts to hijack the central mission of higher education."[50] His unambiguous repudiation of a boycott against Israelis was then turned into a statement published in the *New York Times* signed by 300 other university presidents.

Bollinger's statements speak for themselves and it is hard to deny that he has taken up the challenge of restoring the leadership role of the university president. But he is no saint. Some of the problems he is facing are of his own (or his administration's) doing, or lack of doing earlier on. The political nature of Middle East studies needs addressing at Columbia. Shoddy scholarship and propaganda masquerading as honest intellectual inquiry needs to be better managed.

Bollinger's actions are a beginning. His situation, however, does shed some light on the difficulties a university administrator faces and is high-lighted by the many complaints he also received (many from his own faculty) for being "rude" to an invited world leader.[51] Whichever way one chooses to look at Bollinger's recent actions, he is at least being responsive.

San Francisco State University president Robert Corrigan also deserves a great deal of credit for how his campus has moved forward following what could be regarded as some of the ugliest anti-Israel incidents in the country. He has been exemplary on condemning anti-Semitism and set-ting the tone for his campus. SFSU was the location of both the distribu-tion of flyers accusing Jews of canning Palestinian baby meat and a riot against a Jewish peace rally at which students reportedly chanted "Hitler should have finished the job." In the years following those incidents, Cor-rigan has, publicly and internally, sought to repudiate hostile and aggres-sive methods for political protest on campus and worked to instill a sense of respectful, if still highly charged, dialogue.[52] Compare this to Irvine's Chancellor Drake who has yet to make a clear enough statement on cam-pus about anti-Semitism, sticking more to general condemnations of all forms of hate speech.[53]

Most cases require little more than an administrator doing his or her job well. The University of Southern California provost, Chrysostomos L. Max Nikias, banned the use of a hadith, or Islamic teaching, that calls for the murder of Jews on the university's Muslim Student Association web-site. The hadith states: "The last hour would not come unless the Muslims will fight against the Jews and the Muslims would kill them until the Jews would hide themselves behind a stone or a tree and a stone or a tree would say: Muslim, or the servant of Allah, there is a Jew behind me; come and kill him. . . ." Provost Nikias, alerted to the hadith on university servers by a USC trustee, called it "despicable" and ordered it removed. This trustee did what too many trustees no longer see as their role: paying attention and engaging in the social culture of the university.[54] And the provost did his job.

The uncivil university extends across the border to Canada. York and Concordia universities have been closely linked to the trends on American college campuses and have therefore been included in our analyses. These two universities were sites of mob violence in protest against Israeli politicians and supporters coming to speak and their administrations were roundly criticized for not being able to secure a safe environment for Jews. The hostility, however, eventually turned inward in 2006 when calls were made to oust Jewish members of the York University Foundation for their "Israel connection." The calls originated from a heavily anti-Israel Jewish professor, David Noble. Noble authored a pamphlet titled, "The York University Foundation: The tail that wags the dog" and accused the foundation of being "biased by the presence and influence of staunch pro-Israel lobbyists, activists, and fundraising agencies."[55] Noble accused Jewish community members and Jewish members of the York University Foundation for conspiring to arrest pro-Palestinian students and defraud the university. Noble is likely referring to attempts by the York Foundation members to encourage the administration to act against the worst perpetrators of violence on campus, which the administration should have done anyway.

The university appropriately reprimanded Professor Noble for targeting individual Jews as enemies of the university. Of course, this only endeared him to anti-Israel student groups. The student groups Solidarity for Palestinian Human Rights [SPHR], the Arab Collective and Grassroots Anti-Imperialist Network at York University held a rally calling for the "Israel lobbyists" to be removed from the foundation. SPHR stated in a press release that, "We emphatically support Professor Noble and other like-minded and open-minded professors . . ."[56] In fact, Noble was so emboldened that he sued the university for defamation, asking for $10 million. Due to the university's failure to contact him before the public denunciation, an arbitrator ruled that the university must pay a fine, rejecting Noble's financial claims and his demands for an apology.[57] Though the administration may have erred in its process, it was correct in its intent.

The University of California, Riverside was supposed to host the 2006 Annual Palestinian Solidarity Conference. However, the organizers themselves chose to move off campus after the administration insisted university rules be followed. Namely, according to Stop the ISM (International

Solidarity Movement), a group devoted to lobbying against hosting the annual conference, the conference organizers would have to accept campus security rather than their own, allow filming of the conference, and ensure equal access to attendees, including pro-Israel students.[58] Though it seems simple, at past conferences on other campuses, clear demands were not made to follow university guidelines. As a result, numerous complaints of harassment and exclusion were made. Riverside's clarification was enough for the PSM organizers to move the conference to a nearby hotel. This is an example of the ability administrators have to influence what occurs on campus without inserting themselves into a highly charged debate, or abrogating free speech. Indeed, they were demanding free speech, open access, and normal journalist presence. They were also ensuring the safety of the campus. Demanding free speech, civility, and safety was enough to drive the organizers away.

Dealing with Low-Quality Faculty

Part of the heightened debate about higher education has been an increasing examination of the quality of the professoriate. Are professors teaching effectively? Is their research useful and methodologically sound? Do they enrich or detract from the campus environment? Many approach these questions from different perspectives. David Horowitz, a strident critic of liberal dominance in higher education published a book, *The Professors: The 101 Most Dangerous Academics in America*.[59] Horowitz is certainly the most extreme critic, and uses the most disruptive and media capturing tactics, but he is not alone in his criticism of the actions and quality of faculty on many college campuses. Others include Anne Neal from American Council of Trustees and Alumni; author, historian, and classicist Victor Davis Hanson of the Hoover Institution; and Daniel Pipes, founder of Middle East Forum and Campus Watch.[60]

Faculty have responded in kind to the elevated scrutiny of their work, largely by crying foul and, in turn, accusing those who question their objectivity of attempting to deny academic freedom. The American Association of University Professors (AAUP) released a statement in 2007, "Freedom in the Classroom," written by the committee on Academic Freedom and Tenure.[61] The statement expressly defends the right of faculty, to, more or less, do as they wish in the classroom. In reaction to criticism of faculty for instructing out of their realm of expertise, the statement "defends the right of college faculty to make comparisons, contrasts, and analogies across a whole range of subjects and historical periods—no matter what course they are teaching." Cary Nelson, AAUP president tellingly explained that the statement would allow professors to tell critics, "You shouldn't mess with me."[62]

A similar statement was issued by the "Ad-Hoc Committee to Defend the University" in 2008.[63] One of the five organizers is Jonathan Cole, who has drawn repeated protest for what some consider to be politicized and low quality scholarship. The statement goes further than that of the AAUP and directly fingers defenders of Israel's right to exist as the primary threat to universities. It states that universities have been "targeted by outside groups seeking to influence what is taught and who can teach. . . . many of the most vociferous campaigns targeting universities and their faculty have been launched by groups portraying themselves as defenders of Israel.[64] The Ad-Hoc Committee paints all defenders of Israel as close-minded and anti-intellectual, a nearly exact mirror of the complaints made by Israel supporters against the faculty themselves.

A defensive and aggressive faculty has largely kept administrators at bay. Long protracted and public battles with faculty who are quick to denounce the administration as a tool of political interests are unsavory and have largely been avoided. But the presence of marginally rigorous and politicized faculty has become as much a problem for administrators as attempting to get rid of them. As a result, some universities have dismissed faculty who were undeserving of tenure or who violated academic rules of conduct.

Norman Finkelstein, the now infamous son of Holocaust survivors who has devoted his work to Holocaust critique and criticism of Israel, had been involved in an extended dispute over tenure with his employer, DePaul University. In June of 2007, Finkelstein was denied tenure and dismissed by the university.[65] Charles Suchar, dean of DePaul's college of Liberal Arts and Sciences, who recommended against tenure said "the personal attacks in many of Dr. Finkelstein's published books . . . border on character assassination and, in my opinion, . . . embody a strategy clearly aimed at destroying the reputation of many who oppose his views."[66] Though Finkelstein declared his intent to teach his courses regardless of the university's decision in an act of "civil disobedience," Finkelstein and the university reached a settlement that led to his official resignation. Despite the attempts to frame Finkelstein as a victim of an attack on academic freedom, his denial of tenure and cessation of teaching activities was done within the accepted rules of tenure decisions: his scholarship was judged to be sub-par by his peers.[67]

Ward Churchill, infamous for his declaration that the victims of the World Trade Center bombings were "little Eichmanns," was also denied tenure by the University of Colorado. Among the reasons for his denial was substantial evidence of scholarly improprieties, including plagiarism.[68] Nevertheless, his supporters declared a witch hunt, claiming he was being persecuted for his political views outside the classroom. Hank Brown, president of the university, said in an interview, "This was someone who created fraudulent research and was caught. The universities efforts were focused solely around that."[69] The board voted 8–1 in favor of denial of tenure and adamantly defended their decision as one based entirely on the merit of his scholarship, or lack thereof, rather than on his political statements.[70]

Although both Finkelstein and Churchill both responded to the decisions of their respective universities with defiant declarations that they would continue to teach their courses, both ended up effectively removed from their respective campuses.

Wadie Said, son of the late Columbia professor Edward Said, was a candidate for a position at Wayne State University Law School. Said represented one of Sami Al-Arian's codefendants accused of leading a branch of Palestinian Islamic Jihad.[71] Some also questioned his scholarship and qualifications for the job. In a student interview, he declared, reminiscent of his father's politicization of his professorship, that he would use his position to try to change the university's stance against divestment from Israel.[72] Wayne State University ended up choosing to look elsewhere for a more qualified candidate, despite pressure that framed a choice not to hire Said as nothing more than a political decision. Wayne State proved to be unyielding to political correctness in its defense of academic integrity. The University of South Carolina, however, has since offered him a position.[73]

Kevin Barrett was a lecturer at the University of Wisconsin, Madison when he founded the organization, Muslim-Jewish-Christian Alliance for 9/11 Truth. He has argued that the tapes of Osama bin Ladin were fabricated by the CIA, adding that, "the 9/11 report will be universally reviled as a sham and cover-up very soon."[74] Despite his "9/11 truth" work, a university review decided he was fit to teach the course "Islam: Religion and Culture" which elicited a number of complaints, from community members to representative Steve Nass who said, "Barrett has got to go. It is an embarrassment for the state of Wisconsin. It is an embarrassment for the university."[75] Though the university did uphold his one-semester contract to teach the course,[76] in an uncharacteristic lack of fanfare, he was not invited to return the next semester. Perhaps Barrett's antics went so far beyond the pale that other academics were not willing to come to his defense—despite the fact that it was again community uproar that forced the administration's hand. The question must be asked: Would he still be teaching if not for the criticism from outside the university?

INSTITUTIONAL AND COMMUNAL RESPONSES

It would be reassuring if positive actions taken by administrators were solely the result of the initiative of a university president or dean tackling offensive anti-intellectualism. In some cases, this may certainly be the case. But administrators are also faced with growing communal and governmental responses to anti-Israelism in academia that in some cases force the hand of a normally tepid administration. Alternative faculty associations created to challenge politicized existing associations, federal recognition of the problem of anti-Semitism in higher education, and a slew of Jewish and non-Jewish organizations challenging the campus status quo place increasing onus upon administrative heads to take a stand against intolerance.

Association for the Study of the Middle East and Africa

The "overhaul" of Middle East Studies in America that Martin Kramer outined in his book, *Ivory Towers on Sand*, and that we touched upon as well, includes the Middle East Studies Association. MESA is the primary national organization devoted to Middle East Studies and has been criticized for failing to provide important research and teaching while devoting much of its time to lambasting Israel and all the while tolerating shoddy scholarship.[77] In response to the co-optation of MESA into the anti-Israel or pro-Arab/Muslim movement, two eminent scholars of the Middle East, Fouad Ajami and Bernard Lewis, have established an alternative association. The Association for the Study of Middle East and Africa (ASMEA) is, "a new academic society dedicated to promoting the highest

standards of research and teaching in Middle Eastern and African studies, and related fields. It is a response to the mounting interest in these
inter-related fields, and the absence of any single group addressing them
in a comprehensive, multi-disciplinary fashion."[78] It is encouraging that
some scholars are devoted enough to their field and to the principles of
good scholarship that they would take it upon themselves to provide a
forum for honest inquiry, but disturbing that the need for a new association developed at all. One would have hoped that most faculty would have
spoken up to bring some semblance of balance to MESA, but it has simply
become another forum for groupthink.

The U.S. Commission on Civil Rights and State Department

The defense employed by many in the anti-Israel camp against accusations of anti-Semitism has been that they are merely criticizing Israel,
not Jews. And indeed, this is true for many who, though perhaps flawed
in their assessments of Israel, do not infuse their criticism of some Israeli
policies with anti-Semitism. But as we have illustrated, some cross the line
between legitimate criticism of Israel into anti-Semitism, yet still attempt
to deflect criticism with the same essential argument.

In broad terms, anti-Israelists believe all kinds of accusations are fair
game. They make the specious argument that criticism of Israel is *never*
anti-Semitic, counter punching their own critics who they accuse of being
hypersensitive zealots who see *any* criticism of Israel as anti-Semitic. But
over the past three years, two separate reports by United States government agencies have clearly stated that anti-Israelism and anti-Zionism
are often only thin veneers that mask anti-Semitic sentiments, statements,
and actions.

The U.S. Commission on Civil Rights issued a series of findings
regarding anti-Semitism on campus. The findings unambiguously state,
"Anti-Semitic bigotry is no less morally deplorable when camouflaged as
anti-Israelism or anti-Zionism."[79] Kenneth Marcus, staff director of the
U.S. Commission on Civil Rights at the time of the inquiry, writes that, "a
new strain of anti-Semitism has evolved that targets Israel and Zionism.
Virulent attacks on the Jewish state have assumed the trope of political
discourse. This allows such attacks to pass as constitutionally and socially
acceptable criticism. In truth, this new form of attack is merely a new
adaptation of the age-old virus of anti-Semitism."[80] Mr. Marcus, as well as

the Commission members, rightly acknowledges that aiming one's hatred at the Jewish state does not diminish the bigotry, but only hides it. This action for some is intentional. They do harbor prejudice against Jews, but know that it is socially and politically unacceptable to express this attitude, at least in the United States, and therefore attack Israel instead. The increased activity of white supremacists and neo-Nazis against Israel can testify to this phenomenon.[81] Many others, as Lawrence Summers stated, engage in anti-Semitism, "in effect if not intent,"[82] by forwarding outrageous claims about Israel that are rooted in traditional Jewish stereotypes, but that many, especially young people, identify as unique to Israel.

The U.S. Commission on Civil Rights is not alone in its declaration. The United States State Department also has issued clear condemnation of contemporary manifestations of anti-Semitism. The report entitled "Contemporary Global Anti-Semitism Report" states that, "the distinguishing feature of the new anti-Semitism is criticism of Zionism or Israeli policy that—whether intentionally or unintentionally—has the effect of promoting prejudice against all Jews by demonizing Israel and Israelis and attributing Israel's perceived faults to its Jewish character."[83] The distinction that contemporary anti-Semitism may be unintentional is an important one precisely because most critics of Israel are not anti-Semitic. But the most committed anti-Israelists sometimes use anti-Semitic language. In order to push forth ideas like divestment and boycotts, Israel must be made to be fundamentally evil. The process of demonizing Israel hinges on attacking its identity, a process that employs the use of stereotypes and accusations historically leveled at Jews as a people.

Public Officials

The positions taken by both the USCCR and State Department have spurred elected officials to weigh in on the situation at UC Irvine. Relying upon these reports, questions have been raised about both the role of the UC Irvine administration and the Office of Civil Rights' dismissal of the complaint against the university. The Senate Judiciary Committee sent a letter to the U.S. Secretary of Education, Margaret Spelling, in February of 2008 questioning the decision by the OCR to dismiss the case against Irvine and demanding that the case be pursued. The letter, signed by Republican senators Jon Kyl, Sam Brownback, and Arlen Specter, specifically criticized the narrow interpretation of "Jewish" as solely a religious distinction employed by OCR. The OCR does not pursue cases based solely on religious identity. Of course, Jews are both an ethnic/national group as well as a religious group, and identify themselves as both.[84] The letter references a previous clarification by former OCR staff director Kenneth Marcus that clearly placed discrimination against Jews in education within the realm of the OCR.[85] Moreover, the senators questioned the quality of the investigation: "Why did OCR take over three years to issue a decision? . . . Why did OCR delay making site visits to UCI and interviewing university officials, and why did OCR fail to interview all available witnesses?"[86] The senators cite the findings of the U.S. Commission on Civil Rights to support their concerns.

Worries about anti-Semitism on campus extend across the aisle in Congress. Democratic congressman Brad Sherman issued a public statement detailing a letter he sent to UC Irvine chancellor Michael Drake in which he strongly questions Drake's response to anti-Semitism at UC Irvine.[87] Congressman Sherman relies upon the State Department's recently released report on contemporary forms of anti-Semitism to support his demand that Drake speak out unambiguously against intolerance. Congressman Sherman also calls upon Chancellor Drake to do his duty, when he writes:

> Comparing current Israeli policies to the Holocaust, the systematic murder of the Jewish people of Europe, is clearly anti-Semitic. It wholly demeans the Jewish victims of the Holocaust and vilifies the Jewish citizens of Israel. The United States Department of State has officially declared that such a comparison is a prototypical example of anti-Semitism.
>
> As the leader of a public university, Chancellor Drake also has a duty to condemn anti-Semitism, especially when it occurs at the UCI campus. In my letter to the Chancellor, I asked him to publicly denounce this hate speech. I hope he does so.[88]

Congressman Sherman's request of Chancellor Drake is the same we would make of all university administrators: take a moral stand.

Organizational Response

The recent rise of anti-Semitism and anti-Israelism has been met by a variety of well-established Jewish organizations attempting to define and deal with the growing problem. Many in the Jewish community expected, and continue to expect, that the extensive Jewish organizational structure can and will address safety and security issues. That is, of course, part of the reason why so many American Jews can be counted on to fund the wide network of Jewish NGOs that claim that they are combating anti-Semitism. How have Jewish organizations performed in addressing anti-Semitism and anti-Israelism on campus?

The answer is more complicated than it might seem. In many ways, established organizations such as the American Israel Public Affairs Committee (AIPAC) have had a hard time responding to the situation on campus. These are large organizations with established missions that may or may not fit well with the goals of Israel advocacy on campus or academic reform. AIPAC, for example, has a much larger and more complex agenda than the campus. While AIPAC is adept at training students to become community leaders,[89] the primary goal is preparing them for political action, not educational reform. No one should expect anything different. AIPAC does not fit well into many campus cultures. Furthermore, its professionals charged with campus affairs may not really understand campus culture. The AIPAC director of student programs, Jonathan Kessler, continues to utterly dismiss anti-Israelism on campus, telling the *Jewish Journal* in Los Angeles, "The amount of anti-Israel activity on campus is so negligible that it is almost impossible for students to find unless they are looking on all but maybe three campuses a year."[90] Anti-Israel ideology, as expressed in research, lectures, and student newspapers, seem unimportant in his analysis.

Similarly large and established organizations such as the Anti-Defamation League (ADL), the American Jewish Congress, and the American Jewish Committee, have been limited in their ability to combat campus anti-Semitism. This is not to say that these organizations have ignored the issue. The ADL continues to provide tolerance training to universities and is able to integrate teaching about new forms of anti-Semitism into its programs.[91] The American Jewish Committee has been integral in organizing university presidents to sign petitions condemning various boycott and divestment schemes[92] and runs an excellent program that hosts university presidents on trips to Israel.[93] The American Jewish Congress has actively supported legislative efforts to provide more oversight over federal funding for Middle East Studies.[94] The Jewish National Fund was quick to respond to anti-Israel sentiment by providing speakers to campuses through Caravan for Democracy and instituting a fellowship program.[95] Local Jewish Community Relations Councils also play a role in dealing with campus issues as they arise locally. But the campus is not the prime area of expertise or institutional strength for most well-established Jewish organizations. Moreover, issues diverge from campus to campus and require on the ground attention.

Why have the largest Jewish organizations been only moderately successful in addressing campus anti-Semitism and anti-Israelism? Largely because they cannot and should not be on the front line of the campus. The issues of campus civility, free speech, and anti-Israel political culture are massive problems to tackle. As stated throughout our work, addressing anti-Semitism and anti-Israelism on campus requires coming up against decades-old ideologies, structures, and processes. There is only one national Jewish organization that can claim to be focused solely on the campus—Hillel: The Foundation for Jewish Campus Life. But Hillel, for different reasons, faces barriers.

Hillel is often more focused upon creating a central place for Jewish student life than educating about Israel, an endeavor that does not play to its greatest strength. Even though Hillel has attempted to put Israel at the center of its activities, with the creation of the Israel on Campus Coalition, these efforts have been largely administrative and coordinative rather than action oriented.

Hillel is, itself, intertwined with the campus and is part of the campus culture. In this capacity, it provides a great deal for the Jewish community and the campus as a whole, including sponsorship of Jewish events, welcoming of all Jewish students, and education about Jewish culture. In these it does an exemplary job. However, its marriage with the universities can also limit its ability to address some of the more deeply seated anti-Israel problems within academia for two primary reasons. First, Hillel does not want to be marginalized on campus, appearing to oppose free speech, academic freedom, or aligning itself with "right-wing" forces. Individual Hillels depend upon campus networks and inclusion to be successful in their work. Second, Hillel is inevitably influenced by some of the intellectual obfuscation that characterizes much of the Israel debate on campus.

Considering their permanency on campus and that the campus is, in fact, their workplace, one can understand Hillel's desire, and need, to be well-accepted by the campus community. They accomplish much by this integration and acceptance and it would be foolish to expend good will and hard earned legitimacy by being overly aggressive. But what if the problems on a campus sometimes require a more activist approach? Then Hillel, which must be a peacemaker and provide a big tent for all kinds of Jewish students, may not be in the best position to respond. Nor should it. Israel advocacy should not be Hillel's main activity, and perhaps it should not be involved in this arena at all.

Hillel states on its website that it, "helps students find a balance in being distinctively Jewish and universally human by encouraging them to pursue tzedek (social justice), tikkun olam (repairing the world) and Jewish learning, and to support Israel and global Jewish peoplehood."[96] If one views issues such as "social justice" through the lens of the campus, some might see a contradiction with support for Israel. When so many activists on so many campuses promote Israel as the world's worst perpetrator of social injustice, then Hillel's other stated goal of support for Israel might become a problem. This is a conflict not only for Hillel, but also for many Jewish students, who must simultaneously attempt to be included in campus community efforts to promote social justice and human rights, while also avoiding the rabid anti-Israelism that so often dominates this subject.

However, other traditional Jewish organizations are less shackled by the need to provide a "big tent." The Zionist Organization of America (ZOA) is a well-established Jewish organization that has stepped in to play a major role on campus.[97] For obvious reasons, defense of Israel falls squarely within the ZOA's mission. Moreover, ZOA has not been a major force in Jewish life compared to ADL or others. They have been redefining themselves, and the campus has become an important part of their portfolio.

The ZOA initiated an investigation and subsequent lawsuit in 2004 against the University of California, Irvine filed through the Office for Civil Rights in the Department of Education. The complaint was filed against UC Irvine under a federal statute that requires any body receiving government funding to eradicate discrimination on the basis of race and ethnicity from its programs and activities.[98] The complaint sparked a debate about whether or not Jews are protected under the Federal Civil Rights Act of 1964. The outcome of the investigation was a letter written by the Office of Civil Rights, Department of Education to Chancellor Michael Drake stating that although some Muslim student activities were offensive to Jewish students, the activities were based on opposition to Israeli policies, not the national origin of Jewish students.[99] Subsequently, the United States Commission on Civil Rights issued findings and recommendations regarding campus anti-Semitism that included a request to Congress to amend Title VI to make clear that discrimination on the basis of Jewish heritage constitutes prohibited national origin discrimination.[100] During the writing of this edition, the ZOA case against the University of California, Irvine filed with the Office of Civil Rights in the Department of Education was reinstated following questions by a number of elected officials about the inadequacy of the investigation.[101]

The ZOA has also taken organizations like Hillel to task for not doing enough. Morton Klein, the president of the ZOA said Hillel sometimes contributes to the anti-Israel problems on campus that it claims to be addressing, by hosting programs that unfairly tarnish Israel's image, and giving podiums to college leaders who won't address Israel-bashing on their campuses.[102] But ZOA's very identity as a pro-Zionist organization carries risks on campus and comes with heavy baggage. The term Zionist itself is linked by anti-Israelists to the most offensive of historical ideologies, including Nazism, Apartheid, and white supremacy. ZOA can battle from the outside, but it is not likely to become an equal participant on campus. Perhaps the outsider status both enables in some ways and limits in others, ZOA's effectiveness.

Emerging Pro-Israel Advocacy Organizations

Many in the Jewish community, both on campus and off, feel that more must be done. This is evidenced by the sprouting up of a number of local and national organizations that are dedicated specifically to campus anti-Israelism and anti-Semitism. They are independent and flexible. They are not afraid to make demands of the university and tend to be more focused than larger, older Jewish organizations. Scholars for Peace in the Middle East, StandWithUs, the David Project[103] and others have made impacts far beyond their size, notoriety, and operating budgets.

The David Project made a big splash when it released the film *Columbia Unbecoming*,[104] a documentary, which lambasted Columbia University's Middle East and Asian Languages and Cultures department for bias in its teaching and discrimination against Jewish students. The David Project states that it is involved in other activities such as the creation of student advocates,[105] but its primary contribution has been to utilize popular media as an effective tool to publicize campus issues and mobilize pressure on universities. Other organizations have noted the David Project's success in this realm and emulated it. Interestingly, this was not the David Project's initial intention.

The David Project says that the film was originally produced to communicate to the Columbia community issues that were not being addressed by the administration and was not originally intended to be a documentary. Their goal was to alert Columbia University to the issues so that they could resolve the problems internally. After six months of unproductive private meetings between the students and the administration, the students arranged a press conference as a last resort and decided to produce the documentary and share it with the Columbia community and the press.[106]

Campus Watch, a subsidiary of The Middle East Forum, also created quite a stir when it launched its website, *Campus-watch.com*. Campus Watch reviews and critiques Middle East studies in North America[107] and has been criticized for employing "McCarthyesque" intimidation for creating dossiers on professors who they allege are espousing dangerous rhetoric on campus.[108] Daniel Pipes, the founder of Campus Watch, has been unabashed in his criticism of certain professors and the institutions that house them. He has rightfully defended his website as an expression of free speech, though this does little to stem the tide of criticism against him and his organization. Pipes is also said to have been instrumental in getting HR 3077, the "International Studies in Higher Education Act," an effort to mandate greater accountability by International Studies departments receiving federal funding, introduced to Congress, where it is currently sitting in the Senate.[109] Pipes has himself also been a very active speaker on campuses throughout the country. Pipes' independence has been crucial to his maverick approach, more or less taking on as much criticism as he himself is willing to shoulder. It is unlikely he would have been able to weather the storms of condemnation had he been fettered by the varied concerns of a larger organization.

The Committee for Accuracy in Middle East Reporting in America (CAMERA)[110] is not explicitly focused on the campus. It is a media-monitoring outlet that aims to expose and correct inaccuracies in popular media around the world. However, the close relationship between college life and international media, as well as the central role campus media plays in shaping the university environment, creates a natural entrée to the campus for CAMERA. The result is CAMERA on Campus.[111] They provide free subscriptions to their publication *Camera on Campus*, and encourage students to submit articles about both negative and positive experiences they have had on campus. As part of the publication, it also publicizes inaccuracies in campus media and engages editorial departments to correct the problems. Additionally, CAMERA provides students with printable flyers to counteract and educate against common themes of anti-Israel bias perpetuated on campus. Though CAMERA is not a new organization, its focus upon media-monitoring allows it to extend its work directly to campus. It can clearly frame its campus work as part of its larger mission.

Scholars for Peace in the Middle East, with over twenty chapters across the country, was established by faculty at UCLA and UC Santa Cruz and aims to "inform, motivate, and encourage faculty to use their academic skills and disciplines on campus, in classrooms, and in academic publications to develop effective responses to the ideological distortions, including anti-Semitic and anti-Zionist slanders, that poison debate and work against peace."[112] California universities were some of the first to begin a concerted campaign against Israel. The first chapter of Students for Justice in Palestine was established at the University of California Berkeley, which also launched the first divestment campaign.[113] San Francisco State University was one of the first universities to attract national attention, and rebuke from elected leaders, for the hostile climate on campus.[114] UC Irvine was the first school to be reviewed by the U.S. Department of Education Office of Civil Rights for claims of anti-Semitism.[115] It is not surprising then, that California has also been the launching pad for some of the more targeted initiatives in defense of civility and fair study of Israel and the Middle East.

Scholars for Peace in the Middle East is growing and has taken the lead in attempting to affect change from within academia, an important distinction as many critiques from "outside" observers have been rejected by academics themselves as removed from campus reality. SPME presented a detailed documentation of "one-sided and often inaccurate" portrayals on California campuses of Israel and the Middle East to the UC regents. SPME "respectfully urged" the regents to take measures to ensure that scholarship on the Middle East and Israel is honest and that courses are "forums for inquiry" rather than political polemics. SPME has been among the few organizations countering the anti-Israel bias on campuses that have pressed administrations to respond to the findings of the U.S. Commission on Civil Rights, and to appropriately address the issues identified in them.[116]

Faculty actions in support of campus civility and scholastic honesty are invaluable, representing the silent voices of most faculty. Anti-Israel faculty are a minority, but a rather vocal one.[117] In many cases, the anti-Israel position is presented to and absorbed by students and others simply because there is no equally respected counter argument being made by other faculty. SPME makes clear that, "there is room for negotiation," but is also clear in its concern for the ideals of the university and for the negative impact poor and politicized scholarship has on the prospects for peace in the Middle East.[118]

Another group that was formed to fill a need not being met effectively by established Jewish organizations is StandWithUs (SWU). Started in Los Angeles, SWU "ensures that Israel's side of the story is told in communities, campuses, libraries, the media and churches through brochures, speakers and conferences."[119] SWU organizes events, fields petitions, and in general, serves a community organizing function among Jews and, increasingly, non-Jewish pro-Israel groups. Previously, campus oriented groups devoted to supporting Israel had mostly been student groups and larger Jewish organizations such as AIPAC and ADL. Student groups fluctuate based on the students heading the organization at any given time and are generally narrow in their scope. Their ability to connect issues on one campus to others and to engage in national efforts is limited. SWU develops locally led chapters across the country and, though it does organize off campus, is focused on promoting Israel within the university. At the same time, as an international organization, it has a wide network with which to work and a consistent presence over time.

However, there is yet another quietly growing, but already huge organization on campus. Chabad, perhaps best known to the general public for their giant menorahs erected alongside city center Christmas trees, is an international organization, but one that is very focused on local grass roots organizing. And though Chabad is involved in quite a broad range of activities off campus, it has made a concerted effort to reach Jewish students while they are in college. Chabad is not a political organization nor does it hold explicit policy positions on many of the controversial issues on campus. However, it is slowly laying a competing claim to Hillel as being the home of Judaism and Jewish students on campuses across the country.[120] Chabad is unburdened by nationally directed talking points and the obligation of trying to please everybody at once. Chabad is often quick to condemn anti-Semitism on campus clearly and without reservation. What role Chabad chooses to ultimately play on campus in the long term is unclear. But they are willing to engage in Israel advocacy.

ARE CAMPUSES BETTER OFF TODAY THAN A FEW YEARS AGO?

Questions about whether campuses are calmer today than they were in 2000, when the second Intifada began and, in 2002, when the Iraq war broke out, are difficult to answer. In many ways they are. Signs of success in Iraq and the aging of the Intifada diminish the fervor of student protest and frequency of anti-Israel events. Proactive responses to anti-Israel sentiment on campus by a variety of Jewish and non-Jewish organizations have helped to contradict some of the stereotypes and misinformation about Israel common to campuses. Some university administration heads have spoken up in defense of Israel, particularly in regards to attempted boycotts of Israeli scholars.

In other ways, they are the same or worse. Although the hostility at the University of California, Berkeley has toned down to some extent, the University of California, Irvine has more than made up for any abatement. While some faculty have deservedly been dismissed, others such as Nadia Abu El-Haj have received tenure, ensuring her anti-Israel archeological pseudo-science will taint academia for decades to come. Ahmadinejad's visit to Columbia, despite Bollinger's strong rebuke of the Iranian president, was a troubling development that along with Saudi agreements with the Universities of California and Texas (to name only two), provide invaluable legitimacy to Middle Eastern theocracies and dictatorships.[121]

It is not very productive to debate whether campuses are marginally better or worse than in the recent past. It is enough to know that anti-Semitism and anti-Israelism remain a problem on campus. What is more important to analyze is how the anti-Israel movement has developed: what is new? What can we expect in the near and distant future? In the past, the launch of the divestment campaign and the establishment of the annual Palestinian Solidarity Movement conference marked significant developments for the anti-Israel community. Today, high profile book releases and campus speakers take the stage. Anti-Semitism and anti-Israelism continue to evolve and express themselves within higher education. The uncivil university persists, but there are signs of improvement. In the 1960s, students were urged to "take back the campus." We will make even more progress if the same rallying cry inspires those who are devoted to common sense and common decency.

THE UNCIVIL UNIVERSITY ILLUSTRATED

Protesters at Cornell University equate the democratically elected government of Israel with the brutal policies of the deposed regime of former Iraqi dictator Saddam Hussein. They advocate for violence against Israeli citizens. (Source: AIPAC)

On various Northern California campuses, an American flag, originally modified to protest the influence of multi-national corporations on American foreign policy, has been further altered to invoke the stereotype that Jews—this time through corporate power—control the United States.

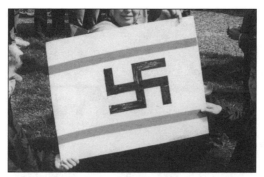

Nazi symbols are often used to characterize Israel, including defacing the Israeli flag.

A slide show at the University of Arizona at first seemed to refute the assertion so often made by anti-Israelists that equates Israelis with Nazis, but only to change the equation to depict Israelis as even worse than Nazis. (Source: AIPAC)

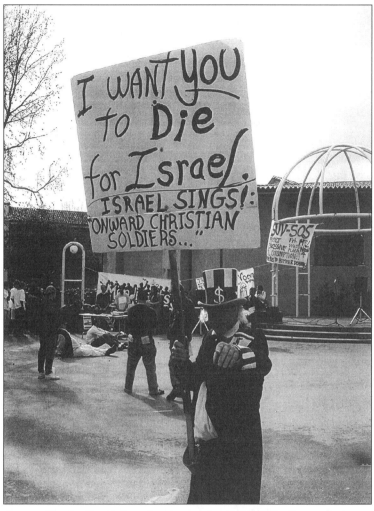

In an odd mix of anti-Americanism and anti-Christianity, protesters at Stanford University conflate several issues into a muddled anti-Israel protest. (Source: AIPAC)

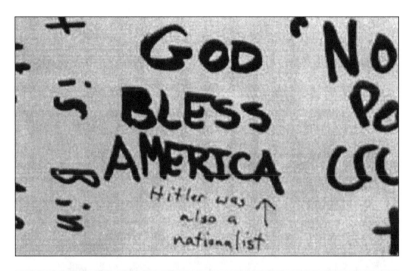

On the day after the 9/11 attacks, a student message board at the University of California, Berkeley, equated American patriotism and a love of the United States with Nazism. Another message recycled old charges of Jewish conspiracy with its call to "Stop the Jewish Lobby."

Anti-Israelists urge universities to pull their investments from companies that conduct business with Israel. Militaristic images are often used to equate Israel with the racist apartheid regime that once ruled South Africa.

In an attempt to weaken the United States' relationship with Israel, a group at the University of California, Berkeley, tries to create a direct link between American support and deaths in the Middle East.

As part of the ongoing campaign calling for divestment from Israel, Palestinians are depicted as the "David" fighting against the Israeli "Goliath."

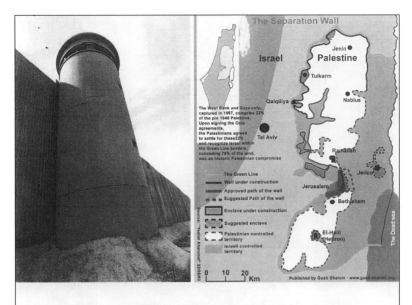

Using both historically and politically inaccurate information, students at The Johns Hopkins University invoke charges of apartheid to protest the Israeli security barrier. (Source: AIPAC)

Ending the UC's Connection to Israeli Apartheid

a Students for Justice in Palestine pamphlet

Many organizations distribute pamphlets on campus as a way to spread propaganda, such as this one from Students for Justice in Palestine.

At Rutgers University, students make the claim that a Palestinian state must include all of Israel, de-legitimizing the idea of Jewish nationalism. The banner was displayed in the student union on university property. (Source: AIPAC)

In the Brown University Daily Herald, *the student artist who created this satire of American ignorance of the "other" invoked the classic anti-Semitic blood libel, perhaps unaware that the anti-Israel campaign uses the same charges to de-legitimate both the Jewish people and the state of Israel.*

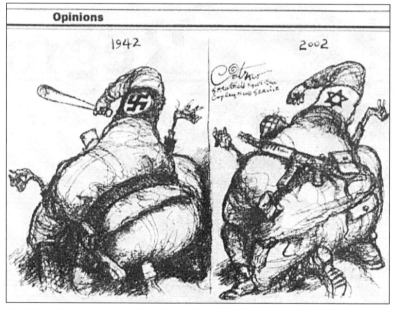

Anti-Israel propaganda often likens Jews to Nazis, as in this cartoon from Texas A&M University, which juxtaposes a Nazi officer with an Israeli soldier by replacing the swastika with the Star of David.

TRY BEING PALESTINIAN FOR A DAY

Go to the Checkpoint at Sather Gate

Checkpoints: The Palestinian Daily Experience

What happens at a checkpoint?

➤ Checkpoints surround Palestinian towns and are a feature of the Israeli military occupation
➤ Curfews and roadblocks: ambulances and emergency vehicles often denied access.
➤ Checkpoints seal off of the Palestinian economy: Palestinian laborers unable to reach their jobs inside Israel. Food and medicine often in short supply.
➤ Arbitrary searches and seizures: NO Due Process for Palestinians.
➤ Random arrests: over 1250 uncharged detainees in the past 4 months.
➤ Legalized torture: Sanctioned by Israeli Supreme Court

= Apartheid, a fundamentally biased system of laws and policies

"*Apartheid*? Wasn't that South Africa?"

ɔm a black South African, and if I were to change the names, a description of what is happening in the ɪza Strip and the West Bank could describe events in South Africa."
- **Archbishop Desmond Tutu**, South African Anti-Apartheid activist, December 25, 1989. *Ha'aretz*

ael claims a sacred law of "return" – any Jew anywhere in the world can easily obtain Israeli citizenship. ɔwever, Palestinians expelled from the same piece of land during the founding of Israel in 1948 cannot ʈurn to the land where they were born. The Palestinian refugees are the oldest and largest refugee ɔpulation in the world, making up roughly one *in four* of the total world refugee population.

ɘ **pay for it**. While the rest of the world condemns Israeli criminality, Israel is the highest recipient of US ʾeign aid, receiving over three times the aid to all of sub-Saharan Africa. It is enough to subsidize the ɔllege education of millions of students in America. Instead, we pay for a state founded on dispossession ɪd violence to continue a systematic state of oppression. We must at the very least **DIVEST FROM ISRAEL!**

Since September 2000, more than 350 Palestinian fatalities and over 11,000 injuries.

Dressed as Israeli border police, protesters at the University of California, Berkeley, harassed other students by setting up "checkpoints" in an attempt to brand Israel a police state.

Part of the traveling anti-Israel road show, Wheels for Justice brought its bus, which is painted to evoke the protests of the 1960s, to the campus of the University of Colorado. The group attempts to link sentiment on campus against the war in Iraq with the Palestinian cause. (Source: AIPAC).

A flyer created by Muslim student groups and funded by the Associated Students of San Francisco State University dredges up the medieval anti-Semitic blood libel of Jews slaughtering children—this time Palestinian children—for ritual purposes.

Anti-Israelists and other protesters, both on and off campus, often use Nazi images as a means to demonize both American and Israeli leaders.

Birmingham University (UK) lecturer Sue Blackwell, who spearheaded the effort to boycott Israeli universities and scholars, is clad in a costume that resembles both the Palestinian flag and an academic robe, the perfect melding of anti-Israelism and the academy.

These kids are innocent.

These Palestinian children were killed by the U.S.-backed Isreali Army...

Are brown lives worth less than white?

The anti-Israel campaign exploits the abhorrence of racism on campus by falsely depicting Israelis as white "colonialists" oppressing brown "native" peoples.

METHODOLOGY

Time frame

The Institute for Jewish & Community Research conducted research on anti-Semitism and anti-Israelism in American educational systems from 2002 through 2005 for the 2005 edition of this book. The revised edition contains research through 2008. We used a number of methods and sources, which are discussed below.

Student interviews

The Institute conducted over fifty personal interviews with students from a variety of campuses. Interviewees included anti-Israel protesters, Jewish students, student leaders, and student "observers," those who were not part of the Israel debate. Our interviews focused on anti-Israel protest, anti-Semitism, intellectual freedom, the conflict in the Middle East, Middle East Studies, and student safety, among other subjects.

Key informant interviews

The Institute conducted over forty key informant interviews with Jewish organizational leaders to assess the Jewish communal response to anti-Semitism and anti-Israelism on campus. Some of these organizations are listed below:

- Aish Ha-Torah (student leadership training program)
- American Israel Public Affairs Committee
- American Jewish Committee
- American Jewish Congress
- Anti-Defamation League
- Caravan for Democracy (the campus division of the Jewish National Fund)
- Chicago Jewish Community Relations Council
- Connecticut Jewish Community Relations Council
- Hadassah Curriculum Watch
- Hamagshimim (helps foster Jewish student groups)
- Hillel (national office and campus divisions)
- San Francisco Federation Israel Center
- San Francisco Jewish Community Relations Council

Campus literature

The Institute completed a content analysis of hundreds of anti-Israel materials distributed on college campuses or designed for student protest. These include divestment literature, divestment petitions, flyers, pamphlets, posters, rally announcements, and other materials. We collected these materials by visiting campuses and gathering them from the tables of anti-Israel student groups, anti-Israel protesters, posted materials, and so on. We also used the Internet, examining activist websites such as electronicintifada.net, internationalanswer.org, and palestinecampaign. org, and we downloaded materials for students such as checkpoint flyers, divestment strategies, and ways to fend off accusations of anti-Semitism. In addition, we conducted extensive content analysis of banners, posters, signs, and sloganeering of anti-Israel protesters by attending rallies and examining photos taken at rallies. We paid special attention to anti-Semitic stereotypes, Holocaust imagery, historical inaccuracies, incitement, misrepresentations, negative slogans, and provocative language.

Newspapers, magazines, internet newswires, and websites

We monitored twenty-five major news outlets on a daily basis, collecting news and opinion articles pertaining to anti-Semitism and anti-Israelism. Most prominent among them were the *Chronicle of Higher*

Education, *The Christian Science Monitor*, *Haaretz* (Israel), *The Jerusalem Post* (Israel), *National Review Online*, *New York Post*, *The New York Times*, *San Francisco Chronicle*, *The Wall Street Journal*, and *The Washington Post*. The Institute also monitored weekly news outlets such as *Al-Ahram Weekly* (Egypt), *Education Week*, *Newsweek*, *Time*, and others. We analyzed articles on anti-Semitism and anti-Israelism for newsworthy incidents, relevant quotes from experts, and for the emergence of general trends.

We systematically read Jewish community periodicals and news services including the *Forward*, the *J.*, and the *Jewish Week*. When an incident of anti-Semitism and/or anti-Israelism arose on a campus, the local community newspaper also was consulted.

Websites

The Institute regularly analyzed the content found on over 30 websites. The types of websites varied and included anti-divestment drives, divestment petitions, faculty organizations, pro-Israel advocacy, pro-Palestinian/anti-Israel student and other groups, socialist movement groups, university information, university organizations/departments/centers, and others.

Anti-Israel groups' websites provided information on anti-Israel campaign goals, links to other anti-Israel organizations, literature and propaganda, and past and upcoming events. Divestment petition websites, as well as anti-divestment websites, were examined as they were created. We searched university websites for administrative responses to anti-Semitism and anti-Israelism on campus. University department websites were examined when they were involved in sponsoring a Middle East forum or teach-in on campus. We reviewed faculty organization websites if their field was related to the Middle East, or if they issued a statement regarding the Middle East in their capacity as professors.

E-mail newsletters

The Institute regularly received, reviewed, and analyzed five relevant e-mail newsletters from Jewish organizations, including the American Israel Public Affairs Committee and the Jerusalem Center for Public Affairs, as well as grassroots pro-Israel organizations such as StandWithUs. We analyzed these newsletters for recent events and incidents on campus.

College and university student newspapers

The Institute systematically investigated fifteen campus newspapers (and other campus sources) selected by geography, campus size, public or private, and other factors. We examined over 1,500 articles, advertisements, and other materials. These universities include:

California
- University of California, Berkeley *(The Daily Californian)*
- University of California, Irvine *(The New University)*
- University of California, Los Angeles *(The Daily Bruin)*
- University of California, San Diego *(The Guardian)*

Michigan
- University of Michigan, Ann Arbor *(The Michigan Daily)*
- Wayne State University *(The South End)*

Texas
- University of Houston *(The Daily Cougar)*
- University of Texas, Austin *(The Daily Texan)*

Colorado
- University of Colorado, Boulder
- University of Colorado, Denver *(The UCD Advocate)*

New York
- New York University *(Washington Square News)*

Illinois
- University of Chicago *(The Chicago Maroon)*

Georgia
- Emory University *(The Emory Wheel)*
- University of Georgia *(The Red & Black)*

New Hampshire
- Dartmouth University *(The Dartmouth)*

In addition to these fifteen campuses, the Institute used campus media at colleges and universities throughout the country. We analyzed the media content for several themes, including:

- Anti-Israel voices (e.g., opinion articles, speakers, and statements)
- Anti-Israel events (e.g., rallies, street theater, conferences, lectures, and courses)
- Anti-Semitism (e.g., graffiti, vandalism, vocal threats, libelous accusations, discrimination, and physical attacks)
- Divestment/apartheid accusations (e.g., examples of campus rhetoric and introductions of divestment campaigns)

We also evaluated news content for bias and accuracy when it pertained to the Middle East or related events on campus. We analyzed editorial boards' writings as well as their decisions as to what submissions to feature on the opinion page. The Institute collected opinion articles and evaluated them for egregious anti-Semitic and anti-Israel content. We also identified, collected, and monitored contributions to student media from outside the university environment.

Participant Observation

Institute staff members attended Jewish community meetings with campus administrators and were included in discussion groups for campus task forces about these issues. Researchers observed pro-Israel and anti-Israel demonstrations on college campuses, attended teach-ins, lectures, and conferences addressing the Middle East conflict.

Notes

Introduction to the Revised Edition

1. Laurie Zoloth, "Fear and Loathing at San Francisco State," in Ron Rosenbaum, ed., *Those Who Forget the Past: The Question of Anti-Semitism* (New York: Random House, 2004).

2. See Gary A. Tobin, Aryeh K. Weinberg, and Jenna Ferer, *The UnCivil University* (San Francisco, CA: Institute for Jewish & Community Research, 2008), p.241.

3. In re University of California, Irvine, OCR Case No. 09-05-2013.

4. Charles R. Love, Program Manager, U.S. Department of Education, Office for Civil Rights, Region IX, OCR Case No. 09-05-2013, Closure Letter to Susan Tuchman, Director, Center for Law and Justice, Zionist Organization of America, dated Nov. 30, 2007. Curiously, OCR later opened a companion case based on more recent allegations.

5. See, e.g., Chaim Seidler-Feller, "Advocacy and Education as Divergent Strategies in the Effort to Support Israel on Campus," in Deborah E. Lipstadt, et al., eds., *American Jewry and the College Campus: Best of Times or Worst of Times?*, p. 32 (American Jewish Committee, 2005), available at http://www.ajc.org/atf/cf/%7B42D75369-D582-4380-8395-D25925B85EAF%7D/AmericanJewryCollegeCampus2005.pdf.

6. See Gary A. Tobin and Aryeh K. Weinberg, *Religious Beliefs & Behavior of College Faculty* (San Francisco, CA: Institute for Jewish & Community Research, 2007), p. 80.

7. *Id.*

8. See Kenneth L. Marcus, Deputy Assistant Sec'y for Enforcement, Delegated the Auth. Of Assistant Sec'y of Educ. for Civil Rights, U.S. Dep't of Educ., Dear Colleague Letter, Title VI and Title IX Religious Discrimination in Schools and Colleges (Sept. 13, 2004), available at http://www.ed.gov/about/offices/list/ocr/religious-rights2004.html.

9. See Kenneth L. Marcus, "Anti-Zionism as Racism: Campus Anti-Semitism and the Civil Rights Act of 1964," 15 *Wm. & Mary B. of Rts. J.* 837, 858 (Apr. 2007).

10. Letter from Kenneth L. Marcus, Del. The Auth. of Assistant Sec'y of Educ. For Civil Rights, U.S. Dep't of Educ., to Sidney Groeneman, Ph.D., Senior Research Assoc., Inst. For Jewish and Comty. Research, dated Oct. 22, 2004, available at http://www.eusccr.com/letterforcampus.pdf.

11. U.S. Commission on Civil Rights, *Campus Anti-Semitism* (Washington, DC, 2006), available at www.usccr.gov.

12. *Id.*

13. See Letter of Assistant Secretary of Education for Civil Rights Stephanie Monroe to U.S. Commission on Civil Rights Staff Director Kenneth L. Marcus, dated Dec. 4, 2006, available at http://www.eusccr.com/lettermonroe.pdf.

14. *Report of the Task Force on Anti-Semitism at the University of California, Irvine,* available at http://www.redcounty.com/rccampuswatch/Orange%20County%20Task%20Force%20Report%20on%20anti-Semitism%20at%20UCI.pdf.

15. *Id.*

16. Letter of Senators Arlen Specter, Sam Brownback, and Jon Kyl to Secretary of Education Margaret Spellings, dated February 27, 2008.

17. See Kenneth L. Marcus, "The Most Important Right We Think We Have But Don't: Freedom From Religious Discrimination in Education," 7 *Nevada Law Journal* 171, 172 (Fall 2006).

18. The Commission's campus anti-Semitism initiative has a virtual presence at http://www.eusccr.com.

1. Something Amiss in Higher Education

1. Unless otherwise noted, all financial figures for higher education come from the *Chronicle of Higher Education: Money and Management* at http://chronicle.com/money/.

2. By far, medical-based research is the research area most heavily subsidized by the federal government. The top institutions receiving federal research and development funds are The Johns Hopkins University, the University of Washington, Stanford University, the University of Michigan, and the University of California, San Diego. They are also in the top ten in overall spending on research and development, indicating the difficulty in locating enough funds to compete at the top levels without relying upon federal dollars. (Source: *Chronicle of Higher Education*)

3. Kelly Field, "Colleges Find Road to Riches in Transit Bill: Transportation Legislation Has Almost $600-Million in Earmarks for Campuses," *Chronicle of Higher Education,* September 2, 2005, sec. A1.

4. Tax benefits for colleges and universities are also found on the consumer end. Parents of college-bound children are allowed to set up tax-free accounts in which they can invest money designated for college tuition. Securities can be bought and sold within the account without taxes on either short-term or long-term gain. When the money is eventually used to pay for tuition, withdrawn funds are not taxed unless the money is not used for college tuition. This is yet another form of government subsidy for higher education. (Source: *Chronicle of Higher Education*)

5. For a good compendium of the issues facing higher education, see Phillip G. Altbach, Robert O. Berdahl, and Patricia J. Gumport, eds., *American Higher Education in the Twenty-first Century: Social, Political, and Economic Challenges* (Baltimore: The Johns Hopkins University Press, 1999).

6. Morris P. Fiorina, *Culture War?: The Myth of a Polarized America* (Upper Saddle River, New Jersey: Pearson Education, 2005), 150.

2. Defining the Civil University

1. Frank Newman, Lara Couturier, and Jamie Scurry, *The Future of Higher Education: Rhetoric, Reality, and the Risks of the Market* (San Francisco: Jossey-Bass, 2004), 215.

2. For a good history of the evolution of the contemporary American university, see Laurence R. Veysey, *The Emergence of the American University* (Chicago: The University of Chicago Press, 1965).

3. Clark Kerr, *The Uses of the University* (Cambridge, MA: Harvard University Press, 2001), 35–36.

4. James B. Twitchell, "Higher Ed, Inc." *The Wilson Quarterly*, Summer 2004, 46–47.

5. Newman, Couturier, and Scurry, *The Future of Higher Education*, 222.

6. Newman, Couturier, and Scurry, *The Future of Higher Education*, 70.

7. Newman, Couturier, and Scurry, *The Future of Higher Education*, 3–4.

8. Stanley N. Katz, "Liberal Education on the Ropes," *Chronicle of Higher Education*, April 1, 2005, sec. B6.

9. Linda J. Sax et al., *The American Freshman: National Norms for Fall 2004* (Los Angeles: University of California, Los Angeles, 2004).

10. Ross Gregory Douthat, *Privilege: Harvard and the Education of the Ruling Class* (New York: Hyperion, 2005), 8.

11. Robert J. Birgeneau, "Frontiers of Knowledge, Frontiers of Education," (induction speech, University of California, Berkeley, April 15, 2005), http://cio.chance.berkeley.edu/chancellor/birgeneau/remarks/4-15-05-frontiers.htm.

12. Kerr, *Uses of the University*, 36–37.

13. Stephan Thernstrom, "Harvard's Crucible: A Question of Academic Freedom, and Meritocracy, and Sense," *National Review Online*, April 11, 2005, http://www.manhattan-institute.org/html/_national_review_harvards_crucible.htm.

14. Gil Troy, "Current State of Academic Freedom," *Organization of American Historians Newsletter*, May, 2005, http://www.oah.org/pubs/nl/2005may/troy.html.

15. "Statement on Professional Ethics," *American Association of University Professors*, http://www.aaup.org/statements/redbook/rbethics.htm.

16. George Dennis O'Brien, *All the Essential Half-Truths about Higher Education* (Chicago: University of Chicago Press, 1998), 53.

17. Unknown, "Academic Freedom Resolution Passed at the Evergreen State College," *Politicalaffairs.net*, March 1, 2005, http://www.politicalaffairs.net/article/articleview/723/.

18. Lee C. Bollinger, "The Value and Responsibilities of Academic Freedom," *Chronicle of Higher Education*, April 8, 2005, sec. B20.

19. Bollinger, "Value and Responsibilities of Academic Freedom," sec. B20.

20. Barry Ames, David C. Barker, Chris W. Bonneau, and Christopher J. Carman, "Hide the Republicans, the Christians, and the Women: A Response to 'Politics and Professional Advancement Among College Faculty,'" *Forum* 3, no. 2 (2005): article 7.

21. Victor Davis Hanson, "Profiles in Diversity," *Claremont Review of Books* V, no. 3 (Summer 2005): 6–9.

22. James O. Freedman, "Ghosts of the Past: Anti-Semitism at Elite Colleges," *Chronicle of Higher Education*, December 1, 2000, sec. B7.

23. Eric Hoover, "Public Colleges See a 10% Rise in Tuition for 2004–5: Rates Also Increase at Private Institutions and Community Colleges," *Chronicle of Higher Education*, October 29, 2004, sec. A1.

24. For further discussion, see Jesse B. Sears, *Philanthropy in the History of American Higher Education* (New Brunswick, NJ: Transaction, 1990, first published 1922); and Merle Curti and Roderick Nash, *Philanthropy in the Shaping of American Higher Education* (New Brunswick, NJ: Brown Book Co., 1965).

25. Roger Geiger, "Research, Graduate Education, and the Ecology of American Universities: An Interpretive History," chap. 6 in *The European and American University since 1800: Historical and Sociological Essays*, Sheldon Rothblatt and Björn Wittrock, eds., (Cambridge: Cambridge University Press, 1993), 243. For further discussion, see Geiger, *To Advance Knowledge: The Growth of American Research Universities, 1900–1940* (New York: Oxford University Press, 1986), 43–57.

26. Geiger, "Research, Graduate Education," 241. Geiger draws from Howard Miller in *Dollars for Research: Science and its Patrons in Nineteenth Century America* (Seattle: University of Washington Press, 1970) and his own work, *To Advance Knowledge*, 80–82.

27. Geiger, "Research, Graduate Education," 241.

28. David L. Kirp, *Shakespeare, Einstein, and the Bottom Line: The Marketing of Higher Education* (Cambridge, MA: Harvard University Press, 2003), 3.

29. Gary A. Tobin and Aryeh K. Weinberg, *Mega-Gifts in American Philanthropy: Giving Patterns 2001–2003 and Mega-Gifts in Jewish Philanthropy: Giving Patterns 2001–2003.* (San Francisco: Institute for Jewish & Community Research, 2008).

30. Colleges and universities depend heavily on their tax-exempt status, which is simply another way of saying that they are subsidized by government. For example, municipal governments derive a significant percentage of their revenue through property taxes. Property owners, including businesses, make annual payments that correspond to the value of their property to their local government. However, in a number of cities and towns across the United States, a primary landowner is a college or university. Campuses have classroom and administration buildings, sports facilities, common areas, student and faculty housing, parking, research facilities, and other land-intensive needs. In addition, some own large swathes of unused land, which they may hold, develop, or sell for an untaxed profit. Universities also receive public dollars indirectly through their heavy reliance on public services. Bringing together sometimes tens of thousands of people between the ages of 18–22, many newly liberated from parental supervision, college campuses have a higher than average need for police services. A university may have independent security, which helps to patrol the campus. However, the campus community extends far beyond the actual physical space that the university occupies. Demonstrations, rallies, and events can require municipal police presence. A wide range of concerns, from altercations between students to the safety of students at night, can tie up time and energy of a municipal police force. The increase in traffic and related parking problems can fall to the police. Even harmless pranks nevertheless require investigation. Other times, the issues are much more serious. All of these services cost public money. For more information, see Bertrand M. Harding Jr., *The Tax Law of Colleges and Universities*, 2nd ed. (New York: John Wiley and Sons, 2001) and the *Chronicle of Higher Education* (http://chronicle.com).

3. The Emergence of the Uncivil University

1. Eric Ferreri, "Democrats Get Lion's Share of Donations at Area Universities," *Herald Sun*, October 23, 2004, http://www.heraldsun.com/durham/4-536228.html.

2. Ferreri, "Democrats Get Lion's Share."

3. For more on the political ideology and hegemony of thought on campus, see Roger Kimball, *Tenured Radicals: How Politics Has Corrupted Our Higher Education* (Chi-

cago: Ivan R. Dee, 1990) and Jim Nelson Black, *Freefall of the American University: How Our Colleges Are Corrupting the Minds and Morals of the Next Generation* (Nashville, TN: WND Books, 2004).

4. Karl Zinsmeister, "Case Closed: There's No Longer Any Way to Deny It: College Campuses Are the Most Politically Undiverse Places in America," *American Enterprise*, January/February 2005, 42.

5. Ferreri, "Democrats Get Lion's Share."

6. William Pilger, "In but Not of Academe: A New Assistant Professor Finds that His Conservative Politics Mean He Will Never Quite Fit in on Campus, " *Chronicle of Higher Education*, December 17, 2004, sec. C2.

7. Thomas Lipscomb, "Students Have Appallingly Weak Grasp of Free Speech," *Chicago Sun-Times*, February 4, 2005, http://www.suntimes.com.

8. Troy, "Current State of Academic Freedom."

9. Amity Shlaes, "It Is OK to Say that Women Are from Venus," *Financial Times*, January 24, 2005.

10. Donald Alexander Downs, *Restoring Free Speech and Liberty on Campus* (Oakland, CA: The Independent Institute, 2005), xv.

11. Alan Charles Kors and Harvey A. Silverglate, *The Shadow University: The Betrayal of Liberty on America's Campuses* (New York: The Free Press, 1998), 355.

12. Robin Finn, "At the Center of an Academic Storm, a Lesson in Calm," *New York Times*, April 8, 2005, sec. B4.

13. Jacob Gershman, "Civil Liberties Official Defends Columbia Professors," *New York Sun*, December 28, 2004, http://www.nysun.com/pf.php?id=6826.

14. Sax et al., "American Freshman Norms for 2004."

15. Ryan C. Amacher and Roger E. Meiners, *Faulty Towers: Tenure and the Structure of Higher Education* (Oakland, CA: The Independent Institute, 2004), 54.

16. Baudouin Loos, "An Interview of Ilan Pappe," *Le Soir (Bruxelles)*, November 29, 1999, translation posted at Ben Gurion University website, http://www.ee.bgu.ac .il/~censor/katz-directory/$99-11-29loos-pappe -interview.htm.

17. Fred Siegel, "Radical Professors: The New Brain Trust?" *New York Observer*, March 21, 2005, sec. 5.

18. *College Access and Opportunity Act of 2005*, HR 609, 109th Cong., 1st sess.

19. President Paul Ansel Chadbourne in his 1873 inaugural address at Williams College. Quoted in Richard Hofstadter, *Academic Freedom in the Age of the College* (New Brunswick, NJ: Transaction, 1996), 274.

20. O'Brien, *Essential Half-Truths about Higher Education*, 226.

21. Karen W. Arenson and N.R. Kleinfield, "Columbia's President, an Expert on Free Speech, Gets an Earful," *New York Times*, May 25, 2005, sec. A1.

22. Diane Ravitch, "Academe Gone Mad?" *New York Sun*, February 10, 2005.

23. Ravitch, "Academe Gone Mad?"

24. Max Boot, "Abolish Tenure," *Los Angeles Times*, March 17, 2005, http://www .latimes.com/.

25. John M. McCardell Jr., "What Your College President Didn't Tell You," *New York Times*, September 13, 2004, sec A23.

26. Eric Foner, letter to the editor in response to "The Clash of Ideas at Columbia," *New York Times*, April 11, 2005, sec. A22.

27. Amacher and Meiners, *Faulty Towers*, 94.

28. Rob Reich, *Bridging Liberalism and Multiculturalism in American Education* (Chicago: University of Chicago Press, 2002), 11.

29. Reich, *Bridging Liberalism and Multiculturalism*, 1–13.

30. For more information, see Beverly Daniel Tatum, *Why Are All the Black Kids Sitting Together in the Cafeteria: And Other Conversations about Race* (New York: Basic Books, 1997).

31. For an analysis of how the politicization of multiculturalism goes unchecked, see David O. Sacks and Peter A. Thiel, *The Diversity Myth: Multiculturalism and Political Intolerance on Campus* (Oakland: The Independent Institute, 1995).

32. Victor Davis Hanson, "Teachable Moments," *National Review Online*, March 14, 2005, http://www.nationalreview.com/hanson/hanson200503010747.asp.

33. Andrew Delbanco, "Colleges: An Endangered Species?" *New York Times Book Review*, March 10, 2005, 19.

34. Kirp, *Shakespeare, Einstein, and the Bottom Line*, 3.

35. Derek Bok, *Universities in the Marketplace: The Commercialization of Higher Education* (Princeton, NJ: Princeton University Press, 2003), 9.

36. Kirp, *Shakespeare, Einstein, and the Bottom Line*, 253.

37. Alison Bernstein, "Is Philanthropy Abandoning Higher Education?" *The Presidency* (Fall 2003): 34–37.

38. Bernstein, "Is Philanthropy Abandoning Higher Education?" 34–37.

39. Newman, Couturier, and Scurry, *Future of Higher Education*, 29.

40. O'Brien, *Essential Half-Truths about Higher Education*, 50.

41. Charles J. Sykes, *Profscam: Professors and the Demise of Higher Education* (Washington, DC: Regnery Gateway, 1988), 4.

42. Sykes, *Profscam: Professors and the Demise*, 4–5.

43. Newman, Couturier, and Scurry, *Future of Higher Education*, 58.

44. Geiger, "Research, Graduate Education," 242–3. Geiger draws from William James in "The PhD Octopus," in *Harvard Monthly* (1903), reprinted in *Educational Review* 55 (1918), 149–57; Veysey, *Emergence of American University*, 180–203; and Hugh Hawkins, "University Identity: The Teaching and Research Function" in Oleson and Voss, eds., *The Organization of Knowledge in Modern America* (Baltimore: Johns Hopkins University Press), 302–4.

45. Newman, Couturier, and Scurry, *Future of Higher Education*, 128.

46. Twitchell, "Higher Ed, Inc.," 59.

47. Jennifer Washburn, *University Inc.: The Corporate Corruption of Higher Education* (New York: Basic Books, 2005), 239.

48. Birgeneau, "Frontiers of Knowledge."

49. Gilbert M. Gaul and Frank Fitzpatrick, "College Sports: What Was Sacred Is Now Up for Sale," *Philadephia Inquirer*, September 14, 2000, http://www.philly.com/mld/philly/.

50. Goldie Blumenstyk, "Income from University Licenses on Patents Exceeded $1-Billion," *Chronicle of Higher Education*, March 22, 2002, sec. A31.

51. Jonathan R. Cole, "Academic Freedom under Fire," *Daedalus: Journal of the American Academy of Arts and Sciences*, Spring 2005: 17.

52. Amacher and Meiners, *Faulty Towers*, 30.

53. Andrei Postelnicu, "Do Your Homework Before You Give," *Financial Times*, June 28, 2005, http://news.ft.com/home/us.

54. Michael D. Cohen and James G. March, *Leadership and Ambiguity: The American College President* (New York: McGraw-Hill , 1974), 2.

55. Cohen and March, *Leadership and Ambiguity*, 198.

56. Cohen and March, *Leadership and Ambiguity*, 198.

57. Martin Kramer, *Ivory Towers on Sand: The Failure of Middle Eastern Studies in America* (Washington, DC: Washington Center for Near East Policy, 2001), 31.

58. Caroline Glick, "Human Rights & Wrongs," *Moment*, August 2002, http://www .momentmag.com/archive/aug02/feat2.html.

59. James Piereson, "The Left University," *Weekly Standard*, October 3, 2005, http:// www.weeklystandard.com/Content/Public/Articles/000/000/006/120xbklj.asp.

60. Jessica Hamm, "Rally Addresses Concerns with Israeli Occupation," *Daily Cardinal*, December 10, 2003.

61. Diane Tobin, Gary Tobin, and Scott Rubin, *In Every Tongue: The Racial & Ethnic Diversity of the Jewish People* (San Francisco: Institute for Jewish & Community Research, 2005).

62. Sid Groeneman and Gary A. Tobin, *The Decline of Religious Identity in the United States* (San Francisco: Institute for Jewish & Community Research, 2004) and Gary A. Tobin and Sid Groeneman, *Surveying the Jewish Population in the United States—Part 1: Population Estimate, Part 2: Methodological Issues & Challenges* (San Francisco: Institute for Jewish & Community Research, 2004). For more information on these publications, see http://www.jewishresearch.org/publications.htm.

63. Earl Raab, "Anti-Israel Prejudice Is Still Bigotry, Anti-Semitic or Not," *J. The Jewish News Weekly*, http://www.jewishsf.com/content/2-0-/module/displaystory/story _id/18799/edition_id/378/format/ html/displaystory.html.

64. Senator John F. Kennedy (speech, Zionists of America Convention, Statler Hilton Hotel, New York, August 26, 1960).

65. "In a Time of Torture: The Assault on Justice in Egypt's Crackdown on Homosexual Conduct," *Human Rights Watch*, http://hrw.org/reports/2004/egypt0304/ egypt0304.pdf.

66. Nissan Ratzlav-Katz, "They Were Victims Once: When the American Left Turned on Israel," *National Review Online*, June 13, 2002, http://www.nationalreview .com/comment/comment-ratzlav-katz061302.asp.

67. Earl Raab, "Anti-Israel Chic Consumes S.F.'s Once-Friendly Left Wing," *J. Jewish News Weekly of Northern California*, December 13, 2002, http://www.jewishsf.com/content/ 2-0-/module/displaystory/story_id/19434/edition_id/394/format/html/displaystory .html.

68. Hala Halim, "Being Among Difference," *Al-Ahram Weekly Online*, February 27– March 5, 2003, http://weekly.ahram.org.eg/2003/627/cu5.htm.

69. Chris Shortsleeve, "Benny Morris' Alamo," *Palestine Solidarity Review*, http:// psreview.org/content/view/34/72/.

4. The Persistent Prejudice

1. For more information, see Jerome Karabel, *The Chosen: The Hidden History of Admission and Exclusion at Harvard, Yale, and Princeton* (Boston: Houghton Mifflin, 2005).

2. Freedman, "Ghosts of the Past," B7.

3. For more information, see Morton Keller and Phyllis Keller, *Making Harvard Modern: The Rise of America's University* (New York: Oxford University Press, 2001).

4. Piereson, "The Left University."

5. For a history of Henry Ford's campaign against the Jews, see Neil Baldwin, *Henry Ford and the Jews: The Mass Production of Hate* (New York: PublicAffairs, 2001). This volume also discusses the anti-Semitism of Father Charles C. Coughlin.

6. For more information, see Charles Y. Glock and Rodney Stark, *Christian Beliefs and Anti-Semitism* (New York: Harper and Row, 1969).

7. For an excellent definition and typology of anti-Semitism, see Yehuda Bauer, "Contemporary Anti-Semitism, Israel and the Holocaust," *Teaching and Learning about the Holocaust*, August 11, 2004, http://www.cyberlearning-world.com/holocaust/ israel/conference3.htm.

8. Bauer, "Contemporary Anti-Semitism."

9. Paul Johnson, "The Anti-Semitic Disease," *Commentary*, June 2005:34.

10. For a discussion of Japanese anti-Semitism, see David G. Goodman and Masanori Miyazawa, *Jews in the Japanese Mind: The History and Uses of a Cultural Stereotype* (New York: Free Press, 1995).

11. For more information about anti-Semitic attitudes and beliefs, see Gary A. Tobin and Sharon L. Sassler, *Jewish Perceptions of Anti-Semitism* (New York: Plenum Press, 1988) and "ADL Survey: Anti-Semitism Declines Slightly in America; 14 Percent of Americans Hold 'Strong' Anti-Semitic Beliefs," *Anti-Defamation League*, http://www .adl.org/PresRele/ASUS_12/4680_12.htm.

12. For a history of anti-Semitism in the Catholic church, see David I. Kertzer, *The Popes Against the Jews: The Vatican's Role in the Rise of Modern Anti-Semitism* (New York: Alfred A. Knopf, 2001).

13. "Nostra Aetate: Declaration on the Relation of the Church to Non-Christian Religions," *The Vatican*, http://www.vatican.va/archive/hist_councils/ii_vatican _council/documents/vat-ii_decl _19651028_nostra-aetate_en.html.

14. Pope John Paul II, "Address at the Great Synagogue of Rome," *Boston College Center for Christian-Jewish Learning, Christian-Jewish Relations Library*, http://www.bc .edu/research/cjl/meta-elements/texts/cjrelations/resources/documents/catholic/ johnpaulii/romesynagogue.htm.

15. "Pope Terror 'Snub' Angers Israel," *BBC News*, July 25, 2005, http://news.bbc .co.uk/2/hi/europe/4715959.stm.

16. General Convention of the Episcopal Church, July 1988, "Guidelines for Christian-Jewish Relations," posted at *Boston College Center for Christian-Jewish Learning, Christian-Jewish Relations Library*, http://www.bc.edu/research/cjl/meta-elements/ texts/cjrelations/resources/documents/protestant/Episcopal_Guidelines.htm.

17. Alexander C. Karp, Gary A. Tobin, and Aryeh K. Weinberg, "An Exceptional Nation: American Philanthropy Is Different Because America Is Different," *Philanthropy* 18, no. 6 (November/December 2004).

18. To see polling data about Jews, see "Religion and Politics: The Ambivalent Majority," *PEW Research Center for the People and the Press*, http://people-press.org/ reports/display.php3?ReportID=32, and "Pew Global Attitudes Project: Nine Nation Survey (March 2004)," *PEW Research Center for the People and the Press*, http://people -press.org/reports/pdf/206topline.pdf. Polling data about Jews show increasing proportions of Americans feel neither positively or negatively about Jews, as they have no strong opinions about a variety of ethnic, racial, and religious groups. Race, religion, and ethnicity matter less in certain ways.

19. For more information about this controversy, see Robert Weller, "Air Force Cadets See Religious Harassment," *SFGate.com*, April 19, 2005, http://www.sfgate.com/ cgi-bin/article.cgi?f=/n/a/2005/04/19/national/w111447D80.DTL, and Steve Rabey, "Christian Emphasis on Evangelism at Heart of Air Force Academy Scandal," *Religion News.com*, June 9, 2005, http://www.religionnews.com/ArticleofWeek60905.html.

20. "Shooting Suspect Returned to L.A. to Face Charges," *CNN.com*, August 12, 1999, http://www.cnn.com/US/9908/12/california.shooting.01/.

21. For more information about global anti-Semitism, see "Report on Global Anti-Semitism," *U.S. Department of State: Bureau of Democracy, Human Rights, and Labor*, January 5, 2005, http://www.state.gov/g/drl/rls/40258.htm.

22. For research about the rise of anti-Semitism in Europe, see "Attitudes Toward Jews in Twelve European Countries," prepared by First International Resources LLC, May 2005, http://www.adl.org/anti _semitism/european_attitudes_may_2005.pdf.

23. Miri Chason, "Anti-Semitism Hits 15-year High," *YnetNnews.com*, April 5, 2005, http://www.ynetnews.com/articles/0,7340,L-3081211,00.html.

24. For more information about anti-Semitism in South America, see "Global Anti-Semitism: Response of the Jewish Community Relations Field," *Chicago Jewish Community*, October 14, 2002, http://www.juf.org/news_public_afairs/article.asp?key=3615.

25. For more information about anti-Semitism in Argentina, see Brian Byrnes, "Acquittals in '94 Attack Spur Protests by Argentina's Jews," *Washington Post*, September 9, 2004, http://www.wpost .com/; "Argentina's Jews Protest Synagogue Attacks in Turkey," *Jerusalem Post*, November 19, 2003, http://www.jpost.com/; and "Terrorist Bombings in Argentina," *Jewish Virtual Library*, http://www.jewishvirtuallibrary.org/jsource/Terrorism/argentina.html.

26. For a look at some violent anti-Semitic incidents around the world, see Lisa Katz, "Jewish in the World Today: Anti-Semitic Attacks in the Wake of the Middle East Crisis," *About.com*, http://judaism.about.com/library/2_antisemitism/bl_antisemitism2000.htm.

27. For more about anti-Semitism in the Muslim world, see "Anti-Semitism on Arab TV: Satellite Network Recycles the Protocols of the Elders of Zion," *Anti-Defamation League*, October 29, 2003, http://www.adl.org/special_reports/protocols/protocols _recycled.asp; "Blast at Tunisian Synagogue Kills Five," *BBC News*, April 11, 2002, http://news.bbc.co.uk/1/hi/world/middle_east/1923522.stm; "Al-Qaeda Claims Tunisia Attack," *BBC News*, June 23, 2002, http://news.bbc.co.uk/1/hi/world/middle_east/2061071.stm; and "Israeli Report Links Kenya Terrorist to Al-Qaeda," *CNN.com/World*, November 29, 2002, http://archives.cnn.com/2002/WORLD/africa/11/28/kenya.israel/.

28. For information on the Arab economic boycott, see "What You Need to Know to Fight for Israel's Security," *Anti-Defamation League*, http://www.adl.org/israel/advocacy/glossary/arab_economic_boycott.asp; and Dina Ezzat, "Boycott Israel? Not So Simple," *Al-Ahram Weekly Online*, April 11–17, 2002: no. 581, http://weekly.ahram .org.eg/2002/581/ec1.htm.

29. Raphael Israeli, "Poison: The Use of Blood Libel in the War Against Israel," *Jerusalem Viewpoints, Jerusalem Center for Public Affairs*, no. 476, April 2002, http://www .jcpa.org/jl/vp476.htm.

30. Brigette Gabriel, "Environments of Hate: Indoctrination in the Arab World and Propaganda Advocacy in America's University Classrooms," (speech, Columbia University, New York, March 6, 2005). The full text of the speech can be found at http://www.americancongressfortruth.com/columbia-university-speech.html.

31. For more information about Jews being expelled from Arab lands, see *JIMENA—Jews Indigenous to the Middle East and North Africa*, http://www.jimena.org.

32. Mike Kepp, "Arab-Latin Summit Angers Jews by Justifying Violent Resistance," *Jewish Telegraphic Agency*, May 17, 2005, http://www.jta.org/page_view_story.asp

?intarticleid=15419&intcategoryid=2. Regarding the summit, Jewish confederation vice president Osias Wurman said, "Brazilian government authorities assured Jewish leaders that this summit would not be political, and instead they imported the conflict between Israel and Palestine to Brazil. Furthermore, the summit only considered that conflict from the point of view of the Palestinians, not the Israelis." Wurman also commented that the summit was used to build Arab nations' support for Brazil's bid to obtain the votes it needed to become a permanent member of the U.N. Security Council.

33. Yasir H. Kaheil, "New Laban and New Nephi," *Utah Statesman*, March 21, 2003, http://www.utahstatesman.com/global_user_elements/printpage.cfm?storyid =396726.

34. Kaheil, "New Laban and New Nephi."

35. Peter McNamara, letter to the editor, *Utah Statesman*, March 28, 2003, http:// www.utahstatesman.com/media/paper243/news/2003/03/28/Opinion/Letter .Accusations.Stem.from.Bad .Source-402407.shtml.

36. Steve Siporin and Arthur Caplan, "Previous Column in Newspaper Borders Religious Hate," *Utah Statesman*, March 28, 2003, http://www.utahstatesman.com/ media/paper243/news/2003/03/28/Opinion/Column.Previous.Column.In.Newspaper .Borders.Religious.Hate-402404.shtml?page=2.

37. Alyssa Beaver, "Perspective: Divestment: Middle East Conflict Hits Home," *Daily Pennsylvanian*, November 26, 2002, http://www.dailypennsylvanian.com/vnews/ display.v/ART/2002/11/26/3de3471390ecd?in_archive=1.

38. Edward W. Miller, "McCarthyism Deja Vu: Zionist Thought Police on Campus," *Coastal Post*, May 1, 2005, 2.

39. Yaakov Lappin, "The Academic Ban—Nazi Connection," *Jerusalem Post*, May 1, 2005, http://www.jpost.com/.

40. For information on Communitarians in France, see Denis Boyles, "Crawling from the Wreckage," *National Review Online*, October 17, 2003, http://www.nationalreview .com/europress/europress20031010948.asp.

41. Josef Joffe, "Nations We Love to Hate: Israel, America and the New Antisemitism," in *Posen Papers in Contemporary Antisemitism*, ed. Robert S. Wistrich (Jerusalem: Vidal Sassoon International Center for the Study of Antisemitism, 2005).

42. For a first-hand account of the rampant anti-Semitism and anti-Israelism at the United Nations World Conference against Racism, see Tom Lantos, "The Durban Debacle: An Insider's View of the UN World Racism Conference at Durban," *The Fletcher Forum of World Affairs* 26, no.1 (Winter/Spring 2002); and Anne F. Bayefsky, "Terrorism and Racism: The Aftermath of Durban," *Jerusalem Viewpoints, Jerusalem Center for Public Affairs*, no. 468, December 16, 2001, http://www.jcpa.org/jl/vp468 .htm.

43. "Israel and the EU: Economic Allies," *Anti-Defamation League*, http://www.adl. org/international/EU-3-EconomicAllies.asp; and "Israel and the EU: Political History, Economic Sanctions," *Anti-Defamation League*, http://www.adl.org/international/ EU-5-EconomicSanctions.asp.

44. David A. Harris, letter to the editor, *Forward*, September 30, 2005, 14.

45. "Needed: Genuine UN Reform," *Jewish Week*, September 16, 2005, http://www .jewishweek.com/.

46. Julie Geng, "C.U. Debates Allegations of Columbia Anti-Semitism," *Cornell Daily Sun*, February 4, 2005, http://www.cornellsun.com/vnews/display.v/ART/ 2005/02/04/420315dfbcfd9?in_archive=1.

47. For a look at how individual European countries see Israel compared to other countries as a threat to world peace, see Robin Shepherd, "In Europe, an Unhealthy Fixation on Israel," *Washington Post*, http://www.wpost.com/; and Alan M. Dershowitz, "Euro Trash: Perversity & Anti-Semitism Lead Europeans to Call Israel Greatest Threat to Peace," *New York Daily News*, November 8, 2003, http://www.nydailynews.com/news/ideas_opinions/story/134989p-120276c.html.

48. Flash Eurobarometer of the European Commission, "Iraq and Peace in the World," *Public Opinion Analysis Sector of the European Commission*, http://europa.eu.int/comm/public_opinion/flash/fl151_iraq_full_report.pdf.

49. For more on the organizations emerging to combat rising anti-Semitism in Europe, see Michael Whine, "International Organizations: Combating Anti-Semitism in Europe," *Jewish Political Studies Review, Jerusalem Center for Public Affairs* 16, no. 3–4 (Fall 2004), http://www.jcpa.org/phas/phas-whine-f04.htm.

50. For discussions of anti-Semitism and anti-Israelism in the United Nations, see Anne Bayefsky, "The United Nations: Leading Global Purveyor of Anti-Semitism," *Jerusalem Center for Public Affairs*, April 1, 2005, no. 31, http://www.jcpa.org/phas/phas-31.htm; Meghan Clyne, "U.N.'s Anti-Israel Propaganda Prompts Congress to Act," *New York Sun*, August 23, 2005, http://www.nysun.com/article/19020; Anne Bayefsky, "Undiplomatic Imbalance," *National Review Online*, December 13, 2004, http://www.nationalreview.com/bayefsky/bayefsky200412130835.asp; Anne Bayefsky, "Your Tax Dollars at Work: The U.N. Discovers the Cause of Anti-Semitism: Jews," *Opinion Journal*, November 18, 2004, http://www.opinionjournal.com/extra/?id=110005908; and Anne Bayefsky, "Fatal Failure (re. The United Nations)," *Standwithus.com*, December 3, 2004, http://www.standwithus.com/news_post.asp ?NPI=167.

51. For more information about divestment, see "United Jewish Communities Opposes Presbyterian Church USA Moves on Divestment from Israel: Resolution Unanimously Passes," *United Jewish Communities*, http://www.ujc.org/content_display.html?ArticleID=131069.

52. For more on the exclusion of Israel from the United Nations regional group system, see Sir Robert Jennings, "Opinion Regarding the Exclusion of Israel from the United Nations Regional Group System," *Israel Ministry of Foreign Affairs*, http://www.mfa.gov.il/; and Alan Lazerte, "Israel Excluded by Three-Tier UN," *The United Nations and Israel*, http://christianactionforisrael.org/un/3-tier-un.html.

53. The American Jewish yearbook lists the world Jewish population at about 13 million. See David Singer, Lawrence Grossman, eds., *American Jewish Year Book: The Annual Record of Jewish Civilization* (New York: The American Jewish Committee, 2004). We believe this to be a conservative estimate by at least 1 million.

54. Johnson, "The Anti-Semitic Disease," 38.

55. For information on repairing America's image, see Steven R. Weisman, "Bush Confidante Begins Task of Repairing America's Image Abroad," *New York Times*, August 21, 2005, http://www.nytimes.com/; and Mike Allen, "Hughes Hopes to Burnish Image of U.S.: Nominee Says Ideas Will Prevail," *Washington Post*, July 23, 2005, http://www.wpost.com/.

56. Rashid I. Khalidi, "Road Map or Road Kill?" *Nation*, June 9, 2003, http://www.thenation.com/doc.mhtml?i=20030609&s=khalidi.

5. Ideology and Propaganda

1. Marc Ballon, "Jewish Students and Activists Call UC Irvine a Hotbed of Anti-Semitic Harassment," *Jewish Journal*, March 11, 2005, http://www.jewishjournal.com/home/preview.php?id=13779.

2. "Hatred at NU," *Northwestern Chronicle*, August 9, 2005, http://www.chron.org/tools/viewart.php?artid=626.

3. Anti-Semitism against Jewish students is not only an American phenomenon. At the School of Oriental and African Studies in the United Kingdom, for example, Jewish students have repeatedly complained about instances of anti-Semitism and the college's failure to act to prevent them. In the spring of 2005, a British Jewish interest group and the Board of Deputies of British Jews submitted a dossier of evidence documenting alleged instances of anti-Semitic behavior to Colin Bundy, the head of the School of Oriental and African Studies. See Polly Curtis, "SOAS Faces Action over Alleged Anti-Semitism," *Guardian*, May 12, 2005, http://education.guardian.co.uk/racism/story/ 0,10795,1481647,00.html.

4. Ballon, "Jewish Students Call UC Irvine a Hotbed."

5. *Columbia Unbecoming*, directed by Avi Goldwasser, DVD (Boston: David Project, 2004).

6. Sadanand Nanjundiah, "The Death of Conscience," *Media Monitors*, May 15, 2002, http://mediamonitors.net/sadu5.html.

7. "AJC Condemns Anti-Semitic Remarks of Prominent Georgetown Professor," *American Jewish Committee*, November 21, 2002, http://www.ajc.org/site/apps/nl/content2.asp?c=ijITI2PHKoG&b =849241&ct=868083.

8. Eliana Johnson, "McCarthyism in Action at Yale," *FrontPageMagazine*, June 3, 2003, http://www.frontpagemag.com/Articles/ReadArticle.asp?ID=8180.

9. Verena Isensee, "Israeli-Palestinian Tensions Run High at Student Meeting," *Daily Texan*, March 25, 2002, http://www.dailytexanonline.com/media/paper410/news/2002/03/25/University/IsraeliPalestinian.Tensions.Run.High.At.Student.Meeting-502636.shtml.

10. "Reports from Campus: Bias Incidents at University of Chicago," *Campus Watch*, July 24, 2002, http://www.campus-watch.org/article/id/101.

11. Adam Weisberg, interview with author, October 25, 2002, San Francisco, CA.

12. Joe Eskenazi, "Jewish Student Politico Claims U.C. Is Lax on Anti-Semitism," *J. Jewish News Weekly of Northern California*, July 18, 2003, http://www.jewishsf.com/content/2-0-/module/displaystory/story_id/20672/edition_id/423/format/html/displaystory.html.

13. Jessika Fruchter, "CU Campus Not Alone in Debate," *Colorado Daily*, April 11, 2002, http://web.uccs.edu/ur/mediawatch/Apr2002/colodaily_4_11_02a.htm.

14. Joe Eskenazi, "Berkeley Chabadnik Attacked in Alleged Hate Incident," *J. Jewish News Weekly of Northern California*, December 21, 2001, http://www.jewishsf.com/content/2-0-/module/displaystory/story_id/17429/edition_id/345/format/html/displaystory.html.

15. Wendy Lee, "Incidents of Violence, Prejudice Followed Last Year's Attacks," *Daily Californian*, September 11, 2002, http://www.dailycal.org/article.php?id=9390.

16. Randy Barnes, "Students Must Not Tolerate Anti-Semitism," *Daily Californian*, October 11, 2002, http://www.dailycal.org/article.php?id =9390.

17. "Reports from Campus," *Campus Watch*.

18. Bronson Hilliard, "Vandals Strike Jewish Symbol in Colorado," *Colorado Daily*, September 21, 2002, http://www.coloradodaily.com/articles/2002/09/22/export6521.txt.

19. Ballon, "Jewish Students Call UC Irvine a Hotbed."

20. "Anti-Semitism in Paris, San Francisco and Elsewhere," *Israel National News*, May 15, 2002, http://www.israelnationalnews.com/news.php3?id=23556.

21. "About Us," *Arab World and Islamic Resources*, http://www.awaironline.org/aboutus.htm.

22. Audrey Shabbas, ed., *The Arab World Studies Notebook*, (Berkeley: Arab World and Islamic Resources and Middle East Policy Council, 1998).

23. Gary A. Tobin and Aryeh K. Weinberg, *Profiles of the American University: Volume I: Political Beliefs & Behavior of College Faculty* (San Francisco: Institute for Jewish & Community Research, 2006). Gary A. Tobin and Aryeh K. Weinberg, *Profiles of the American University: Volume II: Religious Beliefs & Behavior of College Faculty* (San Francisco: Institute for Jewish & Community Research, 2007).

24. David A. Harris, "Letter from the Campus Front," *American Jewish Committee*, http://www.ajc.org/atf/cf/%7B42D75369-D582-4380-8395-D25925B85EAF%7D/Letter_fromCampusFront.pdf.

25. Sarah McDermott, "Transfer is Serious Threat to Palestinian Population," *Miftah.org*, March 1, 2003, http://www.miftah.org/Display.cfm?DocId=1815&CategoryId=18.

26. Gilead Ini, "Joseph Massad's Mangled Lexicon: The Columbia Professor Redefines Anti-Semitism, Jews and Israel to Suit His Radical Agenda," March 30, 2005, *CAMERA*, http://camera.org/index.asp?x _context=2&x_outlet=118&x_article=876.

27. Yasir H. Kaheil, "It's a Joke, But Not a Funny One," *Utah Statesman*, January 29, 2003, http://www.utahstatesman.com/media/paper243/news/2003/01/29/Opinion/Column.Its.A.Joke.But.Not.A.Funny.One-354517.shtml.

28. Sherrie Gossett, *WorldNetDaily*, "WND Goes Inside 'Mainstream' Muslim Conference," January 3, 2004, http://www.worldnetdaily.com/news/printer-friendly.asp?ARTICLE_ID=36430.

29. David Greenberg, "Lyin' About Zion: The Diplomatic Back-Story on 'Zionism Equals Racism,'" *Slate Magazine*, September 7, 2001, http://slate.msn.com/id/114902.

30. Lisa Huynh, "Mideast Stirs up Feelings at UH," *Kaleo.org*, June 27, 2002, http://www.kaleo.org/vnews/display.v/ART/2002/06/27/ 3d1a6efdc42e2.

31. Ali Moosavi, "The Sign on the Road Says We're Going Nowhere," *South End*, June 9, 2003, http://www.southend.wayne.edu/.

32. Brenda Abdelall, letter to the editor, *Michigan Daily*, July 8, 2002, http://www.michigandaily.com/vnews/display.v/ART/2002/07/08/3d29056494c10?in_archive=1.

33. Chris Shortsleeve, letter to the editor, *Brown Daily Herald*, April 20, 2005, http://www.browndailyherald.com/media/paper472/news/2005/04/20/Letters/Ara-Responds.To.Zapendowski-931056.shtml.

34. Ricki Hollander, "Tom Paulin's Poetic Incitement," *CAMERA*, August 11, 2005, http://www.camera.org/index.asp?x_context=7&x _issue=47&x_article=888.

35. Franz Gwiazdon Julio, "Blind Nationalism Leads to False Supremacy," *Golden Gater*, March 30, 1995, http://www.journalism.sfsu.edu/.

36. Julio, "Blind Nationalism Leads to False Supremacy."

37. Ini, "Joseph Massad's Mangled Lexicon."

38. Mazin Qumsiyeh, letter to the editor, *Commentary*, March 2005, http://www.commentary.magazine.com/Archive/DigitalArchive.aspx ?panes=2.

39. Joseph Massad, "Post-Oslo Solidarity," *Al-Ahram Weekly Online*, February 26, 2003, http://weekly.ahram.org.eg/2003/626/op2.htm.

40. Steve Lehtonen, "Tensions Mount between Ideologies," *UCSD Guardian*, April 29, 2002, http://www.ucsdguardian.org/cgi-bin/news ?art=2002_04_29_03.

41. "Schooled in Hate: Anti-Semitism on Campus," *Anti-Defamation League*, http://www.adl.org/.

42. "Schooled in Hate," *Anti-Defamation League*.

43. Stewart Ain, "'Hate Rally' at Carnegie-Mellon," *Jewish Week*, February 25, 2005, http://www.thejewishweek.com/news/newscontent.php3?artid=10568&offset=&B1=1&author=Stewart%20Ain%20&issuedates=oneday&month=02&day=25&year=2005&issuedate =20050225&keyword=hate.

44. Ain, "'Hate Rally' at Carnegie-Mellon."

45. Amir Abdel Malik Ali (campus speech, University of California, Irvine, February 2, 2005).

46. Ballon, "Jewish Students Call UC Irvine a Hotbed."

47. Loren Casuto, "UCI Permits Anti-Semitism," *New University*, August 19, 2005, http://www.newuniversity.org/article.php?id=1120.

48. Anneli Rufus, "Berkeley Intifada," *East Bay Express*, May 19, 2004, http://www.eastbayexpress.com/issues/2004-05-19/news/feature _a.html.

49. "Khalid Abdul Muhammad," *Jewish Virtual Library*, April 1999, http://www.jewishvirtuallibrary.org/jsource/anti-semitism/Khalid.html.

50. Amanda Wheeler, "Muslim Students Celebrate Black History Month," *Guardsman*, March 8, 1999, http://www.ccsf.edu/Events_Pubs/Guardsman/s990308/news02.shtml.

51. Wheeler, "Muslim Students Celebrate Black History."

52. Jonathan Calt Harris, "A Saudi Education, Right Here at Home," *National Review Online*, June 19, 2003, http://www.nationalreview.com/comment/comment-harris061903.asp.

53. Fadi Haidar, "Israel Wages War in Response to Peace Plan," *Daily Cougar*, April 10, 2002, http://www.stp.uh.edu/vol67/127/opinion/oped3.html.

54. Juan Cole, "Sharon's Murder of Yassin Endangers Americans in Iraq and Elsewhere," *Informed Comment*, personal website, March 23, 2004, http://www.juancole.com/2004/03/sharons-murder-of-yassin-endangers.html.

55. Ronnie Friedland, "Interview with Robert Costrell," *Swastika on the Lawn: A Year of Anti-Semitism in Massachusetts*, July 1995, http://www.hebrewcollege.edu/sol/ch06.html.

56. Christopher Neal, "American Apathy toward Palestinian Plight Inhumane," *Daily Bruin*, May 13, 2002, http://www.dailybruin.ucla.edu/news/articles.asp?ID=19761.

57. Farzad Masroor, "Time to Point Fingers at Anti-Arab Racism," *Emory Wheel*, September 10, 2002, http://www.emorywheel.com/vnews/display.v/ART/2002/09/10/3d7d476704449?in_archive=1.

58. Francis Boyle, "The International Laws of Belligerent Occupation," *Information Clearing House*, http://www.informationclearinghouse.info/article5936.htm.

59. Charlie Beckerman, "'He Hit Me First' Is a Weak Excuse," *Washington Square News*, December 4, 2001, http://www.nyunews.com/.

60. Julie A. Belz, letter to the editor, *Digital Collegian*, April 18, 2002, http://www.collegian.psu.edu/archive/2002/04/04-18-02tdc/04-18-02dops-letter-05.asp.

61. Gordon McFee, "Why 'Revisionism' Isn't," *Holocaust History Project*, http://www.holocaust-history.org/revisionism-isn't/.

62. "Truth Triumphs in 2000 Historical Court Victory," *Holocaust Denial on Trial*, http://www.holocaustdenialontrial.org/mjud.html.

63. Mahmoud Abbas, "The Other Side: The Secret Relations between Nazism and the Leadership of the Zionist Movement" (doctoral dissertation, Moscow Oriental College, n.d., translated by the Wiesenthal Center). For more information about Mahmoud Abbas' dissertation, see Rafael Medoff, "Likely PA Prime Minister a Holocaust Denier," *FrontPageMagazine*, February 26, 2003, http://www.frontpagemagazine.com/articles/ReadArticle.asp?ID=6340.

64. Abbas, "The Other Side."

65. John K. Wilson, "Censoring the College Press," *Collegefreedom.org*, 2002, http://www.collegefreedom.org/newspaper.htm

66. "Schooled in Hate," *Anti-Defamation League*.

67. "1999 Audit of Anti-Semitic Incidents: Listing of Reported 1999 Campus Incidents," *Anti-Defamation League*, 1999, http://www.adl.org/1999_Audit/Campus_Incidents.asp.

68. Xan Nowakowski, "Students Organize Sit-In to Support Palestinians," *Columbia Spectator*, April 18, 2002, http://www.columbiaspectator.com/vnews/display.v/ART/2002/04/18/3cbe8e3d6a634?in_archive=1.

69. Christopher Johnson, "Protesters Rally to Stop Israeli Aggression," *Michigan Daily*, March 18, 2002, http://www.michigandaily.com/vnews/display.v/ART/2002/03/18/3c9594b53b687?in_archive=1.

70. Mingyou Cheo, "Mideast Protesters Square off on Israeli Holiday," *Washington Square News*, April 19, 2002, http://www.nyunews.com/.

71. Ghaith Mahmood, "Israel's Occupation, Siege Must End," *Daily Bruin*, April 4, 2002, http://www.dailybruin.com/news/articles.asp ?id=19042.

72. "Pro-Palestinian Rallies on U.S. Campuses and Streets," *Islam*, April 10, 2002, http://www.islam-online.net/English/News/2002-04/10/article37.shtml.

73. Cyrus Farivar, "Scheduled Talk Draws Crowd to Local Theater," *Daily Californian*, November 29, 2000, http://www.dailycal.org/article.php?id=4081.

74. Simone Santini, "Hope Lies in the People of Israel, Not in the Nation's Leaders," *UCSD Guardian*, April 11, 2002, http://www.ucsdguardian.org/cgi-bin/opinion?art=2002_04_11_01.

75. Subooshi Hasan, "Israel Is Telling Lies to the World," *Daily Cougar*, April 5, 2002, http://www.stp.uh.edu/vol67/124/opinion/oped2.html.

76. Joseph Anderson, "Zionist Claim to Israel: Modern Day Apartheid," *Daily Californian*, October 12, 2000, http://www.dailycal.org/ article.php?id=3508.

77. M Shahid Alam, "Extending the Boycott," *Al-Ahram Weekly Online*, August 29–September 4, 2002, http://weekly.ahram.org.eg/2002/601/op12.htm.

78. Lisa Anthony, "Ostracized on My Own Campus," *CAMERA On Campus* 15, no. 2 (Spring 2005), 18.

79. Julio Cesar Pino, "Singing Out Prayer for a Youth Martyr," *Daily Kent Stater*, April 15, 2002, http://www.stateronline.com/.

80. Beverly Lwenya, "Forum Responds to Mideast Violence," *New University*, June 3, 2002, http://www.newuniversity.org/author_lookup.php?id=32&issue_date=#.

81. Salah O. Ahmed, "Suicide Missions Way Too Common," *South End Newspaper*, April 4, 2002, http://www.southend.wayne.edu/.

82. Ashraf Shaqadan, "Let's Be Reasonable," *Utah Statesman*, January 22, 2003, http://www.utahstatesman.com/media/paper243/news/2003/01/22/Opinion/Letter.Lets.Be.Reasonable-349175.shtml.

83. Martin Peretz, "Israel Responds to Israeli Terrorism," *New Republic*, August 10, 2005, http://ssl.tnr.com/p/docsub.mhtml?i=w050808&s =peretz081005.

84. Shaya Mohajer, "Bleeding Hearts Society Intl.: The Vicious Reality of Palestine and Israel," *New University*, April 8, 2002, http://www.newu.uci.edu/archive/2001-2002/spring/020408/opinstory02.htm.

85. Lona Panter, "Suicide Bomber Disrupts Passover Feast," *Red and Black*, March 29, 2002, http://www.redandblack.com/vnews/display.v/ART/2002/03/29/3ca4738794a1d?in_archive=1.

86. Thane Rehn, "Mideast Tension Comes to Campus," *Chicago Weekly News*, April 18, 2002, http://www.chicagoweeklynews.com/print .php?story=171.

87. Mohamad Bydon, "Israel, Palestine and Terror," *Dartmouth*, April 5, 2002, http://www.thedartmouth.com/article.php?aid=200204050202.

88. Nelson Mandela, *Long Walk to Freedom: The Autobiography of Nelson Mandela* (Boston & New York: Little, Brown, 1994).

89. "Nobel Peace Prize Press Release," *Nobel Prize*, 1994, http://nobelprize.org/peace/laureates/1994/press.html.

90. Lwenya, "Forum Responds to Mideast Violence."

91. "Study: Reuters Headlines," *Honest Reporting*, July 14, 2003, http://www.honestreporting.com/articles/critiques/Study_Reuters_Headlines.asp.

92. Hollander, "Tom Paulin's Poetic Incitement."

93. Eric Adler and Jack Langer, "The Intifada Comes to Duke: A University Plays Host to Anti-Semites and Terror Advocates," *Wall Street Journal*, January 5, 2005, http://www.online.wsj.com/.

94. Tyler Bitten, letter to the editor, *Digital Collegian*, April 11, 2002, http://www.collegian.psu.edu/archive/2002/04/04-11-02tdc/04-11-02dops-letter-02.asp.

95. Erin Clements, "Religious Groups Unify to Trash Terrorism," *Washington Square News*, November 27, 2001, http://www.nyunews .com/.

96. Adam Gobin, "Israeli Influence Impedes Objectivity," *Red and Black*, October 1, 2002, http://www.redandblack.com/vnews/display.v/ART/2002/10/01/3d999d385c3a6?in_archive=1.

97. Richard Harvell, "A Time to Protest," *Dartmouth*, April 18, 2002, http://www.thedartmouth.com/article.php?aid=2002041802020.

98. Ariel Sinovsky, letter to the editor, *Daily Illini*, January 22, 2002, http://web.archive.org/web/20030410211115/www.dailyillini.com/jan03/jan22/opinions/stories/letter03.shtml.

99. M Shahid Alam, "What Went Wrong?" *Al-Ahram Weekly Online*, December 12–18, 2002, http://weekly.ahram.org.eg/2002/616/op13.htm.

100. Sarah Kaiksow, "Israel Is an Apartheid State, UC Must Divest," *Guardian*, October 17, 2002, http://www.ucsdguardian.org/cgi-bin/opinion?art=2002_10_17_03.

101. Jonathan Linder, "U.S. Must Learn from Israel, React Responsibly," *Daily Cardinal*, September 18, 2001, http://www.dailycardinal.com/media/paper439/news/2001/09/18/Opinion/U.Must.Learn.From.Israel.React.Responsibly-96159.shtml.

102. Kevin McGuire, "Is Anti-Semitism Ever the Result of Jewish Behavior?" *Oak Leaf*, March 18, 2003, as quoted in Aryan-Nations, http://aryan-nations.org/headlinenews/is_antisemitism_ever _the_result_of_jewish_behavior.htm.

103. Carol Benfell, "Strife No Stranger to SRJC Newspaper," *Press Democrat*, May 10, 2003, http://www1.pressdemocrat.com/apps/pbcs.dll/frontpage.

104. Neal, "American Apathy toward Palestinian."

6. Uncivil Politics and Campus Misconduct

1. The Middle East Media Research Institute (http://www.memri.org) regularly translates what is said in Arabic about the Middle East and other subjects and distributes these translations to the newswires.

2. John J. Miller, "At War: The Failure of Middle Eastern Studies," *National Review Online*, November 19, 2001, http://www.nationalreview.com/.

3. Franklin Foer, "Disoriented," *New Republic*, December 3, 2001, http://www.tnr.com/.

4. Kramer, *Ivory Towers on Sand*, 39. For further discussion, see Richard D. Lambert, *Language and Area Studies Review* (Philadelphia: American Academy of Political and Social Science, October 1973), 47, 59.

5. Barbara C. Aswad, "Arab Americans: Those Who Followed Columbus," *MESA Bulletin*, July 1993, http://fp.arizona.edu/mesassoc/Bulletin/Pres%20Addresses/aswad.htm.

6. Foer, "Disoriented."

7. Martin Kramer, "Arabic Panic," *Middle East Quarterly*, Summer 2002, http://www.meforum.org/article/208.

8. Kramer, *Ivory Towers on Sand*, 28.

9. Edward W. Said, *Culture and Imperialism* (New York: Knopf, 1993), 314.

10. Kramer, *Ivory Towers on Sand*, 37.

11. Ruth J. Wisse, "Israel on Campus: How Did American Colleges Get So Anti-Semitic?," *Wall Street Journal*, December 13, 2002, http://www.opinionjournal.com/extra/?id=110002775.

12. "Federally-Funded International and Foreign Language Studies Programs Important to American Competitiveness, Security, Field Hearing Finds," *U.S. House Education & the Workforce Committee News Update*, April 22, 2005, http://edworkforce.house.gov/press/press109/first/04apr/t6042205.htm.

13. Foer, "Disoriented."

14. Bernard Lewis, *What Went Wrong?* (Oxford University Press, 2002), 159.

15. Fouad Ajami, "In Bin Laden's Mirror," *U.S. News & World Report*, December 24, 2001, http://www.usnews.com/usnews/news/articles/011224/archive_019922.htm.

16. Khaled Abu Toameh, "Attempted Lynching Shuts Down PA Univ.," *Jerusalem Post*, March 1, 2005, http://www.jpost.com/.

17. Bernard Lewis, "The State of Middle Eastern Studies," *American Scholar* 48, no. 3 (Summer 1979): 372–73.

18. Uriel Heilman, "A Lesson in Academic Politics," *Jerusalem Post*, February 27, 2005, http://www.jpost.com/.

19. Juan Cole, "Thoughts on the Middle East, History, and Religion," *Informed Comment*, personal website, February 2004, http://www.juancole.com/2004_02_01_juancole_archive.html.

20. Cole, "Thoughts on the Middle East."

21. "Palestinians Get Saddam Funds," *BBC News World Edition*, March 13, 2003, http://news.bbc.co.uk/2/hi/middle_east/2846365.stm.

22. "List of Signatures," *Columbia University Divestment Campaign*, http://www.columbiadivest.org/sig_list.html.

23. Martin Kramer, "Columbia's Troubles Bubble Up through the Bubbly," *Sandstorm*, March 6, 2003, http://www.geocities.com/martinkramerg/2003_03_06.htm.

24. Hamid Dabashi, "The Hallowed Ground of Our Secular Institution," *Columbia Spectator*, May 3, 2002, http://www.columbiaspectator.com/vnews/display.v/ ART/2002/05/03/ 3cd27f3f03167?in_archive=1.

25. Massad, "Post-Oslo Solidarity."

26. Scott Smallwood, Lila Guterman, and Megan Rooney, "Peer Review," *Chronicle of Higher Education*, February 7, 2003, sec. A7.

27. Nur O. Yalman, "Terrorist Mayhem in America," *Harvard Crimson*, September 21, 2001, http://www.thecrimson.com/article.aspx?ref =121262.

28. Miller, "At War."

29. House Committee on Education and the Workforce, Subcommittee on Select Education, Hearings on Reauthorization of Title VI of the Higher Education Act, 108th Cong., 1st Sess., June 19, 2003 (testimony of Gilbert Merkx), http://edworkforce.house .gov/hearings/108th/sed/titlevi61903/merkz.htm.

30. Martin Kramer, "The Petition Middle East Scholars Would Rather Forget," *History News Network*, April 25, 2003, http://www.hnn.us/articles/1415.html.

31. Kate Zernike, "Professors Protest As Students Debate," *History News Network*, April 5, 2003, http://hnn.us/readcomment.php?id=10452.

32. Robert C. Post, "Academic Freedom and the 'Intifada Curriculum,'" *Academe*, May–June 2003, http://www.aaup.org/publications/Academe/2003/03mj/03mjpost .htm.

33. "Student Comments About Joseph Massad," *Campus Watch*, http://www .campus-watch.org/article/id/63.

34. "Student Comments About Joseph Massad," *Campus Watch*.

35. Ariel Beery, "Middle East Certitude," *Columbia Spectator*, March 10, 2003, http:// www.columbiaspectator.com/vnews/display.v/ART/2003/03/10/3e6c836370420?in _archive=1.

36. Jordana R. Lewis, "Indoctrinating Not Educating," *Harvard Crimson*, November 15, 2001, http://www.thecrimson.com/.

37. Matar Davis, interview with author, September 2, 2005, San Francisco, CA.

38. *Columbia Unbecoming*, Goldwasser.

39. Ron Lewenberg, "Whitewash at Columbia," *FrontPageMagazine*, April 6, 2005, http://www.frontpagemag.com/Articles/ReadArticle.asp?ID=17612.

40. George Archibald, "California Professor Flunks Kuwaiti's Pro-U.S. Essay," *Washington Times*, January 16, 2005, http://washingtontimes.com/national/ 20050115-115940-9997r.htm.

41. Rachel Pomerance, "Africans Say Their Story, Too, Excluded from Middle East Studies," *Jewish Telegraphic Agency*, March 8, 2005, http://www.jta.org/page_view _story.asp?intarticleid=15143&intcategoryid=4.

42. Irshad Manji, *The Trouble with Islam* (Toronto: Random House Canada, 2003), 148.

43. Jerome L. Sternstein, "Ideological Prejudice at Brooklyn College," *Wall Street Journal*, January 28, 2003, http://online.wsj.com/.

44. Adam Dickter, "Tenure Tension," *Jewish Week*, December 27, 2002, http://www .thejewishweek.com/.

45. "DePaul Invites Ward Churchill to Lecture: University Sued by Professor Fired for Supporting Israel," *WorldNetDaily*, September 18, 2005, http://www.worldnetdaily .com/news/article.asp?ARTICLE_ID=46384.

46. Pauline Dubkin Yearwood, "Gag Order: Is Depaul University Silencing a Professor for His Pro-Israel Views?," *Chicago Jewish News Online*, http://www .chicagojewishnews.com/archives_articles .jsp?id=192612.

47. "DePaul Invites Ward Churchill," *WorldNetDaily*.

48. Laurie Zoloth, "Activists at a Jewish Peace Rally Are Confronted by a Terrifying, Threatening Mob," *Aish*, May 9, 2002, http://www.aish.com/jewishissues/jewishsociety/Fear_and_Loathing_at_San_Francisco_State.asp.

49. "Faculty," *Northwestern University Center for Genetic Medicine*, http://www.cgm.northwestern.edu/faculty_bios/zoloth.htm.

50. Ballon, "Jewish Students Call UC Irvine a Hotbed."

51. Ingrid Peritz, "Concordia Bans Talk By Ex-Israeli PM," *Toronto Globe and Mail*, October 5, 2004, http://www.theglobeandmail.com/servlet/ArticleNews/TPStory/LAC/20041005/CONCORDIA05/ TPNational/Canada.

52. Daniel Pipes, "The War on Campus," *New York Post*, September 17, 2002, http://www.nypost.com/.

53. Pipes, "The War on Campus."

54. Adam Bissen, "Students Oppose Campus Watch Founder's Lecture Next Week," *Daily Cardinal*, April 22, 2003, http://www.dailycardinal.com/media/paper439/news/2003/04/22/News/Students.Oppose.Campus.Watch.Founders.Lecture.Next.Week-422835.shtml.

55. Margaret Wente, "Welcome to York U, Where Tolerance Is No Longer Tolerated," *Toronto Globe and Mail*, March 11, 2003, http://www.globeandmail.com/servlet/ArticleNews/TPStory/LAC/ 20030311/COWENT11//?query=zundel.

56. BBC arts panelist Tom Paulin's statement in his interview with the Egyptian weekly *Al-Ahram* is quoted in Tom Gass, "Welcome Voice? Harvard Invites Academic Who Wants Jews 'Shot Dead,'" *National Review Online*, November 12, 2002, http://www.nationalreview.com/comment/comment-gross111202.asp.

57. Aaron Klein, "Students Slam Pro-Israel Speaker, but Welcome Professor with 'Terror Ties,'" *WorldNetDaily*, January 21, 2005, http://www.worldnetdaily.com/news/article.asp?ARTICLE_ID=42480.

58. For more information, see Manfred Gerstenfeld, "Jews Against Israel," *Jerusalem Center for Public Affairs*, March 1, 2005, http://www.jcpa.org/phas/phas-30.htm.

59. Corina Yen, "Nakba Day Remembers Palestine," *Stanford Daily*, May 15, 2003, http://daily.stanford.edu/tempo?page=content&id =11300&repository=0001_article.

60. Stephen Rose, "More Pressure for Mid-East Peace," *Guardian*, April 6, 2002, http://www.guardian.co.uk/Archive/Article/ 0,4273,4388633,00.html.

61. Suzanne Goldenberg and Will Woodward, "Israeli Boycott Divides Academics: Sackings on Two Obscure Journals Fuel Debate on Cooperation with Universities," *Guardian*, July 8, 2002, http://www.guardian.co.uk/Archive/Article/0,4273,4456883,00.html.

62. "Professor Mona Baker Press Release," *In Defence of Academic Freedom*, 2002, http://www.btinternet.com/~reveuse/acbaker1.htm.

63. Stephen Howe, "More Splits over the Academic Boycott of Israel," *Guardian*, July 17, 2002, http://education.guardian.co.uk/higherfeedback/story/0,11056,756713,00.html.

64. Hillary Rose and Stephen Rose, "The Choice Is to Do Nothing or Try to Bring about Change," *MonaBaker.com*, July 15, 2002, http://www.monabaker.com/pMachine/more.php?id=A449_0_1_0_M.

65. Sara Leibovich-Dar, "Scholars Under Siege," *Haaretz*, November 21, 2003, http://www.haaretzdaily.com/hasen/pages/ShArt.jhtml?itemNo=363485.

66. Andy Beckett, "It's Water on Stone—In the End the Stone Wears Out," *Guardian*, December 12, 2002, http://www.guardian.co.uk/g2/story/0,,858314,00.html.

67. Julie Henry, "Outrage as Oxford Bans Student for Being Israeli," *Telegraph*, June 29, 2003, http://www.telegraph.co.uk/news/main.jhtml?xml=/news/2003/06/29/noxf29 .xml&sSheet=/portal/2003/06/ 29/ixportal.html.

68. Beckett, "It's Water on Stone."

69. Goldenberg and Woodward, "Israeli Boycott Divides Academics."

70. Goldenberg and Woodward, "Israeli Boycott Divides Academics."

71. Stephen Greenblatt, "An Open Letter to Mona Baker, Director of the Centre for Translation and Intercultural Studies, University of Manchester Institute for Science and Technology," *In Defence of Academic Freedom*, June 26, 2002, http://www.btinternet .com/~reveuse/acgreenblatt.htm.

72. Letter from Jewish defense groups and the three main Jewish religious streams to Protestant leaders, April 22, 2005, quoted in Rachel Pomerance, "As Protestant Divestment Drive Heats Up, Jews Express Their Ire," *Jewish Telegraphic Agency*, April 29, 2005, http://www.jta.org page_view_story.asp?intarticleid=15356&intcategoryid=4.

73. Francis A. Boyle, "Israeli Divestment/Disinvestment Campaign," e-mail correspondence to AALS Section on Minority Groups mailing list, May 16, 2002, http:// legalminds.lp.findlaw.com/list/forintlaw/msg00844.html.

74. Lawrence H. Summers, "Address at Morning Prayers," *Office of the President*, Cambridge, MA, September 17, 2002, http://www.president.harvard.edu/speeches/2002/ morningprayers.html.

75. Lee C. Bollinger, "Columbia University Statement on Divestment from Israel," *Communications Office of the President*, November 7, 2002, http://www.columbia.edu/ cu/president/communications%20files/israel.htm.

76. Judith Shapiro, "Barnard College Statement on Divestment from Israel," *Barnard News Center*, November 7, 2002, http://www.barnard.edu/newnews/news110702b.html.

77. Alex Garinger, "Keohane Speaks Out, Rejects Divestment Campaign: President Calls Tactic 'Too Blunt for Middle East,'" *Chronicle*, February 5, 2003, http://www .chronicle.duke.edu/vnews/display.v/ART/2003/02/05/3e412adb05409.

78. Marilyn H. Karfeld, "Divestment Advocates Wage War of Lies, Dershowitz Says," *Cleveland Jewish News*, December 12, 2002, http://www.clevelandjewishnews .com/articles/2002/12/12/export9489.txt.

79. Samuel G. Freedman, "Divestment Movement Undercuts Israel," *USA Today*, October 28, 2002, http://www.usatoday.com/news/opinion/ 2002-10-29-freedman-oped_x.htm.

80. "Guiding Principles: Adopted at the Third National Student Conference of the *Palestine Solidarity Movement*, November 7, 2003," http://www.palestineconference .com/principles.html.

81. Thomas L. Friedman, "Campus Hypocrisy," *New York Times*, October 16, 2002, http://www.nytimes.com/.

82. "Background Report: What AJC Is Doing about Israel Divestment Campaigns," *American Jewish Committee*, October 11, 2004, http://www.ajc.org/site/apps/nl/ content2.asp?c=ijITI2PHKoG&b =837277&ct=873255.

83. SUSTAIN Memphis website, "About Memphis Chapter," http://www.sustain-memphis.org/memphis_history.htm. The Memphis Chapter of SUSTAIN (Stop US Tax-funded Aid to Israel NOW!) was inaugurated with two teach-ins that brought outside speakers from Washington, DC, and a local group called "Friends for Palestine" to the University of Memphis campus. According to SUSTAIN, twenty people showed up for the first teach-in, fifty for the second. A SUSTAIN-organized sit-in at Southwest Tennessee Community College focused on "European Perspectives on US Foreign

Policy" and "Global Terrorism," and drew, according to SUSTAIN, eighty people. Protest ended when school security dispersed the event.

84. James Kirchick, "Applauding Falsehoods at a University," *Yale Daily News*, February 26, 2003, http://www.yaledailynews.com/article.asp?AID=21965.

85. Chris Buell, "Speaker: Peace Offers Unacceptable," *Digital Collegian*, April 19, 2002, http://www.collegian.psu.edu/archive/2002/04/04-19-02tdc/04-19-02dnews-05.asp.

86. Jonathan Calt Harris, "Muslim Students at Penn Sponsor Nazi," *FrontPage Magazine*, October 9, 2003, http://www.frontpagemag.com/Articles/ReadArticle.asp?ID =10233.

87. Beth Duff-Brown, "Groups Condemn 'Israeli Apartheid Week,'" *Washington Post*, January 31, 2005, http://www.wpost.com/.

88. Martin Kramer, "Columbia Prof Plumbs the Shiite Mind," *Sandstorm*, April 14, 2002, http://www.geocities.com/martinkramerorg/2003_04_14.htm.

89. Margaret Hunt Gram, "Professors Condemn War in Iraq at Teach-in," *Columbia Spectator*, March 27, 2003, http://www.columbiaspectator.com/vnews/display.v/ART/ 2003/03/27/3e82ec7193097?in_archive=1.

90. Sara Russo, "Columbia Prof. Expresses Desire for 'A Million Mogadishus,'" *Accuracy in Academia*, April 2003, http://www.academia .org/campus_reports/2003/ apr_2003_2.html.

91. Adi Neuman, "Viewpoint: Terrorism, Anti-Semitism and the Conference," *Michigan Daily*, October 10, 2002, http://www.michigandaily.com/vnews/display.v/ ART/2002/10/10/3da501f6dd587?in_archive=1.

92. "Chicago Palestine Film Festival" program, April 18–26, 2002.

93. Courtney Heeren, "Palestinian Drawings Under Fire," *Daily Cardinal*, May 2, 2002, http://www.dailycardinal.com/media/paper439/news/2002/05/02/News/ Palestinian.Drawings.Underfire-249074.shtml. A series of drawings entitled "Innocence Under Siege: Palestinian Children's Perspective of the World around Them," was presented by Palestinian Humanities and Arts Now and Al-Adwa, the Palestinian Right to Return Coalition, at a local café frequented by numerous University of Wisconsin, Madison, students. The drawings included lines such as "Death for Israel," "From North to South it's only Palestine," and "Bloodshed is the language of Israel." Sarah Kaiksow, a UW senior and co-chair of the UW chapter of Al Awda defended the drawings by saying "Our organization put the pictures up because they present a reality and experiences that are completely silenced in the United States media."

94. Joe Eskenazi, "Protesters Use Street Theater to Demonstrate Anger at Israel," *J. Jewish News Weekly of Northern California*, February 15, 2002, http://www.jewishsf .com/content/2-0-/module/displaystory/story_id/17716/edition_id/352/format/ html/displaystory.html.

95. Jennifer Misthal, "Pro-Israeli Conference Incites Riots from Palestinian Supporters," *Michigan Daily*, March 11, 2002, http://www.michigandaily.com/vnews/ display.v?TARGET=printable&article_id=3cb2fb4bca091.

96. "Anti-Semitic/Anti-Israeli Events on Campus," *Anti-Defamation League*, May 14, 2002, http://www.adl.org/Campus/campus _incidents.asp.

97. Steve Sexton and Lally Rezayani, "Activists Hold Wheeler under Siege," *Daily Californian*, April 25, 2001, http://www.dailycal.org/article.php?id=5411.

98. Helen Christophi, "Students Arrested during Protest May Be Suspended: Sanctions Issued for Wheeler Hall Occupation," *Daily Californian*, April 26, 2002, http:// www.dailycal.org//article.php?id=8514.

99. Charlotte Crowly, "Students Should Be Critical," *Broadside*, April 3, 2003, http://www.broadsideonline.com/.

100. Shannon Pettypiece, "Students Hold Pro-Israel Rally," *Michigan Daily*, April 11, 2002, http://www.michigandaily.com/vnews/display.v/ART/3cb58691d87e1.

101. Jessika Fruchter, "Hoffman, Byyny Urge Restraint," *Colorado Daily*, April 18, 2002, http://www.coloradodaily.com/.

102. "ADL and Hillel Calls on CU President and Students to Take Stand against Inciteful Campus Activity," *ADL Press Release*, April 16, 2002, http://www.adl.org/CAMPUS/press_release/pr_campus.asp.

103. Steve Irsay, "Palestinian Supporters Hold Silent Demonstration," *Washington Square News*, April 10, 2002, http://www.nyunews.com/.

104. Soojung Chan, "Students Act Out Funeral Procession," *Michigan Daily*, April 17, 2002, http://www.michigandaily.com/vnews/display.v/ART/2002/04/17/3cbd1f40b1569?in_archive=1.

105. Cheo, "Mideast Protesters Square Off."

106. Tracy Landers, "Rally Highlights Contrasting Views," *Dartmouth*, April 19, 2002, http://www.thedartmouth.com/article.php?aid =2002041901010.

107. Jessika Fruchter, "Peace Activists Back from Palestine with Stories of Violence," *Colorado Daily*, April 16, 2002, http://www.coloradodaily.com/articles/2002/04/17/export2592.txt.

108. William Booth, "On Campus, a Reflection of Middle East Anger: Rally at San Francisco State Leads to Slurs and an Investigation as Tensions Rise at U.S. Universities," *Washington Post*, May 19, 2002, http://www.wpost.com/.

109. Bram Eisenthal, "Pro-Palestinian Hotbed in Montreal Erupts, Canceling Netanyahu Speech," *Jewish Telegraphic Agency*, September 10, 2002, http://www.jta.org/page_view_story.asp?intarticleid=11812&intcategoryid=2.

110. George Jonas, "Academic Fortresses of Repression," *National Post*, February 10, 2003, http://www.canada.com/national/nationalpost/ index.html.

111. "Anti-Semitic/Anti-Israel Events," *Anti-Defamation League*, http://www.adl.org/CAMPUS/campus_incidents.asp.

112. Campus media also include radio and web broadcasts, which were not part of our analysis.

113. Garrett, student from Northwestern (Louisiana) State University, *Associated Collegiate Press ACP Forum*, August 6, 2004, http://www.studentpress.org/acp/forums/~1564.html.

114. "Forget the Past: A Suggestion to Americans," *New University*, April 28, 2002, http://www.newu.uci.edu/archive/2001-2002/spring/020429/opinstory01.htm.

115. "Anti-Israel Fabrication Rocks Arizona Journalism School," *CAMERA On Campus* 6, no. 1 (1995):1.

116. Friedland, "Interview with Robert Costrell."

117. Paula Maggio, "Colleges Struggling with Differences between Free Speech and Hate Speech," *Akron Jewish News*, November 15, 2002, http://www.akronjewishnews.com/.

118. William James Martin, "On the Palestinian Refugees," *Central Florida Future*, April 1, 2004, http://www.ucfnews.com/media/paper174/news/2004/04/01/Opinions/Reader.Views-647354.shtml?page=4.

119. Steven I. Weiss, "College Columnist Fired over Call for Profiling," *Forward*, September 23, 2005, http://www.forward.com/articles/4010.

120. "Anti-Semitic/Anti-Israel Events," *Anti-Defamation League*.

7. Reclaiming the Civil University

1. Tobin and Weinberg, *Mega-Gifts in American Philanthropy.*

2. *College Access and Opportunity Act of 2005*, HR 609.

3. Lee Smith, "The Language Gap: Why Middle Eastern Linguists Are Hard to Find, Even Though the Government Has Been Funding the Field," *Slate Magazine*, Oct. 4, 2004, http://www.slate.msn.com/.

4. National Commission on Terrorist Attacks Upon the United States. *The 9/11 Commission Report: Final Report of the National Commission on Terrorist Attacks Upon the United States* (New York: W.W. Norton and Company, 2003), 92.

5. Committee on Education and the Workforce press release, "Education Subcommittee Approves Hoekstra Measure to Strengthen International Studies in Higher Education, Ensure Programs Fulfill National Security Needs," September 17, 2003, http://edworkforce.house.gov/press/press108/09sep/hr3077psub091703.htm

6. Jennifer Jacobson, "The Clash Over Middle East Studies: Critics Say the Programs Are Biased Against U.S. Foreign Policy and Need a Review Board," *Chronicle of Higher Education*, February 6, 2004, sec. A8.

7. Coalition for International Education, "Memorandum to Members of the House Subcommittee on Education and the Workforce Regarding HR 3077, International Studies in Higher Education Act," *Joint National Committee for Languages and the National Council for Languages and International Studies*, September 22, 2003, http://www .languagepolicy .org/ciehealetter.html.

8. Jacobson, "Clash Over Middle East Studies."

9. Chris Nguyen, "Legislation Aims to Reduce Bias in International Studies Classes," *Stanford Daily*, February 25, 2004, http://daily.stanford.edu/tempo?page =content&id=13288&repository=0001_article.

10. "Letter to Sens. Mike Enzi and Edward Kennedy Regarding the Higher Education Act of 2005," *American Council on Education*, September 7, 2005, http://www.acenet .edu/AM/Template.cfm?Section=HENA&TEMPLATE=/CM/ContentDisplay.cfm &CONTENTID=11845.

11. HR 177, General Assembly of Pennsylvania, session of 2005.

12. HR 177.

13. "Difficult Dialogues: Promoting Pluralism and Academic Freedom on Campus," *Ford Foundation*, http://www.fordfound.org/news/more/dialogues/index.cfm ?print_version=1.

14. "Pats Owner to Calm Columbia?" *Jewish Telegraphic Agency*, n.d., http://www .jta.org/.

15. Ronald S. Lauder, "A New Free Speech Movement, Starting with Alumni," *New York Sun*, December 2004, http://www.nysun/article/5959.

16. "College Presidents Decry Intimidation on Campuses," *American Jewish Committee*, October 15, 2002, http://www.ajc.org/site/apps/nl/content2.asp?c=ijITI2PHKoG &b=849241&ct=868017.

17. "College Presidents Decry Intimidation," *American Jewish Committee*.

18. Jessamyn Blau, "Levin Declines to Sign AJC Statement," *Yale Daily News*, October 14, 2002, http://yaledailynews.com/article.asp?AID =20111.

19. Deborah E. Lipstadt, *History on Trial: My Day in Court with David Irving* (New York: HarperCollins, 2005), 30.

20. Uriel Heilman, "Jewish Columbia Alumni Threaten to Stop Contributions," *Jerusalem Post*, February 13, 2005, http://www.jpost .com/.

21. Gary Rosenblatt, "New Fronts in Campus Wars," *Jewish Week*, February 11, 2005, http://www.thejewishweek.com/.

22. Josh Rolnich, "The Quad Squad," *Moment Magazine*, April/May 2003, http://www.momentmag.com/.

23. Jacob Gershman, "Search Committee for Israel Scholar Includes Two Harsh Critics of Israel: Crisis at Columbia," *New York Sun*, April 29. 2005, http://www.nysun.com/article/13026.

24. *Columbia Unbecoming*, Goldwasser.

25. Owen Hearey, "CU to Create $5 Mil Chair of Israel Studies," *Columbia Spectator*, March 28, 2005, http://www.columbiaspectator.com/vnews/display.v/ART/2005/03/28/4247bba45dc4e.

26. Hilary Leila Krieger, "Profs Combat Academic Anti-Israel Bias," *Jerusalem Post*, May 25, 2005, http://www.jpost.com/.

27. Jewish Telegraphic Agency, "Fund Fights Israel Boycott," *Cleveland Jewish News*, May 19, 2005, http://www.clevelandjewishnews.com/articles/2005/05/19/news/world/fund0520.txt.

28. The Solomon Amendment is currently under heavy attack in a concerted effort by a number of universities to deny military recruiters access to their campuses. A group of colleges and universities has chosen to fight the Solomon Amendment through the courts and has successfully brought the case all the way to the Supreme Court (to be heard December 2005, subsequent to the publication of this volume). The rationale for the current objection to military recruitment lies in the objection to the armed forces' policy of "don't ask/don't tell" concerning homosexuals, which is considered incompatible with the anti-discrimination statutes of, in particular, schools of law. For a discussion of the Solomon Amendment, see Kelly Field, "High Court to Hear Case on Military Recruiting: Justices to Decide If Colleges Can Enforce Restrictions Based on Hiring Practices," *Chronicle of Higher Education*, May 13, 2005, sec. A1; Charles Lane, "Court to Review Military Recruiting at Colleges: Law Schools Challenge Rule Requiring Universities to Give Equal Access or Risk Losing Funding," *Washington Post*, May 3, 2005, sec. A02; and Jeffrey Toobin, "Sex and the Supremes: Why the Court's Next Big Battle May Be about Gay Rights," *New Yorker*, July 25, 2005, http://www.newyorker.com/fact/content/articles/050801fa_fact.

29. Katz, "Liberal Education on Ropes."

30. Gabriel, "Enviroments of Hate."

8. Conclusion to the Revised Edition

1. Chris Isidore, "College Sports' Fuzzy Math: Big College Sports Programs Are Making a Greater Push to Increase Revenue, But Schools Are Having to Kick in More Money Than Ever," *CNN Money*, November 10, 2006, http://money.cnn.com/2006/11/10/commentary/sportsbiz/index.htm.

2. "At University Hospitals, Ivory Towers Become Source of Big Business for Their Communities," *Business World*, March 1, 2004 and Association of American Universities, Council on Governmental Relations, and National Association of State Universities and Land-Grant Colleges, "Statement Expressing Opposition to Indirect Cost Cap on Basic Research In House Defense Appropriations Bill," http://206.151.87.67/docs/WebJointIDCStatement.doc.

3. Scott Jaschik, "A Call to Defend Academic Freedom," *Inside Higher Education,* October 23, 2008, http://www.insidehighered.com/layout/set/print/news/2007/10/23/freedom.

4. Jeffrey Brainard, "College Groups Oppose New Cap on Research Costs," *Chronicle of Higher Education,* November 16, 2007, sec. A23. http://chronicle.com/cgi-bin/printable.cgi?article=http://chronicle.com/weekly/v54/i12/12a02302.htm

5. "Almanac," *Chronicle of Higher Education,* http://chronicle.com/free/almanac/2007/ and "Money & Management," *Chronicle of Higher Education,* http://chronicle.com/money/.

6. Victoria Fosdal, "GU Questioned by Congress on Endowment Spending," *The Hoya,* January 29, 2008, http://www.thehoya.com/print/15159.

7. Stuart Taylor Jr. and KC Johnson, *Until Proven Innocent: Political Correctness and the Shameful Injustices of the Duke Lacrosse Rape Case* (New York: St. Martin's Press, 2007), 117.

8. Taylor and Johnson, *Until Proven Innocent,* 117.

9. Greg Lukianoff (president, *Foundation for Individual Rights in Education*), in discussion with one of the authors, May 2008.

10. Deb McCown, "School, Student Settle Flier Suit," *Washington Times,* May 11, 2003, http://www.washingtontimes.com.

11. McCown, "School, Student Settle Flier Suit."

12. "Duke Lacrosse Players File Federal Lawsuit Against University, City of Durham," *Fox News,* February 21, 2008, http://www.foxnews.com/story/0,2933,331568,00.html.

13. McCown, "School, Student Settle Flier Suit."

14. Gary A. Tobin and Aryeh K. Weinberg, *Profiles of the American University: Volume I: Political Beliefs & Behavior of College Faculty* (San Francisco: Institute for Jewish & Community Research, 2006). Gary A. Tobin and Aryeh K. Weinberg, *Profiles of the American University: Volume II: Religious Beliefs & Behavior of College Faculty* (San Francisco; Institute for Jewish & Community Research, 2007).

15. Tobin and Weinberg, *Profiles of the American University: Volume I: Political Beliefs & Behavior of College Faculty,* 39.

16. Gary Tobin, David Dutwin, Dennis Ybarra, and Aryeh K. Weinberg. Authors, *College Faculty Views about Israel and the Middle East* (Lanham, MD: Lexington Books, forthcoming).

17. Sam Dillon, "Tuition Rise Tops Inflation, but Rate Slows, Report Says," *New York Times,* October 19, 2005, http://www.nytimes.com/2005/10/19/education/19tuition.html?_r=1&oref=slogin&pagewanted=print.

18. Kamil Dada, "Congress Investigates Endowment," *The Stanford Daily,* February 1, 2008, http://daily.stanford.edu/article/2008/2/1/congressInvestigatesEndowment.

19. Anne H. Franke and Meyer Eisenberg, "10 Rules for Avoiding Conflicts of Interest," *Chronicle of Higher Education,* October 12, 2007, sec. B20, http://chronicle.com/cgi-bin/printable.cgi?article=http://chronicle.com/weekly/v54/i07/07b02001.htm.

20. Tobin and Weinberg, *Profiles of the American University: Volume I: Political Beliefs & Behavior of College Faculty,* 39.

21. Myles Brand, "College Sports Are Not Professional," *Chronicle of Higher Education,* June 23, 2006, sec. B13, http://chronicle.com/weekly/v52/i42/42b01302.htm.

22. See Duane Gang, "Christian Group Denied Cal State Charter; Ruling: The University Says the Group Cannot Form Because It Would Exclude Some Students," *FIRE: Foundation for Individual Rights in Education*, December 20, 2005, http://www.thefire.org/index.php/article/6611.html and "Christians 'Too Evangelical' for Christian School: Alliance Defense Fund Asks University to Reconsider Ban on Ministries," *World Net Daily*, October 13, 2006, http://www.worldnetdaily.com/news/article.asp?ARTICLE_ID=52420.

Epilogue to the Revised Edition

1. See Howard Kurtz, "College Faculties A Most Liberal Lot, Study Finds," *Washington Post*, March 29, 2005, http://www.washingtonpost.com/wp-dyn/articles/A8427-2005Mar28.html and Mark Bauerlein, "Research on Faculty Politics and Attitudes," *Chronicle of Higher Education*, June 15, 2008, http://chronicle.com/review/brainstorm/bauerlein/?pg=2 and Alan Cooperman, "Is There Disdain for Evangelicals in the Classroom: Survey, Bias Allegation Spur Debate," *The Washington Post*, May 5, 2007, http://www.washingtonpost.com/wp-dyn/content/article/2007/05/04/AR2007050401990_pf.html.

2. Addressing anti-Semitism and anti-Israelism on America's college campuses is attracting more and more bi-partisan support in the House, Senate, and state legislatures. See the following letters: From Members of the United States Senate Judiciary Committee to Department of Education Secretary Margaret Spellings, Washington DC, February 27, 2008, (http://www.octaskforce.files.wordpress.com/2008/03/senjudiccom0208.pdf) and from Brad Sherman, Linda Sanchez, Steven Rothman, Allyson Schwartz, and Robert Wexler, Members of Congress, to Department of Education Secretary Margaret Spellings, Washington DC, April 30, 2008, (http://www.zoa.org/media/user/documents/publ/ushousetoedsecyretitlevi.pdf), and from State Assemblyman Chuck Devore, "Liberal Groupthink Causes Conservatives to Self-Censor," http://republican.assembly.ca.gov/members/a70/index.aspx?page=OPED&oped=1743. Also, Lynn Munson, "Robbing the Rich to Give to the Richest," *Inside Higher Ed*, July 26, 2007, http://www.insidehighered.com/views/2007/07/26/munson.

3. For further information, see "Findings and Recommendations of the United States Commission on Civil Rights Regarding Campus Anti-Semitism," *The United States Commission on Civil Rights*, April 3, 2006, http://www.usccr.gov/pubs/081506campusantibrief07.pdf and "Contemporary Global Anti-Semitism Report," *United States Department of State*, March 2008, http://www.state.gov/documents/organization/102301.pdf.

4. United States Senate Judiciary Committee to Department of Education Secretary Margaret Spellings (http://octaskforce.files.wordpress.com/2008/03/senjudiccom0208.pdf) and Sherman, et al., Members of Congress to Department of Education Secretary Margaret Spellings.

5. In June of 2008, the ZOA case against the University of California, Irvine previously filed and dismissed by the Office of Civil Rights in the Department of Education, was reinstated following questions by a number of elected officials about the inadequacy of the investigation. See Zionist Organization of America, "Federal Government Initiates New Investigation Into UC Irvine's Response to Campus anti-Semitism," news release, June 6, 2008.

6. The Orange County Independent Task Force on Anti-Semitism, *Task Force on Anti-Semitism at the University of California, Irvine: Report* (Orange County, 2008).

7. Aaron Hanscom, "UC-Intifada," *Front Page Magazine*, February 20, 2007, http://www.frontpagemag.com/articles/Printable.aspx?GUID=D64DF0F8-5E16-4568-AFE4-5D2990DFF375.

8. "U.S. Anti-Israel Activity: Imam Amir Abdul Malik Ali," *Anti-Defamation League*, http://www.adl.org/israel/malik_ali.asp.

9. "The Muslim Student Union at UC Irvine," *Front Page Magazine*, April 3, 2008, http://frontpagemag.com/articles/Read.aspx?GUID=71E533E2-AE2F-487B-9B41-3A36FF1C5308 and "Transcript: Muhammad Al-Asi – Ghetto Jews," *The Investigative Project on Terrorism*, February 21, 2001, http://www.investigativeproject.org/article/239.

10. The Orange County Independent Task Force, *Task Force on Anti-Semitism at the University of California, Irvine: Report*.

11. Kimi Yoshino, "New Muslim-Jewish Discord at UC-Irvine: Program Titles Considered Anti-Semitic by Some at Site of Civil Rights Probe," *Scholars for Peace in the Middle East* (re-post of *Los Angeles Times* article), May 18, 2006, http://www.spme.net/cgi-bin/articles.cgi?ID=523.

12. Jeffrey Rips and Ami Glazer, "UC-Irvine Hillel Executive Director and SPME Co-Coordinators Jeffrey Rips and Prof. Amihai Glazer Report on Dorm Swastika Incident and Vice Chancellor Gomez's Remarks," *SPME: Scholars for Peace in the Middle East*, October 27, 2006, http://www.spme.net/cgi-bin/articles.cgi?ID=1306.

13. Brad A. Greenberg, "Quiet War on Campus: Israel Remains Under Attack Despite Fewer Public Protests, Is Anti-Zionism the New Anti-Semitism?" *Jewish Journal*, August 20, 2008, http://www.jewishjournal.com/education/page2/quiet_war_on_campus_israel_remains_under_attack_despite_fewer_public_protes/.

14. Ron Campbell, "FBI Denies Investigating UCI: Agent Followed 'Suspicious' Truck on Campus, but FBI Says Probe Had Nothing to Do With Student Activism," *Orange County Register*, http://www.ocregister.com/ocregister/homepage/abox/article_1701746.php.

15. Ben-Zion Jaffe, "A Big Jew on Campus: Anti-Semitism Goes to College," *The Jerusalem Post Blogs*, April 16, 2008, http://cgis.jpost.com/Blogs/jaffe/entry/anti_semitism_goes_to_college.

16. *Columbia Unbecoming*, directed by Avi Goldwasser, DVD (Boston: David Project, 2004).

17. Karen W. Arenson, "Columbia Panel Clears Professors of Anti-Semitism," *New York Times*, March 31, 2005, http://www.nytimes.com/2005/03/31/education/31columbia.html and Chanan Tigay, "Report Finds Little Proof of Bullying, but Columbia Spat Likely to Continue," *JTA*, April 5, 2005, http://www.jta.org/cgi-bin/iowa/news/article/Reportfindslittle.html.

18. Joshua Runyan, "Jewish Professor Defiant in Face of Anti-Semitic Vandalism," *Chabad.org*, November 7, 2007, http://www.chabad.org/news/article_cdo/aid/591628/jewish/A-Sign-for-All-to-See.htm.

19. Adam Dickter, "Columbia Prof Defiant After Swastika: Jewish Educator Says Hate Outbreak a 'Clarion Call to the Jewish Community,'" *The Jewish Week*, November 7, 2007, http://www.thejewishweek.com/viewArticle/c36_a976/News/New_York.html#.

20. Karen W. Arenson, "Fracas Erupts Over Book on Mideast by a Barnard Professor Seeking Tenure," *New York Times*, http://www.nytimes.com/2007/09/10/education/10barnard.html?pagewanted=print.

21. Dickter, "Columbia Prof Defiant After Swastika: Jewish Educator Says Hate Outbreak a 'Clarion Call to the Jewish Community.'"

22. Anti-Defamation League, "Annual ADL Audit: Anti-Semitic Incidents Decline in 2005 but Levels Still of Concern in U.S.," news release, April 5, 2006, (http://www .adl.org/PresRele/ASUS_12/audit_2005.htm)

23. "Sukkah at California University Vandalized," *JTA*, October 9, 2007, http:// www.jta.org/cgi-bin/iowa/breaking/104548.html.

24. Salvatore Caputo, "Wildcat Cartoon Flap Raises Issues: Anti-Jewish Message Initially Defended as Satire," *Jewish News of Greater Phoenix*, http://www.jewishaz .com/issues/printstory.mv?071026+cartoon.

25. Philip Kurian, "The Jews," *The Chronicle Online*, October 18, 2004, http://media .www.dukechronicle.com/media/storage/paper884/news/2004/10/18/Editorial columns/The-Jews-1471620.shtml.

26. Kurian, "The Jews."

27. John J. Mearsheimer and Stephen M. Walt, *The Israel Lobby and U.S. Foreign Policy* (New York: Farrar, Straus, and Giroux, 2007).

28. Michelle Goldberg, "Is the 'Israel Lobby' Distorting America Mideast Policies? Two Leading Academics Have Tried to Break the Taboo Against Criticizing Israel's Powerful U.S. Lobby: It's a Worthy Aim, but Their Clumsy Argument May Backfire," *Salon*, April 18, 2006, http://www.salon.com/news/feature/2006/04/18/lobby/.

29. Scott Jaschik, "War of Words Over Paper on Israel," *Inside Higher Ed*, March 27, 2006, http://www.insidehighered.com/news/2006/03/27/israel.

30. Jake Robert Nelson, "John Mearsheimer Speaks on Israel Lobby," *The DoG Street Journal*, April 8, 2008, http://www.dogstreetjournal.com/story/4141, and Daniel Strauss, "Controversial Profs Coming to Campus: Mearsheimer and Walt Authored Book about Israel Lobby on Capitol Hill," *Michigan Daily*, February 8, 2008, http://www .michigandaily.com/content/controversial-authors-discuss-book-us-relation ship-israel and "Dubai School of Government Hosts John Mearsheimer and Stephen Walt at Dubai Press Club," *Maktoob Business*, June 15, 2008, http://business.maktoob. com/NewsDetails-20070423170658-Dubai_School_of_Government_Hosts_John _Mearsheimer_and_Stephen_Walt_at_Dubai_Press_Club.htm.

31. "Israel and Palestinians," *PollingReport.com*, http://www.pollingreport.com/ israel.htm.

32. Walter Russell Mead, "Jerusalem Syndrome: Decoding 'The Israel Lobby,'" *Foreign Affairs: A Publication of the Council on Foreign Relations*, http://www.foreignaffairs .org/20071101fareviewessay86611/walter-russell-mead/jerusalem-syndrome.html.

33. See Norman G. Finkelstein, "When the Talk Gets Too Serious, Send in the Clown," *CounterPunch*, December 28, 2006, http://www.normanfinkelstein.com/ article.php?ar=788&pg=11, and Gabrielle Birkner, "'Israel Apartheid Week' Begins, Reigniting Carter-Led Debate," *The New York Sun*, February 13, 2007, http://www. nysun.com/new-york/israel-apartheid-week-begins-reigniting-carter/48542/, and Ibrahim Nafie, "Peace, Not Apartheid," *Al-Ahram Weekly*, December 14, 2006, http:// weekly.ahram.org.eg/2006/824/op2.htm, and Saree Makdisi, "Academic Freedom at Risk on Campus," *Arab Media Internet Network*, October 17, 2007, http://www.amin .org/look/amin/en.tpl?IdLanguage=1&IdPublication=7&NrArticle=42797&NrIssue =1&NrSection=3.

34. Jimmy Carter, *Palestine: Peace Not Apartheid*, (New York: Simon & Schuster, 2006), 208.

35. Alan Abrams et al, "Malicious Advocacy: The Carter Center Councilors' Letter of Resignation," *Wall Street Journal*, January 11, 2007, http://www.opinionjournal.com/ forms/printThis.html?id=110009510.

36. Dennis Ross, "Don't Play With Maps," *New York Times*, January 9, 2007, http://www.nytimes.com/2007/01/09/opinion/09ross.html?_r=2&oref=slogin&pagewanted=print.

37. "Carter Center Op-Eds/Speeches," *The Carter Center*, http://www.cartercenter.org/news/editorials_speeches/index.html.

38. Griff Witte, "Carter Meets With Hamas Chief In Exile, Defying Israel and U.S.," *The Washington Post*, April 19, 2008, http://www.washingtonpost.com/wp-dyn/content/article/2008/04/18/AR2008041801256_pf.html.

39. Nicholas Kralev, "Hamas Rebuts Carter's Claim of Concession," *The Washington Times*, April 22, 2008, http://www.washingtontimes.com/news/2008/apr/22/hamas-rebuts-carters-claim-of-concession/.

40. Lena Khalaf Tuffaha, "Palestine: Peace Not Apartheid, by Jimmy Carter," *Institute for Middle East Understanding*, November 15, 2006, http://imeu.net/news/article003566.shtml, "Pro-Palestinian Groups Praise Jimmy Carter's Book," *ADL*, January 3, 2007, http://www.adl.org/Israel/carter_reactions_pa.asp, and Norman G. Finkelstein, "When the Talk Gets Too Serious, Send in the Clown," *Counter Punch*, December 28, 2006, http://www.normanfinkelstein.com/article.php?ar=788&pg=11, Saree Makdisi, "Academic Freedom at Risk on Campus," *Arab Media Internet Network*, October 17, 2007, http://www.amin.org/look/amin/en.tpl?IdLanguage=1&IdPublication=7&NrArticle=42797&NrIssue=1&NrSection=3 and Joel Beinin, "Silencing Critics Not Way to Middle East Peace," *San Francisco Chronicle*, February 4, 2007, http://www.sfgate.com/cgi-bin/article.cgi?f=/c/a/2007/02/04/INGFLNSJQJ1.DTL&type=printable.

41. "Merriam-Webster's Words of the Year 2006," *Merriam-Webster Online*, http://www.merriam-webster.com/info/06words.htm.

Truthiness (noun), 1 : "truth that comes from the gut, not books" (Stephen Colbert, Comedy Central's "The Colbert Report," October 2005)
2 : "the quality of preferring concepts or facts one wishes to be true, rather than concepts or facts known to be true" (American Dialect Society, January 2006)

42. Anthea Lipsett and Jessica Shepherd, "Brown Promotes Academic Links with Israel," *Guardian Unlimited*, July 21, 2008, http://www.education.guardian.co.uk/higher/worldwide/story/0,,2291960,00.html.

43. Marilyn H. Karfeld, "'Divestment Advocates Wage War of Lies,' Dershowitz Says," *Cleveland Jewish News*, December 12, 2002, http://www.clevelandjewishnews.com/articles/2002/12/12/export9489.txt.

44. *UCU: University and College Union*, http://www.ucu.org.uk/.

45. "Israel Boycott Illegal and Cannot be Implemented, UCU Tells Members: UCU Announced Today That, After Seeking Legal Advice, an Academic Boycott of Israel Would Be Unlawful and Cannot Be Implemented," *University and College Union*, September 28, 2007, http://www.ucu.org.uk/index.cfm?articleid=2829.

46. "News: UCU Response to Boycott Vote," *UCU: University and College Union*, http://www.ucu.org.uk/index.cfm?articleid=2595.

47. "Past Events: Mahmoud Ahmadinejad, President of the Islamic Republic of Iran," *Columbia University World Leaders Forum*, http://www.worldleaders.columbia.edu/events.html.

48. Anthony Faiola and Robin Wright, "Ahmadinejad's Day One in New York: A Hostile Reception, a Rambling Talk," *Washington Post*, September 24, 2007, http://www.washingtonpost.com/wp-dyn/content/article/2007/09/24/AR2007092400168.html.

49. "President Lee C. Bollinger's Introductory Remarks at SIPA-World Leaders Forum with President of Iran Mahmoud Ahmadinejad—September 24, 2007," *Columbia University News*, http://www.columbia.edu/cu/news/07/09/lcbopeningremarks .html.

50. "Statement by President Lee C. Bollinger on British University and College Union Boycott," *Columbia University News*, http://www.columbia.edu/cu/news/07/06/ boycott.html.

51. Tom Faure, Erin Durkin, Shane Ferro, Josh Hirschland, and Jacob Schneider, "Professors Clash over Bollinger," *Columbia Spectator*, November 14, 2007, http://www .columbiaspectator.com/?q=node/28100.

52. Robert Corrigan, "Anti-Defamation League Award Acceptance Speech," (speech, Anti-Defamation League, New York, January, 2007).

53. "Chancellor Drake Participates in Hillel Summit," *Office of the Chancellor, University of California, Irvine*, http://www.chancellor.uci.edu/080324_hillel.php.

54. Reut R. Cohen, "'Hadith of Hate' Banned at USC," *Front Page Magazine*, August 27, 2008. http://www.frontpagemagazine.com/Articles/Read.aspx?GUID=9E589 DA9-14A5-4147-A755-47E92DA10F2A.

55. Solidarity for Palestinian Human Rights, "Academic Freedom and Dissent Under Attack," news release, December 9, 2004. https://lists.resist.ca/pipermail/ project-x/2004-December/008361.html.

56. Solidarity for Palestinian Human Rights, "Academic Freedom and Dissent Under Attack."

57. Dan Carnevale, "York U. Must Pay Fine for Criticizing Professor," *Chronicle of Higher Education*, http://chronicle.com/news/article/3452/ york-u-must-pay-fine-for-criticizing-professor.

58. Lee Kaplan, "How 'Stop the ISM' Stopped Al Awda at UC Riverside," *Independent Media Review Analysis*, May 15, 2007, http://www.imra.org.il/story.php3?id=34307 and Amy Klein, "Hilton Boycott Organizers Claim Victory as Palestinian 'Right of Return' Conclave in O.C. Attracts Few Participants, *Jewish Journal*, May 29, 2007, http:// www.jewishjournal.com/home/print.php?id=17726.

59. David Horowitz, *The Professors: The 101 Most Dangerous Academics in America* (Lanham, MD: Regnery Publishing, 2006).

60. *American Council of Trustees and Alumni*, http://www.goacta.org/, *The Hoover Institution*, http://www.hoover.org/, Middle East Forum, http://www.meforum.org/, and *Campus Watch*, http://www.campus-watch.org/.

61. "Freedom in the Classroom," *American Association of University Professors*, 2007, http://www.aaup.org/AAUP/comm/rep/A/class.htm.

62. Robin Wilson, "AAUP Goes to Bat for 'Freedom in the Classroom,'" *Chronicle of Higher Education*, September 21, 2007, A9.

63. Joan Scott, Edmund Burke, Jeremy Adelman, Steven Coten, Jonathan Cole, "Petition: Ad Hoc Committee to Defend the University," *Defend.University*, http://defend .university.googlepages.com/home.

64. "Critical Mass: The Partisan Battle Over Academic Freedom," *Chronicle of Higher Education*, November 9, 2007, http://chronicle.com/weekly/v54/i11/11b00401.htm.

65. News Blog, "DePaul Rejects Tenure Bid by Finkelstein and Says Dershowitz Pressure Played No Role," *Chronicle of Higher Education*, June 8, 2007.

66. Michal Lando, "Dershowitz, Finkelstein and a Bitter Tenure Battle, *Jerusalem Post*, April 19, 2007, http://www.jpost.com/servlet/Satellite?cid=1176152838045 &pagename=JPost%2FJPArticle%2FPrinter.

67. Paul Wasley, "Tenure Dispute at DePaul Ends With a Settlement and a Resignation," *Chronicle of Higher Education*, September 14, 2007, A9, http://chronicle.com/cgi-bin/printable.cgi?article=http://chronicle.com/weekly/v54/i03/03a00901.htm.

68. Scott Jaschik, "The Ward Churchill Verdict," *Inside Higher Ed*, May 16, 2006, http://www.insidehighered.com/layout/set/print/news/2006/05/16/churchill.

69. John Gravois, "Colo. Regents Vote to Fire Ward Churchill: Research Misconduct Cited, but Professor Says Decision Was Political and Sues," *Chronicle of Higher Education*, August 3, 2007, A1, http://chronicle.com/cgi-bin/printable.cgi?article=http://chronicle.com/weekly/v53/i48/48a00101.htm.

70. "Report of the Investigative Committee of the Standing Committee on Research Misconduct at the University of Colorado at Boulder Concerning Allegations of Academic Misconduct Against Professor Ward Churchill: Media Summary of Investigative Committee Findings," *University of Colorado at Boulder*, http://www.colorado.edu/news/reports/churchill/churchillreport051606.html.

71. Thomas W. Krause, "Layer Involved in Al-Arian Case Asks Extortion Charge Be Dropped," *Tampa Bay Online*, December 3, 2004, http://news.tbo.com/news/MGB1WHYPA2E.html.

72. Roberta Seid and Roz Rothstein, "Wayne State & Wadie Said," *Campus Report Online*, November 30, 2006, http://www.campusreportonline.net/main/printer_friendly.php?id=1363.

73. "Wadie E. Said Profile," *University of South Carolina School of Law*, http://law.sc.edu/faculty/said/.

74. Gretchen Ruethling, "A Skeptic on 9/11 Prompts Questions on Academic Freedom," *New York Times*, August 1, 2006, http://www.nytimes.com/2006/08/01/education/01madison.html?_r=2&oref=slogin&oref=slogin.

75. Ruethling, "A Skeptic on 9/11 Prompts Questions on Academic Freedom."

76. Board of Regents of the University of Wisconsin System, "Provost Review Clears Barrett to Teach Class on Islam," *University of Wisconsin-Madison News*, July 10, 2006, http://www.news.wisc.edu/12701.

77. Martin Kramer, *Ivory Towers on Sand: The Failure of Middle Eastern Studies in America*, (Washington DC: The Washington Institute for Near East Policy, 2001).

78. "Welcome to the Association for the Study of the Middle East and Africa," *Association for the Study of the Middle East and Africa*, http://www.asmeascholars.org.

79. *United States Commission on Civil Rights, Findings and Recommendations on Civil Rights Regarding Campus Anti-Semitism.*

80. Kenneth L. Marcus, "The Second Mutation: Israel and Political Anti-Semitism," *inFocus*, Volume II, no.1(Spring 2008). (http://www.jewishpolicycenter.org/pf.php?id=114)

81. "Antisemitism and Racism: United States of America 2005," *The Stephen Roth Institute for the Study of Contemporary Anti-Semitism and Racism*, http://www.tau.ac.il/Anti-Semitism/asw2005/usa.htm.

82. Karen W. Arenson, "Harvard President Sees Rise in Anti-Semitism on Campus, *New York Times*, September 21, 2002, http://query.nytimes.com/gst/fullpage.html?res=9B0CE7DD1F30F932A1575AC0A9649C8B63.s.

83. The United States Department of State, *Contemporary Global Anti-Semitism Report* (Washington, DC: Office of the Special Envoy to Monitor and Combat Anti-Semitism, 2008).

84. Barry A. Kosmin, Egon Mayer, and Ariela Keysar, *American Religious Identification* (New York: The Graduate Center of the City University of New York, 2001) and Sid Groeneman and Gary Tobin, *The Decline of Religious Identity in the United States* (San Francisco: Institute for Jewish & Community Research, 2004).

85. Kenneth L. Marcus, Deputy Assistant Secretary for Enforcement at the United States Department of Education Office for Civil Rights, letter to colleagues, September 13, 2004, and Kenneth L. Marcus, Delegated the Authority of Assistant Secretary of Education for Civil Rights, U.S. Department of Education, letter via facsimile to Sid Groeneman, Senior Research Associate at the Institute for Jewish & Community Research, October 22, 2004, http://www.eusccr.com/letterforcampus.pdf.

86. Letter from the United States Senate Judiciary Committee to Secretary Margaret Spellings.

87. Congressman Brad Sherman to Chancellor Michael V. Drake, Washington DC, May 15, 2008, http://www.investigativeproject.org/documents/misc/134.pdf.

88. Representative Brad Sherman, "A California Campus Event Intended to Encourage Violence and Spread Hate," *The Cutting Edge*, May 26, 2008, http://www.thecuttingedgenews.com/index.php?article=517.

89. AIPAC encourages student activism by teaching Israel advocacy and how to be more politically active, while also sponsoring student missions to Israel for non-Jewish students. They also publish a student-focused webpage: The Near East Report, that highlights current affairs affecting the relationship between Israel and the United States. See "American Israel Public Affairs Committee," *Israel on Campus Coalition*, http://www.israelcc.org/members/aipac.htm and "Undergraduate," *The American Israel Public Affairs Committee*, http://www.aipac.org/For_Students/3965.asp.

90. Greenberg, "Quiet War on Campus."

91. ADL runs a program entitled "A Campus of Difference" which they identify as intending to "help college administrators, faculty members and students learn to examine stereotypes, expand cultural awareness, explore the value of diversity and combat racism, and anti-Semitism and all forms of bigotry." See "Anti Defamation League on Campus," *The Anti Defamation League*, http://www.adl.org/awod/campus.asp, and "ICC Members," *Israel on Campus Coalition*, http://www.israelcc.org/members/adl.htm.

92. "American Jewish Committee Weekly News Update," *American Jewish Committee*, August 8, 2007, http://www.ajc.org/site/apps/nlnet/content2.aspx?c=ijITI2PHKoG&b=3121957&ct=4271237.

93. *Project Interchange*, http://www.projectinterchange.org/.

94. "Crisis on Campus," *American Jewish Congress*, http://www.ajcongress.org/site/PageServer?pagename=crisis_on_campus.

95. JNF created Caravan for Democracy in 2002, to bring speakers to campus to discuss democracy in general and specifically Israel's role as a democracy in the Middle East. Since their inception, they have expanded to create fellowship programs. See *The Jewish National Fund*, http://www.jnf.org/site/PageServer?pagename=PR_Caravan_Fellowship.

96. "About Hillel," *Hillel: The Foundation for Jewish Campus Life*, http://www.hillel.org/about/default.

97. The Zionist Organization of America (ZOA) sponsors a campus activism network that includes speakers bureaus, Israel trips, a pro-Israel magazine, and other programs that promote Israel advocacy and education about Israeli democracy. See What is ZOA, "Zionist Organization of America," http://www.zoa.org/content/about_us.asp and "ZOA Campus Activism Network," Zionist Organization of America, http://www.zoa.org/content/on-campus.asp and "Israel on Campus Coalition," http://www.israelcc.org/members/zoa.htm.

98. "American Zionist Group Slams U.S. Government on Campus Anti-Semitism," *Haaretz*, http://www.haaretz.com/hasen/spages/936677.html.

99. *Zionist Organization of America*, "ZOA Condemns Office for Civil Rights' Decision Not to Protect Jewish Students From Anti-Semitic Harassment," news release, December 19, 2007, http://www.zoa.org/sitedocuments/pressrelease_view .asp?pressreleaseID=264 and "U. of California at Irvine Cleared in Investigation of Anti-Semitism," *Chronicle of Higher Education*, December 12, 2007, http://chronicle .com/news/article/3612/u-of-california-at-irvine-cleared-in-investigation-of-anti-semitism.

100. United States Commission on Civil Rights, *Findings and Recommendation on Civil Rights Regarding Campus Anti-Semitism.*

101. Zionist Organization of America, "Federal Government Initiates New Investigation Into UC Irvine's Response to Campus Anti-Semitism," news release, June 6, 2008.

102. "Hillel Hosts Some Programs and Speakers that Harm Pro-Israel Agenda," *Zionist Organization of America*, http://www.zoa.org/sitedocuments/oped_view.asp ?opedID=349.

103. "SPME Mission," Scholars for Peace in the Middle East, http://www.spme.net/, "Our Mission," *StandWithUs*, http://www.standwithus.com/, and "About Us," The David Project, http://davidproject.org/.

104. "Video Transcript," *Columbia Unbecoming*, http://www.columbiaunbecoming .com/script.htm.

105. On their website, The David Project states the following as their long-term strategy, "To populate campuses with educated, trained, and confident college students, to prepare high school students and Jewish teens to be pro-active Israel activists and to activate the Jewish community in response to the growing anti-Israel discourse." See "About the David Project," *The David Project Center for Jewish Leadership*, http://www.davidproject.org/index.php?option=com_content&task=view&id=13 &Itemid=31

106. "About Columbia Unbecoming," *Columbia Unbecoming*, http://www.columbia unbecoming.com/.

107. Campus Watch gathers information about institutions, faculty, and campus involvement in Middle East studies from public and private sources. They make this information accessible on their website and publicize it to the media. They also investigate student complaints of abuse. They describe their focus to be on five problems in Middle East studies: analytical failures, the mixing of politics and scholarship, intolerance of alternative views, apologetics, and the abuse of power over students. "See about Campus Watch," *Campus Watch: Monitoring Middle East Studies on Campus*, http://www.campus-watch.org/about.php.

108. Tanya Schevitz, "Professors Want Own Names Put On Mideast Blacklist: They Hope to Make it Powerless," *San Francisco Chronicle*, September 28, 2002, http://www .sfgate.com/cgi-bin/article.cgi?f=/c/a/2002/09/28/MN227890.DTL.

109. "H.R. 3077," *Library of Congress Thomas*, http://thomas.loc.gov/cgi-bin/bdquery/z?d108:h.r.03077: .

110. The Committee for Accuracy in Middle East Reporting in America (CAMERA) was founded in 1982 as a media-monitoring and research organization devoted to promoting accurate and balanced coverage of Israel and the Middle East. CAMERA educates the general public about Middle East issues and the role of the media in reporting inaccurate and distorted accounts of events in Israel and the Middle East. See *CAMERA*, http://www.camera.org/.

111. "Guidelines for Activism on Campus," *Committee for Accuracy in Middle East Reporting in America*, http://www.camera.org/index.asp?x_context=22.

112. "SPME Mission," *Scholars for Peace in the Middle East.*

113. Eric Hoover, "A Diverse Pro-Palestinian Movement Emerges on College Campuses: Many on the Left Embrace the Cause, While Jewish Students Feel a Rise in Hostility," *Chronicle of Higher Education*, May 17, 2002, http://chronicle.com/free/v48/i36/36a04101.htm.

114. Tom Tugend, "Gov. David Tackles Anti-Semitism at California Colleges," *J. Jewish News Weekly*, July 26, 2002, http://www.jewishsf.com/content/2-0-/module/displaystory/story_id/18615/edition_id/374/format/html/displaystory.html.

115. Zionist Organization of America, "Federal Government Initiates New Investigation Into UC Irvine's Response to Campus Anti-Semitism," news release, June 6, 2008, http://www.zoa.org/sitedocuments/pressrelease_view.asp?pressreleaseID=651

116. "Open Letter to the Governor of California, University of California Board of Regents, Board of Trustees of the California State Universities, Chancellors of the University of California, and the Presidents of the California State Universities," *SPME Scholars for Peace in the Middle East*, http://web.mac.com/spme_at_ucsc/iWeb/Site/Home_files/Open%20Letter%20to%20the%20Govern.pdf.

117. Gary A. Tobin and Aryeh K. Weinberg, *Profiles of the American University: Volume I: Political Beliefs & Behavior of College Faculty* (San Francisco: Institute for Jewish & Community Research).

118. "About SPME," *SPME: Scholars for Peace in the Middle East*, http://www.spme.net/aboutus.html.

119. "Our Mission," *StandWithUs.*

120. Philanthropist George Rohr provides seed grants to Chabad to establish new student centers, and challenge grants to enable the construction of new facilities to serve campus communities. See "Leadership: The Chabad on Campus International Foundation," *Chabad on Campus International Foundation*, http://www.chabad.edu/templates/articlecco_cdo/aid/387556/jewish/Leadership.htm. Currently there are 110 Chabad Houses serving campuses in the United States. (20 abroad) See "Chabad on Campus International Directory," *Chabad on Campus International Foundation*, http://www.chabad.edu/centers/campus_cdo/jewish/Campus-Directory.htm.

121. David Cohen, "Academic Oasis?" *Mail & Guardian Online*, July 31, 2008, http://www.mg.co.za/article/2008-07-31-academic-oasis.

Selected Bibliography

Ajami, Fouad. *The Dream Palace of the Arabs: A Generation's Odyssey.* New York: Vintage Books, 1998.

Altbach, Philip G., Robert O. Berdahl, and Patricia J. Gumport, eds. *American Higher Education in the Twenty-First Century: Social, Political, and Economic Challenges.* Baltimore: Johns Hopkins University Press, 1999.

Amacher, Ryan C., and Roger E. Meiners. *Faulty Towers: Tenure and the Structure of Higher Education.* Oakland, CA: Independent Institute, 2004.

Baldwin, Neil. *Henry Ford and the Jews: The Mass Production of Hate.* New York: PublicAffairs, 2001.

———. *The American Revelation: Ten Ideals That Shaped Our Country from the Puritans to the Cold War.* New York: St. Martin's Press, 2005.

Bauman, Zygmunt. *Modernity and the Holocaust.* Ithaca, NY: Cornell University Press, 1989.

Berman, Paul. *Terror and Liberalism.* New York: W.W. Norton and Company, 2003.

Black, Jim Nelson. *Freefall of the American University; How Our Colleges Are Corrupting the Minds and Morals of the Next Generation.* Nashville, TN: WND Books, 2004.

Bok, Derek. *Universities in the Marketplace: The Commercialization of Higher Education.* New Jersey: Princeton University Press, 2003.

Bollinger, Lee C., and Geoffrey R. Stone, eds. *Eternally Vigilant: Free Speech in the Modern Era.* Chicago: University of Chicago Press, 2002.

285

Brown, Michael, ed. *Approaches to Antisemitism: Context and Curriculum.* New York: American Jewish Committee/ International Center for University Teaching of Jewish Civilization, 1994.

Bryson, Bethany. *Making Multiculturalism: Boundaries and Meaning.* Stanford, CA: Stanford University Press, 2005.

Buckley, William F., Jr. *In Search of Anti-Semitism.* New York: Continuum Publishing Company, 1992.

Chesler, Phyllis. *The New Anti-Semitism: The Current Crisis and What We Must Do about It.* San Francisco: Jossey-Bass, 2003.

Cohen, Michael D., and James G. March. *Leadership and Ambiguity: The American College President.* New York: McGraw-Hill Book Company, 1974.

D'Souza, Dinesh. *Illiberal Education: The Politics of Race and Sex on Campus.* New York: Free Press, 1991.

Dershowitz, Alan. *The Case for Israel.* Hoboken, NJ: John Wiley and Sons, 2003.

Douthat, Ross Gregory. *Privilege: Harvard and the Education of the Ruling Class.* New York: Hyperion Books, 2005.

Downs, Donald Alexander. *Restoring Free Speech and Liberty on Campus.* Oakland, CA and Cambridge, UK: Independent Institute/Cambridge University Press, 2005.

Emerson, Steven. *American Jihad: The Terrorists Living among Us.* New York: Free Press, 2002.

Fiorina, Morris P., Samuel J. Abrams, and Jeremy C. Pope. *Culture War? The Myth of a Polarized America.* New York: Pearson Education, 2005.

Foxman, Abraham. *Never Again? The Threat of the New Anti-Semitism.* San Francisco: HarperCollins, 2003.

Geiger, Roger L. *Research & Relevant Knowledge: American Research Universities since World War II.* New Brunswick, NJ: Transaction, 2004.

———. *To Advance Knowledge: The Growth of American Research Universities, 1900-1940.* New Brunswick, NJ: Transaction, 2004.

———. *Knowledge and Money: Research Universities and the Paradox of the Marketplace.* Stanford, CA: Stanford Unversity Press, 2004.

Glock, Charles Y., and Rodney Stark. *Christian Beliefs and Anti-Semitism.* New York: Harper and Row, 1969.

Hale, Frank W., Jr. ed. *What Makes Racial Diversity Work in Higher Education: Academic Leaders Present Successful Policies and Strategies.* Sterling, VA: Stylus Publishing, 2004.

Harding, Bertrand M., Jr. *The Tax Law of Colleges and Universities.* 2nd ed. New York: John Wiley and Sons, 2001.

Herzl, Theodore. *The Jewish State.* Mineola, NY: Dover Publications, 1988.

Hofstadter, Richard. *Academic Freedom in the Age of the College.* New Brunswick, NJ: Transaction, 1996.

Hollander, Paul, ed. *Understanding Anti-Americanism: Its Origins and Impact at Home and Abroad*. Chicago: Ivan R. Dee, 2004.

Karabel, Jerome. *The Chosen: The Hidden History of Admission and Exclusion at Harvard, Yale, and Princeton*. Boston: Houghton Mifflin, 2005.

Keller, Morton, and Phyllis Keller. *Making Harvard Modern: The Rise of America's University*. New York: Oxford University Press, 2001.

Kerr, Clark. *The Uses of the University*. Cambridge, MA: Harvard University Press, 1963.

Kertzer, David I. *The Popes against the Jews: The Vatican's Role in the Rise of Modern Anti-Semitism*. New York: Alfred A. Knopf, 2001.

Kimball, Roger. *Tenured Radicals: How Politics Has Corrupted Our Higher Education*. Chicago: Elephant Paperbacks, 1998.

Kirp, David L. *Shakespeare, Einstein, and the Bottom Line: The Marketing of Higher Education*. Cambridge, MA: Harvard University Press, 2003.

Kors, Alan Charles, and Harvey A. Silverglate. *The Shadow University: The Betrayal of Liberty on America's Campuses*. New York: Free Press, 1998.

Kramer, Martin S. *Ivory Towers on Sand: The Failure of Middle Eastern Studies in America*. Washington, DC: Washington Institute for Near East Policy, 2001.

Langmuir, Gavin I. *History, Religion, and Antisemitism*. Berkeley: Regents of the University of California, 1990.

Lewis, Bernard. *Islam and the West*. New York: Oxford University Press, 1993.

———. *Semites and Anti-Semites: An Inquiry into Conflict and Prejudice*. New York: W. W. Norton and Company, 1999.

———. *What Went Wrong? The Clash between Islam and Modernity in the Middle East*. New York: Perennial, HarperCollins, 2002.

Lipstadt, Deborah. *Denying the Holocaust: The Growing Assault on Truth and Memory*. New York: Plume, 1993.

———. *History on Trial: My Day in Court with David Irving*. New York: HarperCollins, 2005.

Lowen, Rebecca S. *Creating the Cold War University: The Transformation of Stanford*. Berkeley: University of California Press, 1997.

Manji, Irshad. *The Trouble with Islam*. Toronto: Random House, 2003.

Martin, Jerry L., and Anne D. Neal. *The Intelligent Donor's Guide to College Giving*. N.P.: American Council of Trustees and Alumni, 1998.

Moody, JoAnn. *Faculty Diversity: Problems and Solutions*. New York: RoutledgeFalmer, 2004.

National Commission on Terrorist Attacks Upon the United States. *The 9/11 Commission Report: Final Report of the National Commission on Terrorist Attacks Upon the United States*. New York: W.W. Norton and Company, 2003.

Newman, Frank, Lara Couturier, and James Scurry. *The Future of Higher Education: Rhetoric, Reality, and the Risks of the Market.* San Francisco: Jossey-Bass, John Wiley and Sons, 2004.

O'Brien, George Dennis. *All the Essential Half-Truths About Higher Education.* Chicago: University of Chicago Press, 1998.

Prager, Dennis, and Joseph Telushkin. *Why the Jews? The Reason for Antisemitism.* New York: Touchstone, 1983.

Reich, Rob. *Bridging Liberalism and Multiculturalism in American Education.* Chicago: University of Chicago Press, 2002.

Rhoads, Robert A. *Freedom's Web: Student Activism in an Age of Cultural Diversity.* Baltimore: Johns Hopkins University Press, 1998.

Rosenbaum, Ron. *Those Who Forget the Past: The Question of Anti-Semitism.* New York: Random House Trade Paperbacks, 2004.

Rothblatt, Sheldon and Björn Wittrock, ed. *The European and American University Since 1800: Historical and Sociological Essays.* New York: Cambridge University Press, 1993.

Rubin, Barry and Judith Colp Rubin. *Hating America: A History.* New York: Oxford University Press, 2004.

Sacks, David O., and Peter A. Thiel. *The Diversity Myth.* 2nd ed. Oakland, CA: Independent Institute, 1998.

Said, Edward W. *Orientalism.* New York: Vintage Books, 1978.

———. *Covering Islam: How the Media and the Experts Determine How We See the Rest of the World.* New York: Vintage Books, 1997.

Shain, Milton. *Antisemitism.* London: Bowerdean Publishing Company, 1998.

Shapiro, Ben. *Brainwashed; How Universities Indoctrinate America's Youth.* Nashville, TN: WND Books, 2004.

Shermer, Michael, and Alex Grobman. *Denying History: Who Says the Holocaust Never Happened and Why Do They Say It?* Berkeley: University of California Press, 2000.

Stone, Geoffrey R., Louis M. Seidman, Cass R. Sunstein, Mark V. Tushnet, and Pamela S. Karlan. *The First Amendment.* New York: Aspen, 2003.

Stone, Geoffrey R. *Perilous Times: Free Speech in Wartime, from the Sedition Act of 1798 to the War on Terrorism.* New York: W.W. Norton and Company, 2004.

Sykes, Charles J. *Profscam: Professors and the Demise of Higher Education.* Washington, DC: Regnery Gateway, 1988.

———. *A Nation of Victims: The Decay of the American Character.* New York: St. Martin's Press, 1992.

Tatum, Beverly Daniel. *Why Are All the Black Kids Sitting Together in the Cafeteria and Other Conversations About Race.* New York: Basic Books, 1997.

Taylor, Stuart, and K. C. Johnson. *Until Proven Innocent: Political Correctness and the Shameful Injustices of the Duke Lacrosse Rape Case.* New York: St. Martin's Press, 2007.

Tobin, Gary A., with Sharon L. Sassler. *Jewish Perceptions of Anti-Semitism.* New York and London: Plenum Press, 1988.

Tobin, Diane K., Gary A. Tobin, and Scott Rubin. *In Every Tongue: The Racial & Ethnic Diversity of the Jewish People.* San Francisco: Institute for Jewish & Community Research, 2005.

Veysey, Laurence R. *The Emergence of the American University.* Chicago: University of Chicago Press, 1965.

Wallis, Jim. *The Soul of Politics: Beyond "Religious Right" and "Secular Left."* San Diego: Harcourt Brace, 1994.

Washburn, Jennifer. University Inc.: *The Corporate Corruption of Higher Education.* New York: Basic Books, 2005.

INDEX

Utah State University, 75, 94, 112

van de Mieroop, Marc, 129
Vatican II, 70
Vermont, funding for education in, 4–5
Vietnam War, xxix
violence, 36
virtual programs, 50

wage-earning capacity, higher
    education influencing, 20
Wahhabi extremists, 92
walkouts, 153
The Wall Street Journal, 116, 247
Walter Cronkite School of
    Journalism, 159
Walt, Stephen, 201–3, 205
War of 1973, 62–63
Washburn, Jennifer, 53
The Washington Post, 247
Washington Square News (New York
    University), 102, 248
Wayne State University, xxxiii, 95, 112,
    212, 248
Weaver, Clarence Mason, 185
Weinberg, David, 88–89
Wente, Margaret, 141
What Went Wrong? (Lewis, B.), 127
Wheels for Justice, 240
white supremacy, 93
Wilkie, Andrew, 145
Williams College, 40
Wisconsin Policy Research Institute, 50

Wisse, Ruth, 126
women's rights, 62
World Council of Churches, 71
World Jewish Congress, 72
World War I, 20
World War II, i, 20, 65, 67, 74, 96, 103,
    109, 115
Wurman, Osias, 260n32

xenophobia, 68

Yale Alumni Fund, 27
Yale University, 19, 87, 97, 147, 149, 171
Yalman, Nur O., 130
Yemeni government, 93–94
Yiftachel, Oren, 144
Yom Ha'atzmaut. *See* Israel
    Independence Day
Yom Kippur attack, 63
York University, 141, 209

zero tolerance, 10
Zilbering, Noa, 98
Zionism, 81, 93–101, 161
Zionism Awareness Week, 97
Zionist-Arab conflict, 63
Zionist Organization of America (ZOA),
    xxviii, xxxiv, 61, 195, 219, 276n5,
    283n93
ZOA. *See* Zionist Organization of
    America
Zoloth, Laurie, 90, 139
Zundel, Ernst, 141

ABOUT THE AUTHORS

GARY A. TOBIN, Ph.D., is president of the Institute for Jewish & Community Research. He was the director of the Center for Modern Jewish Studies at Brandeis University for fourteen years, after spending eleven years on faculty at Washington University, St. Louis. He is the editor of two volumes about race in America, *What Happened to the Urban Crisis?* and *Divided Neighborhoods.* His books include *Jewish Perceptions of Antisemitism; Rabbis Talk About Intermarriage; Opening The Gates: How Proactive Conversion Can Revitalize The Jewish Community; In Every Tongue: The Racial & Ethnic Diversity of the Jewish People;* and *The Trouble with Textbooks: Distorting History and Religion* with Dennis R. Ybarra. Dr. Tobin and Aryeh K. Weinberg coauthored two volumes on American college faculty entitled *Political Beliefs & Behavior of College Faculty* and *Religious Beliefs & Behavior of College Faculty.*

ARYEH K. WEINBERG is a research associate at the Institute for Jewish & Community Research. He received his B.A. from the University of California, Berkeley. He is currently completing his Ph.D. at Baylor University in sociology of religion. Mr. Weinberg's areas of research are anti-Semitism and anti-Israelism, American religion, as well as philanthropy in America. His latest publications include an article entitled, "An Exceptional Nation: American Philanthropy Is Different Because America Is Different," *Mega-Gifts in Jewish Philanthropy: Giving Patterns 2001–2003,* and *Mega-Gifts in American Philanthropy: Giving Patterns 2001–2003.* He is the coauthor of two volumes on American college faculty.

JENNA FERER is a former research associate at the Institute for Jewish & Community Research. Ms. Ferer formerly lived in Jerusalem, where she worked as a news, feature, and photojournalist for The Media Line, a nonprofit news agency that specializes in countering media bias against Israel. While in Israel, she produced an independent photographic study on schoolchildren in areas of violence. She was an editor and writer for the *College Campus Initiative E-News and Information Brief* for the Jewish Federation of Los Angeles.